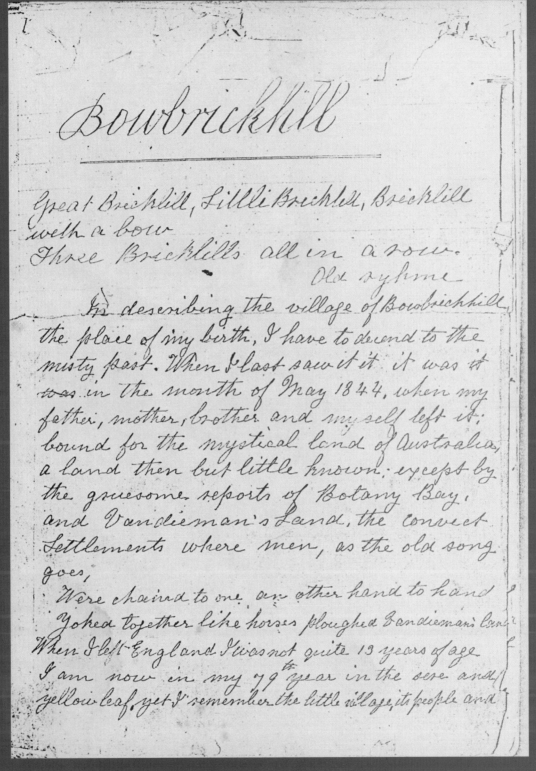

The first page of Henry Mundy's original manuscript.
Written in 1909.

Dedicated to:
Harold Mundy
Les Hughes Snr
Bronwen Hughes
Tristan Hughes
who totally believed in Henry

First published in the United Kingdom by Next Century Books.

Next Century Books
P.O. Box 6113
Leighton Buzzard
Bedfordshire
United Kingdom, LU7 0UW

Design and production by Hughes Graphics and Design, P.O. Box 2455, Mansfield, Qld 4122 Australia.

A CIP catalogue Record for this title is available from the British Library.

ISBN 0-9544011-2-3

A YOUNG AUSTRALIAN PIONEER

A YOUNG AUSTRALIAN PIONEER

Henry Mundy

CONTENTS:

ACKNOWLEDGEMENTS – To all those who contributed

The final result of a book like this is clearly the result of a huge amount of input contributed by a massive number of people, many of whom I have not met personally. I hope to acknowledge all of them here, but there is a very great possibility that I will miss more than one, and to them I apologise, but do appreciate their efforts in bringing Henry to life again.

In a chronological order acknowledgement must begin with Henry's great grandson Harold Mundy who rescued Henry's original manuscript and had it transcribed. When I knew Harold he was an old man, and a friend and neighbour of my father. He lived only a few doors away, but I could never have imagined the impact he and his ancestor would have on my life many years later.

Fortunately, he gave a copy of his transcription to my father, and while Harold had died many years before I saw it, my father loved Henry's writings and we began to trace his life. Sadly, my father, also Les Hughes, didn't live to see the final result, but I know he would be deliriously happy about it.

My wife Bronwen and son Tristan too have been living with Henry for many years, and have not only heard the story countless times when asked what this book was to be about, but have travelled back to Bow Brickhill, throughout Victoria, and encouraged me to head off to the Western District and back to England more than once to photograph and research life in those places now - and then.

This entire book though may have remained an unfulfilled dream on my computer screen had it not have been for the enthusiastic help and willingness of Sue Malleson in Bow Brickhill. Sometimes things come together in a way which could never be planned, and when I arrived back in Bow Brickhill for the second time in 1999 I knew nobody, and was purely there on a personal quest to take more photographs and trace Henry's words. While standing outside a group of houses in Church Road where Henry was born, Helen Hart, who lived in one of the cottages, came out and was curious. She then stopped Alan Preen who was driving home for his lunch, and after a chat he then sent his wife Mary along. Mary in turn went to her friend Sue Malleson - and the ball was rolling! Sue is a former school teacher who now operates a PR business with her husband Andy, and her researching skills, love of history in Bow Brickhill and elsewhere, and sheer enthusiasm, produced a raft of often long lost facts, stories which enlarged on Henry's writing, and photographs which made this entire project even more exciting from my viewpoint.

Sue Malleson and Mary Preen in Bow Brickhill, mid-winter.

It was Sue who located publisher Tim Purcell, and in turn Tim embraced Henry and this book with more positive energy and co-operation that I could have hoped for. In a staggeringly short space of time Henry was 'reborn'.

In Australia I discovered, after I was well into the book, that Don Reid, who lives in Kialla near Shepparton, had also spent a huge amount of time and effort in researching Henry. Don had even published 'In the land of their Adoption' and another book embracing all of the members of the extended Mundy clan because he is the local historian, and his wife is directly related

6

to Henry's brother.

While I spent a few days in Shepparton and Mooroopna discovering more about Henry's life after his manuscript ended, I didn't have the chance to meet Don, much to my regret and through no fault of his, but we spent many hours on the telephone and he sent me a huge amount of his own research.

The only direct relation of Henry's that I met, apart from Harold Mundy, is Syd Hill.

Syd's great grandmother is Jane Mundy, whose tragic story is explained at the end of this book. I met Syd only a few weeks before this book went to the printer, but we had corresponded electronically for some years when he gave me more information. Again, the association with Henry made our meeting great fun, and our time together was very satisfying.

Many old friends turned out to have an association with aspects of Henry's era which I had no previous knowledge of, and they helped enthusiastically. Here then is a list of people, associations, and publications which need to be thanked for all of their efforts, and I apologise that they could not be acknowledged in greater detail - however, please know that your assistance is of equal importance. I hope that in your seeing this book published you too gain pleasure, and a feeling of having had a hand in it.

In no particular order, there is the Bletchley Archeological and Historical Society, Ballarat Genealogy, the State Library of Victoria, Central Highlands Regional Library, Jean Stevens, Kevin A. Quick, Eve McLaughlin, the Buckinghamshire Genealogical Society, Julie Grante, Myrtle Rands (a Mundy descendant) and Roy and Di Williams in Geelong.

Michael Cannon's superb books 'Perilous Voyages to the New Land', 'Old Melbourne Town Before the Gold Rush' and 'The Roaring Days' were a wonderful source of stories and explanations about life in the 'old days'. Also 'Old Gold Towns of Victoria' by John Darbyshire and C.E. Sayers showed and explained a lot about towns which are rapidly disappearing back to dust.

Chris Patterson in England is a Munday ancestor, and contributed, as did Alan Cook another Munday relation in England, Sue McKeegan and Andrea Johnson. The Clunes Museum helped me finally locate the grave of Ann Mundy and her two children after I had searched their cemetery a number of times, and given up hope of finding that very sad Mundy resting place. With my living over 1000 miles from Victoria, I was given great assistance by friends such as Lachlan Story who drove to Clunes, rediscovered more of the Mundy family history there and photographed it.

A number of visits to Sovereign Hill and the Sovereign Hill Gold Museum were fruitful and the staff very co-operative, as was the Eureka Stockade Museum. Thanks also to Andrea Johnson, George R Blanke, Ada Ackerly, the Milton Keynes Open University and another good friend Max Joffe and his wife Lorraine Finley who works with the Old Victorian Treasury.

Then there was the staff at the Mooroopna Historical Society, the Geelong Historical Record Centre, Susie Zada, Dianne Hughes (no relation), and the books 'Melbourne on the Yarra' by Marjorie Tipping, 'One People, One Destination' by John Ross and the 'James Flood Book of Early Australian Photographs'.

My apologies to anybody who wasn't named.

Most off all, thanks to Henry. He must have been a fascinating man, I only wish I had known him better.

Les. Hughes
Brisbane
14.09.2003

Bow Brickhill and neighbouring places relevant to Henry Mundy

Official Ordnance Survey Map 1846

* Green line denotes the route described by Henry from Woburn to Bow Brickhill.

9

INTRODUCTION – meet Henry Mundy

Henry Mundy would be shocked, amazed and probably delighted, that almost 100 years after his death, and a full 170 years after his birth, his writings have been widely published.

The purpose of doing that now is a desire to introduce contemporary readers to a 'normal' life from ages past, and to illustrate in words and pictures the places which were so familiar to Henry both in the Australia and the England of his childhood, teenage and formative adult life. His thoughts have not been altered from those he originally hand-wrote (save for some transcription errors and punctuation) and that keeps them enchantingly readable and true to his character.

Henry wrote this very intimate story for his family in the first person, and it takes us into his world as though he was having a conversation with us - a most unusual way of writing for the early 1900s.

Henry's story is captivating, so to understand it better it was vital to revisit to all of the places he lived and worked in, to see them first-hand, to photograph them and to understand just what he was describing. In doing that his memories could be verified. Places have obviously changed, or even mostly disappeared along with the family and friends he tells us about. Proving their authenticity though was very important.

Some dedicated people helped out, and because of that it is hoped readers will be able to derive a feeling for Henry's life, while understanding just where the places were, or are still, and what they had evolved into at the start of the 21 century.

Henry would almost certainly not agree that he was a remarkable person, but having been born

The hill in Church Road, Bow Brickhill
exactly as it would have looked when
Henry knew it and described the scene.

into a poor, and illiterate but upright family in rural Buckinghamshire, the legacy of his colourful life can be appreciated by people in both England and his adopted homeland.

The Munday (sometimes also recorded as Monday - but in the UK only 'Mundy' once because this depended upon who filled in the parish record) family has roots dating back to 1755 in the tiny farming village of Bow Brickhill. That is according to parish records for the All Saints church which stands at the very top of the steeply hilled village. Mundays, from that date up until Henry's time, lived there and were all farm labourers.

Families were employed on a casual basis by landowners to work on their farms, thus remaining illiterate and ignorant. They very seldom, if ever, ventured out of the village or its nearby surroundings because they didn't have the means nor the necessity to do otherwise.

They were subservient to the gentry, as Henry explains with a passion, but he was different to most - and was granted an exciting opportunity to fulfill his potential when his family took the very bold and courageous move to sail to remote far-off Port Phillip to better the lives of themselves and future Mundy generations. Their mission succeeded, but most modern Mundys are oblivious to why they live where they do, and what they owe their ancestors. Henry understood that would happen, and that was one of the main reasons for his writing his memoirs.

He was clearly very bright, ambitious, observant of everything around him, had a remarkable memory - and thankfully - wrote about the first twenty-seven years of his life in 165,500 words of enlightenment. He lived through an important era which shaped the foundation of the State of Victoria at least, but the years he describes had long ended before he wrote this story for his future generations.

By 1909 Henry realised he had lived through an age which heralded the white establishment of an Australian State (Victoria) which, when he wrote this, was the capital of Australia.

Although he only ever received one letter from his family in Bow Brickhill, he understood he had left behind an old way of life in England which didn't exist any more. He realised that without putting his story down nobody would know about the old ways which he, his parents and brother John left behind them forever.

Henry was almost entirely self-educated, and documented a unique account of an ordinary working person who lived a long time ago. His recordings provide a genuine historical insight into how things really happened in those days. His life is not romance, fiction, nor the writings of aristocracy, the government, or even a very important person - his was an average life explained wonderfully well.

Henry would be surprised to know that until his writings were brought to Bow Brickhill in 1999, nobody in his old county had a clue what life there was like for the poor majority of the population there in the 1830s and '40s.

Because 99% of the working class could not read or write, their personal thoughts and working habits were never recorded on paper. Equally, shortly after the Munday family left Bow Brickhill in June 1844, life there changed drastically.

The establishment and expansion of the railway, which encompassed the industrial revolution, meant that the way of living which Henry wrote about, disappeared within a very few years of his departure when masses moved away from their home villages for the first time.

The industrial revolution put thousands of farm labouring families out of work, and previously quite villages, including Bow Brickhill, Little Brickhill, Fenny Stratford, Wavendon and Simpson were subjected to riots by unemployed labourers who smashed and burned harvesters and other implements which replaced the need for their labour.

There have not been many Mundays living in Bow Brickhill since almost the beginning of the

1900s. The last to be buried in the village church were interred in 1949 and 1972. Before then, many had been buried there in unmarked paupers graves. As if part of his tradition, Henry, his brother and his mother (she later received a headstone thanks to Henry's brother John) were also buried in unmarked graves in different parts of Victoria, and generally only the place of their burial can be found, not the specific graves. That is despite the fact that Henry became a very successful gold miner, farmer, builder and undertaker.

His recollections and the recording of this era is virtually unmatched. Illiteracy, a short life span, and disinterest by almost everyone else ensure his words are not only fascinating, but historically very important.

He writes about his own life, his family, the problems they encountered, his endeavours to keep his wife in comfort and security, arriving in Melbourne when it had been established for less than ten years, Geelong, the earliest days of the prosperous Western District of Victoria, aboriginal life there, and most fascinatingly, the early gold rush era covering Geelong to Ballarat, Bendigo and beyond.

Henry was not a saint, and tells us of his running and selling illegal alcohol to troopers who operated 'grog shops' on the Ballarat goldfields, conflicts with other family members, and particularly, problems with his drink-ravaged father-in-law.

Henry Mundy's account of Bow Brickhill and Australia is more than merely a good story. A very small selection of his words have been quoted in a book written about the goldfields of Victoria and California, but the author cast grave doubts on the accuracy of Henry's words. Should that author ever read this, I can assure that academic that at least 99% of what Henry writes about is absolutely precise.

This may sound difficult to believe, having been written so long after the events occurred, but having visited Bow Brickhill at least eight times from Australia, and traced the exact routes he describes (Bow Brickhill is remarkably well preserved despite being on the edge of the plains which today make up the boom area of Milton Keynes), Henry's descriptions NEVER fail.

His recollections are so precise that in Bow Brickhill and nearby areas it is possible to find the exact spots he describes including road details, buildings, farms and even old Munday homes. In Victoria that is also the case, despite the sheer scale of the travels he undertook largely on foot.

When they arrived in their new country class structures which dominated the Munday labouring life in Bow Brickhill, suddenly did not exist. There were no old rules, no expectations and they had a clean sheet of paper to work with. As the reader will soon discover, Henry vehemently detested the English class system.

There were wealthy families in Port Phillip and the Western District, of course, but they too were newly landed and fighting to establish themselves. Together they worked to found the places which sometimes exist still.

Henry didn't travel more than about four miles from home in the first twelve years of his life, but the moment the Mundays were loaded onto the train with their meagre belongings at Bletchley Station, their lives were transformed by the 'big smoke' of London, the mammoth adventure sailing under canvas to the other side of the world, then having the total freedom to be their own masters in Melbourne, Geelong, the Western Victoria and later Mooroopna.

After shepherding for the first five years, the Mundys had sufficient money to buy a new house in Geelong, own cows, horses and, generally be as free as they hoped to be when they left England, destitute but full of optimism.

Henry grasped the chance to 'reach for the sky' and achieved much more than he ever could have in England. Eve MacLachlin, an historian in Buckinghamshire, read Henry's writings on his Bow Brickhill life, and stated that today somebody with his abilities, even those from a poor background, would be recognised and snapped up by a university and carefully nurtured. In those days though, Henry would probably have been quickly brought into line and become subservient if he remained in England.

He died aged eighty having recorded the first twenty-seven years of his colourful life. After read his original document, it was a shock to find the written 'conversation' stop almost mid-sentence. Suddenly, he was gone.

He had just described the birth of his first living son, but the man who now felt like a close friend, died shortly after writing: "Gribble, I and the blacksmith forthwith went to Jimmy Quaid's to wet the job (registering the birth of his son George Henry)".

... But there had to be more.

What happened to Henry, his beloved wife Ann, his son George Henry, how many more children did they have, where did they live, what did they do for the rest of their lives, and what happened to his mother, brother John, Gribble, Fanny etc., etc?

Fortunately, after a huge amount of research we know the answers. It is not all happy - but this was the real world.

The biggest surprise was to learn that technology aside, the problems which people had to deal with in their daily lives in these 'old days' were no different to right now. Henry talks about family rivalries, the deep sadness shared with his relatives in Bow Brickhill when the Mundays left for Australia, money problems, illnesses, death and all of the usual struggles we endure in our not-necessarily-exciting daily lives.

He takes us into a world which was only known from school books or through folklore. Suddenly they aren't the 'old days' any more - they are 'now', modern, vibrant and brand new.

Being a man who loved words and wrote so very well, I'm sure Henry would be very pleased that we now know **him** - and that he left a more important legacy to England and Australia than he ever imagined.

When he died in Euroa, Northern Victoria on January 28, 1912, his doctor described his death as being the result of Arteriosclerosis (thickening of the arteries resulting in a lack of blood flow), Asthenia (lack of strength and debility) - and Senility.

'Senility', despite the fact that Henry wrote almost half of his words in the last six months of his life. It is interesting to note from his death certificate (on which a number of other deaths in Euroa were included) that two other people of a similar age, who died under that doctor within two weeks of Henry's passing, were also described as having succumbed to 'Asthenia and Senility'.

I am sure Henry is still having the last laugh ...

LES. HUGHES

One hundred and sixty years after Henry left Bow Brickhill, the junction of Church Road and Station Road is still the centre of his home village. He described it then as widening to occupy several acres. The building on the left which is now white, was the bakery of Mr Britten.

The Rectory Farm can be seen in the centre, while the site of the Chapel Henry attended was to the left behind the buildings.

BOW BRICKHILL – Henry's birthplace

As already mentioned, Bow Brickhill was the centre of the Munday family's world for many generations, and remained that way until George and Mary took their two sons to Port Phillip in May 1844. It is the place Henry grew up in and which he describes so well.

Today the village remains remarkably the same as it was in Henry's era - given the assumed modernisations. It is situated close to the M1 Motorway, is around 44 miles north of London, and close to Woburn and Milton Keynes.

However, before the age of the car and motorways, the main road was Watling Street. It came from London, went through St. Albans, Dunstable and Fenny Stratford, then onto north west England. It is the old Roman road to the north. In Henry's times the road was already divided into sections controlled by trustees who were permitted to erect gates, or turnpikes, and demanded tolls be paid for traversing their section. That continued until 1874.

The road Henry describes to Bow Brickhill runs off Watling Street, and this secondary road becomes Church Road at the top of the hill into Bow Brickhill. It then runs into Station Road.

Civilisation in Bow Brickhill has been dated back to 43AD when the Romans occupied this part of Britain for four centuries. Ancient Romans coins and other artifacts were common-place when the fields were ploughed, and the site of an Iron Age fortification has been unearthed on the hill near All Saints church. Ironically, Bricks have never been made in the region.

The village is situated on the side of a now thickly wooded sand hill, and the open plains at the foot of the village are home to ancient villages such as Shenley, Simpson and Milton Keynes. It was simply 'Milton' to Henry, and the new city of Milton Keynes, which took its name from the village, is a booming housing and industrial area 160 plus years after Henry's time.

The farms on which he worked are now mostly modern businesses ranging from Jaguar

Racing's Formula 1 team (a genuine stone's throw from the back yard of the old Munday home in nearby Caldecotte), to computer component suppliers. Fortunately, important parts of the old villages can still be found amongst the modern facilities, and even some of the old farms Henry and his family worked on still exist. Bow Brickhill has mostly dodged the notice of developers - fortunately - and remains amazingly pristine.

The parish occupies nearly 200 acres, and is the most northerly of the three Brickhills (Bow, Little and Great). For centuries it has been surrounded by thick forests and farms producing wheat, barley and beans. The hill on which the village stands rises about 500 feet from the plain to the peak on which the village church, All Saints, stands loftily. In older times it was a very prominent landmark, but today is mostly lost in the trees which abound on the hill.

The largest nearby town to Bow Brickhill is Bletchley which is a major rail stop, and which grew mightily after Henry's time, thanks to rail. The once tiny mediaeval village of Caldecotte is now a 'new' town, part of Milton Keynes, and boasts a massive man-made lake for thousands of executive townhouses. Amazingly though, in one tiny isolated pocket, the former Munday home survives isolated in the mainly empty Simpson Street!

A huge and historic 17th century farmhouse with thatched roof and half-timber building survived in the village until being burnt down in the 1980s.

The River Ousel and the Grand Union Canal meander through Caldecotte and are referred to by Henry. The Grand Union is one of the few canals which didn't fall into a derelict state when road and rail offered a different means of moving manufactured goods. It is the main canal through the centre of England, and opened the Midlands up to Europe as a manufacturing hub. It begins in Birmingham, and ends in London where it passes through Regents Park. The Grand Union eventually enters the River Thames after passing through Primrose Hill and Camden en route to ships on the docks, which once took the goods which came through Bow Brickhill to all parts of the world. The Grand Union Canal was opened in 1805.

On April 9, 1838 the London and Birmingham Railway was opened between Euston Grove Station in London and Denbigh Hall. It continued again from Rugby to Birmingham after a coach journey between the two points. Denbigh Hall is on the northern outskirts of Bletchley, and for a few years, until the railway lines from north and south met, it was a popular place where passengers were off-loaded and taken to Rugby by stage coach. Three coaches a day ran between the two stations. Today there is only a simple bridge marker to remind us of Denbigh Hall, but very few understand its significance.

In 1777 a coach journey from Birmingham to London took twenty-seven hours; when the first train journey was made that had been reduced to five and a half hours. A central station at Wolverton replaced the wooden building at Denbigh Hall.

In 1846 a new line, running from Bedford to Bletchley, was opened and a station built at Bow Brickhill. Life in the village changed immediately, with people employed by the railway, and others using it to travel away to new lives.

The name Bow Brickhill derives from the old English title 'Bolle Brichelle'. Brichelle was the Norman spelling of Bryk - a British word for 'Hill Top'. Hylle was an Anglo Saxon word meaning 'Hill'. At the end of the 1100s the village was associated with a family named Boel.

This is the rail bridge at Denbigh Hall as it was, and as it survived in 2003. It is insignificant to most people now, but was a bustling village site at the end of the rail line for some years in the earliest times.

15

From 1086, a number of different families owned the land on which the area stands. They had the rights to collect rents from tenants whose homes were in the manor of Bow Brickhill. Through disputes and changes of ownership, Bow Brickhill eventually, through inter-marriage, came into the De Laps of Monellan family in the late 1700s.

The manor eventually was owned by the Duke of Bedford, but the De Laps are believed to still be major landowners in the area. Throughout the centuries the village maintained a steady population of around 400 inhabitants. In 1931 that stood at 381.

The village church of All Saints dates from the 1100s, but was completely remodelled in the 1400s. The records there state that in 1185 there was a transfer of the advowson (the right to earn an ecclesiastical living). The structure, built of sandstone rubble, in large blocks, and dug from the greensand escarpment on which it stands, is situated at 535 feet above the village. Before the 1400s the building probably consisted only of an aisleless nave and a chancel, but the north and south aisles were built in the 1400s along with the west tower.

In 1630 the nave was reroofed, but after falling into decay the building is believed to have been derelict and unused for around 150 years.

Eventually, the entire church was restored in 1756-57 under benefactor Browne Willis, who rebuilt the east wall of the chancel in brick. The church was restored again in 1883, when the porch was added. Services are held most Sundays, and there is an enthusiastic choir. The bells cannot be rung for fear of damage to the tower.

In fact All Saints has a long choral tradition, and in 1847 Thomas Webster, a member of the Cranbrook Colony, painted his famous picture 'A Village Choir' using the church for his subject, and the Bow Brickhill residents as its characters. The original painting stands in the Victoria and Albert Museum in London as part of the Sheepshanks Collection. All of the people in the painting were known in the 1930s, but typically, their names were not written down, and the only person known today is Mr Kent who is depicted wearing a smock.

Thomas Webster's *A Village Choir* painted in 1847 and set in All Saints church featuring residents of Bow Brickhill. The only known person mentioned by Henry Mundy is 'Old Mr. Kent' who is wearing the smock and orange scarf. Undoubtedly, all of the older residents were known to Henry. Not all members of the 'establishment' were liked by him.

The Wesleyan Chapel which Henry mentions, and his family attended, has gone, and its site is the car park of the school in Station Road at the foot of the hill. It dates from 1880. The Wheatsheaf Inn was originally a picturesque half-timber and brick building built around 1600. It had a thatched roof, and was run by at least two Munday families in the 1800s before burning down and being replaced by a modern soul-less building bearing the same name.

The parish was enclosed in 1790 when an allotment of land (known as Rectory Farm) was assigned to the Rector in lieu of tithes (a tenth part of the annual produce of agriculture paid as a tax for the support of the Rector). At the same time, an area known as 'Black Ground', and mentioned by Henry, was awarded to the parish 'for use of the poor for firing'. In 1844, and soon after the Mundays left, an Act of Parliament was passed to enable the Rector, Churchwardens and Overseers, who were Trustees of this land, to sell part of it.

This caused a great deal of trouble in the village, and a memorial stone was put into the wall of a house opposite the Plough Inn, which remarkably for those times, denounces those Trustees and named them - adding exclamation marks at the end of their names ... It remains there today.

The River Ousel marks the boundary of the parish, and runs through Caldecotte (the old spelling was Caldecot) which has been developed enormously. A large section of the land in Caldecotte was excavated in the 1970s to form Caldecotte Lake. Caldecotte and surrounds came under the redevelopment of the entire Milton Keynes area.

Despite threats from sand mining and housing developers, Bow Brickhill citizens continue to fight to preserve the integrity of the village which Henry has probably helped promote through his writing.

Above Left: The notorious stone placed in the wall of April Cottage in Bow Brickhill proclaims the treachery of having the land set designated as a source of fuel for the poor, returned to the wealthy parish council. Names are named and the reasons for having the stone made and placed are quite clear. A very bold statement by the poorer villagers, in those times especially, when they were meant to be humbled by the establishment.

Left: Bow Brickhill as it was seen from the Rectory Farm around early 1900 - virtually unchanged from the scenes Henry describes. The school is behind the wall on the right, and while Henry didn't know the school, it is also the site where his Sunday School was held and his father went to church services. The cottages on the hill can be seen to the right. The large building is where the village bakery was housed.

THE MUNDAY FAMILY - to 1844

Today we know much more about the Munday/Mundy/Monday family than Henry ever did. He talks about his grandmother, grandfather, uncles, aunts, and friends, but he omitted a huge range of cousins and other uncles and aunts who proliferated in Bow Brickhill. This suggests that like so many of us, their own lives were so intense that they were not terribly close to those members outside their immediate circle of involvement. However, Henry's writings have stirred a great deal of interest in his descendants both in Australia and back in England.

It is believed that the Mundays originally came to Bow Brickhill thanks to William Monday whose family came into the parish records first on November 16, 1755.

That was the date William Monday married Elizabeth Allen (father Richard Allen). It is probable William Monday was born in Westbury (a small village near Brackley, about 20 miles west of Bow Brickhill) about 1730 and baptised in Simpson in 1743. His parents were probably Richard and Judith Munday. Richard was born in Water Stratford (a village next to Westbury) where they married.

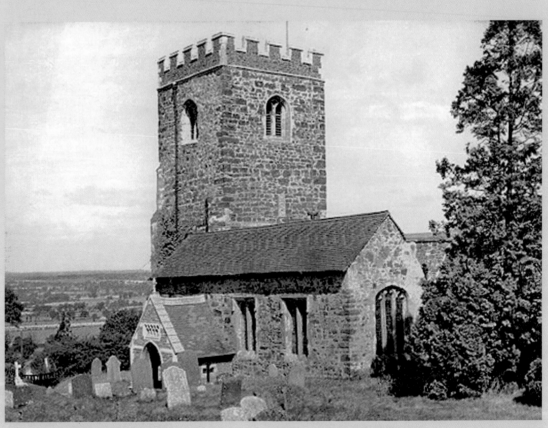

The ancient church of All Saints was not liked by Henry, but its grounds contain the remains of many Munday family members.

William (buried at All Saints February 15, 1804) and Elizabeth (buried November 16, 1755), had five children of whom only one lived to become an adult. That son, William Munday (baptised May 15, 1758 buried April 10, 1836 aged 81), was married to Susannah Cook in All Saints church on May 12, 1778. Susannah too lived to a very good age, and was buried

This old grave at All Saints contains the remains of George William Munday and his wife Lizzie.

in All Saints grounds on March 16, 1835. She was baptised on April 30, 1758 making her 77 years old when she died. They were Henry's great grandparents and, no doubt, theirs and other family funerals, had a profound effect on him. He poignantly mentions that old bones were piled thick on the ground when the holes were dug for Munday burials, and all relics were simply shovelled back after the body was interred.

They had seven children, but as an indicator of the infant mortality rate then, only four survived - two boys and two girls.

The boys were John and James, the girls Hannah and Dinah. Hannah would marry into a wealthy publican family named (William) Fowler. Dinah married William White who we know nothing of at this time. James was Henry's grandfather. James' older brother John would have many children who became the mainstay of the Mundays in Bow Brickhill.

James was baptised on July 17 1785, and married Elizabeth Fowlkes in 1804. The Fowlkes family too was very strongly represented in Bow Brickhill over many generations, and prominent in the church and hierarchy.

Sadly, Elizabeth died in childbirth in 1811, having previously given birth to Henry's father George (1805), and his favourite aunt, Jane, in1808. Their third child died with Elizabeth, and was named Thomas.

James Munday remarried Susannah Smells in 1812, and together they had a son, John who was christened on January 18, 1818.

19

Munday family snippets

William Fowler was baptised on May 1, 1804. He and Ann (Munday - Henry's grandfather's sister) had their son William baptised in BBH during 1833 despite living in Watford. Their daughter Ann Fowler was buried in All Saints on September 27, 1838. Her family lived in Watford, and she was 18 months old.

Baby Thomas Munday (brother of Henry's father) was buried in All Saints on Nov 1, 1811 - his parents were James and Elizabeth, Henry's grandparents.

HENRY'S GRANDFATHER'S BROTHER'S SIDE

Maria Worby was a single woman who had Joseph Munday baptised at All Saints in 1888.

William George Munday and Lizzy had their banns annulled by his father - William George - who claimed he was too young. George William Munday (Snr) was a carpenter in Wolverton. William George Munday (Jnr) was a labourer in London.

John and Lizzie eventually married and had their children John and Elizabeth baptised at All Saints in 1884.

The grave of Henry's mother lies in rural northern Victoria, an incredibly long way from 'home'. Her son John is thought to have erected it.

The road through the woods from Woburn described by Henry runs by Bow Brickhill's All Saints church which is out of view on the left. It then passes the back of the Rectory and heads down the hill where it becomes Church Road leading on to Station Road.

A YOUNG AUSTRALIAN PIONEER

Henry Mundy

REMINISCENCES OF MY NATIVE VILLAGE –
as it was 70 years ago (written 1909)

WRITTEN BETWEEN 1909 AND 1912 BY AN OLD PIONEER, HENRY MUNDY - BORN JUNE 1831.

BOW BRICKHILL:

"Great Brickhill, Little Brickhill, Brickhill with a bow

Three Brickhills all in a row" (Old rhyme).

In describing the village of Bow Brickhill the place of my birth, I have to descend to the misty past. When I last saw it, it was in the month of May 1844, when my father, mother, brother and myself left it bound for the mystical land of Australia, a land then but little known, except by the gruesome reports of Botany Bay and Van Dieman's Land, the convict settlements where men, as the old song goes:

Henry's dreaded thought - a Humber flying machine at nearby Aylesbury in 1910.

Were chained to one another hand to hand
Yoked together like horses ploughed Van Dieman's Land.

When I left England I was not quite thirteen years of age, I am now in my seventy-ninth year, in the sere and yellow leaf, yet I remember the little village, its people and its surroundings as if it were only yesterday.

In those days there were no telegraphs, no telephones, photography was unknown, no steamships - I cannot say there were no railways. In my memory's longest span I remember my mother taking me to see the railway being made at Bletchley, the line from London to Birmingham, which was in working order long before I left. And God save us there were no flying machines.

Bow Brickhill is situated in Buckinghamshire within three miles of the confines of Bedfordshire on the east; where is the ancient town of Woburn, Woburn Abbey and the domain of the Duke of Bedford, and 44 miles from London. There were three Brickhills: Great, Little and Bow Brickhill. I was in Great Brickhill once, sent on a message. The only thing I remember of it was seeing a number of men and women sitting on stools picking red, white and black currants and an old lady giving me some to eat. I have no recollection of any hill.

Little Brickhill church.

I also remember of once going to Little Brickhill with my mother when I had the measles, to see the parish doctor, Dr Ghent, who gave us a very abrupt and unwelcome reception. Dr Ghent was one of the old style of brutes who think it undignified to say a civil word to the poor, he had no sympathy either physically or psychologically with the lower classes. Mother told father when we were home: "He swore awful."

Where the Brickhills derived their name is difficult to say. I have often thought that perhaps in old

21

Bow Brickhill looking from the Bletchley direction.

times bricks were manufactured there, but the only hill in the three villages is in Bow Brickhill which is a hill of red sand of great depth, which a deep incline cutting to make traffic possible testifies, so as far as Bow Brickhill is concerned, I cannot see how a brick factory comes in.

In the description of Bow Brickhill and its surroundings, I must take my reader to Old Woburn, or near it on to the turnpike road to London, as it would appear in the month of May. The stage coach is passing drawn by four horses, the driver conspicuous in his heavy brown overcoat with many capes. The coach, a capacious lumbering vehicle crammed with passengers inside and on the top of the coach. Protected by an iron railing, were the second class passengers sitting as conveniently as they might on the roof. The guard, a conspicuous individual, sits on an elevated perch behind, significant with his long horn. The coach is now approaching Woburn: the guard blows

The grandness of Woburn Abbey.

the signal announcing the coming coach, and notice to have a relay of horses ready for the onward journey.

The coach has passed, let us proceed west towards Bow Brickhill. Off the turnpike road, we enter through some large gates into a pine wood; in Australia it would be called a forest. This wood has been planted by hand. It must have been established for generations, the trees are of uniform height about forty feet. It is, as far as I could understand, within the domain of the Duke of Bedford where he keeps his game.

The entrance of the Woburn Road into the Woods was marked by a gate as mentioned.
On the right and top is the same road looking for either direction (Longslade Lane) and which is the entrance to the forest as described by Henry. The Keeper's Lodge was on the right but it and the gate are long gone.

On the right hand side as we enter is the keeper's lodge, built fantastically of sods of hazelwood unbarked. A caretaker, or keeper, as he is called, is established to protect His Grace's hares, rabbits, pheasants, partridges etc. Although pedestrians are allowed to pass through the roads, or ridings, as they are called, God help anyone caught poaching the reserves. Not withstanding, poaching was done by night to a considerable extent. The law against poaching, if caught, was three months imprisonment, and often fights occurred between poachers and keepers when the penalties were very severe. In my grandfather's time many a poacher was transported to Botany Bay or Van Dieman's Land for stealing of a horse or hare. Of course that was exile from home, wife, children and country forever. They never came back. I remember a scrap of an old poacher's song:

I can wrestle and fight my boys
I can jump over anywhere
It's my delight on a shiny night
At the season of the year.

'Magnificent trees, ferns growing thick between.' In 2003 a grand but unobtrusive golf and country club was operating on the sands past the Heath.

The Heath - still the same one hundred and sixty years later.

But let us get on through the wood. We see hazel bushes, which bear the famous hazel nut (these are for the squirrels to feed on), beautiful flowers - snapdragons, rhododendrons, tulips, shrubs, laburnum, sunflower, lilac, laurel, cypress and others; the perfume of all is delicious. The delicious scent of Australian flowers bears no comparison to the English. The huckleberry bush is conspicuous - this in season bears a berry - single, about the size of a black currant which makes delicious puddings. The poor people are allowed to pick them which they can sell at a penny or two pence a quart.

After proceeding about two miles through this wood, turning to the left slightly we come on to what is called the Heath. An open plain, nothing grown on it but furze and ling, it is about 200 acres. It is reported that some benevolent man, some generations back left it for the benefit of the poor of Bow Brickhill; to supply them with fuel. The furze is a thorny thick set short bush which is cut into bundles and when tied up is called a faggot. The ling is a different affair. The top is a leafless shrub used to make

Henry's 'wood of a different kind'.

rough brooms, or as they are called, bessoms. The bottom is a mass of fibrous roots for three or four inches in the sand. The people use an implement like a half moon shovel, called a turfing iron to pare it up the depth required and turn it upside down to dry in the sun. This is called turf and makes excellent fuel. Wild thyme is abundant with various kinds of vegetation. The ground is all sand and sandstone to the depth of fifty feet as far as it has been pierced.

We pass over a corner of the heath, next come to a wood of a different kind, larch, spruce and the wide spreading beech; magnificent trees, ferns growing thick between. A little further on the scene is abruptly changed; hitherto we have been passing over level ground, but now we have reached a steep decline for about half a mile, then flat almost level country. The view is magnificent beyond words; reaching for miles.

The village stands partly on the hillside and partly on the flat beyond. The country further on as far as the eye can reach is divided into squares (fields) enclosed with hawthorn and blackthorn hedges with large trees; oaks, elm, ash or willow here and there at intervals. A mile away is Caldecot, with its two farms, houses and six labourers' cottages. In old time this was a small village, but decaying into its present insignificance, is reckoned as a suburb of Bow Brickhill. Two miles is the village of Simpson; to the right Walton, Wavendon. To the left two miles distant is Fenny Stratford, a place of 300 or 400 inhabitants which is dignified by the name. A town fair is held there once a year. The turnpike runs through it and it has its mail coach to London.

Farther is Bletchley, Shenley and Denbigh; small villages. Like a band of sinuous silver a river meanders through green meadows from Fenny Stratford to Simpson. What its name is I never knew, and

Woburn village.

GRAND UNION CANAL

Henry's mysterious canal is the Grand Union Canal. It originates in Birmingham and terminates in London where it runs through Paddington, past Regents Park, Camden (bottom) and down to the docks where it enters the Thames. "I remember working barges on the Grand Union Canal as a child in 1950s. Nowadays it's just leisure traffic, but unlike many other canals in the UK, it never fell into total disrepair and boating holidays are increasingly popular."

SM

Church Road at the top of Bow Brickhill. Milton Keynes is straight ahead, Walton and Simpson to the left. Some farms are visible.

then a little farther on is the canal with its long narrow boats drawn by horses, which brings coal and merchandise from goodness knows where. Whence this canal comes and whither it goes I know not.

We are now standing on the highest pinnacle view alongside the old parish church built in the days of monkdom, many generations ago, a most conspicuous object, dominating the country to the west for miles. What a history, if it could speak, could this old pile unfold.

'Like a band of sinuous silver a river meanders through green meadows' - the River Ousel.

The baptisms of babies, the happy couples in the heyday of their youth under the merry peeling of the bells came to the marriage altar, and the solemn sound of the funeral bell summoning the dead to their last resting place in its little acre.

From the time the church was built it has swallowed the bodies of the whole parish in its little church yard. Human bones are a foot thick. What a great upheaving there will be when the last trump shall sound. The lower class never travelled except in their helpless old age to the workhouse. Where they were born, there they died and were buried, mixing their bones with their forefathers.

Labourers' cottages at the hill top - Church Road as it was.

Well, let us proceed down the hill through the village, down the narrow crooked street (if such a track can be called a street). The first place we come to next is the back of the parsonage, a large magnificent garden with a capricious mansion fenced in

The Rectory - once the home of Parson Davies.

with high walls to exclude the vulgar gaze. The parson is a personage of great import. He is generally a man of property, keeps his carriage, receives a fat stipend annually assured to him by government. When a poor man meets him he has to doff his hat or a poor woman she must curtsey low. I have seen them in due reverence nearly squat to the ground; of course, you know the parson belonged to the aristocrats and his cloth must be considered. It was the duty of the poor and humble to be subservient.

How it makes an Australian's blood boil at this day, to think of the arrogance, the contempt, the tyranny and oppression of the lower classes which was obtained in the days of which I write. Knowledge has spread education among the masses, has aroused a recognition of what is their natural rights. The labourer and producer has come at last to know his value, and is valiantly asserting his rights against the despotism and tyranny of the capitalist. But this is digressing from our subject. Let us proceed down the hill.

On the right hand are farm labourers' cottages graded step by step, each lower than the other; the walls are built of bond timber and half brick in thickness; roofs thatched with straw. If we enter one we shall see a brick floor, naked joists on the ceiling, one or two rooms on the ground floor; the bed rooms are on the second storey. The largest room is set off with a chimney, with eight or ten feet opening, gathered in high up so that anyone sitting by the fire can see the soot above head. On each side of the fireplace is a niche built in the wall with a wooden seat likewise built in. This seat is called the 'settle', generally occupied by the old people. On the left side of the hill are no houses, but half way down is an ever flowing spring of cold pure water.

We are at the bottom of the hill now. On the right is the 'Plough Inn', I think it was called. On the left is a number of labourers' cottages, in one of which your humble servant first saw the light. A grocer's shop the only one in the village. Another spring. Here the roadway sprawls out to a considerable width, one or two acres. What was the reason of this large space left unoccupied? I do not think anyone living

The Rectory garden from the house.

had any idea, but I can infer from what I remember, to have seen in two adjacent villages, namely Simpson and Milton, that the open space here referred to was where the ancient Druid's Oak was standing and held sacred for religious rites; under whose spreading branches the Druid's worshipped and offered their human sacrifices, burning young children in wicker cages to appease the wrath of Thor or Woden, as told by Julius Caesar who invaded Britain 40 BC. In an open space, as above referred to, I remember seeing on a high mound a large hollow trunk of an oak, it was large enough to hold three or four people standing. If I am not mistaken, this old ancient stump collapsed during my time. In Milton there was a wide spreading oak, a close fence was built around it for say fifteen feet, and filled in with earth about the trunk. This was called the Druid's Oak.

The open space in our village was bounded on one side principally by the sacred domain of the Rev. Parson Davies. I only remember once being within its precincts when Queen Victoria was crowned. I was about six years old. All the poor children of the parish were invited to a grand feast which consisted

Houses on the hill

"Henry's description of the farm labourers' cottages on the side of the hill is correct. The walls are indeed built of single brick in thickness. We used to live in one of them, and found decaying wood in the structure of one wall. I researched this building habit, and was told that the constructors used timber every so often in a wall to accommodate settlement."
SM

THE PLOUGH INN

"The Plough is still much as it was." SM

The cottages opposite the Plough Inn - Henry was born in one of these homes.

Social standing

"To this day a Rector or Parson is regarded as belonging to a different social strata to the ordinary middle class - on a par perhaps with a medical doctor or head teacher of a school - although these days we don't curtsy!"
SM

The old Druid's Oak in Milton.

Stephen Davies was the Rector at All Saints from December 23, 1832 to June 23, 1839. J.M. Jackson succeeded him.

CHURCH STREET, BOW BRICKHILL

The bottom of Church Road. The Plough Inn is on the left and Henry was born opposite.

These buildings show the village is well preserved. The old shop is on the right with the faded sign still evident.

MISTLETOE
"Henry mentions the church having mistletoe - it's not something you often find in churches - it's associated with pagan rituals."
SM

of a piece of cake and a glass of wine. Next to the parsonage was the pound where any delinquent straying donkey or dog might be incarcerated. Close by was the stocks in which any erring human animal could be exposed in the open public to expiate his small sins. The stocks consisted of a horizontal slab on edge in two parts one end joined to a vertical post. In the centre were two round holes to admit the culprit's shins; the upper part of the slab opened upward on a hinge to admit the prisoner, then lowered and locked. If obstreperous his wrists were placed in iron clamps on the vertical post. A man in the stocks was great sport for the boys and rowdies, especially if the individual in trouble was disliked. They would jeer, taunt and laugh at the poor wretch, remind him of all his misdeeds - not one of his sins would be forgotten, and a heavy burden added to the list, throw dirt or filth in his face. It was a great opportunity for anyone who owed him a grudge, to perhaps pelt him with rotten eggs. No authority interfered at these exhibitions. The indignity of it was the punishment. I must admit I never witnessed a man in the stocks, but I have heard my father and grandfather tell of them. However, the stocks remained a memorial of the brutal past.

Labourers' cottages on both sides in all kinds of nooks and corners. But the next thing of importance we come to as we travel on are two farm houses, one on each side of the road. I must dwell a little here in order to explain to the reader what an English farm house is like, as there is little comparison between a farm in Australia and one in England. I will describe one that I remember well, and that will be typical

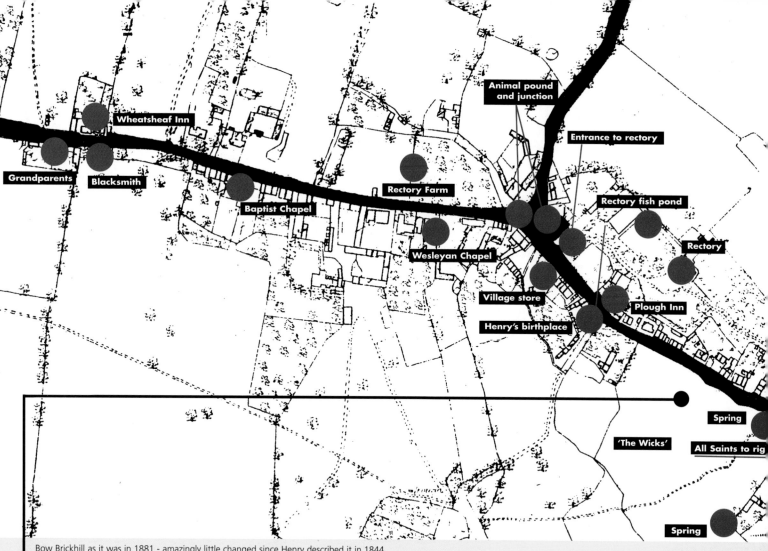

Labels on map:
- Animal pound and junction
- Wheatsheaf Inn
- Entrance to rectory
- Rectory fish pond
- Grandparents
- Blacksmith
- Rectory Farm
- Rectory
- Baptist Chapel
- Wesleyan Chapel
- Village store
- Plough Inn
- Henry's birthplace
- Spring
- 'The Wicks'
- All Saints to rig
- Spring

Bow Brickhill as it was in 1881 - amazingly little changed since Henry described it in 1844.

The view of old Bow Brickhill from The Wicks halfway down the very steep hill.

of the rest.

A spacious gabled mansion built of brick, three stories or two stories, and a garret which is in the roof lighted by dormer windows. Roof covered with red tiles; outside walls white washed. The interior - Master's room, parlour, servants, hall, a large room, furnished with a large fire place with brick oven on one side (this is where the yule log was burnt at Christmas), cellar, dairy, kitchen and pump all included in one building. Next to the back door is the pigsties with its odoriferous tanks of sour milk. The farm yard is next, a square open space about half an acre. Around the inside of this square are built stables, cart sheds, cow houses, cattle sheds and threshing barns.

In England the snow covers the ground in winter for many weeks, and consequently the grass is covered sometimes three or four feet. Cattle and sheep have to be kept yarded and fed in the farm yard from the straw from the threshing. The barns are high capacious buildings, a threshing floor in the centre. The material to be threshed is stacked on each end. When winter comes men are put on to thresh out the grain, the straw is thrown to the cattle over the yard for them to browse over and tramp into manure. On the back is the stackyard, where what grain cannot be placed in the barns is stacked on frames built on stone or wooden pillars. The farm lands extend from the back of the village, divided into fields (paddocks) from three to twenty acres each, surrounded with a thorny hedge consisting of hawthorn, blackthorn, briar, alongside of which is always a ditch for drainage. About half the land is cultivated for the growing of cereals, peas, beans, turnips, clover and vetches. The other half is devoted to grass for grazing, and for hay for feeding the cattle in the winter. The hay is all made from grass, mown by the scythe in the month of June. The rich land produces wonderful crops if mown and gathered in

favourable weather. Whoever has experienced the fragrance of English hay will never forget it.

After this digression, we pass an obtuse angle to the left, more cottages, very few on the right. We come now to the Wesleyan Chapel where I used to attend Sunday School twice, and listen to two sermons, and very likely a prayer meeting to finish with. Hell, fire and brimstone, the devil and damnation were dealt out here freely, with a glimpse now and then of the great glory of heaven and happiness of the elect. The saved were few, as many were called, but few were chosen. The great magnificent, almighty God was worshipped more out of fear than love or reverence. The effects of this severe creed on the youthful mind suggests horrible inexpressible cruelty, casts a gloomy terror over his existence, so that he is apt to fly to reason to satisfy himself that it is untrue, and perchance he may despise religion altogether, or worse, become an atheist. My father believed in this creed wholly. He was a sincere good man.

When we came to Australia we lived in the bush for the first five years, during which time we never saw a church or heard divine service, yet my father never faltered in his faith to the day of his death.

On the opposite side of the road lived old Mr Groves, a retired butcher, and my teacher in the Sunday School on occasions. He was none of the rabid sort, but took delight in imparting useful knowledge to children. He kept in the school a little box of books to distribute among the scholars. Being a constant applicant to his little library, I was a great favourite with him. Poor old Mr Groves, he must have been mustered with his fathers for many years, his bones in the old church yard.

Next to the chapel lived our only baker, Mr Britten, one of the local preachers, a just and honest man, but he held himself a bit above the common, his puritanical principals were rather extreme.

Progressing onward, we come to the largest farm in the parish. It was owned by a blasphemous wretch named Colonel De Laps. He would swear sometimes so horribly, I was told, enough to make the natives' hair stand on end. Luckily, however, the Colonel himself did not live on this farm being, as reputed, a very rich man. Likely as not, he herded with the aristocracy. The farm was let to a farmer from Suffolk.

Cottages again till we come to the Baptist chapel which I know little about only that my uncle and aunt belonged to it. On the right was another farm of small pretensions. Lastly, we come to another inn, I think called the 'Wheatsheaf' and opposite the only blacksmith's shop in the village, half a dozen cottages - my Grandfather lived in one.

We have now practically come to the end of the village containing about sixty cottages, six farms, including two at Caldecot, one bakery, one blacksmith, one wheelwright, one shoemaker, one carpenter, one grocer, two inns and one recognised church. Those of the poor class who professed any religion were either Wesleyans or Baptists. All those who had any pretension to a higher position went to the Church of England, the old church on the hill. The farmers one time made an attempt, under the instigation of the parson, to compel all dissenters to attend the English church or give them no work, but it failed. As it was, however, no baptisms, marriages or burial services were legal except if performed by the minister of the Church of England. The inhabitants of the village I could say, all told would number about four hundred; four-fifths are farm labourers. The size of each farm, from 200 to 400 acres, employing from five to fifteen men and boys each. The wages for men is 8/- or 9/- a week during the winter. In harvest time they are allowed to earn 2/- or 3/- more, in cases of emergency, by working very long hours from light to dark, say sixteen hours. Boys start work at seven or eight years of age and get at start 1/-, when they reach the age of eleven they get 2/-. It must be remembered the scale of wages above stated is without food. Each farm, as a rule, keeps two servants - a man and a woman who board and live in the house. The man receives five pounds a year; the woman three pounds; their year of servitude lasts from Michaelmas to Michaelmas (September 29).

For an example I choose the farm I worked on as a type of the rest. Three strong horses, stable fed on grass or clover hay, chaff, cut by hand to which split beans were added; a good bedding of straw with sack overhead filled with hay last thing at night.

At 6 o'clock in the morning in the winter the oastler had to be in the stable to grind the beans, feed the horses, rub them down, water them (often he had to break the ice in the pond to allow them to drink), harness them ready for ploughing. As soon as it was light the ploughman and a boy started for the field. The plough was a single furrow, wooden beam and handles, the mould board was wood sheeted over with an iron plate, two wheels, one in the furrow and one on the land. Three horses yoked in a line, one before the other all walked in the furrow. The ploughman held the handle, and the boy, with a long whip, drove the horses. At eleven o'clock a halt was made for 'bever'. The man and boy sat on the plough beam to munch a piece of dry bread for a few minutes, and if thirsty drank face downwards out of the ditch. Then onward again till 3 o'clock when they unyoked and went to dinner. An acre was considered a fair day's work. The ploughman tended the horses after dinner, cut chaff, ground beans, cleaned out the stable, cleaned his horses, etc. The boy did odd jobs.

Some of the grain was sown broadcast, some drilled in and some dibbled in; this was a slow process, a man walking backwards armed with an implement in each hand about three feet long with a crutch at the top, fitted at the bottom with a lump of iron resembling a pointed plumbob with which he punched holes guided by a line; two boys followed him with pouches of grain hanging in front, dropping three or four grains in each hole.

A typical old Bow Brickhill farm worked on by Henry - this was 'Poplar Farm'.

The hands at this time were employed variously; some trimming the hedges, cleaning out the ditches, others carting out last winter's manure from the farmyard and stacking it in a heap to ferment. Old manure heaps of last year were carted on to the land left fallow, much of it was spread over the grass land, others were put on to the threshing floors. The farmer kept a dozen milking cows. One of the hands was appointed milkman to milk and feed the cattle and store calves. His situation was an arduous one, at his work earlier and later than others. He had to attend to his work, of course, on Sundays. For his extra work he was allowed a basin of bread and milk in the morning and same in the evening. The churning came once a week, at which operation the milkman and a boy were employed to turn a large rotary barrel with a crank at each end, on which occasion they were favoured with a horn of beer and a bite of bread and cheese.

The horses, cattle and sheep were always in good condition, though the sheep were often affected with the disease called scab and also footrot, fluke and maggots from flies blowing them under the wool. The breeds of sheep were Leicester and Southdowns. Fowls and pigs were largely reared. The standard meat was the pig - bacon was the only meat the poor ever got, eggs never. Some of the poor did manage to rear a pig, the neighbours contributing feed in the way of pot liquor scraps, bad potatoes, etc, and when that pig was killed portions of it were distributed far and wide. A pig was not killed every day, hence the custom I presume of today in the event of killing of a pig, neighbours must have a bit.

Most of the tenements owned a garden, flower garden in front, kitchen garden at the back or side where

Life was tough for people on the land as witnessed by this photograph of a Shenley farm covered with snow.

The Rectory Farm in Simpson is typical of such places in the region then.

An old decaying example of the farm cart described by Henry.

culinary vegetables were raised. Currants red, white and black, gooseberry's were abundant. The better-to-do class owned some grand orchards two or three acres in extent, apples and pear trees fifty to sixty feet high, generations old growing in the grass - never cultivated. Apples and pears sold at a shilling a bushel, damson, plum and cherry trees grew proportionately high. There were many isolated orchards where owners and every vestige of habitation had disappeared, unknown in the memory of living man.

Having described the methods of ploughing, seeding and general winter farm work, I will now proceed to the hay making and harvesting. In the month of June mowers grind and prepare their heavy, clumsy scythes for the hay. In the early morning three or four mowers meet in the field to be operated on, a long whetstone hanging behind their waist in a pouch. The boy appears with a large can of beer. They drink a couple of horns each (the horns hold about half a pint) and then make a start. The best mower is the leader and goes first, the second best follows and so on. The ground is well graded and level, the grass is cut within an inch of the ground into swathes even and straight. I never, in Australia, saw a man who could handle a scythe properly except my father. The mowers go to the end of their bout, say fifteen chains, then return to the starting point. The next operation is what is called tedding. Men, boys, perhaps women with two prong forks shake the mown grass evenly over the ground to dry. After this work is completed, as soon as the hay is wilted enough, it is raked into small even rows, next into larger rows and so on. When considered dry enough, it is heaped into large cocks. The haymakers at eleven o'clock have a short respite to have 'bever', sit down for a few minutes to drink their beer. The men have two horns, boys and women one each. This is good strong ale, brewed by the farmer himself in the winter. Besides, there is always plenty of what is called 'small beer' to drink at anytime. At four in the afternoon the bever process is again repeated. When the hay is ready for stacking the carts come on the field drawn with one horse driven by a boy.

I will give the reader an outline of these old fashioned carts - heavily built, wooden axles with a plate of iron on underside of arm, run in iron bushes, rim of wheel eight inches wide strapped with two separate tyres in three feet sections spiked on to the felloes with large headed spikes. In front of the cart was a frame reaching as far as the horse's shoulders, supported in front by bars reaching to the shafts. This frame was called the 'copses', behind was a short frame held by leverage (hind ladder), short frames also projected over the wheels. These carts, though clumsily constructed, would carry an enormous quantity of hay and one horse was able to draw them with ease. Two men with long forks pitch up the hay, one man loads, two boys follow with dray rakes cleaning up all as they go. What with strong limbs, strong muscles and plenty of beer the work goes merrily on.

We have done haymaking. Let us skip a month and go harvesting. All harvest work is done by hand, no reaping machines in those days. Let us suppose the wheat is ripe and ready for reaping. Five, six or seven men armed with sickles start in rotation each taking half a land, cutting the straw about six inches high from the ground. Boys following behind lay down a band on which the reaper deposits his handful. When the end of the cut is reached all hands turn round, bind and stook as they go all that has been reaped. Oats and barley are cut with the scythe, peas are gathered with sickle having a long handle, cut close to the ground. Beans are chopped off near the ground and made into sheaves. All through haytime and harvest time bevers at eleven o'clock and four o'clock, with small beer 'ad libitum' is continued. The last load of grain is a stupendous affair - 'Harvest Home', boggins of beer and bread and cheese. The boys on the top of the load sing 'Harvest Home', cut all manner of silly tricks. Fun runs riot. If the farmer is of the kindly sort, and has had a successful harvest, he invites all hands to supper and they have a real jollification. At the end of the season comes the apple gathering. Men and boys with long ladders and baskets gather in the golden fruit. Bever times now are over, no more beer.

THE SOCIAL, MORAL AND SUPERSTITIOUS CHARACTERISTICS OF THE PEOPLE

Everybody

Paying the turnpike toll.

Residences in Church Road at the bottom of the hill.

in the village knows everybody else. Among the poor there is no reverence for age, everyone is called by his christened name or half of it; Tom, Dick, Sam, Bett, Sall, Moll, etc. People of any means are called Mr or Mrs.

As a rule the community were peaceful, but sometimes a little fracas would arise, especially among the women. One day I recollect seeing two women scratching and leering at each other's faces, pulling hair, screeching outrageously: a man coming along in a soothing way enquired what the grievance was, the row, about. "Peg?" he enquired, "Oh-oh-oh the hus-s-sy she call-led me a bit-bitch. I-I-I'm no more a b-bitch than she is, if I have a bas-bastard, she had one afore she was married. I'll tear her eyes out I will. The miserable shurocks she ain't got a smock to her back. I'll pay you out for this Sall West that I wull; see if I don't you leerups." Sally's wrath rose again at that - she retorted: "Yah, you mean thing, you think Sam West is going to marry you; not he; when he marries he'll have a decent gal not a trapes like you. You can't earn a shillen a week at lace making, you can only do tatten." The intercessor here took Peg by the arm saying: "Come along Peggy don't mind 'er." Peg commenced to wind up her straggling hair and twisting it into a knob at the back of her head, when the man said: "Why don't you and Sam get married?" "We're going to," she replied. "We are waiting till he gets money enough to start. Sam's only getting 7 shillings a week, an he has to allow me eighteen pence a week for little Tommy, so we'll have to wait."

It is an indisputable fact that one half of the young women have a child before marriage. It is called a chance child, but the men are, as a rule, very honourable, marrying in the long run. If a young fellow seduces a girl and abandons her he was despised. Illegitimacy among the poor is of no great consequence. I knew some cases of wife beating, but they were rare. The severe application of the rod was a specific remedy for all sins. Old Solomon's proverb was implicitly believed in, "Spare the rod and spoil the child." If a child did anything wrong, the only corrective was a good basting or lacing down, even up to the age of puberty. I remember fathers thrashing their daughters unmercifully. They were cautious, however, with their big sons because they would not stand it. Castigation in the schools was carried on to a fearful extent. I went to a school in Woburn (fee 2 pence a week) where the master did nothing else but thrash. There were 400 boys, the larching was carried on by ushers (pupil teachers). If any boy misbehaved himself, was unusually stupid or had dirty hands or face he was sent up to the master to get a leathering, either with the strap or cane. This old fury did his work with a bitter

There were many Cooks, Harts, Bodilys, Kents and Perrys in BBH in Henry's era.

Members of the Woodward family of Bow Brickhill. Seen at the bottom is William Woodward (born in Bow Brickhill about 1849, died in Bow Brickhill in June 1923) and two pictures (left below) of his wife Sarah Elizabeth Tansley (born in Bow Brickhill in October 1849 and died in Bow Brickhill in March 1934). The lady in the shot under this caption is William and Sarah's daughter Caroline Woodward (born in Bow Brickhill in October 1868 and died in Bow Brickhill in December 1937).

31

SOCIAL BENEFITS

While modern thinking at the time of publication may have us believing we are well advanced over people from the time of Henry's childhood, we owe folk from that era more respect. It might surprise most readers to know that all villages had their own Friendly Societies which were brought in to protect most of the working men and their families against sickness by joining these societies. One was the Ancient Order of Foresters. It was formed in 1834 and lodges were set up in villages and towns. The Societies provided funds for sickness, old age, funeral benefits, unemployment or other infirmities. Contributions averaged 4 pence or 6 pence per week for sickness which paid out 12 shillings per week for twenty-six weeks. Children could be enrolled for a death benefit on a contribution of 1 penny per week providing about 10 pounds at death. Wages for farm labourers during the 1800s averaged 8 shillings per week at the start and had risen to 15 shillings per week at the end of the century. Men's wages were often supplemented by their wives and daughters engaged in the lace or hat trades. An expert lacemaker could earn 6 shillings per week. Bow Brickhill had 125 Society members at the end of the 1800s. The population in the 1911 census was stated as being 432.

The Wests were recorded as being labourers in Bow Brickhill. Descendants were still in the village in 1950.

LACE MAKING

Lace making and hat making as cottage industries began to decline from the middle of the 1800s faced with competition from factory-made products from Nottingham and elsewhere.

"Bobbin lace is described very accurately - I've done some. Tatting makes similar fancy work, but not anything like as fine, so the insult made by Sally is quite a strong one.

"Henry is right about Bucks lace which is made with fine cotton and incredibly intricate - one of the finest and most sought-after types of lace. It's still regarded that way amongst lace makers. He obviously observed the whole process very carefully because his description is just right.

"He refers to the Dunstable hat making industry - there are still several hat makers in the Dunstable and Luton areas."
SM

complacent smile. Of course, was he not executing the only pennance for all evil boys. Lord how this old wretch was feared and execrated.

The principal occupation of the women in Buckinghamshire and the surrounding counties was lace making, this lace at one time world famous for its elegance and beautiful texture. As far as I am able, I will describe the operation. First we have a globular bag stuffed hard with straw two feet in diameter, this is placed on a stand of convenient height; on the top a bow projects out on one side over the operator's lap. The bow is about eighteen inches in diameter. The globe, or pillow as it is called, is placed in this bow where it is held firm. On the pillow is placed the pattern, pricked out in parchment, of the lace to be made. A thousand pins more or less are stuck into the pillow at the top of the parchment. Next comes the bobbins - little sticks about five inches long something like a pen holder, a neck is formed on the top to receive the thread to be used which is wound on with an implement called the bobbin wheel. The bobbins (a hundred or so) and the ends of the threads, to start, are fixed to pins in the pattern. The operator sits with her knees under the pillow, and deftly handling the bobbins with her fingers, sticks in a pin where required, always bringing pins from the back to the front. When threads get short the bobbin is unwound a little and fixed by a half hitch.

The lace sold from 1/- to 10/- a yard. Lace-making was a very unhealthy occupation, sitting from early morning till late at night was a great cause of consumption. In winter on a brick floor the cold was very severe, the only means of warmth used was an earthenware pot with live coals put under their petticoats.

Another industry carried on by women to a small extent was straw plaiting. Dunstable straw hats and bonnets were famous at one time. In harvest time when the last sheaf of wheat had been carted out of the field, a crowd of women and girls would be standing at the gate ready to rush in to pick up any stray ears that may have been dropped. The smartest picking often took home large bundles which they threshed and cleaned by hand which the miller ground for them, keeping the bran and pollard for the grinding.

Education among the labouring class was almost nil, some children of my generation were taught a little reading, writing and perhaps a little arithmetic. Geography and grammar was unheard of. I do not remember one of my grandfather's generation who could either read or write. My father, being a sincere Wesleyan, succeeded in learning to read his hymn book, but he made a terrible hash of it. The higher classes were of opinion, and said: "What is the good of education to a working man; it only puts bad things into their head."

People being ignorant are, of course, correspondingly superstitious. They believed in ghosts, witches, bogies, warnings, etc. A thunder storm was the sign of an angry God. I have seen people crazy with terror; old men take off their hats and pray silently to the Almighty for protection. It was sinful to point at the lightning or thunder. A story was rife of a wicked farmer who had hay in the

Education is now fundamental in Bow Brickhill, and the school's car park is on the site of the old Wesleyan Chapel in Station Road (see the picture on the right).

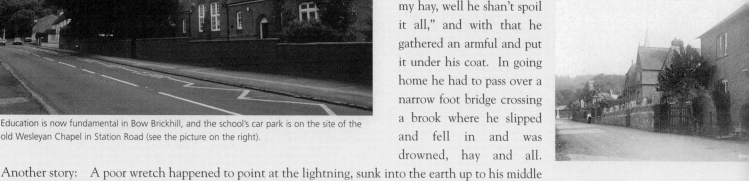

field ready for carting in. A heavy thunderstorm coming on, he said: "God Almighty means to spoil my hay, well he shan't spoil it all," and with that he gathered an armful and put it under his coat. In going home he had to pass over a narrow foot bridge crossing a brook where he slipped and fell in and was drowned, hay and all.

Another story: A poor wretch happened to point at the lightning, sunk into the earth up to his middle and not all the picks, spades or shovels could dig him out.

Cursing and swearing was held in great disfavour. If one used the word "damn" he was looked upon as an extraordinary sinner, because he made use of the great oath. Not one half of the people attended a place of worship of any kind. The superior, or upper class, when they did attend service, patronise the English Church. The labouring people were all dissenters, either Wesleyans or Baptists, though Christmas morning, for what reason I do not know, they attended the Church of England, which on this occasion was profusely ornamented with holly and mistletoe presenting a pretty sight, provocative of a feeling of intense reverence. From the solemn responses of the old clerk, and the people on these Christmas mornings, I always felt more impressed than at any performances at my own chapel.

In the Wesleyan chapels the services were conducted by local preachers selected from the parishes around. Carpenters, shoemakers, bakers, etc., being a step higher than the common, with a little education had been converted and saved from the wrath to come, perfectly sure of their reward; sincere, honest souls no doubt. Some preached in a quiet, undemonstrative manner, but the majority were of the self-satisfied, thoroughly self-convinced kind who interspersed their discourse with hell, fire and brimstone, the 'Last Day', resurrection, God's wrath, etc. and many repetitions of the text. Any forcible assertion he would make was driven home with sledge hammer force on the pulpit, making the candle sticks dance and the nervous to start.

After Sunday services, the last thing at night, a prayer meeting was held for all the members and those who cared to stay. Most of the members and new converts uttered a prayer. There were also two prayer

Religions

'Non-conformist' religion was strongest in the area in Newport Pagnell from the mid-to-late 1700s. An academy was set up in 1780 to train and educate young men to be ordained Ministers of the Independent Church.

Groups were formed in nearby villages including Bow Brickhill in 1799.

An endowment of £1000 was granted to Bow Brickhill and a chapel built. Monies invested produced £25 per year. The chapel and chapel house were demolished in the 1930s.

In 1819 Bow Brickhill had 100 hearers and 50 Sunday School members.

The first records in BBH of families mentioned by Henry are Wootton (1705), Cripps (1634), Cook (1605), Atterbury (1634), Brise (also Brice, 1660), Perry (1790).

All Saints has an extensive graveyard which is now mostly in ruins. Very few graves are marked or can be identified. No Mundays have been buried there since the early 1970s, and no direct Mundays are known to live in Bow Brickhill at the time of publication.

meetings at night during the week held in the chapel, also meetings between nights were held at members' houses in rotation. It seems to me their only hope lay in constant prayer. Well, poor souls, according to their faith, were they not justified - their chances of going to hell so great and to heaven so little. What, through poverty, religion and superstition life was not worth living.

At intervals, red hot evangelists appeared on the scene to hold revival meetings which then, as now, were a great attraction. A pandemonium was nothing to be compared to it. These evangelists seemed to possess mesmeric power over the congregation, especially over the women, jumping, shouting, praying, singing, whispering to one and then to another, denouncing sin and sinner, disclaiming on the awful consequence of evil ways, the never ending agony in fire and brimstone among gibing devils in the pit of hell. "Repent, repent, repent, now, if ye will be saved."

A form was placed in front of the pulpit called the penitent bench. Men and women crying out with tears and groans, women fainting through excess of terror and emotion. It was not uncommon for a woman to go into a fit. Repentant sinners rushed to the penitent bench amidst cries of,

The main door to All Saints. The porch was added in the late 1880s.

"Hallelujah, Amen," "Praise the Lord." So many souls saved, snatched from the burning. Then a hymn would be sung out of pure glorification, and so the game went on. Some of the converts remained steady, though very few. The most of them backslided in two or three weeks or less.

On old view of Bow Brickhill Woods which leads from Woburn off the main road.

JACK CLARKE
Born in 1799, married in 1826 and had eight children. He died in 1879.

One convert I remember very well was named Jack Clarke. Jack was married and had seven or eight children who ran about barefooted and in rags. Jack had a bad reputation. He was seen in the public house often, was heard to swear, even making use of the great oath. He was captured one night and persuaded to attend a revival meeting. Jack was converted, and

The Grand Union Canal near Bow Brickhill goes to London and the Thames.

horrified at the magnitude of his sins the way they were explained to him, prayed with all his might. He remained firm in well doing for three or four weeks, made very long, loud prayers at the meetings, too long some of the members thought and often coughed or gave some other hint for him to cut it short, but Jack heeded them not. He kept on the even tenor of his way to the end. But the devil had not done with Jack, he tempted him again and he fell. He disgraced himself; he was a backslider. His well wishers, greatly grieved at his relapse, used every means to reclaim him and bring him back again to the throne of grace. Bitterly ashamed of himself, he succumbed at last and was once more within the fold. His praying and demonstrations of repentance were louder than ever, but it was of no use, he lapsed again, again and again; the devil, it was said, had claimed him for his own. It was of no use; the brethren said (out of heart) let him slide, he must go to the devil.

Another convert, a girl about eighteen, I remember well, was converted at a revival meeting. Her name was Moll Perry. She was considered the wildest girl in the village, she was called an "out and outer." What Moll's especial sins were I never knew except that she was fast and very noisy, choosing boys' company rather than girls. She could fight too, as was like a Briton. Moll was an assiduous attendant at the prayer meetings, and could pray with such earnestness and vigour as to eclipse the most of them. She became a prominent Sunday school teacher. Moll had a harsh, loud voice. Where the hymns were given out during the service, with eyes lifted towards heaven and open mouth, she would let her vocal powers loose sufficiently to drown all other voices. Moll was a great acquisition to the flock. Her conversion happened not long before we left our home. She remained staunch to her conversion as far as I know.

The average duration of life was low, exceptional cases were rare. A few attained the age of eighty, but were generally in their second childhood. I once saw an old man, said to be near his ninetieth year, who was like a baby in talk and action. The poor were not actually allowed to starve when out of work or incapable of work from old age. There were the parish relief fund and the workhouse, superintended by an official called the 'Relieving Officer'. In cases of distress, this functionary was appealed to, who allowed in cases which he considered real want, perhaps two loaves or three, it depended on the number in the family, and a shilling a week; either that or go into the workhouse. The thought of going to the workhouse was so repugnant and detestable, that some would steal or starve rather than submit to enter it, where brothers and sisters, man and wife, no matter how old, were separated. Able-bodied men were seldom allowed to stay long in the 'House', as all employers were financially interested in the support of the institution. A job of some kind would be found for him at some kind of wages. The food in the workhouse consisted of water thickened with flour; thin so thin, it was called 'skilly'. No doubt the reader has read Oliver Twist. When Oliver wanted more, Mr Bumble, the parish beadle, pre-decided that he would come to a bad end - be hanged or die from over-gorging. It was considered a disgrace to go to the workhouse, but where was the alternative.

It was considered a sacred duty by the upper classes to prosecute with the utmost rigor of the law, any thefts of property committed by old or young. In fact, there was a combination pledged to that effect. With the exception of poaching, stealing was rare, though I remember two cases of sheep stealing, sheep killed and taken out of the field by night. To prevent these depredations, the farmers formed a hunting club. They kept a pack of those vicious, blood thirsty, uncanny looking dogs called blood hounds. These hounds were kept regularly trained. A boy would start early in the day, dragging a bladder at the end of a string, filled with blood. The boy had three hours start, running as fast as he could, trailing his bladder of blood over fields, ditches, through hedges till finding a convenient tree to climb, which

The grave of Will Clark.

Bow Brickhill 40 years after Henry left but unchanged and admirably described.

he clambered up leaving his bladder on the ground, awaiting events.

In the meantime the hunters had assembled on the best of horses suitable for the occasion. The kennel is let loose, yelping and roaring. They are led across the scent and off they start, with a sonorous yell like hell broken loose. Following after came the huntsmen pell-mell over fields, ditches, over or through hedges. Being farmers, mostly the bladder boy is warned not to trail over corn land to avoid doing any damage, but through grass or fallow land. Sometimes the trail is lost, then there is a promiscuous searching in all directions till one of the hounds re-discovers it, and then with a yell, well known to all, off they start again till the bladder is reached; which is instantly torn to shreds. The boy up the tree looks calmly on.

As I have stated before, I remember two cases of sheep stealing. In one case the thief killed the sheep, skinned it, cut off the head and took out the inside which he left for the owner. After this obnoxious crime was discovered, a world wide sensation ensued. The blood hounds were hurried out; everyone who could raise a horse or donkey rushed to see what was going to happen. The great cavalcade arrived at the spot where this daring crime had been perpetrated thinking the hounds would pick up the thief's tracks and trace him to his lair. Nothing of the sort. After scoffing the remains of the sheep (saving the hide) in spite of all persuasions, the hounds could not be induced to proceed any farther in the business. So to the great and righteous indignation of the farmer folk the culprit got off 'scot free'. The criminal was never found out.

In the other case of sheep stealing, the criminal was caught red handed. He was tried and was condemned to be transported to Van Dieman's Land for fourteen years, which meant for life. I do not suppose he ever came back. This man was suspected of poaching, and consequently bore a bad character. The farmers would not give him work; he declared he would sooner steal than go to the Workhouse. He had a wife and four children.

Great Brickhill Manor and Bletchley Park Mansion were typical of the types of grand homes recognised and recalled by Henry all those years later.

There was another kind of chase - fox hunting, which was patronised by the high class, nobility, Dukes, Earls, Barons, Princes, etc. and those snobs of lower degree who could manage to purchase and keep a hunter. It is necessary to explain here who and what was the so called nobility - owners of large estates of ten, fifteen, twenty to thirty thousand acres. The Duke of Sutherland owns today 1,358,600 acres.

A large mansion, perhaps what was called in feudal times an impregnable castle, with beautiful gardens carefully tended. Beyond is the park, a domain of maybe a thousand acres all securely fenced with a close high fence to prevent the vulgar outside from looking in, and to prevent the hares, rabbits and deer from straying. The entrance to the castle was through two superb gates, a rampant lion on each post, or lion and unicorn. Inside the gates was the lodge, where resided the lodgekeeper, a functionary of commanding presence who was stationed there to ascertain who was approaching the great house.

The circuitous road to the castle was magnificent and impressive. Flowers, large old trees the

How the gentry lived - the view to the old gatehouse at Woburn Abbey from near the Abbey. Bow Brickhill lies in the distance near the large aerial.

The De Laps and their estate Monellan, Ireland

"Monellan isn't much of a place now, but you should have seen it in my young days when there was upwards of 50 men employed on it. They kept three men trimming and repairing and cleaning the avenues and a small boy to brush up after them. Woe to the man who would have dared to break as much as a twig that size in them days and soon there won't be a twig left. Rev. Robert De Laps was the owner but he wasn't the first of that name.

"The first De Laps in Monellan was a Colonel in the British Army. He was given the estate in repayment for "services rendered to the Crown" *(this is the De Laps who owned the largest farm in Bow Brickhill).* It might be as far back as 1798. The Colonel had a brother Sam who was the first to start building the 'Big House'. Sam had a son Robert who was a King's Counsel. He only pleaded one case, and lost it. He told me often that it preyed on his conscience and he gave up the law altogether. Reports have it that the old Colonel (his uncle) was a very honourable old soldier who loved truth and straight-forwardness. He persuaded him to give up by saying 'it was too sinful' a life, and to take up the church. Robert became a clergyman. He died on July 28, 1885 aged 83.

"Robert's daughters lived there until the 1920s, when the estate was sold to a timber merchant who cut down all the timber.

"Monellan Castle was built during the 1700s, and part of the 35 room dwelling was underground, to be used as a place of safety. The castle and its grounds were in full glory for some time after the Catholic Emancipation Act in 1775, until its demolition in the 1930s.

"The subsequent division of the estate to the poor local farmers, was much welcomed."

growth of centuries, oak, elm, beech, etc. spreading over an immense area intermixed with other foreign vegetation.

What this great man does not require for his own especial convenience and pleasure, he lets to gentleman farmers - 200 to 400 acres. This farmer employs labourers at 8/- or 9/- a week on whose labour depends the living of the whole family.

These, so called nobles, are of a different caste to the common people with well educated, highly refined manners, delicate features, small feet and hands innocent of all kinds of manual labour - supercilious, haughty, overbearing or when condescending to speak to one below them, extremely patronising. Snobs and toadies bow and scrape to them, only too proud if His Highness would condescend to notice him, and never forgets ever after to boast of his friend Lord....... or Baron.........

But what are these nobles in reality when boiled down? They are no more than the descendants of thieves, plunderers and murderers of the 11th century when William of Normandy, called The Conqueror, fought for and grabbed the English crown. He dispossessed the Saxon land holders (who fought for their home and country) of their homes, because they opposed him in his capacity and then divided it among his rascally followers.

The Reverend Davies even had his own fish pond which exits still.

By the law of primogeniture, these vast estates and titles descended to the eldest son or first of kin. The younger scions of the family had to shift for themselves, but were easily accommodated by governmental and aristocratic influence to the most lucrative positions: perhaps mere sinecures. The head of the family who bore the title had a seat in the

The De Laps' church in Monellan.

37

Caldecotte House was ancient but burned down in the early 1980s.

House of Lords for the term of his natural life. All superior officers of the British Army were selected from the younger sons of nobility, brains or no brains. Old soldiers, veterans of many years, had to submit to be hectored and be bullied by these scions of a noble house. A common soldier was seldom promoted beyond a corporal.

Many of the nobility had magnificent mansions in London, different estates in the country, kept in proper order by a band of caretakers all in order for his mightiness' pleasure when he choose to change his residence.

Also estates in Scotland, estates too in Ireland cut up into small farms which were let to the poor for as much rent as he could extract. The landlord seldom resided in Ireland, but employed agents to superintend their estates and collect the rents.

The nobility have rendezvous in the season in Italy - Venice, Naples, Rome; in France - Paris, Bologne, Notre Dame, etc; in Germany - Baden, at the spas where they swallow mineral water to repair their vitiated stomachs. In Switzerland they must climb Mount Blanc and capture a sprig of edelweiss, at the risk of their lives. Only for the dexterous use of their alpine stocks, they would have fallen a million feet to certain death. Good Lord!

In the leading newspapers of the day, the principal and most important news of the time was concerning the aristocracy, their comings and goings, their adventures, laudable deeds, duels, elopements, morganatic marriages, etc. All seemed to conduce to their glorification and command of admiration.

"His Royal Highness the Prince of Humbug, visiting our shores for the improvement of his health, was yesterday suddenly attacked with severe pains in the abdominal viscera (pains in his guts). His physicians speedily prescribed to his ailments and gave him almost instant relief; by bulletins received during the night, he is satisfactorily improving and will soon be on his feet again."

Another. "We are happy to report that the Duchess of Bumbledon, to the great delight of her Lord, has borne him a son; heir to that vast estate. Her Grace, who is notable for her benevolence and charity to the poor, we are glad to add, is doing well."

Another. "A pleasant episode occurred last week in the county of Bobbleton. The late Earl's demise, as well known, occurred a few months ago. His heir, the successor to the title of the Earldom of Bobbleton, was on his travels in foreign lands, nobody knowing of his whereabouts. He

Looking from the Rectory into the garden and on to Bow Brickhill village.

Cottages just below All Saints church.

FOX HUNTING
"The account of fox hunting is accurate from my own knowledge. I used to go and see the Whaddon Chase Hunt. Whaddon Chase is referred to by Henry when his family left Bow Brickhill, and is a small area of forest near Bletchley. I don't know of a time when hunting came to Bow Brickhill. My father was very strongly against hunting in Buckinghamshire because it damaged crops and property just as Henry described it, and was not performed by the landowners over their own land, but over that of other farmers who had no say in what went on - and probably dared not to say too much anyway."
SM

came home suddenly a few days ago - to claim his title and estates. The present Earl of Bobbleton having taken high honours at Cambridge, won many prizes as an athlete, and having travelled nearly all round the world, is a man of high culture, of a kindly and benevolent disposition. The event of his arrival was signalised by a grand dinner given, and supper followed by a ball to his fellow magnates. All the poor and workmen living on the estate were regaled with a sumptuous meal and beer (a good blowout). Hilarity was the order of the day. It is pleasant to be able to record the generosity and geniality of our noble Earl of Bobbleton." What snobbery and toadyism.

This great nobility on their vast secluded domains rear hares, rabbits, foxes, deer, pheasants, partridges, etc. which, when they are satiated with every other pleasure, delight in slaughtering just for the fun of it. The contest is who can succeed in committing the greatest slaughter. The victor is looked upon as a man of merit.

We will have to proceed now with the fox hunt.

A nobleman of high degree kept a kennel of sixty or seventy fox hounds, nice medium sized dogs, white, with large black or red spots. The man employed to feed, train and conduct the chase was called the Huntsman. When on duty he wore a red jacket, in his hand a long brass horn with which he directs the movements of the hounds, which perfectly understand the different signals. I was never at a starting of a fox hunt, but have seen the hunt in full swing. Tom Day and I were in a grass field one day spudding thistles, when Tom, ceasing his work, suddenly said: "Hullo: What's that nighs, the foxhunters are out, I can hear the hounds." So could I. "I'd lay a penny," I said, "they can see the fox too." Lord how the dogs do holler, "Tally ho! Tally ho!" was getting nearer and nearer. At last after an interval of a few minutes reynard darted through the hawthorn hedge making right for us; a few seconds after, a swarm of hounds were through, yelling like a thousand devils, and then the huntsman with a mighty leap showed his red jacket over the hedge. The fox, on seeing us, shied off at an obtuse angle through a hedge into a crop of nearly ripe wheat, and after him rushed the hounds; after them the huntsman. But what attracted our attention most was the scramble of the noble lords and ladies over the first hedge. Some went over clean and straight, some searched for low places or gaps, some went through it. The ladies followed their lords or favourites; one lost her tall hat hanging on a thorn bush. "My lord," cried Tom, "how them women can jump." Some, however, scrutinised round for a gate. Two unfortunate lords came to grief. "One," Tom said, "tumbled head over horse and all." One, whose horse stuck in the hedge, was propelled over his horse's head, and was landed in the water; nevertheless they recovered themselves in a very short time and followed on. The chase was now through the wheat field and the havoc they made was pitiable to see. The farmer came shortly after to view the destruction done. By his angry looks he must have cursed under his breath, not loud but deep. I heard afterwards the fox had been run down some miles farther on. The foremost at the death claimed the brush (fox's tail), a trophy and an honour to be hung in the ancestral hall and boasted of for all time.

Rectory Farm was owned by the Reverend Davies and now is a playing field in the centre of Bow Brickhill. It was established in the 1970s.

A modern harvest in Caldecotte looking towards Simpson. No more manual labour!

GYPSIES
"It has been said that Bow Brickhill was originally a gypsy encampment - who knows? Travelling people are still frequent visitors in the region."
SM

Goliath Draper, son of Spencer and Elizabeth, was baptised October 12, 1817.
Elenor Draper was buried November 7, 1838 aged 70.
Israel Draper was baptised at All Saints on October 28, 1834 to parents Nelson and Esther.

Perhaps we have had enough of the nobility. We will turn our attention to beings of lesser degree, namely gypsies and tramps. Gypsies, a nomadic race to be found, I understand, in all European nations, said to be 'one of the lost tribes of Israel', were very common in Buckinghamshire, especially hated by the farmers. They could hardly be called wild, but nearly so. They intermarried among themselves and thus, like the Jews, kept the race intact. They lived in clans or tribes. The head man, or leader was called 'King of the gypsies'. Being in possession always of one or two horses and a travelling van to convey their belongings from place to place; short journeys. Their camping places were in nooks and corners on the roadside. When one saw a van, round hooped tents, a three legged triangle and pot suspended over fire, you might conclude it was a gypsy camp.

The men got their living by playing the fiddle, accompanied by a girl with the tamborine at country dances, in public houses at feast time. There was an annual feast in every village. A tin whistle and lolly affair, sometimes the wonderful and laughable farce of Punch and Judy would be exhibited.

The annual feast was supposed to be the anniversary of the foundation of the old churches built in Monkish days. The gypsies did a bit of poaching, horse and donkey dealing, thimble rigging, card sharping, anything but work. A Gypsy was never suspected of honesty.

The Gypsy women told fortunes, knitted cabbage nets, sold matches, little fancy brooms and other small articles; and sometimes under stress of circumstances, would beg. They were excessively polite; would flatter and fawn with such honeyed sweetness that one was almost persuaded to believe them. One singular old woman whom I remember so well was called Betty Draper. Betty was a unique singularly eccentric woman. She was sixty years more or less within a decade; she wore a grey hooded cloak down to her heels and on her head she wore a very tall napless long steeved hat, fastened with a strap under her chin; a stick in her hand, like the witch of Endor's: "We'el shod wee brass."

She would approach our door with a face as smiling as a full moon, saying to my mother: "God Bless you my dear lady and all the little ones, how are you all?" My mother would say: "We are all purty well Betty, how are you getting along yerself this cold weather?" "Oh badly - badly - badly my dear, can't get nuff to eat. Oh, my dear it is a sore trial, I haven't had a mossel in my lips since yesterdy morning. Oh, heavenly father but this is hard times. O'dearie cross my palm with a penny un I'll tell your fortune true as death." Mother would decline, but offer the old hypocrite a crust of bread, upon which she would hobble off invoking all the blessings God could bestow on her benevolent soul.

The gypsies were a class by themselves, inter-married strictly among themselves, never lived in houses, never were seen in a church, never known to tell the truth when a lie would answer the same purpose, and would never work except in their own particular callings. Gypsies had no friends except among their own class. The poorest English labourer despised these wandering sons of Ishmael who lived in tents.

Beggars or cadgers were very numerous in England in my time there. Some were blind, led by a dog or a child, some crippled on crutches, plenty of ship wrecked sailors with their pitiful tales of suffering,

40

Once the common land for the poor people of Bow Brickhill. Much of it is now a golf course.

whole families who would rather beg than go to the Workhouse - most mendicants were barefooted and in rags, some were brought to begging through misfortune. For a typical case of this class read Dicken's 'Old Curiosity Shop'. The wandering of Nell and her Grandfather. Others begged through disinclination to work believing in the beggars song,

Of all the trades of England
Begging is the best
For when you are a tired
you can sit down and rest.

At our little hamlet on the country roadside we had applicants every day begging in the name of God for a morsel of bread, a potato or a halfpenny, or to buy a penny worth of clothes pegs or matches - matches made by themselves consisted of thin slips of deal dipped at the point in melted brimstone; this match point applied a spark dropped into tinder by a flint and piece of steel struck together. It must be remembered there were no lucifer matches in those days. Beggars slept in hovels, strawstacks, under the hedges or any shelter they might come across when night overtook them when in the country. When in London or any big towns, a beggar's bed of straw could be procured under shelter for two-pence upwards; when the two-pence was not forthcoming any corner available was made use of for shelter. If the police spied them they had to move on.

There was another class - wandering musicians - hurdygurdy men, wearing a large hat hung all round the rim with small bells. As they ground out the tune they would shake the hat in accompaniment. Perhaps two or three small monkeys or a dancing bear would be added to the show.

Another class, German girls selling small fancy brooms. All these girls wore a red handkerchief on their heads, tied by the corners under the chin. They sang a song which was always the same words and tune.

Buy a broom, buy a broom, good lady.
A large one for the gentleman, small one for the lady.
Buy a broom, buy a broom, dear lady.

The description of my native village is now finished. The only apology for writing it I have to give is that it is true, and with a small very faint hope that it may be preserved by my descendants in the years to come to remind them of the birthplace of their ancestor, a pioneer of 1844, when his bones are mouldering, not in Bow Brickhill church yard; but (most likely) in some obscure spot on the continent of Australia, the land of his adoption.

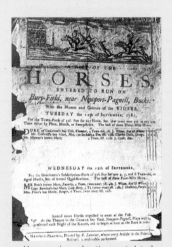
Horse racing advertisement dated September 11, 1791 for Newport Pagnell. These types of events were for the gentry and most people could not even read the poster.

The expanded Caldecotte, with now much smaller Bow Brickhill on the hill beyond.

THE HISTORY OF MY LIFE IN ENGLAND

WILL DAY

Will Day was baptised in BBH on October 13, 1793, he was a bricklayer. He married in 1813 and his first daughter, Jane, was baptised December 25, 1814. His second was Ann who was baptised November 1, 1818. He remarried to Sally and had three more children - June, Maria and Caroline.

Right: Henry was probably born in one of these cottages off Church Road in June 1831. Helen Hart lived in 2 London End Lane, and was delighted when she heard the Mundy story for the first time in 1999.
Below: Next door to Henry's birthplace are these picturesque cottages - the one on the left is April Cottage, bearing the commemorative plaque concerning the sale of common land.

Before reading the history of my life in England, I request the reader to read the description of my native village, which I have already written. It will save both the reader and myself, the recorder of this humble but true narrative, many explanations.

Although there is no ascertainable record in the parish church Register, my mother told me I was born at the foot of Bow Brickhill, the hill opposite the parsonage, on the twenty-fifth of June in the year 1831. When I was about a year old my parents shifted their residence, a mile from Bow Brickhill, to a little hamlet called Caldecot, it consisting of two farm houses and a few labourers' cottages. The house we occupied was one of a terrace of four, two-storey houses. Each house had a small garden for growing its own vegetables, also a damson or plum tree. The well, where all drew water from, was opposite our door. We lived there for about seven years, during which time I had made the following observations. Our next neighbour was a man about fifty years of age. He was married to his second wife, who had a chance child of her own and two by her husband. Her husband Will Day, as he was called, had two daughters by his first wife who were grown up. They were kept at the lace pillow from early morning till late at night. Yet according to the stepmother's estimation they did not do enough. Sally Day was a termagant. She had the tongue of Hantippe. When Will came home she would emphasise the idleness of his two sluts till the poor man, driven beside himself, would get his stick, which was always ready, and give one or both of them a good basting. Poor wretches, I fancy I can hear them squeal now. The eldest one eventually left home and took a situation in Fenny Stratford, and came home in course of time with a baby in her arms. I have only a faint recollection how it ended so I will say nothing about it.

Will Day was a farmer's man par excellence. He was the leading mower, the leading reaper with the sickle, the leading pitcher of hay and corn, that the master, Mr Wynter, had. Will Day was also oastler and boss ploughman. My father was head milkman and cattle tender.

As for the second neighbour, he was a nondescript.

This is the house the Mundays moved to in Caldecotte when Henry was a child. It is comprises three homes, and remains the only dwelling in an empty rural street. It now has a major highway directly behind.

Caldecotte
"In 1970 Caldecotte was just one row of cottages, the farmhouse, a couple of modern houses and a splendid low thatched cottage. The latter was burnt to the ground some years ago - a great shame. Opposite the farmhouse is a meadow, the site of the medieval village of Caldecot. It has not been, and presumably never will be, built on because of its historical importance as a 'shrunken medieval village'. It was acknowledged as a site of importance when modern Milton Keynes was surveyed."
SM

WILL CLARK
Born in 1796, married Bet and had one son Joe born in 1824. He was buried on January 8, 1843.

BETSY CLARK
Died in 1885 aged 85.

Henry's parents, George and Mary (Matthews), were married in All Saints on November 15 1830.

According to the description of him that I can recollect, he was good for nothing, a lazy, drunken wife beater. How he gained his livelihood I cannot say. One thing I do very well remember, he was lowbelled (tin-kettled) for beating his wife. This was a custom in those days by neighbours to show disapprobation and contempt for any such offender's conduct. The man's name was Tom Lovel. Tom at the time was about half drunk, and pretended to be jolly over it. He brought some bottles of beer out to treat the invaders, as if the affair was only merely a jollification. But before it was over he got outrageously angry against his visitors (he pretended for treading on his vegetables).

The third neighbour's name was Will Clark, and his wife's name was Bett. Will was a quiet, inoffensive, easy-going man, but Bett was a spitfire, ever in hot water with someone. I remember well, with her apple-round face and her broad, high-starched frill cap, altercating with someone about her grievances. Bett had a chance child too, who was much older than I, nevertheless Joe and I were great chums; being a small kid, he took me under his wing for protection.

One day about Christmas time, Joe, I and other boys were playing ball games near the lake where we usually played the games, but the day and night before heavy rain had fallen, which in places partially melted the ice. Reckless, however, we started the game. In the middle of the fun Joe Clark, stepping on a weak part, went through. He dropped up to his armpits. Stretching his arms on the surrounding ice he kept himself afloat, he raised himself up till he managed to get his knee on the top, and was hopefully laughing at the fun, when the ice gave way again and down he went again. A second time he tried, and a third without result. We were horror-struck at poor Joe's situation. With his hands spread out holding himself from sinking, I ran to him as near as I could and held out my hand. "Go back, go back," he cried out, "it won't hold the both of us." Just at that time, Mark Wynters, the master's younger brother, came forward with a long pole, stretching it to Joe, which he grabbed and was dragged safely out.

Will, the father, was a farm labourer, he went to his daily work about a mile to a place called

The old Dropshort Farm White Inn and an ancient drawing of the farm (below).

Dropshort Farm

"Dropshort Farm is still on the A5 - Watling Street - just south of Fenny Stratford, and amazingly, still operates as a farm."
SM

DICK BODILY
School teacher, born in 1812.

Dropshort, near Fenny Stratford, both a farm and an inn on the turnpike road to London. One day Will took ill, and he never went to his work again. He fell into consumption and lingered for about a year, at the end a walking skeleton. Bett came to our door one night near the morning and called: "Mary, poor Will has gone."

I think I can safely say that not one of the families in the terrace ever went to a chapel or place of worship except just about our own family.

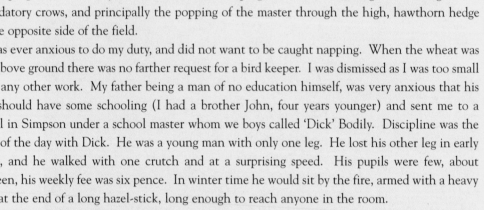

The church in Simpson.

As it happened, when I was about seven years old, Mr Wynters, my father's master, wanted a boy to keep the crows off the land where wheat had been sown, so I went to work for the first time. My wage was a shilling a week. It was dreadfully cold weather I remember. I built what the boys called an elcho, consisting of four upright forked sticks, and cross sticks along the top and sides, and closed it in with haulm, that is stubble after the reaping. I divided my attention between keeping warm and watching the coming of the depredatory crows, and principally the popping of the master through the high, hawthorn hedge on the opposite side of the field.

I was ever anxious to do my duty, and did not want to be caught napping. When the wheat was well above ground there was no farther request for a bird keeper. I was dismissed as I was too small to do any other work. My father being a man of no education himself, was very anxious that his boys should have some schooling (I had a brother John, four years younger) and sent me to a school in Simpson under a school master whom we boys called 'Dick' Bodily. Discipline was the order of the day with Dick. He was a young man with only one leg. He lost his other leg in early youth, and he walked with one crutch and at a surprising speed. His pupils were few, about eighteen, his weekly fee was six pence. In winter time he would sit by the fire, armed with a heavy strap at the end of a long hazel-stick, long enough to reach anyone in the room.

I do not remember getting the strap but once, when I insisted on spelling 'egg' with only one 'g'. 'It was the idea of those days if a child was a bit puzzled or stupid, to liven him up by flagellation. However, according to Dick's account to my mother, I was a very apt and promising scholar. This schooling, however, did not last long at Mr Bodily's. My father caught a severe cold and was laid

An old house in Shenley, the village Henry lived in with his aunt and uncle for a time.

44

This decaying old farm was just down the street from the Munday home in Caldecotte in 2000 - amazingly missing all of the other development in the area.

up with pleurisy (inflammation or something of that sort) and was in bed some weeks. There was great trouble in our house. My father was a very respected member of the Wesleyan chapel and was much beloved, as the prayers around his sick bed could testify. Father had a pig in the sty fattening up to kill. Mr Wynters, his master, ordered it to be taken, for the time, to the farm to feed with his own. Mr C. P. Wynters was a thoughtful, benevolent, good man whose care for others brought poor C. P. W. to grief, as I will tell farther on.

My father being laid on a bed of sickness, we had to seek aid from the parish and I had to leave school; nevertheless it was contrived to send me to a school in Woburn, where the fee was two-pence only. I have given a description of this school elsewhere, so that there is no necessity to describe it here again.

After my father had recovered from sickness and was following his occupation again, I returned to Dick Bodily, where I soon picked up the rudiments of reading, writing and arithmetic. The curriculum of teaching was pupils reading a verse, each in turn, in the New Testament, committing to memory long columns of spelling. In arithmetic we were given sums in short addition, multiplication, subtraction and division. Grammar and geography were never mentioned in the programme. I was at that school for only about six months, and that ended the term of my education; that was when I was about eight years old. What I have learned since is due to my own energy and perseverance, reading instructive books and examples of self-taught men.

Old Denbigh Inn.

After I left school, I was employed by Mr Wynters in doing all sorts of boy's work, sometimes, in winter, keeping the crows off the sown grain, in harvest time, frightening the sparrows off the headlands of ripening wheat, fetching home the cows to milk. At ploughing time, following the single furrow plough, armed with an implement similar to a very narrow spade, with a long handle to relieve the coulter when it got clogged. The height of my ambition was attained when I was promoted to drive old Depper with a load of grain from the harvest field to the stockyard.

Two or three years passed, when Mr Wynters met trouble. His father, a very old gentleman, got into difficulties some way financially and was unable to meet his liabilities and Charles Phillip, his son (our employer), volunteered his security for the debts. After some months the bailiff made his appearance on the scene. After another month or so an auction sale took place, and poor C. P. was sold out. The farm was let before the sale took place, to a man as I understand, from some part of Huntingtonshire named Thomas Brice. He was a lusty, tall, powerfully built man about twenty-eight years of age, lately married. He was said to be worth two thousand pounds. Mr Brice, immediately after sale, took possession when the little band of employees, six men and two boys, assembled to request that they might be retained in his service, and when casting a critical eye over the lot, noticing my father being a small man, said to him: "I shall not want you," and I, being his boy, was not wanted either.

The Grand Union Canal at Wolverton.

Will Day (poor Will) making himself rather prominent by his knowledge of the farm, was cut short by Brice telling him he wouldn't be wanted as he thought the work could be carried on with fewer hands. So here we were, father and me, both out of work. It did not matter so much for myself as

SOCIAL BENEFITS

my earnings were insignificant (a shilling a week). Father tried all round among the different farms in the parish but without success. The complaint was they all had more hands than were required, and why had not Brice kept us on? In a farming community in those days, it was incumbent on each parish to employ its own poor, or to either afford them parish relief, or support them in the workforce. The burden of supporting the workhouse was a tax on the parishes in a certain district, and I think the parish relief fund was contributed to by the parish one lived in, so it was to the advantage of the ratepayers to employ all the poor at wages so low as they could barely survive its extreme economy.

The working class was so numerous that it was with great difficulty work could be found for all. Agriculture was the only staple industry in the parish. My father had been unemployed for about three weeks, when our baker, Mr Britten, a local preacher in father's Chapel, advised him to apply for parish relief, remarking: "If I keep supplying you with bread, you will be contracting a debt. If you make application to the Poor Law Board they will be obliged to find you work, or give you so much a week as parish relief, or send you and your family to the Workhouse" (the 'Workus'). When I heard this doleful news, young as I was, I made up my mind I would never go. The horror of that destination is so drilled into youth that it stood next to going to Aylesbury jail.

No, I would go to London. I knew by the milestone it was only 44 miles, and London was such a big place, I had been told; there ought to be room for a small boy. I said nothing to my parents about my resolve to make a bolt for London in case this consignment to the Workhouse should happen, but I had a confidential chum, Tom Day, to whom, under his promise not to tell anybody, I confided my intended desperate journey to London.

Tom, two years my senior, I fancy I can behold him now, standing before me in his grimy smockfrock, a black greasy cap on his head, wherein was a large hole in the crown, admitting his bristly hair to protrude a couple of inches, his eyes gleaming with admiration. He blurted out: "I'll go with yuh." Then after a little thought, he added: "But I ain't got to go t' the Workus." "You might," I said, "your father ain't got no job yet nur more nur mine." Tom wished "he wur in Lunnon. If we runned away," he said, "they'll fet us back, they'll be sure to ketch us." The outlook to us two boys looked gloomy enough, especially to Tom whose first enthusiasm seemed fast oozing away. I, myself, was fully determined to make the attempt if the worst came. However, the 'Workus' scare happily blew over. My father got work on the other farm in Caldecot, and Tom's father, Will Day, got a job in Brickhill.

After a while I got a job too at 1/6 a week. My former master C. P. Wynter, after being sold up, went to live with his brother, the Rev. A.B. Wynter who lived at The Woolpack; in former years the name of a wayside inn, now converted into a gentleman's dwelling. The Rev. A. B. kept one man servant, who fulfilled the duties of groom, footman, gardener and errand boy all in one. These multifarious duties in the Springtime required extra help, so C.P. recommended me as a smart boy, whereat I was installed in the situation. The Rev. A.B. was a younger man than his brother and of a nature quite different. He was a proud, vindictive, austere man, eminently typical of his class, having great aristocratical pretensions; a would-be terror to all evil-doers, and a bitter hater of all dissenters, as became him as a clergyman of the established church.

As generally with his class, he was the owner of an estate, though in his case not very large. He had married a retired clergyman's daughter from whom it was supposed he derived what he had. He officiated in the church twice every Sunday, one sermon in one church in the morning, and one sermon in the afternoon in another church. The Rev. A.B. was partial to the good things of this life, as his wine hamper could testify. As errand boy I often went for beer a quarter of a mile for his dinner, which happened at the time when common folks were having their supper, and I never forgot to take a swig out of the jug myself.

My daily functions were chopping wood, cleaning out the stable, cleaning knives and forks, boots and shoes, post letters, errands to the shops, weed the flower beds, clean the carriage wheels, etc., etc. The servant man, Bob Cripps, was about twenty nearly, in his ways, as much a boy as I was. We took things very easy in the early morning as His Reverence, on week days, never got up till eleven. Sometimes we had a game of cricket, did a bit of birdnesting etc. One morning he allowed me to have a ride on a favourite pony in a small close near the house, during which ride I came into contact with a clothesline and got a terrible spill. One morning Charles Phillip, paying an early visit, caught us at play, but he did not split on us.

About this time we shifted our residence from the terrace of four houses to an old fashioned lonely cottage rendered vacant by the death of its owner, an old shoemaker, who had long lived alone; an eccentric unsociable individual, many strange tales were rife about this old man. After his death he haunted the house, and many eye-witnesses could testify to having seen him through the window, working and stitching away as usual. My father, sensible enough not to believe these tales, said as long as the living did not injure him he had no fear of the dead.

The house was very old, built after the style of ages ago. The walls were of bond timber filled up with bricks between small windows with leaded lights. The floor was of brick. The roof was thatch, a marvel of perseverance, and industry enough to excite one's wonder how it was kept up. It must have had at least a coat of superincumbent thatch every fifty years. The rafters, perhaps a century before, were seen to be giving way in the middle, when some ingenious person contrived to run a strong beam and secure it on each side of the roof under the centre of the rafters to prevent them from collapsing. However, in the course of time, and no doubt more thatch, the longitudinal beams were giving way when iron plates were fixed under them to prevent them from breaking. This was in the garret, or what we called 'upstairs' where no one ever slept. The ground floor consisted of a spacious room with an enormous fireplace; a good sized bedroom, a pantry and a stair hole. There was another small room attached, built by the old shoemaker with abundance of window light to accommodate himself in way of his trade.

But the garden (about a quarter of an acre) of our new home was the best part of it. I have never known any soil equal to it for productiveness, it had been cultivated and manured for generations. The vegetables, cabbages, carrots, parsnips, beans and potatoes were something phenomenal. Three sides of the garden were edged with currant and gooseberry bushes. In the season we had abundance of red and black currants. In the hedge forming the enclosure, were two large damson trees and two large muscle plum trees, also an apple tree. So we had plenty of fruit. Notwithstanding, my brother, I and other boys did not hesitate to help ourselves in the neighbours' orchards, if we thought their's was better than our's, and many a scrape we got into by so doing.

Old Aylesbury gaol.

An old view of the chapel in Station Road which the Mundays frequented. The chapel is the building on the far right with the present school beside it. The school was not there in Henry's time, but the rest of this view is generally identical to old Bow Brickhill in 1844. The Rectory Farm was on the left in this picture which looks up Station Road to the old animal pound. The chapel was demolished many years ago.

47

The home of Henry's grandparents in Station Road.

At least one Munday was still living in Bow Brickhill during WW1 and is commemorated on the war memorial.

BETSY COOK
Born in 1817, died in 1856.

BURIALS IN WOOL.
Up until the end of the 1600s one of the most important industries was wool, but then its dominance was threatened by imports of cotton, flax, hemp and silk.
So by an act of Parliament coming into effect from 1678, every person had to be buried only in woollen garments, while the inside of a coffin could only could only be 'lined or faced with sheep's wool'. An affidavit had to be signed and lodged within eight days after a funeral with a clergyman or Justice of the Peace to say this law had been complied with.
The penalty for not complying was £5 from the estate of the person buried, or the householder or persons connected with the deceased. Ministers or overseers who failed to ensure the affidavit was complied with would have to pay the £5 if caught.
To ensure it worked, £2.50 would be paid to the Poor Box - and £2.50 to the informer!
The act was repealed in 1814 and had only partially been obeyed.

My father paid rent, namely a shilling a week, for a few weeks when two other claimants turned up as being the next of kin to the old shoemaker and were heirs and rightful owners of the property. Three rightful owners each claiming the right to the rent. Father told the claimants: "The place is not mine I know, I have a right to pay rent, and when you agree among you who has a right to receive the rent I am willing to pay him, but I will not pay any more 'til all that is settled." Nobody, however, proved any title. There was no more said about it, so we lived rent free till the day we left for Australia and might have been there yet, no doubt, if the old house had not fallen about our ears.

During the time I was in the Rev. Wynter's employ, my grandmother, who had been infirm and almost helpless ever since I remembered her, sitting over the fire one day, caught her dress in the flame. She was alone, her daughter, my aunt, being absent, and ran out into the street all aflame. Seeing no-one but a little boy, she ran into the house again. The boy gave the alarm, the neighbours rushed in and found poor old grandmother standing on the floor all on fire. They stripped off her clothes as quickly as possible but it was found she was terribly burnt. She lingered in great pain for several days, her sister was sent for from some place in the north. My mother, aunt, with her sister attended her, neighbours dropping in casually, and at the end of the ninth day it was said she was dying. Father and I after our day's work went to see her. When we got there father went upstairs to see her, I could hear him praying by her from below. She wanted to see me. I was taken up the stairs to her bedside. I was stricken with awe; her poor old face and arms were almost hidden with wet cloths, she could scarcely speak. All she said to me was "be a good boy." She took a sudden craving for a drop of beer. After she drank the beer she went off into a doze. I then went downstairs and sat by the fire in the big chimney on the settle. Several old women were congregated around the hearth telling gruesome stories of ghosts, warnings, death signals and foreknowledge of the coming end, my strained ears taking it all in as gospel truth.

One woman told the story of Betsy Cook who was walking in the road one night when she saw a grave rail travel past her. A grave rail is a board running the length of the grave with a post at each end sunk in the ground. On the board is inscribed the name of the occupant of the grave. "Yes," the old dame continued, "it trotted by her, tit up, to tit up, to tit up, to tit up." Waving her hand up and down to keep time with this nocturnal visitor, Betsy said she "saw it as plain as plain could be." When she got home she told her gal Sally, but Sally only laughed and made fun of her mother, but as sure as we are all sitting here Betsy Cook died within a week. After this dead silence reigned for a while only broken by the moans of grandmother overhead.

The next one to speak was Jenny Baldwell. She told the story as how her one-time neighbour

Judy Lane was one night sitting up late waiting for her man, who had been sent by his master to Newport Pagnell with a wagon and team of horses for a load of something. It was near 11 o'clock and a very, dark rainy night; it was all so quiet and lonely-like, the children had all gone to bed for a long while, when all at once as she sat dozing by the fire she was wakened up suddenly and she saw a glance (a flash) which terrified her almost to death, and a short time after there was another glance. A little after another, by which tokens she knew that something had happened to her poor Will. About one o'clock someone gave a loud knock at the door to tell her that her man was killed; he had been run over by the wagon and was picked up on the road quite dead, and was brought home to poor Judy a corpse, and she a "widder" with four small children. Of course, they had all to go to the "Workus."

Some other weird stories were told about knockings, screechings and scrapings at doors, the particulars of which have escaped my memory. About eleven o'clock my father came down and told us boys to be ready to go home. We had a mile to go. I was wide awake enough, but my brother about seven years old had gone to sleep, tucked away in some corner. Father pulled him out, one hold of each hand we dragged him along between us much to his disgust at being roused at that unreasonable hour. I do not think father slept that night as he was up before it was day. He said he was anxious to know how grandmother was before he went to work. We boys got up too as I did not care to be alone. About half way on our journey we met grandfather, he went straight to my father and said: "George, she's gone. Yes, she's gone, and I had a warning, I knowed she was goin - about two o'clock as I was a sitting in my chair I heard three knocks as plain as I ever heard anything; I knowed when her end had come." My father administered religious consolation and resignation to the will of God as well as he could, but the poor old man was greatly cut up. Grandfather was not a religious man. I never knew him to attend church, or chapel, though in a letter from home after we had arrived in Australia we learned that he had been converted.

Three days after, grandmother was buried in the old churchyard on the hill in a rough elm

Old Newport Pagnell.

Henry's step-grandmother is buried in an unmarked grave in All Saints churchyard, as were most people.

The unused 'Wicks' land in Bow Brickhill below the church and where there are many springs which prevent buildings being erected.

ALL SAINTS' BELLS
"The tower and bells are not in good order now, and the bells can only be chimed, not rung."
SM

ALL SAINTS - TELEGRAPH STATION
All Saints church was used as a telegraph station in the early 1860s, but for a century was not used because of its decay until restored by Browne Willis in 1756.
However, there was no break in the parish registers which date back to 1600.

49

unadorned coffin, carried to the grave on the shoulders of four men, the two shortest in front, the two tallest behind, so placed to suit the climbing of the hill. The coffin was draped with the parish pall, relations following behind. The church bell began its melancholy tolling as soon as we started, and kept up its monotonous sound with its "come-come-come poor weary soul to your everlasting rest and join the thousands already gone before you." As soon as we entered the churchyard gates the bell ceased to toll. The coffin was reverently placed on the edge of the open grave, most of the followers weeping and sobbing. The solemn burial service was then read by the Minister of the Church of England. The coffin was then tenderly lowered down after the solemn words "from ashes to ashes, from dust to dust" were spoken. The sexton began to shovel in the earth until it was about a foot above the coffin, when he brought forward a wheelbarrow load of human bones which he had come across in digging the grave, a miscellaneous heap of skulls, ribs, leg bones, arm bones, etc. and tipped them into the grave. The grave was then filled up and patted over with the sexton's spade. That was all the monument grandmother got, an oblong heap of sand.

Father and I followed our occupations as usual. My brother was sent to Dick Bodily's school, but going to school did not suit his taste, and he constantly played the wag. He learned but little. About this time, after a great flood, a man was drowned in the river which ran by the Rev. A.B. Wynters' residence, which caused a great sensation in the neighbourhood. Different parties up and down the river were dragging for the body day after day, till at last after a fortnight's searching the body was found floating a quarter-mile up-stream. One day I saw a crowd running and converging at a certain spot, nothing to do but I must needs go too. The drowned man had been dragged on to the bank. The body was a ghastly sight to see, swelled to extreme dimensions, arms and legs standing out straight, clearly uplifted from the trunk. I never experienced such a frightful shock. I mention this incident particularly as it affected my mental sanity to a certain degree for many years, but gradually grew less. It recurs even now after long intervals, but does not trouble me.

When the spring and well into summer had passed, the Rev. A.B. told me he would not require my services for a while, and I must look out for another job. Hunting around for work to do I called on farmer Middleton at Walton and asked him if he could give me a job. Mr Middleton was a Huntingshire man and not been long on that farm. He said: "What can 'e do boy?" I said: "Anything sir." He was a pleasant kind of man. He shook his sides a little at my quick answer, then said: "Can 'e ted hay?" "Oh, yes, I can do that sir," then he told me I could come tomorrow and what field to go to. On the morrow morning I was punctually on the spot, a hay fork was given me, and forthwith in company of two other boys bigger than I, began to scatter the newly mown grass with all the energy I was possessed of. I became a favourite of farmer Middleton's and was kept on till all the hay was carted in.

Being the smallest boy, I was picked out to fetch the beer for bever, morning and afternoon about a quarter of a mile. When all hands sat down to have the midday meal I was posted off to the house for two-gallons of small beer. By the time I had come back they had all finished their dinner, and I had barely time to eat mine when the hour was up. I did not like that, but I was only a small boy, a nobody, I had to start work with the rest. When the haymaking was over Mr Middleton said: "As soon as the wheat is ready, if you get two or three more boys to join you I will let you a five acre field to reap." I was quite proud of the prospect and told him I would.

Being out of work again, Mrs. Hart, a lady who owned the farm close to where we lived, wanted a boy to keep the sparrows off the now-ripening wheat, and employed me for the purpose. Armed with a pair of clappers and yelling at the top of my voice, I travelled round and round the hedgerows all day to frighten away these nefarious depredators. For this I got 1/6 a week. The field was near the farmyard so that the fowls had got into the habit of creeping through the holes in the hedge destroying the crop, so my brother was also employed to keep them out, for which service he obtained 1/- a week. So all hands for a short time were engaged.

When my work at Mrs Hart's was finished I went to see Mr Middleton about the reaping contract. The wheat was ready he told me, so if I could get some more boys to join me he would set us to work. Accordingly, I picked up three boys. We formed into two companies, two in each company. George Atterbury and Ephraim Wootten were mates, and Tom Day and I were mates. Each firm had a separate piece of the field allotted to it. We were all very anxious to signalise ourselves and do our utmost, for the more work we did, the more money we would get. Wasn't it

BONES AT ALL SAINTS

"It was necessary, for the good of All Saints structure, to dig out several feet of slipped sand in the early 1990s. It had accumulated around the south and eastern walls of the church, and many bones were uncovered. They were formally interred in another part of the churchyard."

SM

EPHRAIM WOOTTEN

Ephraim Wootton lost a daughter Emma, who was buried in All Saints on August 17, 1856 - they lived in London then. His father was the wheelwright in Bow Brickhill.

GEORGE ATTERBURY

George Atterbury was baptised on April 30, 1826. George married Sarah and had a son Edward, baptised on October 28, 1866. George was still a farm labourer and Atterburys were still in BBH in 1919.

a glorious thing having a contract! The moon was about at its fullest, a grand bright harvest moon. We agreed among ourselves in order to do a lot of work in a short time, to work all day and half the night. So one heavy dewy morning, I remember, we all four arrived at the scene of operations with victuals enough to last three days and our sickles, and commenced work in good earnest. After we had been working about an hour, the master made his appearance, accompanied by another man. He said: "Bohs, you're getting on well, but ye are cutting too high, cut the straw nearer the ground." We had not bargained for this, but we said: "Alright sir," and to bend our backs six inches lower. He remarked to his friend: "I like to break young'uns in properly." They left us then to visit the other two boys. After a time Tom says: "My back aches." I said: "So does mine. I wonder what old Middleton wants it cut so low for, the men don't do it." "Well, becus it seaves bagging the halm" (cutting the after stubble). After a while George Atterbury came over to us to report the same command had been given to him and his mate, which they did not relish either.

George was the biggest boy of the four. He had neither father nor mother, and had been brought up in the 'Workus'. He was the most intelligent amongst us, so we looked up to him as our spokesman. "Look'e here," he said, "we're harvesting now you know and w'll hev to get some beer, we must have bever." We all coincided in his opinion on that point, but the job was how to get it. George offered to go to Wavendon (a quarter of a mile) to Roger's Inn and explain matters. He went, and in a short time returned with a can containing four half pints of beer. We drank our beer and ate a crust of bread in a very short time, and tackled work again like heroes.

We worked on till one o'clock when we ate our dinner, washed down with a drink of water out of the ditch. Half an hour we thought was enough for dinner so we started work again. About four o'clock in the afternoon George went for afternoon bever. After that we reaped a little longer when we thought it was time to bind and stook. We thought we had done very well and were proud of it. Supper over and a little talk for an hour. The moon was shining round and full. We tackled work again, working for a considerable time when we unanimously agreed that we were tired; so each one picked out a stook for himself, and with butt under his hip another under his head, we retired to rest. There is no question about sleeping. I awoke after a time shivering with cold. I tried to sleep again, but it was no use. Crawling out of my stook I saw Tom, who occupied the next bed chamber, with his head between two sheaves looking out. I said: "Hullo Tom, what's the matter" "Oh," he said, "I'm so cold." We heard George and Ephraim talking a little distance off by another stook, so we went to them to know why they were not asleep. George said: "Gypsying does not do without blankets, we will have to get summit to cover us tomorrer night. I feel as stiff as an old man and so does Ephraim." Ephraim was a mild, unobtrusive kind of boy, and he was a shining light among the Baptists. He had lately been converted, and signalised himself greatly at the prayer meetings. It was anticipated he would become a promising local preacher.

Ephraim's teeth were clacking in his head. All he said was: "I've catched a cold, I wished I'd went home to bed." Ephraim had been more tenderly brought up than the rest of us. His father was the only wheelwright in Bow Brickhill. He was the only undertaker. He was also a Special Constable. His mother kept a small shop. I cannot remember what she sold, but they were a little above the common folks.

We sat and chatted waiting for day. George, our oracle, told us strange, amusing stories principally relative to his life in the 'Workus', which are so misty in my memory that I could not repeat them, but when the sun was rising over the top of the hedge, he rolled out in a clear, round, sonorous voice: "Behold the sun is rising in the east, but every year it is getting farther north and when it comes to rise in the west it will set to rise - no more." After this impressive oration, we started to have breakfast about four o'clock in the morning, and began work as soon as the sparse meal was over. We worked

TROUBLES IN BOW BRICKHILL
The industrial revolution changed the need for intensive farm labouring, and many of those who had been employed rioted and smashed the new harvesting equipment. Around the same time the train line was built through Bow Brickhill from Bletchley to Bedfordshire, and it enabled people to be employed on it at twice the wage they received on the farms, and it also allowed them to readily move away from their villages. Many did.

POPULATION OF BOW BRICKHILL
It is estimated that at the time of the Domesday Survey in 1066 Bow Brickhill had a population 300 to 500. In the 1801 census it boasted 431 residents, and in the middle of the 1800s that stood at 394. It then had 116 houses, six were vacant and one was under construction.
By 1931 the village had a population of 388 (176 males and 212 females) with 113 dwellings.

SOCIAL CHANGES
From the middle of the 1800s, and because of the opening of canals, the railways, more contact with the larger world and wider choices of employment, people began to be baptised with two names and not simply one.

Great Brickhill in 1900.

Little Brickhill, 1945.

Manor Farm, Broughton.

all day, but not with the spirit of yesterday. We all felt very stiff and out of sorts. As soon as the sun was down we had a meeting and George our oracle spoke and said: "Look here Ephraim, Tom and Henry, we can't work allus; it ain't natural, after a day's work we're tired, we must go to bed and sleep, therefur I think the best we can do is to come to work early in the morning and at night go home and go to bed". We all agreed with George without a dissentient voice that he was right.

We then, each in a different direction, went home. When I reached home father and mother were at supper. Mother wanted to know how we had got on. I told her how tired, stiff and sleepy I was. She said: "You must be a 'gallus' fool to think you can work allus day and night werout going to bed, sarve you right." Father did not laugh. but he had a very broad smile on his face, and said: "My boy, never kill yourself to keep yourself." I, after years, often called to mind my father's words when I was worrying to complete some task I had in hand. We finished our little field in a little over a week. After paying for our beer we had a shilling or two apiece. I forget the exact amount, but it was not much, I know.

Mr Middleton offered more reaping in another field at the same price. Tom and I agreed to do it but George and Ephraim got a job somewhere else. The first day Tom and I went to start our new job, it came on to rain heavy. My memory about this contract is rather misty. There were other reapers in the field all squatting under the hedge or the spreading oak trees, waiting for the rain to cease which it didn't. The men clubbed together to send for some beer. Tom and I promised to pay plenty of it. We sat under that hedge for hours, talking and drinking beer. The men seemed in devilish delight in pressing the boys to drink. In the long run, I felt very queer and said I thought I had better go home, so I started. After I had gone a hundred yards, I began to unload some of the beer and successively on my way home I had several violent throes of upheaval. As I entered the door mother said: "What ails you boy, you look as white as a sheet." "Oh," I said, "I'm sick." "Why didn't you come home afore, and not stop out in all this rain all this time. You look as if you was going to have the ague, guh to bed und I'll get yuh some hot gruel." Going to bed was welcome enough, but the gruel I did not want that. However, I had to swallow it, but the mess and I did not agree very long, we soon parted company. When father came home, he came to see me and inquired what was the matter. I dare not tell father a lie or dissimilate, so I told him all about what had happened. He looked very grave and vexed and said: "You're not to go to that job again, stay home and try to get somut to do sommer else." I stayed home, and with the exception of a small job now and again, I had very little to do all the winter.

About mid-winter my father bought some turf on the common, two miles away. Father arranged

Old Bow Brickhill houses on Station Road near the former home of James Munday.

This impressive grave lies outside the main door of All Saints church - but the identity of who lies there has been lost in time.

with old Mr Kent, one of his co-religionists, for the loan of his donkey and cart, and as my brother could not go to school on account of the flood of the river he had to cross (brother John was ever ready for an excuse for not going to school) we were ordered to cart home the turf. We put on a good load well stacked fore and aft. When we began to descend the hill the weight in front brought the donkey to his knees. We had to tranship some of the turf to the back. When we got to the bottom, we discerned it was too light on, so to compensate for that we both got on to ride in the front well forward; and thus, we drove home. When we got home, as there was only a very narrow bridge over a ditch to the house, we had to unload in the road and carry the turf in. So I, unthinking, commenced to unload the front first. After chucking a portion off I stepped to the back to unload there, but no sooner had I got on the back than up went the donkey into the air. Mother, who had been watching ran out, I can see her now in her broad frilled cap, cried out: "Whatever are you doing, you'll choke that donkey." The three of us got hold of the shafts and tried to pull the donkey down, but without avail. At last a bright idea struck me to unload the back. I yelled to my brother to help me, and thanks to our united efforts the donkey went down and our trouble was over; much to our great relief. We carted more loads after that, but owing to our first experience, we had no further trouble.

During that winter I got odd jobs now and again, but they did not amount to much. Toward summer my Aunt Jane, my father's sister, got married. Since grandmother died she kept house for grandfather, but domestic affairs did not go smoothly, and she became dissatisfied. Aunt was a good looking, loveable woman about thirty. Every Sunday my brother and I used to have dinner at grandfather's, after we had been to Sunday School in the morning, so as to be ready to attend chapel and school in the afternoon, as we had a mile to go and back to our home.

Some man named John Brown, from a village three miles away called Shenley, met aunt somewhere. I cannot tell how it happened, but they made it up to get married. John Brown was a widower about forty-five. A man of a not prepossessing appearance, he was short, had a shuffling gait, his lower lip minded of an inverted shovel which gave him a dictatorial appearance, which did not belie him one bit. I took a dislike to Uncle John Brown, not so much for his uncomely appearance, as perhaps, for carrying away my aunt. I was very fond of her and she was very kind to us boys. They were married in Bow Brickhill church and merrily did the bells ring. I was not at the ceremony, but joined in the procession later on in the village, where old shoes were flung after the

The pathway from the All Saints church leading to the top of the hill and the road through the woods which Henry described precisely.

Mr William Kent

Mr Kent was the All Saints' sexton and a tailor.
He was born on February 14, 1781 and died in 1862.

St Marys at Shenley Church End, with the village war memorial in the foreground.

newly married pair, and heart-felt good wishes and blessings were showered upon them. My aunt was highly respected in the village.

We continued our tramp to Shenley. There was a good dinner awaiting us and gallons of beer, so we had a jolly good time. The most of us slept there that night. The lodging was pretty rough. The Bow Brickhill party camped upstairs under the thatch. My brother and I in one bed, father and mother next, and farther on two of father's cousins, Nance and Mary Mundy, who cracked many a funny joke about the occasion which I had better not reproduce. One, however, was that we were sleeping upside down (heads and tails). In the morning, father talking to Uncle John, told him he thought his master, Mr Harvey at Cold Harbour, wanted a boy. He would speak to him.

Uncle went to his work as usual and I stayed with Aunt that day. When Uncle came home at night he said Mr Harvey wanted to see me. Accordingly, I went with Uncle next morning to interview Mr Harvey, who employed me straight away for 2/-a week. I went home forthwith to tell Mother. Be it understood that Uncle John would give me lodging, but I had to provide my own tucker and as my work was three miles from my home I had to take it with me, and come home every Saturday night with my wages.

Mother, well pleased that I had got work, packed up some food in a reticule which contained a loaf, and some fat bacon and sent me off to aunt's ready to go to work next morning. I slept upstairs under the thatch, and next morning went with uncle to work. There were several boys on the farm and all had nicknames, one was Smoker another Nipper etc. I was called "Brickull" because I hailed from Bow Brickhill. The haytime was over so the ricks had to be thatched. Mr Harvey asked me if I could make yalms. I replied in the affirmative (I was an expert in yalm making so I performed my duty to satisfaction). Next job was picking up couch roots and docks off fallowed land. This was back aching work, so after a while when my back got sore, I commenced to rest one arm on my knee to ease my back. Farmer came suddenly behind, hit me a solid thump on the back with his paddle, saying at the same time: "Here you Brickull, use both hands, we'll have no laziness here." Nipper alongside had seen him coming, and was consequently clawing away with both hands.

Farmer Harvey was a man about sixty, of pretentious wealth, his two sons fully grown men kept each a hunter, two noble horses and a groom to look after them. The groom stuttered badly. One day he came to me and said: "Bub-bub-Brickul ca-ca-can you ride?" "Yes," I said. "W-w-well get on the hoss-hoss and ec-ec-exercise him." He led a big powerful hunting horse by the bridle, covered with a rug fastened with a surcingle. So he gave me a leg up with this caution: "Jus-jus w-w-walk him ro-ro-round the feel-feelfield, an-an-and if-if you hap-happen to h-h-hear the h-hounds, cum-cum in dreckly." After two hours travelling round the four hedges, as I had no saddle, riding bareback I began to feel chafed and sore, the groom came and said: "Brickull th-that'll ddo today," when I gladly slid off and went to my work which I had left.

As I had done so well one day, the next day the groom called me to exercise again. I would have gladly declined if I dared, for I felt very sore. However, the groom gave me a leg up again. I continued going for about an hour, when the idea struck me it would be good to get down and walk to lead the horse. As soon as I was on the ground pulling the bridle rein off his neck to lead

The farm above is believed to be the Cold Harbour in Shenley, below is Church End Farm, Shenley.

'YALMS'
Could also be spelt as 'yealms' and is the name for a bundle of straw used in thatching.
SM

POPULAR NAMES
In the 1700s the most popular boy's name used for baptisms in Bow Brickhill was 'John', while 'James' was fourth. The most popular name for girls was 'Elizabeth'. Unusual christian names were found mostly amongst 'travellers', but in nearby Little Brickhill, which is on the then main Watling Road, contacts with the wider world led to more unusual christian and surnames.

The Almhouses, Shenley.

him, he commenced rearing up before and behind in such a frisky manner that it took me all my wits to keep clear of his hoofs. I was in a funk to know what to do with the brute, I was getting afraid of him. At last I managed to engineer him to a five barred gate, and with some trouble patting and coaxing I got on his back again. That seemed satisfactory. He was walking quietly as usual, when his owner, young Harvey came up, saying: "Put him into a canter Brickul, we'll see how he goes." With that I had to obey orders. I loosened the reins and stuck my heels into his side. Off he went like a flash at the rate of forty miles an hour, perhaps I would be safe in saying sixty. I'm not able to tell for certain. I dropped the bridle rein and held on to the mane for all I was worth. My cap flew off, I thought my hair would too, but it didn't.

We sailed along like an arrow shot from a bow. At the corner of the field we were approaching was a high gate, we were making straight for it, I calculated the horse would be certain to jump it, if only out of pure devilment. But just as we were nearing the gate on one side, old Mr Harvey was standing on the other. He wore a longtailed coat and hands in his tail pockets. At our approach he spread out his two tails like a pair of wings and yelled out: "Hoo-oo." At this apparition and yell, the horse was frightened, turned suddenly round at a right angle and landed me on the ground. As it luckily happened, I was not hurt much but got a nasty shake up. The young master saw what happened, rode up and asked if I was hurt, I said: "No, not a bit," then he rode after to capture the runaway. As I was still sitting on the ground trying to collect my scattered senses the stuttering groom came up: "Hullo B-B-Brickull, wha-wha-whatld let the hoss bolt for?" I said: "He ran away, I could not hold him." The old gentleman looked vexed. He said to the groom: "Don't put that boy on that horse again, if I hadn't happened to have been here the horse would have jumped the gate and he might have been killed."

I worked for farmer Harvey all through the harvest, during the week days, going to Aunt's to sleep, eating my solitary supper and breakfast there, and taking my dinner with me, which consisted of bread (pretty dry at times) and bacon. Mother gave me two-pence a week to buy cheese. I slept upstairs under the thatch. Uncle John had grown a small bit of wheat in his garden. He used to thresh it by night, the only time he had, in the next room upstairs; and kept on long after I had gone to bed. Thump, thump, thump, on the board floor, singing at times a dolorous ditty, something about needles and pins, when a man marries his sorrow begins. The refrain was so very tiresome, I mostly went to sleep under it.

The work I did was so various that I cannot remember it all, but one event I do particularly remember. One day all hands were carting loose barley. The man on the load on the barn floor was heaving the stuff on to the mow, which was pitched to where it was required by relays behind. I was placed the farthest back, and struggled with all that was in me to keep it clear until I got deeper and deeper involved till I was up to my armpits in barley, till I could no longer wag the fork. Treading my way upwards as well as I could, the groom, who was second to me, sang out: "Wharls, wharls, whar's Brickhill?" I cried out: "I'm here, but I can't get out." They then began to pitch the stuff in another direction, taking no farther notice of me. However, I trod barley till I got to the surface, I was then told to run round and tread the stuff down.

When the wheat and bean crops were being carted in, my work was to drive in the loads from the field to the stack. Nipper was employed the same way. We each had our own horses. One forenoon being near bever time, I was told to fetch the beer when I returned. Accordingly I applied to the maid for the beer which she handed me in an open mouth tin can with a swinging handle over the top. The tin held about 2 gallons. I was allowed to ride back when empty, but having the beer I was supposed to walk and carry it, but this time I planned to get into the cart and carry it; rather a difficult matter it was, to get the can into the cart without spilling some, as the cart had racks sticking out all round, like so many wings. I found a place on an outside rail onto which I placed the two gallons of beer, giving it a shake or two to make sure it was firm, then proceeded to clamber into the cart. I had just landed on the bottom when the cussed horse moved on and over went the beer, the can was on the ground bottom up. I cannot describe my feelings at this horrible

The Bedford to Bletchley line seen in 1870.

THE RAIL DISSECTS BOW BRICKHILL AND CALDECOTTE

The Bedford to Bletchley railway was opened on 17th November 1846, the first railway to serve the county town of Bedford.

In 1851 the line was extended west of Bletchley to Oxford and in 1862, east of Bedford to reach Cambridge. Thus, by 1862 the 16.5 miles Bedford to Bletchley line was part of an important 77 miles long cross-country railway, linking the major University cities of Oxford and Cambridge.

Attempts to close the whole rail route began as early as 1959 but local pressure succeeded in winning a reprieve.

There was some relief when Dr Beeching did not include the Oxford to Cambridge line in his closure proposals in 1963, but there was dismay when, just one year later, the British Railways Board published closure plans for the whole route. Sadly, despite vigorous opposition, all except the original Bedford to Bletchley section was to lose its passenger services on the last day of 1967. Since then the remaining line has seen little investment, falling passenger figures and has twice more been on the brink of closure. In March 1980 the Railway Development Society called a Public Meeting in Bedford at which was formed the voluntary Bedford to Bletchley Rail Users' Association. The new group was charged with the order to 'breathe new life into the railway' and thus help to prevent closure.

From tentative beginnings the association grew to a 2001 membership of over 500.

From then all stations between Bedford and Bletchley saw significant refurbishment.

There was also real optimism that the East-West Rail Link Consortium might be given Government approval to start rebuilding the Oxford - Bletchley - Bedford - Cambridge line to provide a renewed cross country rail route.

catastrophe. I did not know whether to go back for more beer or go straight on. I eventually decided on the latter. When I arrived with the empty can, there were serious looks all round. When seeing my dejected appearance, some began to laugh knowing the can would be refilled at the master's expense as they were working on day wages. If they had been on contract they would have had to pay for their own.

The charm of Bow Brickhill, even in the depths of mid-winter, are obvious as the soft sun shines in the forest.

'New' Caldecotte boasts hundreds of houses and a man-made lake.

One man held up the empty can upside down to the master who was not far away, signalising what had happened, and he came striding up to me in great wrath and said: "What, what have you been done Brickull, spilt all the beer?" Not expecting any mercy, and becoming valiant in despair for I expected to be sacked right away and sent home without a character, I told him the truth how it happened. "Do you know," he answered, "you've no business to ride when bringing beer, you ought to walk and carry." "If you please, sir" I said, "I meant to carry it in my hand when I got up." I do not know whether it was at my penitent attitude, or for the straight-forward story I told him, he burst into a good humoured laugh. "Get away with that load, the men at the stack will be waiting. Here Smoker, go and get this can refilled, I can't trust Brickhull after this." Smoker was in his glee to see me in trouble.

All the boys had a set on me because I came from another parish. This antagonistic feeling among boys was at that time universal. I had rather a rough time while working at Cold Harbour, plain bread and bacon and a bit of dry cheese during the week and water only to drink. My dear aunt would smuggle some little extras to me when she had the chance, but Uncle John Brown did not believe in feeding other people's brats, so if I got anything from Aunt it was by stealth.

He had some dried onions kept where I slept. He accused me to my Aunt for stealing some of them. This was too much for Aunt Jane; they had some angry words about it. Aunt was very indignant and told him a bit of her mind, whereupon he rushed upstairs to me where I was munching my dry bread and bacon, to accuse me of stealing his onions. Knowing I was innocent of the crime, I blurted out: "You're a liar, the onions I've got in my basket mother give me, the're not your'n." "Lookee " he said, "tomorrow is Saturday, and mind you get out of here and don't come back, I ain't going to keep yer aunt's relations and be insulted like this, after getting you the job and this is the way you're sarving me," and his shovel lip nearly went to his nose.

After a pause he continued: "Where did you get them apples I found in yer basket last Monday night?" This question nonplussed me. I did not answer, for the way I got the apples was in no way what the law would call honest. It was in this way; leaving home about three o'clock on Monday morning I had to pass by an apple orchard, the fruit I had sampled many a time. It struck me to enter and get a good supply for the week. The owner's house was about a furlong off. It was close to a farm yard where the orchard was. A large Newfoundland dog was chained near which heard me coming along the road (whistling I suppose) and began to bark. Not heeding the dog I passed in, and supplied myself with as much as it was convenient to carry. I passed out through the gate and was a hundred yards on the road when I met Tom Holmes, the owner of the orchard, the incessant barking it seems, had attracted his attention and thinking someone was robbing his orchard, came out to investigate. He didn't see me coming out of the gate, it was too dark. "Hullo Henry," he said, "what are you doing out at this time of the night?" "Going to Cold Harbour to work sir." "Cold Harbour, all that way?" "Yes sir, I have to start soon sir to get there in time." So I passed on without any more said. He did not suspect me, not one bit. I was very glad because I had done odd jobs for him at times, and had gained his approbation as a smart, active, trustworthy boy. Uncle John Brown, however, concluded the apples had been stolen, that was some satisfaction to him. So I left Cold Harbour and was out of work for a while.

It had somehow happened that father had got into T. Brice's favour, and was working there on the old farm where he had worked from a boy until C. P. Wynter left and Tommy Brice so heartlessly refused to employ him. After a time father became a favourite of Tommy's, when he asked him if his boy was working. On father's replying that he had nothing to do he said: "Let him come, I'll find him something to do for a short time." From that time till we left for Australia, father and I were employed on the old farm. After a time my work was principally among the horses. I was promoted to plough driver, that is driving three horses in the furrow, dragging a single furrow plough, double furrow ploughs then were not used. The young man at the handle named Jack Timms did the guiding business and the bossing.

Jack was about eighteen. He was the house servant hired by the year, fed and housed with a wage of five pounds per annum. Jack and I had grand times when we were sure master was away from home. Our day's work was to plough an acre and knock off at three. Sometimes we would run the horses for all they were worth and finish the acre by two o'clock, then go a birds nesting for an hour. Other times he would give me the handles and he would drive, in which position I felt myself every inch a man. We unyoked at three o'clock, each riding a horse home; after feeding the horses we went to dinner, taking an hour for that. Jack went to milk the cows, feed calves, etc. I had to tend the horses, keep them feeding, clean them down, clean out the stable, fetch beans from the barn, crack them in a mill, and sometimes cut chaff excepting when there were cavings in the chaff house which had to be put through a riddle.

About two hours after dark the horses had to be racked up, that is going up into the loft and pitching hay into racks just above their heads so that they could feed during the night. After bedding them down with plenty of straw, I could go home.

In the morning, two hours before it was daylight (in the winter time), I had to be there to feed the horses. To make sure I was at my duty, I had to rattle the gate just below the master's window, to satisfy him I was there. One morning mother overslept and didn't call me in time, about an hour too late. I scrambled out of bed and was bundled off without breakfast. When I arrived at the stable door, which was open, Tommy was there feeding the horses. He rushed at me bawling out: "What time of day do ye call this to come to feed horses?" Before I had time to utter any excuses he said: "Go back home and see you can't be in good time tomorrow morning," and with that he kicked me out of the stable door.

Next morning I was there in extra good time, rattled the gate, master popped his head out of the window and said in what I thought quite a mollified tone: "Alright Henry, go on about your work." I subsequently learned from the housemaid that Mrs Brice had rebuked master for his harsh treatment to me the morning before. I was in favour with the mistress for the way I cleaned and brightened the brasses of the gig harness, a trick which I had learned when with the Rev. A.B. Wynter.

Events went on quite smoothly after that with regard to work, but more important family events occurred about that time. My Uncle Frank died in Bletchley; my mother's brother. He must have been about thirty-five years of age. He had been bedridden for twelve years. He had what people called 'Kings evil' whatever that was - scrofula I suppose (tuberculosis in the neck glands). He lived

JACK TIMMS
Born 1826.

57

Henry's grandfather's home in Station Road - as it was in 1998.

Grandfather and Aunt Jane married

Henry's grandfather, James, announced his wedding banns to Mary Ann Norman on the same day as James' daughter Jane Munday announced her wedding banns to John Brown of Shenley.
That date was July 24, 1843. James married Mary at All Saints on August 10 of that year, Jane was wed to John on August 27.
Henry and his family would leave England forever less than ten months later.

Mary Ann Norman was baptised on September 11 1791.
Members of the Norman family lived in BBH as late as 1950.

Another Henry Munday was baptised at All Saints on November 14, 1847 - rather - a William Henry. He was born to Mary Munday. Henry and his wife Sarah had William Henry baptised at All Saints on April 17, 1870.

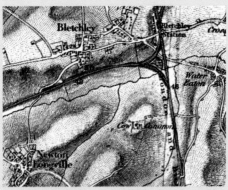
Newton Longville near Bletchley.

with mother's sister, Aunt Bett. I remember from early infancy going to visit him with mother. His poor white face and head covered with a light white nightcap tied under his chin. I was Uncle Frank's favourite, and was elected to be his heir to inherit all he left behind which, poor soul, did not amount to much. On the day of the funeral all uncle's relations were there in attendance. He was buried at Newtown Longfield, a mile from Bletchley. My brother, I and the smallest of the children stayed home, we were not allowed to go to the burying. The mourners returned home about dusk. Solemnly and tearfully, tea was taken. After a considerable time when we were preparing to go home, mother mentioned my right to Uncle Frank's belongings, which he had promised at his death should be mine. Aunt Bett got into a great rage, saying she did not care what Frank had promised; he should not have a stick nor a stitch of anything, whereupon there was a terrible quarrel between the two sisters, mother and Aunt Bett. I do not remember anyone else joining in the turmoil, but as we were leaving for home mother slammed the door with all her might saying: "I'll never darken your doors again Bett, while I have breath in my body," and nor did she, until a day or two before we left home forever, which I shall mention later on.

Uncle John Munday, my father's half brother, kept single whilst his mother was alive but was married shortly after her death. Shortly after, John Brown came along and took away Aunt Jane who was keeping house for grandfather, thus leaving the poor old man quite alone. This situation he rebelled against, having been married for so many years, and having been used to the loving and tender care of a wife. Sitting by his lonely fire in the big chimney he felt very lonely. Odd relations dropped in now and again to see him and cheer him up. Talking to father he said: "George, I am sick of it, I know a woman who'll have me, and I have a good mind to marry her." Father gave him his best advice according to his light. "Father, you are getting old. I know it is very hard but you must trust in the Lord, love and respect the memories of those who are gone, and prepare yourself to meet them in Heaven, where there will be no more parting. If you marry again at your time of life, you'll find all your people set against you."

Grandfather's reply to this was, as far as I can make out, something like this: "George, I love and reverence the memory of the departed more than I can say, and shall do to the last hour of my life, but they are gone, can give me no further comfort, and I am in this world. I am living, yet I want comfort now more than ever I did. All those who used to comfort me once are either dead or left, and here am I all alone. There is no comfort in thinking of the dead, it only makes one more miserable, the least you think of them the better for you. They can never comfort, or care for, or love me any more. Why should I stay lonesome and miserable like this, just to please relations, they'll all come to in a while."

So grandfather proposed marriage to a widow named Mary Norman. She was a strong, active, masculine woman, supposed to be overbearing and aggressive. It was rumoured around that Jim Mundy and Mary Norman were going to be wedded. All relations ceased to visit the old man, and as they were all so distant he asked none of them to the wedding. So the nuptials, except for the attendance of a few of Mary's friends, passed in a solitary way.

Grandfather's relations clubbed together and agreed to boycott the poor old man to serve him out for the heinous crime he had committed, and not go near him. Mother forbade my brother and me to call to see him as we went by. Father said nothing. In fact he called to see his father whenever he passed near the house. Affairs went this way for a considerable time. When going home from Sunday school, grandfather was standing at his gate waiting for us. On seeing him, we went to him, and he said: "Why boys, do you go by now and not come in?" I said: "Mother won't let us." "Oh," he answered, "come in, I've got a nice lot of nuts and crabs, I've been saving up ever so long for you." The temptation was too great. We went in and met our new grandmother. She was delighted, made no end of fuss over us, called us to sit by the fire, gave us hunks of bread and butter, talked to us, and told us pleasant stories of which she had a great fund. Grandfather sat complacently by with his hat on (he always wore his hat in the house). All of a sudden he sprang up and went to a secret corner of his, and took out a quantity of nuts and crabs (being midwinter crabs were the only thing in the shape of apples we could expect). We filled our pockets, and after a while got up to go home, after many promises to Mary (we never called her grandmother) to call every time we passed.

When we got home we told what had happened. Mother said nothing and father looked quite pleased. After that John and I never missed calling to see grandfather and Mary when we passed.

Old Holly House at the end of Station Road.

After that I believe the other relations thawed in due course, but we did not remain long in England after.

Things went on smoothly enough, both father and I were favourites with Tommy Brice. Both master and mistress looked upon me as a clever, active, industrious boy. I continued to please Mrs. Brice immensely by the way I shone the leather and polished the brasses of the gig harness. I pleased the master more so, by the grand condition I brought the horses into. They throve he told me, under my care, better than they ever did under anybody else's management. Very proud of the praise, I said: "I want to see 'em look well sir." "I hope," he answered, "you don't give them more beans than I told you." "Oh, no sir." The fact was, having the run of the barn where the corn was kept, I could help myself and took half as much again as the prescribed allowance. This caused me to have more to grind, but I did not care for that, the team gave me less trouble to drive, looked well and I was proud of them. Master was very stingey in his feed for his live stock.

When the ploughing was over and the crops in, I was otherwise employed in various ways. One day, two more boys and myself were set to grub up turnips. We were not far from the hedge that enclosed the field. Happening to look round, I saw the top of Tommy's white tall hat passing by, the other two boys instead of minding their work were larking. I was working steadily, but put on an extra spurt and made the turnips fly. The other boys were too far off for me to warn them. When Tommy (we always called him Tommy) bounced through the hedge and was at them, he kicked both of them behind and sent them sprawling, snapping out: "I teach you to mind your work, d'ye think I pay you to come here to play? Henry's worth a dozen of ye."

Time went on till near the advent of Spring in the year 1844 when emigration agents were ranging the agricultural counties in quest of suitable emigrants for Canada, Sydney and Port Phillip. They had to be of good character, strong and healthy, must have had the smallpox or have been vaccinated. The inducements were a free passage, two suits of clothes, boxes for clothes, cooking utensils on board ship, all free. In fact, all expenses paid from starting from home till landing in work at the end of the passage. Father, who had seen pretty hard times at home, thinking he might better himself and his boys too, thought a good deal over it. In order to make sure it would be the right step to take, he consulted several of his friends who knew more than himself, one especially Squire Pinfold, who lived in the next village, Walton.

Now Squire Pinfold was a very eccentric old gentleman. The popular story about him was he had been an officer in the Peninsular war, a very fast-going young fellow, and in the siege of Badajoy he got wounded in the head. The doctors, to save his life, placed a silver plate in his skull, after which he was very abnormal in his ways, and in fact he was looked upon as a bit mad.

However, he had considerable method in his madness. The Squire owned a considerable stretch of land around Walton. After his return from the war and his recovery, he was found to be heavily in debt. In those days if a man was in debt and had probable means to pay it, in course of time, was placed in the debtors' prison. The Squire had a very large house on his property with a flat roof floored with sheet lead. So as the law could not arrest him in his house, he chose to lock himself in, and there remained for seven years. He could be seen often taking exercise over the parapet, over his leaden promenade. The rents coming in during the seven years liquidated his liabilities

Walton Hall in the 1930s.

SQUIRE PINFOLD

One of the people Henry recalled most fondly was Squire Charles Pinfold. That was unusual because as readers will have gathered, Henry had little time for members of the 'establishment' because of their ways of making the less educated and poor feel 'unworthy'. However, Squire Pinfold was not like that, and clearly Henry believed he was a major influence on the direction the Munday's took with their decision to leave England for a new life in Australia.

When Henry knew him, Squire Pinfold owned most of the land around the village of Walton, and his home was Walton Hall which was owned by his family from March 15, 1700 until 1903 - 203 years.

Walton Hall was one of two manor houses in the village (the Pinfolds owned both) and was first mentioned in 1189.

The village church is St Michael's, which dates from the same year, and the current building from 1340. It is the church much associated with the generations of Walton Hall owners.

Walton appears first in 1201 as an individual manor. Following the Norman Conquest, the lands on which Walton is situated were included as part of Bow Brickhill. They were owned by Walter Giffard who was the lord of BBH. The lands descended to his daughter Margery who married Nicholas de Hemington. They divorced seven years later and she married Roger de Brailsford. Their son, John de Brailsford, inherited the lands, and within twenty years Nichlolas Hunt of

59

Fenny Stratford, a descendant, was the owner. His grand-daughter Joan married John Longville, and their descendants held Walton Hall until 1622.

It was purchased by Bartholomew Beale, and sold by his grandson in 1665 or 1695 to Richard Gilpin. In 1697 Richard Gilpin (grandson) sold the estate to Sir Thomas Pinfold, Knt. LLD. who was buried in Michael's in 1701.

St Michael's church, Walton.

After 1697 the greater part of Walton Hall was pulled down and the Pinfold family lived in Walton Manor. He was succeeded by his elder son, Dr Charles Pinfold, LLD. who was the Provost of Eton. He died in 1754, and was succeeded by his son (also Charles) who died unmarried in 1788 aged 81. He had been Governor of Barbados from 1756 to 1766.

He left the estate to his nephew, Captain Charles Pinfold, son of Joseph Pinfold. Charles Pinfold was around 12 when he inherited the grand estate, so could not take control until he reached 21. At that time the Hall lay in sixty acres of well wooded park.

Henry's much admired Captain Pinfold rebuilt Walton Hall during 1830 in brick and stucco. He was married to Maria A C Pinfold, and they also resided in London and Welbeck Street, Cavendish Square, Middlesex.

It is believed Captain Charles Pinfold served in the British Army during the Napoleonic wars (when Britain fought Spain on the Iberian Peninsula at San Sebastian between April 1808 and June 1809). From 1816 to 1828 he resided at Chichley Hall which was only a few miles north of nearby Newport Pagnell. In addition to owning most of the land in Walton (755 acres), Captain Pinfold also owned land in Simpson. He was termed 'more than usually

The Pinfold family grave at St Michael's.

and he left his compulsory retirement and was safe to be at large. Owing, 'tis said, to his cranky ways, his wife left him and went to live in London.

After a year or two his wife died. The Squire yoked up two horses into a four-wheeled farm wagon, went to London for her body, rattled her at full gallop down to Walton, and buried her in Walton churchyard.

Squire Pinfold was a man of athletic build, about six feet in height, his age when I knew him must have been between fifty-five and sixty. One ear I remember was very large and long. He dressed always as a labouring man with smock frock, billcock hat, his legs encased in leather leggings. He drove a team of his own horses, and often I have heard him from where I was on the next farm working, on a cold frosty morning yelling in his stentorian voice: "Sultan, Captain," at the highest pitch of his vocal powers. He was a recluse as far as the higher class were concerned; he associated solely with the labouring classes. One of his idiosyncrasies was to erect a large marquee on his ground between Walton and Simpson and cultivate a large vegetable garden. Whatever use he made of his vegetables is unknown to me, but it seems to be a freak of his own for pastime.

Walton Hall - resplendent in 2003.

The Kitchen Garden at Walton Hall is now part of the Open University, and still provides an inkling of the grandness of the home in which Captain Charles Pinfold lived. Remarkably for those times, he maintained a bond with those people considered of a 'lesser class', and encouraged George Munday to take the opportunity to find a new life for his family in Port Phillip. Henry was forever grateful.

Although a rich landholder, he was a genuine and liberal friend to the poor. Perhaps I ought to apologise for digressing so far in describing Squire Pinfold, but I feel grateful to him because I believe it was principally through his advice, that we left that downtrodden country of our birth. Not a very approachable man was the Squire, but father plucked up courage and called on him and stated his case to him, and asked his advice telling him there were three chances, either to go to Canada, to Sydney or Port Phillip, adding that he thought Canada might be the best as Van Dieman's Land and Botany Bay was where all transported felons were sent.

Squire Pinfold had travelled considerably it was said. He had been all round the world, but it is questionable if he had ever been in Australia. Nevertheless, he was pretty well up in general knowledge of the globe. He seemed pleased that father had consulted him on so serious a matter as emigration, and advised him strongly to choose Port Phillip, adding: "There are no convicts sent there. There is very little cultivation, the staple product is wool, the settlers there keep large flocks of sheep. There is plenty of employment for shepherds, which are very much in demand at present. You and your boys ought to go and take up some land and make your fortune, you know well what your prospects are if you stay in England." Father thanked him and said he would take his advice, whereupon the Squire put his hand into his

The beautiful entrance designed by Pinfold.

Walton Hall when privately owned.

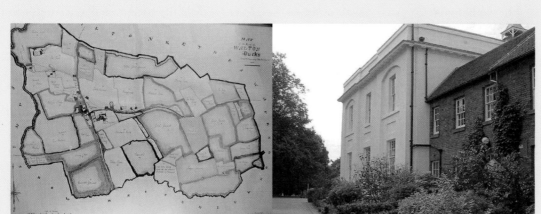

The Walton estate as it was when owned by Squire Pinfold.   The brick section of Walton Hall dates from the early 1700s.

eccentric' when he and his son resigned from the Newport Pagnell Cricket Club on the first day of play (May 11, 1819).

He was a member of a Union Club in Newport Pagnell, formed to keep a pack of hounds.

Before Captain Pinfold died on August 29, 1857 he intended to leave his wealth to his son Rev. Charles John Pinfold, but this only child died in November, 1856.

The estate was therefore inherited by his grand-daughter Miss Fanny Maria Pinfold, who remained unmarried.

She let out Walton Hall from 1866 to 1891 to William Schoolcroft Burton JP. When she died in 1902 the property, including the Manor House, plus Walton Hall, was acquired by Dr Vaughan Harley MD (of Harley Street, London fame). In addition to the manor, he became the chief landowner in Walton along with farmer David Cook.

Mrs Harley retained possession until 1931. By then the manor house was owned by Captain James Fitzgerald who also owned most of the farm land. In 1935 it was acquired by Major Eric Earle DSO.

Walton Hall was occupied by the army during WW2 when electric light was first installed in the house.

Today it is part of the Open University of Milton Keynes which also occupies most of the land around Walton Hall. St Michael's Church is part of the Open University, and while it is generally closed, it is occasionally used for special services and university functions.

pocket and drew out half a sovereign, which he handed to father observing: "This will help you a little Munday. Good luck to you and God speed."

Father came home full up with Port Phillip, and mother and he made up their minds there and then to make application for a passage to Port Phillip. Accordingly, father consulted the parish officer, and told him of his resolve, who forthwith set to work about the necessary business and secured a passage in the good ship Abberton to Australia in about three weeks time; about the beginning of May. It was necessary that we should have to see the doctor who would certify we had had the smallpox. Mother and father passed for smallpox, I had been vaccinated but my brother had not, so he had to undergo the operation.

The three weeks soon passed. I recollect the last day's work in England. It was on Saturday. I was leading the foremost of three horses drag-harrowing fallow land, and father had hold of the two long handles. Tommy Brice came to us and said: "I'm sorry you're going away Henry, I intended to give you another sixpence a week." That would have brought my wages up to half a crown. With Australia in my head, I would not be induced for the magnificent sum of two half crowns. It was arranged that we would take the train at Bletchley station for London on Monday morning, so we had not much time to say goodbye to our relations.

That Saturday night we went to see Uncle John and grandfather. Father was grandfather's special favourite. I shall never forget the old man's broken-hearted state. Dear God, how he did cry. Mary could not help shedding a few tears. She said to me: "When you are in the train, watch Bow Brickhill church as long as you can and say, "Goodbye church, goodbye steeple, goodbye to all Bow Brickhill people."

One final look up old Church Street as Henry knew it.

The grave of Captain Charles Pinfold.

Old Bletchley Station.
Below: Looking back to Bow Brickhill in the distance.

ESTABLISHING THE RAILWAYS

The railway companies had a great deal of trouble getting an Act of Parliament passed because many influential land-owners had their properties dissected by it. There was also conflict with the Grand Junction Canal (now the Grand Union) because the rail took trade away from the waterways.

The train line from London to Birmingham, running through Bletchley and stopping initially at Denbigh Hall (a coach service was used to take travellers to the next link), was opened in 1838. Discussions were held about a possible link from Bletchley to Bedford, through Bow Brickhill.

The first turf for the line was cut in December, 1845. The new line opened in 1846.

From 1870 people from many outside areas were frequently being baptised at All Saints.

A Munday was working for the LNW Railway in 1901.

Next day being Sunday, we started early in the morning to visit our other relations. First visit we paid was to Aunt Jane Brown in Shenley, where we stayed to dinner. Poor Aunt Jane was in a terrible state. "You are going away, and we'll never see you any more, and you are taking them poor boys away to the other end of the world to be killed. I shall never, never see them again." And that was true. Uncle John Brown did not say much, but I fancy he was a bit softened. We had not much time to spare, as we had to walk a couple of miles to see mother's relations in Bletchley, so after sundry huggings and kissings from Aunt Jane and shaking of hands from Uncle John, we bade them goodbye, goodbye forever.

We started then through a wood called Whadden Chase to visit Aunt Bett in Bletchley, the first time we had been there since the row at Uncle Frank's funeral. We were very welcomly and hospitably received by both Uncle Jim and Aunt. Another sister of mother's was there too to meet us. Aunt Jane was younger than mother and very good looking, but had married badly, married to a drunken carpenter who used to beat her. She was mother's favourite sister. The evening went off pleasantly enough, but Aunt Jane burst out suddenly at parting with an hysterical sob and said: "Oh Mary, I wish I was going with you, you're going away to the end of the world to foreign parts. I shall never see you again." Uncle Jim tried to mollify matters and said: "Oh, go on, they might make their fortune out there and come home rich." However, there was a general blubber all around. We stayed at Aunt Bett's that night, and in the morning when I was dressing happened to turn my pants upside down, a quantity of coppers dropping out, making a considerable rattle on the bricks (farewell donations to John and me from friends). Uncle was near when the rattle occurred, and said: "Boy you are rich, I don't happen to have any pennies, or I would gladly give you some."

We had to start to catch the Birmingham train to London. We called on Aunt Jane as arranged, on our way, and the two aunts went to Bletchley station to see us off. Father had disposed of all his worldly goods, except what was supposed to be useful in Australia, which consisted of a large, filled chest about five feet by three feet. It was the duty of the parish officer to attend us to look to our safe guidance to the depot at Deptford.

The Birmingham train came in, then there was more shaking hands, kissing and tears. The parish officer and another family from Shenley were with us. This family was also going to Australia on the same ship. Their name was Moubray. The whistle blew, the train started. With waving of handkerchiefs and uplifting hands our friends were left behind forever, aye forever. I thought of grandfather's wife's injunction and watched the old church steeple for miles. At last it disappeared, when I uttered the words "goodbye church, goodbye steeple, goodbye all Bow Brickhill people."

After a few miles, the train plunged into a dark hole and daylight soon disappeared until it became quite dark; we were in Watford tunnel. We were told it was seven miles long. Break o'day appeared at last, and so many scenes and sights crossed my view. I became so confused that I cannot remember anything particularly till we came to a great railway station in London. The trains and number there was quite bewildering.

Mother's oldest sister Nance, met us there. She had been advised of our coming, and was come to see us and bid us goodbye. There was no great display of emotion between Aunt Nance and mother. They had not met for years. Our conductor, the parish officer, procured a large van into which we and the Moubray family got in, destined for the Deptford Emigration depot. We travelled through Westminster, over Westminster Bridge; as we were going along people cried out: "There go the poor prisoners to Botany Bay." As I was gaping about in an idiotic way, a piece of mud hit me on the face. Looking around I could not discern where it came from.

In due course we reached the depot where were located about three hundred of our destined fellow passengers, men, women and children, mixed up in a noisy medley. Having seen us safe to our destination, the parish officer's duty was over. He wished us goodbye and a safe passage. Adding to John and me: "If you go out into the street and the boys annoy you, tell 'em to kiss your backside." The sleeping accommodation was not very orderly, families all in rotation in rough bunks all in a row. My first night's repose was not pleasant as we had no sheets, we had only blankets, and the prickly covering so irritated me I had little sleep. Father and mother complained of the same trouble. On the morrow was a day of medical inspection to ascertain if we were sound physically and mentally, if we had the smallpox or had been successfully

So many ships were leaving for Sydney, Port Phillip, Canada and later New Zealand, that a permanent fair was established.

Bletchley Station in 1998.

Henry saw London only briefly and was not impressed. This Sovereign Hill depiction of a scene in the city is probably fairly accurate of a tough life in a then grimy place.

vaccinated. Next day we were supplied with two suits of clothes, shirts etc., and two small boxes to put them in - a thorough rig-out, though of not a very superfine description. In a day or two more we were in several lots taken on board in a little steam tug. The young men were stowed away abaft, young women aft and married people and families amidships. A row of bunks two deep ran on each side of the ship with a wide table running through the middle, divided in the centre to accommodate either side. All the ware for use was of tin. Our boxes holding clothes required during the voyage were stowed under the table.

The emigrants were divided into messes, twelve or fourteen as the case might be. Food requiring cooking was ticketed with the number of the mess and taken to the cook's galley to be boiled or baked as the case might be. At meal-times the crowd would be standing round, and as the cook would fish out of his big boiler or extract from his oven, he would call out the number, and each applicant would claim his own.

The third day after boarding, early in the morning we made a start. A small steam tug hauled us out from the mouth of the Thames by Greenwich, Dover, etc., the river widening perceptibly as we proceeded. I was astonished at the number of windmills both on the Kentish and Surrey coasts. These were flour mills (steam mills were few in those days). Towards night the shores were wide apart, the ship began to roll a little when a boy came and said: "Come to the front of the ship, it's rolling about up and down, it is like being in a swing boat," so we went. It did seem a strange sensation. I enjoyed it for a while, then my inside seemed turning upside down, I felt as if I was rising through the upper deck and very giddy. I went back again to the middle of the ship where the motion was not so great. When twilight came on I went again on deck. The shores on each side were scarcely visible, the land was just visible for a short time and then disappeared. The ship went plunging on in the darkness, making for the other side of the world to Australia.

Above: A ship typical of the type which brought the Mundys to Australia.

Left: The same Deptford Immigration Depot, and former port of most often no return, in 2000.

63

WHAT HAPPENED TO THE MUNDAYS?
After Henry left for Australia

It is probably unnecessary to go into details on John Munday, the brother of Henry's grandfather, James, but his family was certainly much more numerous than that of James.

James (christened 17/7/1785) long outlived his son in Australia, but didn't know that. James was buried on September 29, 1861 aged 76, while his third wife, Mary (Norman) was buried on November 1, 1864 aged 73. Mary had previously been married to Samuel Norman in 1832 and they had one son. They were the last of Henry's direct line of Mundays known to live in Bow Brickhill.

James' first wife was Elizabeth Foulkes. They married in 1804. She was the mother of Henry's father George and Aunt Jane - plus Thomas who died at birth, and whose birth also resulted in Elizabeth's death in 1811. James was remarried to Susannah Smells in 1812, and they had one offspring - John. We know from Henry that Susannah was not a well woman, and according to him, a cold and cruel person. She was buried on February 16, 1843 and, no doubt, the fact that James remarried only four months later (24/6/1843) was enough to set the family against him and Mary for some time.

In the year of Henry's departure for Australia, sixteen Mundays were buried in All Saints graveyard. When George and Mary Munday took their family to Australia, George's sister Jane had already moved out to Shenley after marrying John Brown. One of very few irregularities in Henry's recollection is the marriage date of his uncle, John Munday. Henry wrote that John married after his mother had burned to death in 1843, but in fact John married Mary Ann Page, who hailed from nearby Fenny Stratford, on January 22, 1841. John was 23 and Mary Ann 21. His sister Jane was a witness at the marriage.

John and Mary Ann established a successful timber merchant business on Simpson Road in Fenny Stratford. In 1871 he employed five men. They had two sons, George, christened on November 8, 1841, and Joseph christened at the same church on December 17, 1843, plus a daughter Mary Ann who was baptised in 1850 - all of those ceremonies were carried out at Wavendon.

John and Mary moved to Simpson where they lived for many years. Sadly, Mary Ann died in 1855, but not before her son George who died in 1854. Joseph too did not live to become an adult, and in 1860 was buried in the church graveyard at Wavendon with his mother and brother.

Daughter Mary Ann married George Gates, a teacher, at Simpson on August 7, 1878. They are both buried in the Fenny Stratford cemetery.

John was a devout Wesleyan, and became a lay preacher in his church. He remarried a lady named Elizabeth on a date unknown, but they appear on the 1871 census. She was born in Adstock in 1813, and is described in the census as a 'mealswoman' - a term unknown today. She died in May 1873.

John married for a third time, on this occasion to Hannah (also known as Susannah). She was born at Adstock. John died on November 5, 1900 aged almost 83, and he is buried with Hannah in the Fenny Stratford cemetery. She died on 16/8/1907 aged 87. Hannah and John are buried together, and their headstone reads: 'In loving memory of John Munday who was a Wesleyan local preacher in this circuit for over 40 years. Born 17 Dec 1817 died 5 Nov 1900. Also Hannah relict of the above, died 16 Aug 1907 aged eighty-seven years. The memory of the just is blessed.' John left a considerable sum of money in his will.

THE LAST MUNDAYS BURIED AT
ALL SAINTS:

1902 Anne (72).
1915 David (79) lived in Harrow, Middlesex.
1922 George William (62).
1922 Lizzie (63).
1934 Sarah (81).
1945 John 88 (Ormskirk, Lancashire).
1949 George William (65) living in Wolverton.
1972 Amelia (85) Bromyard Hospital, Hereford.

All were descended from Henry's grandfather's brother.

The grave of John Munday and his third wife Hannah lies in the churchyard at Fenny Stratford. John died a wealthy man and gave a lot of money to various charities.

Munday graves as they remain at All Saints, and members of the Munday family who remained in England.

They were all descended from John Munday, Henry's grandfather's brother who had many children. He died on September 2, 1852 aged 70. It appears the families were not very close despite living together in the region as Henry does not refer to any of them.

The standard route undertaken by the Abberton is the large sweep to the left from England and Ireland and going straight to Melbourne without a stop! Not only a feat for the times, but in many cases passengers died en route.

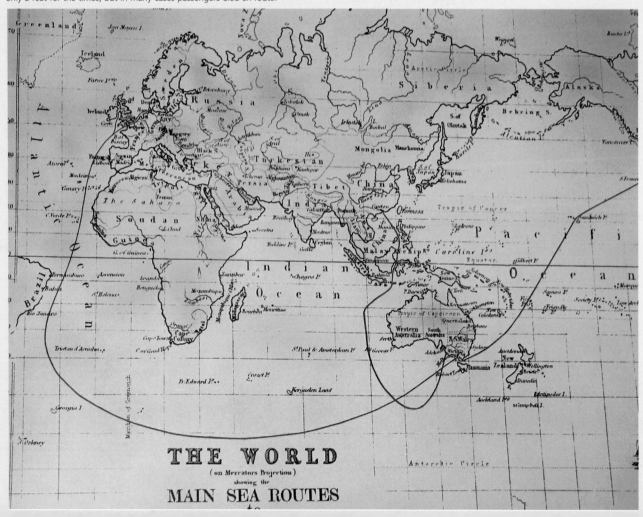

OUR VOYAGE OVER THE SEA TO AUSTRALIA IN THE YEAR 1844

'A life on the ocean wave,
A home on the rolling deep'
- Old sea song

 having written the description of my native village, I had no idea of proceeding farther, but having so much idle time on my hands I wrote the history of my life in England. I am now in my eightieth year, yet the scenes and events of my youth are as clear and vivid as if they happened yesterday. So to pass time I am now writing the story of our passage over the sea to Australia. I have nothing very stirring or romantic to relate, but just a common account of the passage of an emigrant ship in those days of the long ago.

The travellers across the sea at the present day have little idea of ocean voyages in the early part of the nineteenth century. A few small steam boats were employed about the harbours, but no steamships to sail long voyages. The ocean going craft were all sailing ships depending solely on the winds of heaven to waft them over the globe. A ship of a thousand tons was considered large, built more for safety in floating than speed; with prows, only for the keel running up the centre, much resembling the side of a washing tub. They had to rise and jump over waves encountered in their wake. The average speed of a sailing ship was seven or eight knots. Under the most favourable winds the fastest ships never attained to over twelve knots, which was reckoned greyhound speed.

The steamships of the present, of thousands of tons of narrow build and sharp prows, go through a wave instead of tumbling over it, and any wave striking amidships (so I am told) only causes the vessel to shiver, with average speed of twenty knots, so that seasickness is very little experienced.

A voyage from England to Australia is practically a pleasure trip.

Well, let us not digress from the past to the present, which is none of our business.

Picking up our narrative from the close of my History of my Life in England, as I have stated, we went to bed and went to sleep. We slept sound enough till near morning when we simultaneously awoke, when my brother said "how the ship is rolling about." After a while when daylight came (we had a port in our bunk, a pane of glass about eight inches square and one inch thick) we peeped out. Sometimes we could see out pretty clearly, at other intervals it was darkened with the frothy waves. We tried to dress in the bunk, which was only three feet from the upper deck and not being used to such close quarters for dressing, we scrambled down past father's and mother's bunk about five feet on to the lower deck; dressed and went up the hatchway to the upper deck in order to reconnoitre. To our astonishment, there was nothing but water - "Water to the right of us, Water to the left of us" - but not a sign of land in any direction. The little steam tug was gone and the canvas was hoisted; our sole dependence now to the end of the voyage. Presently many curious faces were on deck wondering about our whereabouts. My brother and I leaning over the bulwarks, saw what we considered a monster of a fish, it was lying on the retreat of a wave and broadside to our view, it must have been quite four feet long.

We were approaching the notorious Bay of Biscay, of which so much has been said and sung. The sea got higher before night, and many of the passengers became pale and listless, the motion of the vessel was affecting their stomachs. There was a good deal of vomiting that night. Next day was very rough. That day was, according to the regime, soup day - said soup was prepared by the ship's cook (doctor as he was called) in large boilers for each kind and served out to applicants at 12 o'clock. The soup consisted of bouilli, peas, and some other mess which I cannot remember the name of.

The call on that day, I recollect, was for pea soup principally, yellow peas boiled down to the consistency of thick paste, the flavour of which seemed to appeal to the squeamish stomachs of the passengers, like the craving for oysters and pickled salmon to a man half drunk.

There was consequently a great gorge of pea soup that day, the consequences were disastrous. Men, women, and children were congregated on deck, and all seemed to be unloading pea soup. Sailors were busily

THE GREAT SOUTH LAND

For many hundreds of years there had been rumours in Europe of a great south land mass located south of Asia. The imagined continent was visited by the Dutch and other traders hundreds of years before Cook and the French reached the eastern side. They had landed on the west coast but did not know the extent of the continent. The imagined land was marked on maps and called 'Terra Australis'.

67

engaged swabbing it up, as if at their usual occupation. Some with more regard to decency held their heads over the bulwarks discharging the yellow fluid into the sea, or oftener down the ship's side, causing streaks of yellow down the vessels black hull.

It is beyond my power to describe the scene of the succeeding night. The bunks were all open in front facing the opposite side and the majority sat on the forms in a comatose state; others in a distressed condition, heaving and lamenting, others cursing the day they ever started for Australia. One couple in particular, who had married three days before leaving home for the occasion, I never learned their names, but for convenience we will call them Potts. Mr and Mrs Potts had only met for the first time a week before they were married in view of emigration to Australia. They abused each other soundly as to the way they had both been taken in. The altercation kept on for a considerable time. Augmented to by a wag of a fellow - next bunk - called Bodicott, who sided with Mrs Potts in all her arguments. Poor Potts crawled out of his bunk at last, a vanquished man and collapsed on the seat in front of his bunk, a spectacle of melancholy; whether he slept or not I cannot say, but I know I did and saw no more of that night's troubles.

The next day was rougher than ever, so we rolled and tumbled about in the "Bay of Biscay 0" till many wished they were dead and buried. The day after was calm and warm yet there was a considerable roll, and the heat of the sun on the ship brought out the flavour of dried pea soup to my organs of smell - almost unbearable.

A cessation to our troubles was at hand. We were destined to call at the 'Cove of Cork' for an additional number of Irish emigrants, so in due time we came to anchor on the coast of Ireland. We were delayed there for about a week so everyone recovered from seasickness. I saw the Emerald Isle but had not the pleasure of putting my foot upon it, as we were not allowed to go ashore.

In a few days a batch of about eighty strange looking individuals - men, women and children - of all sexes, arrived on board, accompanied with their friends and relatives to bid them a last farewell. It was a motley crowd and picturesque gathering. The men clad in knee breeches, long stockings and nondescript hats. The children and women were mostly barefooted. After two hours or so the parting had to take place and such a scene of hugging, tears, and kissing, I never beheld. This sight, even at the present day, with the elapse of so many years, when I come to

SAILING TO AUSTRALIA ON THE ABBERTON

After a depression in the economy in the early 1840s, the economy improved slightly in 1844, and squatters again demanded cheap immigrant labour through a government bounty system. Six ships loaded with migrants arrived in Port Phillip that year. The 860 ton *Wallace* was already notorious from an 1841 voyage on which one mother and eleven children died. It was followed by the 530 ton *Royal Consort,* the 410 ton *Sea Queen,* the 400 ton *Dale Park,* the 440 ton *Lord William Bentinck* and the 450 ton *Abberton.*

Little had been learned from the earlier tragedy on the Wallace, and A. B. Smith & Co crammed 340 people onto her for a ninety-one day voyage from Liverpool. Eleven adults and twenty-seven children died of typhus. More died on land, and Smith shipped no more migrants to Port Phillip that year after Governor La Trobe tried to overcome the legal system by appointing a new Harbour Master to supervise new head doctors on the Immigration Board of Inspection. The remaining ships were controlled in Melbourne by J. B. Were in conjunction with Carter & Bonus in London.

The *Royal Consort* carried one hundred and forty-eight migrants, and this time only two adults died of cholera on the voyage.

The *Sea Queen* brought one hundred and seventy-six adults and eighty-three children from Plymouth and Cork. One mother and four children died.

The *Dale Park* sailed on Henry's route from Deptford in London, and Cork. Eight children died, but it was recorded that some who boarded in Cork were in a 'dying state'.

The *Lord William Bentinck* lost seven small children who all died of croup and intestinal disease.

The *Abberton* was not quite so

Ship life then, depicted at Sovereign Hill, Ballarat.

fortunate. It arrived at Williamstown on September 22, 1844 where the surgeon, Dr Edward John Waring, reported that thirty-five year old Mary Wheeler had died while giving birth, and her infant daughter died four days later.

Three other small children died of atrophy (wasting away of the body from malnutrition), while sixteen year old Thomas Foot died of inflammation of the brain.

Dr Waring suggested that emigrant ships could be improved by 'the establishment of two baths between decks,' so that passengers could cleanse themselves without venturing on to the exposed upper deck.

A total of 1406 individuals had been brought to Port Phillip in 1844.

"The system has been a fruitful source of regret," said an official document. "While the single migrants can at once get situations (three hundred and seventy-nine of them) at very handsome prices, couples with large families are still faced with long periods of unemployment and distress.

"Single women should be more carefully selected. Many had lied about having experience as domestic servants, and were proficient only in lace making and straw plaiting for which there was no demand in Melbourne."

recall it, impresses me deeply.

It is a notorious fact, at that time of segregation, the English lower class had an inimical feeling against anything Irish. Scotch or especially French, even the next counties were antagonistic to a degree. In this case, the poor Irish emigrants were looked upon as foreigners and undesirable neighbours, and were boycotted with sneers and jeers, which treatment happily ceased after a time.

With regard to Mr and Mrs Potts who kept up their quarrels incessantly, desiring and praying to go back home, the Emigration Authorities condemned them as undesirable emigrants and sent them back to where they came from and another English couple were located in their bunk.

Coincidentally, the new arrivals, Mr and Mrs Pells were a repetition, as near as possible of Mr and Mrs Potts. They had been recently joined together with the intention of emigration to the other side of the world, with bright visions of making their fortune as it afterwards proved, it was an ill assorted couple, and a butt for the joker Bodicott.

We went to our bunk one night, little thinking of starting so suddenly. When we went on deck in the morning Ireland had disappeared. The ocean, the wide expanse of water was alone visible. We were fairly now on the voyage. The majority of those who had suffered from seasickness were jubilant and jolly, thanks to the recuperation from our delay at 'Cove of Cork'; but this pleasant state of things was not destined to continue long. 'Mal de mere' soon came on again, more evident than before, people of both sexes in all kind of disordered conditions in a "I don't care a damn what happens" state.

The poor Irish, if it was possible, were in a more distracted state than the English. To make things worse, according to the routine of the weekly provender, it happened to be pea soup day. The cook prepared his usual quantity. The Irish partook of some, but those who had had a previous surfeit refused . their previous experience of the abomination was enough. I may as well add here, that from that time out till the end of the voyage, although the cook prepared the mess, once, or twice, after no one applied for the nauseous stuff, and so the cook ceased to make it, and the pea soup day came to an end.

While we had been in port or near, soft tommy (baker's bread) had been served out to us, but as we advanced on the voyage, the ship's rations (the ship's fare), deemed good enough for emigrants was doled out daily, which consisted of hard biscuits, brown and hard as a rock, taking a hammer or something similar to break them, ship's bread it was called, dried potatoes, resembling bread crumbs, salt pork, salt beef in turn, one day in the week rice was served out, already boiled at the cook's galley. A small amount of flour and lime juice on certain days which I think comprehends the whole bill of fare, excepting what was called fresh water which had been pumped out of the river Thames, into large wooden butts stowed in the hold to serve as ballast, which after a month in the wood stunk worse than bilge water; not at all drinkable, unless boiled. It was said the water went

FASTER TRAVEL
While it may have taken three or even
four months to sail to Australia when
Henry made the voyage, by 1877 that
had been reduced to 40 days by Orient
steamer.

bad three times before it became permanently sweet.

Sea sickness prevailed generally, for several weeks among the emigrants. My mother seldom ever left her bunk from the time we started till we anchored at William's Town. My father was never sick at all, my brother and I had three weeks of it and were then ourselves again.

The outlook over the bulwarks was monotonous enough, continuous rolling and pitching of the ship, the unlimited expanse of water seemed so weird and strange to us who had never witnessed the like before. A little change however was a relief, we passed through some islands called the Cape Verde Islands and saw and passed a number of Portuguese fishermen in small boats; in passing them, the captain threw a glass bottle overboard amongst them, supposing to contain a letter for the owners of the vessel, relative to our safety at that stage. After that we saw no sign of land for many a day.

After the sea sickness trouble had passed over and the people as it were, were on their legs again, they began to create amusement among themselves. A young Welshman, one of the sailors, could play the violin very well, so when the deck was anyway steady, dances were got up to the delight of those who desired to shake their legs. Then there was a young Scotchman named Peter Sinclair, of superior education, good naturely formed a school class on deck to teach any who chose to attend. I was one of his pupils, where I renovated my small knowledge of reading, writing and arithmetic.

With the exception of a few squally days, which we thought were terribly rough, and the sailors called good weather, the daily progress was monotonous enough. The sameness of our lives was often broken by incidents happening among the passengers.

Our principal amusement arose from the frequent altercations of Mr and Mrs Pells. They had become very much dissatisfied with all things, themselves in particular. Jangling at intervals during the day, their great outbreak was when they went to bed. This pair hailed from Suffolk. Pells was a big, round-shouldered, slouching fellow, quiet enough if he had half a chance, but Mrs Pells was a real xantippe. Mother said she had a tongue like a mill clack. Bodicott - next bunk - put in a word now and again in Mrs Pell's favour, which increased her ire till she screeched to the amusement and laughter of all around; abusing him as a lying, deceitful, treacherous ugly wretch, not fit to live among decent folks; she did not swear because she knew it would not be tolerated. The climax came at last. Mrs Pells kicked him out of bed one night, declaring he should never sleep with her again as long as she should live, so poor Pells with blanket to cover him slept on the narrow form running along the front of the bunks. He couched that style for many nights, the neighbouring married women cried shame on her and called her an unnatural brute for treating her lawful husband the way she did; he was a fool to put up with such treatment; they advised Pells to go to his own bed; if she did not choose to stay let her try the form and blanket herself. Whereat Mrs Pells must have become thoroughly ashamed of herself, collapsed, and Bodicott being expostulated with to discontinue his silly jokes. Mr and Mrs Pells became quiet and respectable neighbours for the remainder of the voyage.

Day after day followed each other plunging and rolling over the dreary watery waste; one day was very much another, sometimes we could discern a whale spouting in the distance, other times a school of porpoise would be seen springing up and plunging down again. When off the Cape of Good Hope many birds were seen flying round the ship. Shoals of flying fish were plentiful, skimming through the air for two or three hundred yards then down into the sea again. Many albatrosses too were evident, but no land. Nothing to be seen over the ship's side but the everlasting ocean.

The ship's diet by its sameness and coarseness, became so objectionable and repulsive that the strongest appetites became disgusted with it; my digestive apparatus was at its best then, but I felt as if I was on the point of starvation. Mother, an invalid ever in her bunk, father did up the messes as well as he knew how, all the flour we had he made up in messes for mother. For us boys and himself he made up various nondescript dishes, one was biscuits soaked in cold water and baked in a tin, the effluvia of which abomination was strong enough to take one's hair off, my brother and I, at sight of our dinner, would run up the stairs to the upper deck to be clear of the smell, much to the anger and vexation of poor old father, for our ingratitude for the trouble he had taken to prepare such an appetising dish for us. The salt pork and beef were alright, and so were the boullie soup and rice as far as it went.

There was no seasickness now, almost everyone was hearty and hungry with the exception of a few chronic invalids. Three deaths and three births occurred during the voyage. A funeral at sea is a melancholy spectacle, the body is sown up in canvas, a cannon ball or some iron weight placed at the feet. The coffin as we may call this, is placed on a wide plank, carried by four men on to the deck feet foremost; the carriers at the foot place their end on the bulwarks, the men at the head remain stationary, supporting the body, while some one appointed reads the funeral service; when it comes to the words "Ashes to ashes, dust to dust" the carriers behind tilt up the board, when the canvas bundle slides over into the vast deep, and sinks like a stone. On one occasion of a funeral, I, with other boys sat on the bulwarks so as to be able to watch the canvas bag sink; the sea was calm and placid; we saw it sinking for several seconds, down, down into the depths of the interminable ocean.

One memorable event of the voyage was crossing the Line, that is crossing the Equator from the northern to the southern hemisphere. Great wonders we were told were expected to happen. It was, I remember, on the 7th July, the sea was calm and quiet, in the evening after dark about a cable's length astern appeared a boat containing two strange looking creatures, one holding in his hand a blazing torch the other a large three pronged fork, a good many suggestions were hazarded as to what kind of fork it might be, one said he knew it was a dung fork. A sailor standing by hearing the remarks of the crowd rebuked them for their ignorance, said: "That individual you see standing hup thar is Neptin the King of the Sea, and that thar thing he's got in his 'and is the Trident which he rules with." "Well, but what's the other one?" was the query. "Well that's Britaniar, his wife," was the reply. The captain was standing, accompanied by other cabin passengers, on the extreme end of the poop, when the man in the boat carrying the fork roared out: "Ship Ahoy. Captain H. H. Nep. What ship is that?" Captain: "The Abberton from London." Nep: "Whither bound?" Captain: "To Australia with emigrants." Some further dialogue was interchanged between the captain and Neptune when the latter stated the necessity of his coming on board to examine and make sure that all things are shipshape. Accordingly, with great condescension, the captain invited His Majesty on board with his consort. The gangway was opened and steps lowered to the boat. Neptune and Britannia arose majestically on to the deck. The captain said: "Welcome Neptune, Monarch of the sea and Britannia your queen, would you step into my cabin and take a glass of rum." Neptune turned to his spouse to enquire if she was agreeable to partake refreshment, to which she acknowledged acquiescence. The captain and first and second mates preceded their Royalties into the cabin and that was the last we ever saw of them.

WEAVILS
Were a blight for travellers on ships in that era.

1841
It was noted that in 1841 Melbourne had grown to the point where 394 of its buildings were constructed of brick or stone, 375 in timber while 200 were unfinished and 2 unoccupied.
The Depression of 1842 and 1843 slowed that expansion for several years.

EARLY MELBOURNE
While the main shopping for the city of Melbourne is now conducted in Bourke Street, originally it was located in Collins Street between Queen and King Streets.

It afterwards transpired that Neptune was our boatswain and Britannia one of the sailors.

But the main fun came on next day. A mainsail, abaft the main mast was stretched on deck, with the four corners lashed high up and pumped as full of water as it could hold. The shaving operation on crossing of the Line was to be performed. The barber's opened at half past nine. On time the barber, and with him, the barber's clerk, came onto the scene, ready for business. The barber was clad in a nondescript suit, which had seen better days, an inverted billy can on his head with the handle under his chin, by his side was dangling a flattened iron hoop, in imitation of a sword which jingled and rattled as he pranced round. The barber's clerk was dressed in bear's skin from the top of his

THE FIRST 'NEW SETTLERS' IN VICTORIA

Port Phillip Bay in which Melbourne and Geelong are situated, was explored by Lieutenant John Collins in 1802 followed a few months later by Matthew Flinders. For the next 25 years the only visitors to the south coast were sealers and whalers, but in 1824 Hume and Hovell made it to Port Phillip overland from Sydney and a military port was established at Westernport in 1826 but abandoned in 1828.

head to the soles of his feet; fastened with a rope round his waist, was a long heavy chain, with which he was supposed to be tied up.

The barber and his clerk marched up and down the deck several times, one holding the bear by the chain for fear he might get away and scoff some one.

The captain sang out: "It's half past nine, the saloon is now open, any gentleman wishing to be shaved according to the custom of crossing of the Line, let him step forward, every man who wishes to be considered a sailor, or traveller, on crossing the line, must either undergo the process of shaving or provide a bottle of rum." Of course the emigrants were exempt. The cabin passengers, who were few, were looked upon to accede to the custom of shaving or pay their "footing."

At the opening of the saloon the barber and his clerk leaped over the edge of the mainsail into the water and sat down in the water, just their head and shoulders out awaiting custom. The barber's lather was a mixture of hog's dung and Stockholm tar, mixed to a thick paste, the lather brush was a lump of spun yarn half the size of a house mop. The client was blindfolded, hurled into the arms of the barber, soused about in the water until his clothes were soaked through, then commanded to sit up straight and answer the questions put to him. The first was: "What's your name?" Obedient to this request he would open his mouth to reply, the lather brush was rammed into his mouth with a command to speak out.

That settled, he was asked his age, where he was born, etc. etc. with the same application of the lather brush, until he became dumb. When the operation of shaving commenced; every visible part of his face was thickly lathered over, when a formidable razor was applied, a foot of iron hoop fastened to a handle at right angles, with this, the lather was scraped off with considerable vigour till the operator considered his part of the work finished satisfactorily. With an alert movement tipped his subject head over heels to the clerk for him to be washed, cleaned and finished. The clerk claws hold of him, souses his head under water repeatedly till he is half drowned, then telling him he is finished, he has had the honour of being shaved, he has crossed the line.

The foregoing process of shaving was the fate of those who refused to contribute a bottle of rum, those who acceded to the rules, although for the honour of the custom went through the process, got off lightly.

THE SIZE OF VICTORIA
Victoria takes up less than 3% of the entire land area of the mainland.

There were two young men who signed articles at Deptford, as apprentices and merchant sailors, prompted and almost compelled to do so by their parents; being wild and uncontrollable subjects, it was considered that a dose of the sea would bring them to their proper senses. There were many of the ilk in those days, banker's sons, merchant's sons, doctor's and parson's sons etc. of the reprobate class; useless rubbish on land, were sent to sea to be cured and made useful subjects of the realm. If there was anything a sailor disliked, nothing could beat his detestation aboard ship for these land swabs, as he called them.

Two of those apprentices were consigned to our ship, every common sailor presumed a right to order them about, to fetch and carry with no thanks, I cannot say the captain, the first and second mates treated them with any severity, just only with contemptuous indifference. These apprentices, on crossing the line, according to ancient custom, had to be shaved, not through any respect to the lads or to ancient custom, but from pure devilishness, they were put through the process with extreme exactness.

When the shaving business was over being a hot calm day, every body on deck was splashing water at everybody else, so that no one had a dry thread on their body.

The rum began to make itself evident among the sailors; they began to take undue liberties with young girls, who did not resent taking it all as innocent jolly fun, but the captain and doctor put an end to it, by the doctor ordering the girls below and the captain sending the sailors to fo'castle or to their separate duties. And so ended the day of shaving on the crossing of the Line.

The crossing of the Equator is so common in these days that this old and ancient custom of the bye-gone years has become totally discontinued and obsolete.

About this time, we experienced a number of calm days, rocking and rolling with all sails set, but our progress was inconsiderable. After a week or so the weather altogether changed, intermittent squalls, and then came for days and nights, winds enough to take away your breath, roaring through the bare shrouds. Oft-times, nothing but the main or mizzen sheet were hoisted; ship sometimes on one tack- then on the other. It was a difficult matter to walk the deck without being precipitated on to the bulwarks and there from the water at times, oozing through the scuppers, one would find himself up to his knees in sea water. Very few went on deck in this weather, except being obliged to. One night rougher than usual, an extra heavy wave boarded us, and a ton or two of it came down the main hatch just opposite our bunk and continued pouring down for several seconds. An elderly woman two bunks from us sprang out, crying out: "My poor boys! My poor boys! We are all going to be drowned. Oh God, let me see them before we die." The boys were quartered in the fore part of the ship with the young men, in her nightie, disabled, she ran under the weight of water and beat prostrate. Screeching, howling, praying. Tin ware was fling in all directions; what a sensation it was. All of us thought the ship was filling with water and our latter end had come. When the wave had ceased coming down, the doctor made his appearance down the hatchway, to reassure us that there was no danger. He pooh-poohed the idea of any danger whatever; such an occurrence which had happened was nothing; talked cheerfully and laughed at the terrors of us land people for being so scared at so trifling a thing as a drop of water coming down the hatchway. When he went up, he, however, ordered a tarpaulin to be extended over the hatch.

After this the weather moderated considerably, favourable winds blew, sails were hoisted; first on one tack and then on another, sailors were pretty hardly worked taking in sail and letting out sail, climbing about the yard arms like so many monkeys. Little could be done on deck in working of the sails in those days.

THE FIRST PERMANENT SETTLERS
Free settlers in Van Dieman's Land were keen to acquire more land and a group known as the Port Phillip Association led by John Batman and J.T. Gellibrand applied to the NSW government for land at Westernport in 1827.
They were denied, but took the law into their own hands and the first to squat were Edward Henty and his brothers who moved into what became Portland.

BATMAN AND GELLIBRAND
Batman and Gellibrand followed the lead of the Hentys, deciding that once they had established themselves the government would not deny them. Batman brought legal documents, and in June 1835 bought half a million acres around what was to become Melbourne, from the aborigines. He found a large fresh water river which was later named the Yarra Yarra.

THE TRAGEDY OF JOHN BATMAN

John Batman was born in Parramatta in 1800, but had lived in Van Dieman's land when he came to this part of the Yarra in 1835 to establish a settlement. He recognised that the aborigines owned the land and compensated them for his lease. He built a house and established the place which would be the capital city of a new country. Sadly, he was disgraced within a few years and died tragically young at 39 on May 6, 1839.

Batman had been diagnosed with syphilis in 1833 which progressively disfigured his face and left him unable to walk. It was indeed a sorry sight to see the man who laid claim to the foundation of the European settlement of Melbourne being wheeled around in a bath chair, his nose partly eaten away by disease.

His son John died aged eight when he fell into the Yarra River while fishing at the Falls in 1845.

It is believed his brother Henry Batman died unexpectedly on October 17, 1839.

John's wife Eliza, who had one son and seven daughters to him, left him to live with one of his workers, and remarried to William Willoughby in 1841, then William Collyer in 1846 and finally William Dunn in 1853. She was murdered in mysterious circumstances in Geelong.

With favourable winds and weather we sped satisfactorily onward for weeks; little occurred to break the monotony of our progress. The doctor every Sunday morning read the Church of England service. Peter Sinclair continued his day school; once we had a physicking all round. A tub of salts was placed anent the cabin door and every emigrant had to pass by this tub to receive his or her dose. Some said the salts were mixed in sea water. It was nauseous in all conscience, if one could judge by the wry faces made and no sugar stick to suck either.

From some reason or other it seemed that the captain and the doctor were apprehensive of some complaint being made on our landing, as to the treatment of the passengers on the voyage; everyone who could not write his name, of which there were many, were urgently requested to learn to write, if only their own name. My father was one, who set to work in good earnest to improve his education by learning to write, he succeeded so far, as to be able to shape his autograph into some sort of hieroglyphics, which were considered legible, and that is as far as he ever got.

Some time before we reached Port Phillip Heads, we sighted an island on the starboard side called St. Paul's. The captain spoke to a vessel or two about that time. After a while the sailors began to catch barracoota by a hook trailing astern, baited with red rag. Then sea-gulls made their appearance, which increased in numbers as we proceeded. One morning, sometime about the 19th September; what seemed like a dark cloud low down on the horizon loomed out dimly at first, on the larboard bow. As we advanced it became more distinctly visible and was said to be land - "Australia, Australia, the promised land." All eyes were turned wistfully towards it, some said they could see rocks, others said they were not rocks but trees. Presently the trees became plain enough and the land seemed to rise like magic out of the sea. Scarcely a soul sick or well but what was on deck looking with wondering eyes at the land, that through all the weary months, they had come sixteen thousand miles to see, and thereon make their future home. A written document was passed around among the passengers requesting all adult male immigrants to sign to the effect that we had had proper treatment during the voyage, eulogising the captain, the doctor and the ship's company for their great kindness and assiduous attention to our comfort while on ship.

There had been, during the voyage, some threatenings of complaints when we landed, but the joy of coming so safely to the haven, those dissatisfied feelings died out, and all, or almost all, signed the paper.

At dark, we were close in land, I stood watching the shore till I could no longer see it, standing near the mainmast, the bosun came along parading the deck. He accidentally stumbled over a light, iron charcoal stove and nearly fell; with a few pretty-heavy swear-words, he picked up the

MELBOURNE BY ANOTHER NAME

When the tiny settlement of Melbourne was founded by John Batman in 1835 it was also suggested to be named Batmania (!), Bearbrass, Beargrass, Gutigalla or Glenelg.

For some time it was unclear if Melbourne or Portland would become the major city in that part of Australia. Today Portland (below) is remarkably untouched and looks still very much like early Melbourne did in the 1840s and '50s.

Williamstown as it was when the Mundys landed in 1844, and the same view 160 years later includes Naval dockyards - but it retains much of its village charm.

thing and pitched it overboard. The captain, happening to be standing in front of the poop, cried out: "Bosun, what's that gone overboard." Bosun answered: "Don't know sir" and stalked on.

I went below after, mounted into my bunk and slept. I have no idea how long I slept, when a terrible explosion occurred which shook the ship from stem to stern, the consternation was great, some declared the ship had struck a rock.

It was shortly ascertained that one of our two old cannons had been fired to summon the pilot. In half an hour another was fired. Being a foggy morning the pilot could not discover our whereabouts, about break of day the pilot came on board and took command; the fog cleared; it was a clear fine morning before twelve o'clock. The cable ran out and we were anchored at Williamstown, Port Phillip, about 22nd September, 1844.

EARLIEST MELBOURNE

In 1835 the new settlement of Melbourne numbered 142 white males, 35 white females and 1000 aborigines within a 30 mile radius. Buildings consisted of a small gathering of five weatherboard huts and slab dwellings plus a number of tents of various sizes.
By November 1837 it boasted 100 houses and stores.

Melbourne and to the west as it was in 1847.

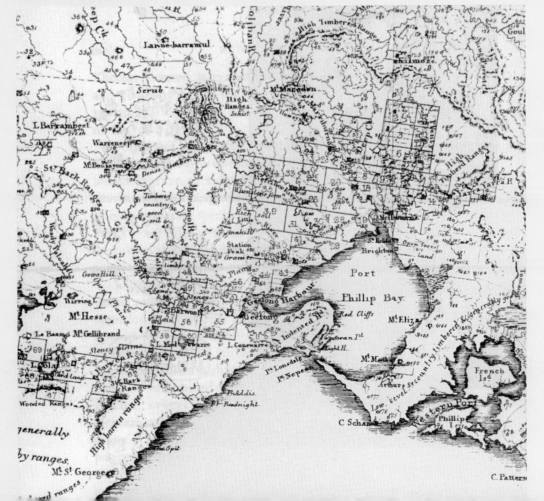

1839

The majority of buildings in Melbourne in 1839 were located in Flinders Street and Flinders Lane. Only one single storey timber and brick building existed away from there, plus several wooden two storey buildings.
Every structure was contained in nine blocks between Flinders, William, Lonsdale and Swanson Streets. Only eight private houses existed on Eastern Hill.

MELBOURNE'S POPULATION IN THE 1840S

In 1841 the population of Melbourne had risen to 11,7000 which included 518 male and 6 female convicts.

Melbourne in 1837 painted from 'Canvas Town' or South Melbourne as it became.

Melbourne from the Williamstown foreshaw with Port Melbourne directly on the other side.

A NEW LIFE OPENS UP ...

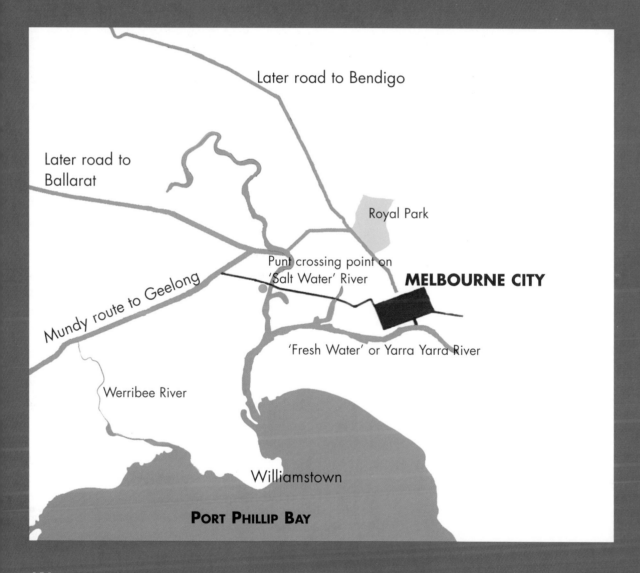

Later road to Bendigo

Later road to Ballarat

Royal Park

Mundy route to Geelong

Punt crossing point on 'Salt Water' River

MELBOURNE CITY

'Fresh Water' or Yarra Yarra River

Werribee River

Williamstown

PORT PHILLIP BAY

WILLIAMSTOWN

While Williamstown provided the best anchorage
for large ships, and was considered for the main
city, like Portland it lacked sufficient fresh water
and remains charmingly quaint and untouched by
too much progress.

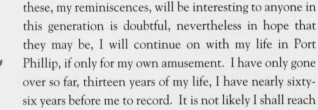

Williamstown remains a retreat which retains all of its seafaring heritage.

PURE YARRA YARRA

The original Yarra Yarra River was a small stream almost covered over by lush foliage and described by the first settlers as 'beautiful'. The area around it was almost swamp, but pure to the point where a number of people were lost in the undergrowth for a short time. Both banks teemed with ti-tree and wattle, wild ducks and other birds. The fresh water above the natural rocky falls where the Queen Street Bridge now stands was perfect for the population - until it began to be used for industrial purposes.

MY LIFE IN PORT PHILLIP

WILLIAMSTOWN

By the turn of the 21st century Williamstown had come back into vogue as a stylish housing area and visiting destination. It remains delightfully detached from the hustle and rush of Melbourne, and is a charming seafaring village surrounded by industrial areas which were forged along the Salt Water (Maribynong) and the Fresh Water (Yarra Yarra) Rivers.

Whether these, my reminiscences, will be interesting to anyone in this generation is doubtful, nevertheless in hope that they may be, I will continue on with my life in Port Phillip, if only for my own amusement. I have only gone over so far, thirteen years of my life, I have nearly sixty-six years before me to record. It is not likely I shall reach that far but intend to continue for the present. My life in Australia is more eventful and, I should think, more interesting than anything that preceded it. I intend to write a portion daily and if God spares me I may finish it; and, thus live my life over again.

We had not been anchored more than a couple of hours when the health inspectors came aboard to investigate our condition, as to the sanitary state and well-being of all on board, also the captain's and doctor's report of the voyage. All things being found satisfactory, before the evening, a number of visitors came aboard bringing various commodities for sale, fresh meat, vegetables, bakers bread, fruit etc. Didn't we have some glorious feeds from that night and after.

Williamstown to our left consisted of a few scattered low houses built on a narrow point of land jutting out into the sea. A few craft were anchored near us, the largest was the Lord

78

The city of Melbourne is on the left with the Yarra River leading from Williamstown to the far right. The wharves are at Port Melbourne. This is it in 2003.

Bentink, a previous immigrant ship preparing for 'Homeward bound'. Farther away on the right was Sandridge (now Port Melbourne) a low mass of black scrub, no human habitation was visible from our point of view. Watermen were daily crossing from Sandridge, the nearest out to Melbourne, to Williamstown and to vessels anchored in the bay; so we had plenty of visitors. Two small steam boats also were continuously plying up and down the Yarra to us from Melbourne - one was called the Governor Arthur, I forget the name of the other.

Two days after our arrival in Williamstown, father, with others paid Melbourne a visit to cash a draft which he had received from the emigration agents. They went by boat to Sandridge, thence walked into Melbourne. There had been heavy rains previously, the Yarra was overflowing, father said people in places were rowing through the streets in boats.

Squatters from the back blocks and other employers came on board to engage servants of their various capacities. The squatters chief demand was shepherds and hut keepers. Father in the old country had had a considerable experience among sheep, was interviewed by a squatter named Sprott, a young Scotchman who owned a sheep station far away back in the Western District on Muston's Creek (now called Caramut). Father telling him he was a married man and exhibiting his two boys John and myself. Mr Sprott made him an offer of twenty five pounds a year with free conveyance from the ship to the station with all his luggage and supply us with rations for the twelve months. Father there and then agreed with him. The offer at the time was very small pay, but considering all things, it was for the best.

The next day, Mr Sprott arrived in a steamboat requesting us to be ready, ourselves, and our belongings as quickly as possible to go in the return boat to Melbourne. We were soon in readiness and started on our journey for the first time up the Yarra. The progress was slow up the crooked narrow river. We landed on a platform opposite Elizabeth Street. On landing my brother and I ran up and down the landing, in excessive joy of having a run once more on terra firma.

Our belongings were transferred a short distance to a public house, I think called the Club Hotel in Elizabeth Street, kept by a small little man named John Hasset or

LANDING
This scene is re-enacted at Ballarat's Sovereign Hill and shows new arrivals aboard sailing ships.

THE YARRA MOUTH
The mouth of the Yarra Yarra River with Williamstown on the right, and Port Melbourne on the left. Many foul smelling industrial factories were built on the right hand side of what was called then called Salt Water River in Footscray and Yarraville. The other bank was very swampy and flat so remained under developed for very many years.

1842 brewery in Flinders Street, Melbourne.

The huge city of Melbourne in 1912 - the year Henry Mundy died.
This marks the place on the corner of Flinders and Elizabeth Streets where Henry and John first stepped on Australian soil.

Johnny Hasset as he was popularly called. The hotel was a low weatherboard building situated a small distance from Flinder's Lane, northward, on the west side of Elizabeth Street, very near the site now occupied by the Australian Buildings.

The bar was liberally patronised during open hours. I recollect only one boarder beside ourselves named Larry who passed most of his time with drinking and courting the cook, Bridget, a lump of an Irish woman about forty, a kind, pleasant woman withal. The accommodation as far as food went was alright, but the bed furniture according to mother's ideas all wrong. On our arrival, the host said to mother: "Here is your bedrooms, two nice clean stretchers, not a bug in'em"; the blankets were anything but clean. What was meant by bugs puzzled mother. However the first night in bed cleared up the mystery, without any further doubt what bugs were.

Next morning at the breakfast table, mother complained of what a restless night she had had, things crawling over her, what with itching and scratching she hadn't had a wink of sleep all the night, her arms and neck were covered with bumps. Larry said: "Woman, that was bugs; look under the stretcher underneath the canvas, if there is any they will be there." Mother went to work there and then to investigate and sure enough the vermin were thick enough where Larry had predicted. Bridget supplied mother with hot water and wholesale slaughter ensued the bugs and no further trouble.

A typical much hated bed-bug.

Larry was a communicative old chap, he told us many stories of Australia especially of the 'Other Side' meaning Van Dieman's Land; how cruelly prisoners were treated, gave us the character of Governor Arthur, talked of the feats of bushrangers, Brady and others. Larry gave us boys great encouragement, prophesying we had come to make our fortune. "In ten years," he said, "you will have a sheep

The houses and hotels in Flinders Lane when the Mundys landed.

Elizabeth Street from Collins Street. The railway station is in Flinders Street and the Yarra behind that. This road was being metalled when Henry came to the city, and was the only made piece of road. It is where Henry and John first set foot on Australian soil.

station of your own - you will be wealthy men" - which prophesy I am compelled to say, never came true.

The Moubrays, our messmates, came ashore on their own, and rented a small house in Flinder's Lane, a few doors from Elizabeth Street, Mr Moubray being a carpenter, thought to get work in the town. We paid them one or two visits. Betsy Moubray was, I thought, the prettiest girl that I had ever seen, her skin was so fresh and pure, revealing the bloom on a peach; in my boyish way, I fell in love with Betsy; though I didn't dare to tell her so, or anyone else. I dreamed of Betsy for a long time as her initials on trees in the lonely bush could testify. Those immigrants who were not hired on the ship, were taken to the Immigrant's depot, till employers engaged them.

When we had been at the hotel two days, Bill Doyle, Mr Sprott's bullock driver called on us to see what we were like, and what cargo we had to take. He was pretty heavily loaded he said, rations and slops etc. He would do all he could to make us comfortable. Father and Bill had a few drinks at the bar and became quite friendly, he said his bullocks were now paddocked, he would let us know when we were to start. The bulls he said wanted a bit of a spell, as he had a pretty heavy load to go back with one hundred and eighty miles. We saw Bill nearly every day.

My brother John and I made daily excursions around the neighbourhood, we mostly watched the boats and traffic on the Yarra; sometimes went into Collins Street. The bullock teams were a novelty - eight, ten, twelve, fourteen bullocks with iron collars dragging heavy drays over such bad roads; every few yards was a mud hole where the wheel went down to the axle, with much cracking of long whips, cursing, calling out with blessings the name of every bullock in the team; the wheel would slowly rise to higher ground.

It often happened that a team got hopelessly stuck, the next driver coming along would stop his team and go to his assistance by cracking and yelling at the off side; if that did not avail (bullockies would never leave a brother driver in trouble) he would unhitch his own team and hook on in front, out it must come then or something give way. The latter often happened; a link would break or a yoke get disabled.

The north side of Collins Street was mostly occupied by Jews; one mostly standing at the door of his shop inviting passers-by to come and buy, everything so cheap, on one or two occasions I saw the would-be vendor take hold of the reluctant customer by the arm and drag him inside to just let him see how "cheap" his wares were.

There were no buildings of any kind between Great Flinders Street and the Yarra. I do not recollect a bridge of any kind over the river.

Flinders Lane, at that time was a reputed residence of the street girls. I often saw half a dozen or

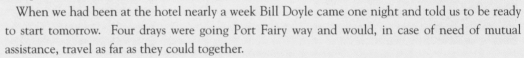

so standing at the corner in Elizabeth Street discussing their various businesses. Their language was anything but select so I will not soil this paper with it, only they called us bloody "jimmigrants." I told Larry about their conversation. "Oh," he said, "they are othersiders, they're no good, bad gurruls."

The only bit of made road I saw was between the Yarra and Collins Street, where a barrier was placed while that portion of Elizabeth Street was being metalled.

When we had been at the hotel nearly a week Bill Doyle came one night and told us to be ready to start tomorrow. Four drays were going Port Fairy way and would, in case of need of mutual assistance, travel as far as they could together.

In the morning we were making final preparations for a start, awaiting the bullock dray, collecting a few articles we were told would be necessary in the bush, as there were no shops there besides the squatters slop cheat. I went to a small weatherboard variety shop on the corner of Elizabeth and Collins Street, where the Royal Bank of Australasia now stands, and bought two bundles of goose quills for making writing pens out of, and two bottles of ink, intending when we were settled in our new home to write to our friends at home, to give them full particulars of the land of our adoption and what we thought of it.

About ten o'clock, Bill Doyle arrived with a team of eight, well loaded with stores, tea, sugar, flour, wheat etc. etc. Our belongings were soon placed on top of the load. Bidding goodbye to the host, Bridget and Larry, father standing drinks with mutual good wishes all round, we parted. Mother was helped to an elevated though comfortable seat on the load, Bill picked up his long bullock whip with loud demands on Spot, Yellerma, Redman and an explosive crack on his whip - we were off.

Henry could not recall the flat swampy land he travelled over when leaving the city, but this is the scene as it looked in 2003.

Salt Water River (Maribynong) at the spot the party crossed by punt and stayed the night to camp. This is taken 'on the farther side' with the old swamp on the right.

We travelled for an hour or more, till we came to some low lying ground, which Bill called 'The Swamp'. Where this swamp was at the present, I have no idea. When we arrived at the edge of the swamp, two loaded drays were waiting there.

One dray, double banked, had gone on over the punt across the Salt Water River. That was the way the four teams crossed the swamp of black, deep, soft clay. The convoy camped on the farther side of the Salt Water, near a thick bush of ti-tree scrub. Four teams, eight bullocks in each, thirty-two bullocks in all were there unyoked, several of them hobbled, and turned out to graze; grass was abundant.

The company consisted of the four drivers. Our driver, Bill Doyle was an ex-convict. One was a New Zealander called Harry, his face was tattooed over from forehead to chin with black ornamental lines, another a big Irishman called Larry Burke. The other was a Van Dieman's Land native, under whose care were Mr Thomas Gibson, his wife, family of two young children with a young woman, their servant, who was sister to their driver, John Moss. Our employer, Mr Sprott had built a new slab public house, and Mr Gibson with a drayload of necessary stock was going to open it. I do not know to what station the other two teams were destined, but they left us before we arrived at our journey's end.

A fire was quickly made after camping, firewood was plentiful, a large kettle was soon boiling, tea was made, a good hearty meal was partaken of. Then the sleeping arrangements were seen to, for us a tarpaulin was stretched over the pole tightly and pegged down on each side. Bill slung his hammock under the body of the dray. The drivers all had hammocks. A small tent was pitched for the servant girl and the children. We had neither candles nor lamps, a large fire was built up which gave us all the light required. After supper was over and things settled, the bullockies sat around the fire, one would sit on the kettle handle, another on a stick laid across the top of the water bucket or on a convenient log etc. all found seats, if not the most comfortable, served the purpose. Extraordinary yarns, not always too decent, went round. Bill Doyle was the champion pitcher and according to my opinion, the biggest liar. His stories were mostly of the 't'otherside' (Van Dieman's Land) where had been mostly engaged in bull punching as he termed it, there is no doubt he was a thorough expert in that calling, he was as clever in handling bullocks as anyone I ever saw.

Convicts from 't'otherside' had suffered dreadfully.

The New Zealander, Harry, was a simple, childish kind of fellow, his greatest ambition was to perform funny tricks to make the women folk laugh. He was an excellent bullock driver. Larry Burke and John Moss were quiet steady going men, their talk was principally about bullocks, blacks and station work.

Mr Gibson, the intended new hotelkeeper, was a man about thirty-five, an ex-officer of an Indian regiment, with two children, the eldest about eight.

In the morning the thirty-two bullocks had to be found and yoked up. John Moss kept a horse, which when travelling was hitched behind his dray, in case of the cattle being out of sight, which often happened - it came in useful for bringing them up. It was wonderful how the old stagers would go into their places beside their mates and stand while the yokes were fixed. In case of a young steer which had not been perfectly broken he would bolt away, thereat there began a cursing, cracking of whip and yelling till he stood to have the yoke fixed.

EARLY BUILDINGS
The banks on the Salt Water River at the punt later became home to a slaughter house and a smallgoods factory but today some of the finer buildings have been preserved. This S.T. Gill drawing for the smallgoods business is 'a little romanticised'.

WERRIBEE
The Werribee River was the second night's stopping point for the bullock wagon party as they moved towards Geelong en route to Mustons Creek.

A small piece of Cowies Creek remains relatively untouched.

LITTLE RIVER

The travellers camped at Little River for their third stop. That town has long been by-passed after the Geelong Road was relocated and was transformed into Australia's first freeway built in the late 1950s. However, Little River became world famous when the name of the town was picked up in the early 1970s by the pop group 'The Little River Band'.

COWIES CREEK

The massive Ford car plant is located on the banks of Cowies Creek on the Melbourne to Geelong road. It was the original name of the area now referred to as 'Corio'.

BATESFORD

Batesford is located on the Midland Highway which leads from Geelong to Ballarat and over which Henry travelled dozens of times.

It was mostly ten o'clock before a start was made. Just as we were starting from our first camp a boy ran up to my brother and me, followed by a red dog and said: "Here boys, do you want a dog, father says he'll drown him if I can't give him away." This was a chance, we had never possessed a dog, so we accepted his offer. We got a piece of rope off Bill and led him on till camping time, with great care for fear he would escape.

We camped that night on the Werribee. Next day being Sunday, we stayed there till Monday. The weather was all that could be wished for. The bullock drivers washed their clothes, told yarns or slept. The New Zealander put on a pair of hobbles and pretended to be a bullock. John and I traversed the banks of the river, leading our dog, enjoying ourselves immensely.

Monday morning at ten we were again on the track. Little occurred on the road worth recording, just one slow monotonous drag over the plains.

That night we camped at Little River. Next night at Cowies Creek, three miles from Geelong. Camping early, father and Bill and Larry walked to Geelong to inspect the rising town. It was pretty late when they returned. Father stood Sam pretty freely, so that they were fairly jolly. Next day we passed over Bate's Ford and reached a swamp, near where the old Separation Inn used to be on the road to Ballarat. The water in the swamp was milky white and had to be scooped with a pannikin; mother declared was not fit for a cow to drink, but after it was boiled and skimmed, went down alright. Bill said: "Misses, if you never get worse water than this you'll be lucky." Which remark as proved afterwards was true enough. Here we ventured to let Ponto our dog loose, having had several good feeds we thought he could be trusted, he did not belie our confidence, hunted through the swamp and many a quail and snipe he nearly caught, but didn't.

Our next stage was the Leigh. There was a hotel and store, father fancied he would like some

The long and steep hill leading down to the Barwon River and Batesford.

The hotel on the River Leigh - the place where Henry's father bought his much talked of cheese.

GARDNERS CREEK
It was Gardners Creek when Henry knew the small town. Today it is Skipton.

cheese, got a pound for which he was charged 1/6. The exorbitance took his breath away. He told of that cheese for days after.

Next stages were Gardener's Creek, Fiery Creek and Lake Bolac. Larry and Harry diverged off there. We went on. I am a bit confused about the route after, but I think it was over the Hopkins River and on to Russell's Run next to Mr Sprott's.

After a journey of about ten days we arrived at our destination, Muston's Creek. We received a cordial reception on our arrival. The principals on the station were entirely Scotch. The squatter, Mr Sprott was called the Laird. One of his legs was shorter than the other, so to make up the deficiency two inches was added to the boot of the short leg, but still he limped considerably. He was called 'Hopping Sprott'. As a coincidence, his neighbouring brother squatter had a short leg who was called 'Hopping Sheen'. Our employer, Mr Sprott a young man of means had lately come from Scotland with the intention of going in for sheep farming, bought Mr Mustons station; he brought

FIERY CREEK
Like so much of rural Australia, the town at Fiery Creek changed its name. It is now Beaufort.

The town which became Caramut was settled on land owned by J. Muston in 1839. It is on the site of the Gibson's hotel at a cross-roads on the main route to Penshurst. The newer hotel can be seen directly behind the white fence - home of the Gibson pub.

LAKE BOLAC
Lake Bolac is spectacular and remains one of the larger towns on the old road which the Mundys took to Mustons Creek, but which today is too far north to be used for the same trip.

BILL CURLEY
Died in 1870 aged 61.

Thomas Gibson was licencee of the
Collingwood Hotel from 1842 until they
moved to Mustons Creek with the Mundys.
Their daughter Alice Elizabeth was born at
Mustons Creek in 1847 and Robert at
Gisborne in 1854.

WESTERN HOTEL

Gibson's hotel was established at Mustons
Creek in 1844. The town was formed
around it and it became known as the
Commercial then later the Western Hotel.

Caramut was a very tiny and fading country town in 2003.

SCOTTISH SETTLEMENT

Many of the major squatters in the
Western District were from wealthy
Scottish families and most retained many
of their traditions. The names of areas
such as Hamilton, the Grampians,
Dunkeld, Glenelg and Glen Thompson
bear testament to their influence.

with him a manager, Peter McVicar and family, an elderly house keeper, Mrs Bruce, and her son.
The few tenements on the station were slab huts, but the Laird had built a small house for himself
and housekeeper, of bluestone. The station was not large, it would only run three flocks of sheep,
about 1500 each, besides a few cattle and some horses. The only fenced paddock was 400 acres
where the best horses were kept. The Laird kept some pretty good horses and a groom who was
an expert rider; no horse of four legs could throw Tommy, it was said.

The first two days after our arrival we did nothing; on the third day I was sent out to an
outstation in command of two bullocks with shepherd's ration - Strawberry and Brindle, two of the
largest bullocks I ever saw, their pace was one mile and half an hour, neither more nor less. We
arrived at the hut in course of time. The hutkeeper was surprised to see a stranger, asked a lot of
questions about the old country which I answered as well as I could. He made me welcome with
a plenteous feed of damper, mutton and tea out of the kettle which he said was only post and rails
tea. I did not like to display my ignorance so much as what he meant by post and rail tea.

I stayed with the hutkeeper over an hour, Strawberry and Brindle in the meantime had strolled
off with the dray among the green grass and white clover which was then fresh and abundant.
When I "jeed" them up for the return journey, they would not move an inch, I called the hut
keeper, Jimmy Hooligan, to help me move them, but in spite of our exhortations to proceed, they
remained stolidly enjoying the luscious green pasture. "By Holy Moses," Jim said, "I'll get
something to liven yer." He went into some ti-tree scrub, got a stick, pointed on one end and three
or four feet long prodding them behind energetically quickly drew their attention. Commencing
to move, Jim said: "Look here bohy, pwhen you want 'em to go to the right, poke the near bullock
and pwhen you want to go to the left poke the offsider."

With these first lessons in bullock driving I got on the main track and had no further trouble.
Once on the track, they would not leave it. It was a pleasant sunny afternoon, I lay on my back,
letting the bullocks go at their own sweet will.

When I had got half way home a thought struck me, there may be blacks about, starting up, to
my dismay, I saw a tall, single blackfellow with all his implements of war, walking at the tail of the
dray, as I looked at him in a scared way, he said: "Good morning." I said: "Good morning"; from
the blacks we had seen on the road to the station and Bill Doyles yarns, I had picked up some of
the black's lingo, and asked: "Where you pullaway?" He said,: "Along a missuh Splott." I asked
him to jump up, which he did. Our talk was something like this. "You come along Melbun?"
"Yes." "Plenty black fellow Melbun?" "Not many." "You quambie along Missus Splott?" "Yes."
"Merrigig, Mr Splott plenty give at damper, Bulgams good fellow. You got 'em bacca?" "No."
"Ugh too much piccanniny." "Yes." There was silence then for a while when I enquired: "Where
your lubra?" "Giggo Missuh Splott, plenty blackfellow quambie, Missuh Gibson, big one collobre."

A typical aboriginal group as Henry knew them.

PROPERTY OWNERS

The property on which Henry and his family worked was established by J. Muston in 1839 and sold to Ostrey and Smith in 1841. In 1843 Alexander Sprott purchased the place and owned it until 1847 when he sold it to Dr Palmer. In 1851 it was acquired by the De Little brothers.

Robert De Little, with brothers Joseph and Henry, came to Victoria from Van Dieman's Land. They were the sons of John of Dublin and became squatters at 'Bung Brungle', 'Caramut' and 'Mepunga.

One of the brothers became the sole owner of 'Caramut' in 1871.

Coming to the new hotel I saw a black's camp of about fifty or sixty men lubras and piccaninnies fixed for the night. My passenger here sprang off the dray, met by a black woman with a kid slung behind her back in a bag net. She was clothed in the usual blanket, only that the men fastened their's over their shoulders, but mothers fastened their's round the waist for the convenience of the infant. The child was so supported in the bag that its head was above the mother's shoulder and in administering nature's supply, she could lift the nipple of her breast to the child's mouth. In such an attitude I met my passenger's wife.

After unyoking Strawberry and Brindle, having no more to do, I strolled back to the black's camp; a dozen mia-mia or more had been erected. A mia-mia consisted of a forked stick in front, several lighter sticks lodged in the fork forming a half circle, covered with bushes in fine weather and sheets of bark in wet, with a sheet of bark to lie on, a small fire was made on the open side, next to which the man sat, or squatted, behind him his wife and family crept. The piccaninnies scarcely ever numbered more than two.

When I returned to the camp many were busy cooking the spoils of the chase, native cats, opossums, bandicoots, birds, kangaroo rats etc. The process of cooking was primitive enough and performed by the head of the family, who was located near the fire. The animal was held by the tail and beaten with a waddy till all bones in the body was pulverised then thrown, with the hair on, on to the hot coals there frizzled and turned, turned and frizzled, till satisfactorily cooked and ready for the table (a sheet of bark). I was watching my former acquaintance particularly whose name was Jim Crow, as I afterwards ascertained. Jim after gorging himself to repletion, threw the remains behind him to his wife and family. New arrivals were continually dropping in until darkness set in. The blacks had a dread of being alone after dark, they had a fear of some supernatural being which they called Bugelcarnie or devil-devil, some evil or malicious spirit which only boded disaster, several new arrivals were added to the tribe. The whole company must have mustered nearly a hundred.

This is the land on which Henry and John shepherded when they arrived at Muston's Creek.

COMMERCIAL HOTEL CARAMUT

The Western Hotel has links to the original Commercial Hotel. The Commercial Hotel was initially roughly built in wattle and daub on the site of the glorious bluestone home at the junction of the road from Geelong. The home is based on the bluestone Commercial Hotel built in the 1850s by two Jewish businessmen who drowned while crossing Burchetts Creek new Hexham Bridge.

It was owned in 1855 by a man named Bryson, burned down and the existing hotel is the third version.

87

A family of Victorian aboriginal women and children photographed in 1863.

After resting a while following their pretty liberal gorge, the men cast off their blankets or opossum rugs or any other habiliment, chance had thrown in his way. With regard to costume they had not the slightest taste whatever, I have seen a black dressed up with an old cast-off belltopper, a swallowtailed coat, may-be minus a sleeve or perhaps a shirt that had once been white. I have seen lubras, with the conscious pride and dignity of a queen, strutting about with a mob cap, frilled all round tied under her chin, her body habited in a woman's dress, which anything but fit.

The men after throwing aside their daily costume painted their naked bodies, face and limbs with red and white streaks, preparatory for the corroboree; from a string round their waists were suspended short branches eighteen inches or so in length. The dancers arranged themselves in a circle. The skill of the dance consisted in shaking the boughs, quivering the limbs and manipulating the war implements. The lubras supplied the music by chanting dolorous ditties, keeping time by knocking two sticks together. The music was not what an European would call harmonious. Most of the hands from the station and some from Gibson were at the corroboree.

When we had been at the home station a week, we were sent to the outstation where Jimmy Hooligan was. Mother had to cook for the shepherds, father was to shift the sheep yards, so John and me was allotted a flock of sheep to shepherd together, so that the two did one man's work. Jimmy was called to the home station. The station where we were located had formerly been the homestead. It contained the woolshed and two huts. Three flocks of sheep were kept there so mother had two shepherds to cook for besides ourselves, father had to look after the folding yards and act as flour miller, for be it known we did not get flour but wheat to grind in a kind of large coffee mill. This wheat ration did not continue long, in two months or so we received flour instead and mother learned off the overseer's wife, Mrs McVicar how to manufacture yeast and made excellent bread in the camp oven.

Meat was plentiful enough, so was tea, called posts and rails, and very black with sugar. These items made up the bill of fare with the exception of plenty of salt. Vegetables, except at the boss house were unknown. The land was exceedingly rich but was useless to plant as the men were shifted about so often, the sower had little chance of reaping the harvest.

John and I appreciated our position, our care was 1500 sheep let out of the fold at sunrise, feeding at will to the boundary of the run, which was known only by a simple ploughed furrow. If the day was hot the sheep would leave off feeding, to bunch together under the shade of the trees and there remain till three or four o'clock, then commence feeding homeward, at sundown they were again yarded.

We had an old Smithfield sheep dog given to us, he had a significant name, Boco, because he was blind of one eye. Boco was our chief amusement; he was a devil for kangaroo rats, native cats and bandicoots; if he was sent to turn the flock, he would turn often to wait for orders to proceed, which was given by wave of the hand. Kangaroos were very scarce there. One day when the sheep were coiling, we were camping in the shade, we heard an unusual noise, thump, thump, thump. John looking up cried out: "Oh, here comes a donkey," and there, a very large kangaroo coming right at us. We started up scared, and scared it also off at right angles. Our greatest pastime was climbing trees, bird nesting - a pastime we enjoyed much in England.

One of the shepherds named Baxter a reserved, disagreeable Scotsman; what his antecedents were, no one knew and nobody cared. The other whose name was Tom Salt. Tom was an original in his way, openminded, was an ex-convict according to his own confession, but never was known to tell what he was lagged for; but whatever it was for, he had suffered severe and cruel punishment. His age was not more than forty. According to his statement he was condemned to work in Macquarie Harbour unloading boats; their being no jetty, he with other convicts had to go up to their waists to carry ashore the passengers or cargo ashore. After a long duration of this toil, he contracted a severe attack of rheumatism, which in the end shrunk one leg shorter than the other, so that he halted sadly. His fingers, too, were so drawn to near the palm as to be almost useless. Nevertheless Tom was a jolly good sort, good natured to a fault. Tom had a very old sheep dog, which he called Blackbird. As far as common sense went, it was agreed that Blackbird knew more than his master.

It happened at times by night that the wild dogs would make a raid on the fold and cause a panic among the flock, one side of the fold would be sure to give way when the sheep would run anywhere for their lives, unless the sleeper in the watch box should awake and hoot the nocturnal visitors away. In the morning the flock would be goodness knows where. Tom would call Blackbird and indicate what was the matter, tell him to off and fetch them back. The old dog knew what was demanded of him. Making a circle round till he got on the trail, would start leisurely on his journey. About midday the flock would appear slowly in sight. One day when Tom was drunk he sold Blackbird for ten pounds to a passing stranger. Three days after he came back to his old master. Tom's run reached nearly to Gibson's pub, so one day, having got an order off the boss, and leaving Blackbird with the flock; went to Gibsons and got a bottle of rum, went back and had a glorious solitary drink, being very hot he doffed his shirt and went to sleep in the shade till near sundown; but the sun had not stood still. Tom had been roasting in the sun over four hours lying on his face, the consequence was, his back was terribly blistered, he came home in great pain cursing the sun, Gibson and himself, in no very select language.

Shearing being over the sheep had to be attended to for scab and foot rot. Two or three men were sent out for the occasion. Scab at that time was a terrible scourge among the flocks, peculiarly, a skin disease and very infectious; causing great damage to the wool, as a sheep affected with it would rub itself on the nearest tree, leaving wool, and consequently infection following with great damage and loss of wool; which was of the finest merino kind or perhaps in extreme cases, the death of the animal. The remedy for scab was then, to dip the sheep singly after shearing, in a solution of corrosive sublimate and water, a quarter of an ounce to the gallon and keeping a portion of the run vacant for twelve months, when it was supposed to be clear of infection.

Stringent laws were enacted for the eradication of scab, scab inspectors travelled the colony to see that the rules were carried out. The methods and endeavours proved a great success after several years; for I have not heard of scab in sheep for many years.

The other disease in sheep is footrot which is only prevalent in low lying land, the hoofs grow hollow and long; they cripple along in the rear of the sheep and are called crawlers; hence the name a 'crawler' in colonial slang.

The time now was about the middle of January. The grass near the home station had got alight from some cause or other, and was burning very slowly towards our station, but as its progress was so slow, no notice was taken of it, as it was burning against the wind, not nearing us more than half a mile in twenty-four hours. One

TOM SALT
Died in Hamilton during 1887 aged 85.

SHEEP AND CATTLE
Sheep were the first major industry in Victoria and a massive export earner. Official approval was given and sheep sent there for breeding from Van Dieman's Land.
In 1836 there were 26,500 sheep and 100 head of cattle, but by 1838 there were twelve times more sheep and 100 times as many cattle.
In 1840 that had blown out to 500,000 sheep and 15,000 head of cattle.

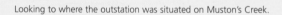
Looking to where the outstation was situated on Muston's Creek.

The foreground marks the border of the Sprott land at Burchett's Creek, and is at the foot of Caramut.

SPROTT'S IMMIGRANTS

The Geelong and Portland Bay Emigration Society (including Port Fairy) operated in 1845 and 1846 to bring workers to the properties. They were brought over to Victoria from Tasmania by the Society which was formed by squatters and merchants along the southern seaboard and into the hinterlands of the ports of Portland Bay, Port Fairy and Geelong. The Society was formed because of continued concerns about the lack of availability of a labour force. Subcribers included the likes of the Manifolds, Learmounths, Connolly and Griffiths (Port Fairy), William Rutledge & Co, Sprott, Campbells, Roadknight and other landed gentry. The greater majority of the migrants were ex-convicts. The agent in Hobart commented that the search for quality exiles was difficult, so many having already emigrated.

morning, quiet and calm, the north wind rose suddenly, the air became dark with smoke. The men working (dipping), old experienced colonials, saw what was coming. A raging grass fire with a north wind, ran to us boys who happily were not far away, collected the flock and hurried them on to the already burnt ground. When within two hundred yards of safety ground, a piercing yell came from Scotty Baxter from the direction of smoke. The men then left us, John and me, and ran to the rescue of Baxter's flock. Choosing a spot where the flame was lowest. With the aid of Boco we hurried the flock on to the burnt ground. After driving the sheep for a short distance we stopped. The black smoke from the burning grass, and from the decayed fallen timber, was choking us with thirst. Not caring much for the sheep, we made back on to the grass in front of the fire to get our breath freely. Presently my brother said: "Oh I'm so dry, let's go home and get a drink." I said: "We can't leave the sheep, but don't you remember a bottle of tea we left hanging on a tree some days ago, let's go and get it." Accordingly, we went through the long grass for about a quarter of a mile, and found our bottle of tea hanging from a string to the neck on a low limb, a drink we had brought with us some days before, being a cool day, not wanting it, we slung it on a tree for a future need. Taking turn about at the bottle of the nauseous stuff we thought it nectar.

The north hot wind was blowing strongly at the time when all at once we heard a terribly cracking, thundering roar; looking in the direction we saw a sheet of flame and smoke reaching to the tree tops. Our first thought was to run back to the burnt ground. The fire was chasing us at horse-gallop speed; knowing no other escape, I seeing a leaning tree, ordered John: "Up quick, quick." Up we scrambled as high as possible. I told him to go higher, he said: "If I do the limb will break." We were clothed in thin fustian. We took off our short jackets, lapped them over our faces and awaited results. The fire was on us instantaneously. Merciful God, we or at least I was roasting.

We both yelled, and screeched to Heaven for mercy. It was not the grass altogether that caused the flame but the thin bark which the eucalyptus sheds yearly hanging on the limbs and on the ground. My jacket caught fire, I threw it down. After the heat had subsided John said: "Are you burnt?" I looked down to my naked shins, they were black, rubbing one against the tree, a piece of skin came off about the size of the palm of my hand, leaving a bare red patch. I enquired if he was burnt. "Yes" he replied: "I'm burnt all over." I hastened down, John following.

As soon as we were down amongst the flaming dead timber and smoke, I commenced to tear away homewards as fast as I could, leaving John to follow. I had not gone far when he cried out: "You're running away from me - to leave me behind to die." At that, I waited for him to come up - poor little fellow. I fancy I see him now gasping, I got him by the arm and dragged him on as fast as I could. I felt on the point of dropping myself. The distance was about half a mile. At last we came to our home, at least to where it used to be, taking little notice of the change, we rushed to the waterhole in the ti-tree scrub, lying flat on our bellies, dipped our faces into the water and had a drink. Oh such a drink. I never relished one like it in my life before, nor ever since.

Looking around, the aspect was a mere desolation, on the site of the huts was a heap of smoking embers. The woolshed the same, over twenty sheep were lying blackened, burnt to death with their legs stiffened straight out, among the smouldering timber. Not a human soul was to be seen. We dropped on the ground in sheer exhaustion, among the ruins feeling like Jugurtha among the ruins of Carthage. I might have cried out with him "Quo redo quid agam." After which, we thought a very long time, some-one of the hands made his appearance. I asked where mother was, he told us she had run away to the home station over the burnt ground and: "Your father is out looking for you boys." I said we were caught in the fire and got burnt. "Much?" I showed him my burnt legs. "Good God! You come to the home station and let Peter McVicar see you." With difficulty I got on my feet; but walk I could not. In a short time father came and ascertaining the affairs, got a horse from somewhere. I was lifted on the horse and taken to the station where Peter McVicar attended to my burns. Peter had studied medicine with the help of books. He had studied Dr Buchan and "other chaps" as Burns has it, had been brought out by the Laird, and a medicine chest complete with all kinds of medical requisites for emergencies in a new colony.

As I was leaving the ruins I caught sight of Scotty Baxter's flock, the wool on many of them was singed black, some had legs shrivelled up. I was told after, some had died or had to be killed. Luckily for Tom Salt and his flock, having gone through the dipping, had a few days before been sent to another and clean run, so situated that they escaped danger.

Arriving at the home station, I was made as comfortable as circumstances would permit. Peter McVicar was assiduous in his attention, with his lotions and scissors clipping blisters. Examining John's burns, which only amounted to one small patch on one of his legs: "Hoot man," he said, "Yerle nae burnt at a'yer brither has got the wor'st olit."

Everything we had had been consumed in the fire, we had nothing but what we stood in, but sympathy was excessive from all quarters. Besides Mr Sprott, the hands on the station, the visitors at Gibson's Public house made a collection for us, so that I do not recollect being in want for necessaries of any kind; in fact we were as well off after the fire as before; only of those dearly valued things we had brought from home of which there was not a scrap saved.

My injuries being considered critical, Mr Sprott sent for a doctor from Port Fairy, who arrived in

DR JOHN BUCHAN
Died in 1874 aged 66.

Sprott's land on which the Mundys lived and worked.

WOOL TAKES HOLD
In 1837, 175,000 pounds of wool were exported from Melbourne for £11,600 in earnings. By 1841 that was 1,715,000 (£85,700), in 1846 6,407000 (£350,400) and in 1850, before the gold rush, had jumped to 18,091,000 to earn the colony £826,200.

Above and below are typical farming workers residences of the 1840s.

SQUATTERS
Were early arrivals in Australia who took large amounts of land for farming without paying for it.

due course, examined me and, giving Peter full instructions what to do, I was confined to bed for 6 weeks and it was two weeks more before I was myself again, thanks to dear old Peter with his dressings and cosseting. Another hut was built for us on the site of our former residence, where we were sent. There had been copious rains since the fire, the grass was growing green again. Three nights before we left the homestead for our new home, a large number of blacks camped not far from Gibson's public house. They appeared much disorganised and in a very distracted state, there was a continuously knocking together of sticks and thumps and at about hour intervals, a breaking out of piercing yells and screeches as if bedlam had broken loose. In the morning I visited the camp and enquired of Milk and Water: "What for you make big one yabber along a night?" He said: "Wild blackfellow along a mount louse come kill 'em blackfellow quambie here, no sleep." The meaning of it was they had surreptitiously speared two Mount Rouse blacks and killed them according to their custom, out of revenge for two of their own tribe who had died recently.

It was a deep rooted idea among the aborigines, that none of themselves died a natural death. If one died he met his "quietus" either by violence or incantation of the evil spirits of a neighbouring tribe. Tribes were isolated within their own recognised boundaries. If any encroachment happened, there was sure to be a fight, the victors cut out the kidney fat of the enemy killed and rubbed their bodies over with it. I've heard it said they eat it out of gratified revenge, that may be, but I feel thoroughly convinced that as low as Australian blacks were in the scale of creation, they were not cannibals.

NED KEARNEY
Died in 1862 aged 38.

So one morning, we found ourselves with our belongings, behind Strawberry and Brindle on the track to our renovated home. We had only one flock at first, as the grass had not sufficiently grown to support more. In a few weeks two more flocks were sent, my brother was given charge of one, I had a flock of merino ewes and at lambing time about September, Ned Kearney, a sort of underoverseer and I, emigrated

with the flock to a nice sheltered grassy spot called Lubra Creek about three miles distant. A hut had been built for us according to Ned's instructions. The hut was of a very primitive construction as well as the furniture, the walls were built with sod, that is, turf cut into squares like large bricks, a spacious chimney on one end, a sack for a door at the other. The wall plates were saplings, same as rafters, which were enormously long in imitation of Gothic style, finished off with a thick thatch of long grass. Some collar ties were nailed firmly to the rafters leaving ample room to stand without knocking our heads. On the ties was placed a hurdle, on top of the hurdle sheets of green bark, on the bark was placed a thick layer of dry grass on top of which our blankets were spread and there we had a furnished bedroom. We undressed on the floor, and by the aid of a very rustic ladder of three rungs we mounted to our repose, entering head first; on rising in the morning we came out feet first to dress. Our table was a sheet of bark, our seats one at each end of the table were sods built up to the convenient height and finished with bark on the top. Ned had lived with the Henty's some years at Portland Bay and had learned how to devise and make the best of things. We kept roaring fires by night, through making dampers, reviving half perished lambs (Ned had as a bonus over a certain per cent of lambs). We passed the time happily enough.

Wild dogs were plentiful and troublesome at that time. About two hundred yards from our hut was the notorious Lubra Creek, so called from the murders of several lubra's a few years back. The bed of the creek for a considerable width was overgrown with a thick mass of ti-tree scrub, impenetrable to man in places, where the dingo made his lair coming out when hungry, pleasure or inclination prompted him. We lost several lambs in the daytime as well as a few ewes, the lambs they would carry away into the scrub bodily, a full grown sheep they would attack in the flank and tear out the entrails after throwing it on its back. But dingo seldom showed himself in the daytime, except when travelling from one lair to another. They were handsome creatures, a little less than the size of a common shepherd's dog of a yellow colour, sharp pointed head, ears erect, heavy bushy tail and as active as a squirrel. Dingo's depredations were mostly carried out by night, he loved deeds of darkness rather than light; one night pretty nigh to morning Ned and I were suddenly startled out of our sleep by hearing a sudden rumbling, crashing noise. Ned shot out, I after him, partly dressed, we ran to the sheep yard and found the yard smashed down, hurdles lying flat and sheep scattered in all directions. On leaving the hut, Ned had snatched up what we called the blunderbuss - an old carbine fitted with a flint lock of ancient design, which was always kept loaded, in case of emergency, with as much powder and shot as was consistent with safety; keenly watching for the depredator, but of course, he was invisible. The only thing to do, was to discharge the blunderbuss and being a still quiet morning, it made a startling report. A few minutes later, we heard the short, snappy howl of dingo about three hundred yards off, which set our dogs howling for all they were worth. Dingo, lifting his voice now and again, kept the music up for nearly an hour. "It is no good going to bed again," Ned remarked, "so light the lamp lad and I'll do up the fire."

In these days of kerosene, gas and electric light, the reader will have little idea of what our lamp

Lubra Creek as it was in 2003 - when almost nobody understood the significance of the name.

consisted. An old pint pannikin with or without a handle, if with a handle so much the better, three parts filled with tightly rammed soil, nearly filled with melted fat; the wick a slip of deal or the bared cone of honeysuckle with a strip of greased rag on one end wound round to the thickness of half an inch: the other the bare end pushed into the soil in the centre of the pannikin. This is called a slush lamp. Housekeepers of higher pretensions acquired a mould and made candles.

The fire ablaze and the lamp lit, we composed ourselves for a yarn. Ned had many tales to tell, especially about the Henty's and the whalers who were the first white inhabitants of Portland Bay. Whales were very plentiful there at one time and the whalers had built huts for themselves, made small gardens and had each captured a lubra as a wife for himself. The stories this morning turned on wild dogs, how cunning and difficult they were to catch. The most effectual way to kill them known, was running them down with a fleet horse and shooting them.

Ned told of a case of Edward Henty being out on the run one day, spotted a dingo, gave chase and having no fire arms killed him with his stirrup iron. Day broke at last, so the billy was slung (the kettle put on) for breakfast. Our kitchen utensils consisted of a kettle, a camp oven which served for baking, frying and boiling, two pint tin pannikin's, two tin plates and two knives and forks, a safe a bag (lengthwise tacked along the wall plate, a board in the bottom to receive the meat and tied at the end). Salt, tea and sugar were kept in anything. While I fried the chops, Ned had gone out to inspect the damage. One sheep had been bitten, though not severely and several hurdles broken.

As I have mentioned before, Lubra Creek derived its name from a wanton slaughter of several lubras by an enraged band of squatters whose sheep had been stolen, slaughtered and eaten by the blacks. It was usual when anything of that kind happened to band together for the squatter, and hunt for the delinquents and shoot down the first blacks they caught innocent or guilty. In the case of the Lubra Creek tragedy, it appears they could not drop across any black fellows and finding the lubras hidden in the scrub, ruthlessly shot them down. The seat of government at that time was in New South Wales; ordering strict injunctions and penalties to the outlying districts against ill treatment of the natives. Nevertheless it was hard to decide and come at the truth. Every shepherd and hutkeeper practically alone during the day carried his life in his hands. Among the timber or scrub the shepherd knew not a moment when a spear might not be thrown at him from some hidden foe or the hutkeeper might be sneaked upon and killed in his hut; true both shepherd and hutkeeper were armed and did not hesitate to use their guns on the least provocation. The hutkeeper had the best chance if he happened to be in his hut and had time to close the door. The slabs were perforated on the four sides to admit the muzzle of a gun so that the man inside had the advantage over his enemy. The huts were mostly thatched with long wire grass; the blacks would often take advantage of this by throwing lighted spears from a long distance and possibly setting fire to the roof.

So it may be said the settlers of Port Phillip had practically to defend themselves against their

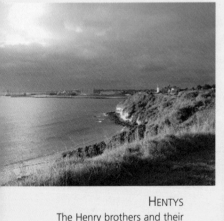

Site of the murders on Lubra Creek.

This home in Portland was built for Frank Henty.

black foes. Later on Captain Pulteney Dana formed a small company of blacktracker's in 1842 to assist in keeping order between blacks and whites but they were a failure. Train them how they would, they were savages still, the most incorrigible race on earth. The wanton massacre at Lubra Creek however got to the knowledge of the government authorities. An investigation into the affair was set on foot, and the ringleaders brought to trial. According to Bill Doyle's story, a squatter named Whitehead and his overseer Beazley were nearly getting hanged, only escaping by the skin of their teeth. This happened five or six years before our arrival, but the bones were lying there as evidence in my time to testify to the carnage, as the bodies had never been buried.

It was the end of September, lovely sunny weather, abundance of grass. We had had a prosperous lambing season and we were ordered to shift back to where we had come from to where mother and father were. As shearing time was near a new woolshed had to be built etc. to replace the destruction of last year's fire.

In the meantime a year had rolled past, our year's engagement was complete. We were hired again for another year for £50, being double the amount of last year. My brother and I were each entrusted with a flock of 1500 sheep, there was another shepherd with another flock, being three flocks altogether on the station. Mother kept hut for us, father tended to the shifting of the sheepyards daily. Ned and some more hands were employed building a temporary woolshed, a shearers hut and preparing the sheep wash, which consisted of fixing poles on the surface of the water, the length of the pool forming a lane about ten feet wide. On the entrance end was laid a sloping, slippery floor of slabs on to which the sheep were dragged, and slipping into the water swam guided by the lane toward the outlet not far from which was a sunk platform two feet six inches. Under the water, where two men stood facing each other, the sheep passing between them were manipulated, soused, dipped under and shoved under a cross pole towards the landing. On dry land they would naturally enjoy a good shake which finished the sheep washing.

Out of the last year's wages, as our wants were very few, father speculated and bought a draught mare with the intention of breeding; she was not a very handsome beast according to my criticism. He asked me what I saw wrong in her, I told him she was too long and small in the neck with a too big head at the end. "A good fault," he retorted, "is a big head, it throws more weight in the collar." The first horse he ever owned, he was very proud of her and called her 'Flower'. Flower was a success in the long run, we reared three good foals from her and a few years later I earned many pounds in Geelong with her carting goods, bricks, water etc.

In due course shearing began. There were only four shearers in the shed who averaged from eighty to one hundred sheep a day. Very decent men, though they all talked Van Dieman's Land, which was almost a certainty they were discharged convicts either from Van Dieman's Land, Botany Bay, Macquarie Harbour or Norfolk Island.

It was inadvisable to question them as to their history, though some unsolicited relate it freely enough. Anyone having come out free to any of these settlements would not forget to talk about it loud enough.

There was another class who came to Port Phillip free, broken down gentlemen, discarded sons of the nobility, parsons and lawyers sons sent to the far end of the earth, anywhere, so as to be rid of them;

ABORIGINAL MASSACRES
'They were nothing better than dogs ... it was no more harm to shoot them than it would be to shoot a dog when he barked at you'.

Reverend William Yate

DIFFERENT OPINIONS
'Our first goal was win their affections, and our next move was to convince them of the superiority we possessed, for without the latter, the former we knew would be of little importance'

Watkin Tench

MUSTON'S CREEK BRIDGE
The first bluestone bridge was built over Muston's Creek by Thomas Dickson in 1855.

these were a useless, undesirable class. They were easily known by their ceaseless blowing about what they were at home, the wealth and grand houses of their people.

About the time I am writing of, 1845 or 1846, a still more objectionable class of subjects were shipped from England to be landed in Port Phillip, a shipload of

The remains of the early track and bridge over Muston's Creek.

Pentonville prisoners, young men and boys serving sentences in Pentonville prison; vagrants, pickpockets, petty thieves, in fact the low scum of the streets of London. The English Government elected to send the best of them as it was said, in the name of exiles, and dump them down on the shores of Port Phillip and there set them free to be hired by any employer who liked to engage

This ship, and later convict hulk, 'Success' was anchored off Williamstown for many years, and became something of an attraction.

them. But only one shipload came. They were a bad lot. All classes protested against them, even the ex-convicts hated them "painted villains" they called them. They had not been out long, before one murdered his mate in a brawl. Meetings in Geelong and Melbourne were held protesting against the Government sending their refuse to our shores. After a while England took the hint and no more convicts were sent this way.

The shearing was over at last, there was no dipping for scab this year, as last year's process had lessened the disease considerably. I had, under the tuition of Peter McVicar and Ned Kearney, become an expert in the detection of the scab disease, and was granted £5 by Mr Sprott (for the year) for hurdling the flock two or three times a week, an hour before sundown to search among the flock for any signs of the disease and check it at its outset. It was an easy matter to detect it. A sheep feeling the itching would either rub and disorder the wool over the spot or pluck a tuft of wool out with its teeth. Catching the sheep and examining the spot, a blue lump could be seen, from the size of a pea to the breadth of half an inch. The wool had to be plucked off round the blue part and the skin scarified with the point of a sharp knife and strong corrosive sublimate water rubbed in. This treatment was mostly effectual to stay the spread of the disease.

There could be no question of the great fertility of the soil at Mustons Creek. I never saw native grass before nor since grow so thick and high. Kangaroo grass often four feet high in the spring and on the old folding ground where sheep had been yarded successively, was thickly abundant, masses of white clover which must have been of spontaneous growth, as it did not grow elsewhere.

The rains in winter and spring were plentiful enough. The main creeks were high and rapid, subsiding in a few days. The country was rocky and undulating, but had a considerable declivity. In all creeks after the rain flood was over, there was no water left, except in water holes here and there in the bed of the water course, which from the daily demands of the cattle and sheep during the hot summer, became low and at times dried up. The water hole near the hut was always preserved with care for domestic use, but from weeds and vegetable growth and constituents of the soil, it became detestable toward the end of summer. In fact there was no water fit for a human being to drink at times. Water was boiled and skimmed before one could drink it and after a pannikin of tea had been drunk the inside of the pannikin would show a coat of red paint. Miniature lakes formed in winter, would dry up in summer, leaving a thin crust of salt on the surface.

In consequence of bad water, diarrhoea was very common, two I knew died of it, and most were affected by it little or much during the hot season. Peter McVicar with his doctor's book and medicine chest, was much in evidence during these epidemics, dysentery he called it. Castor oil and laudanum was his remedy; and there is no doubt he did a deal of good. There was no hesitation in giving Peter credit for being clever.

During the hot summer days the sheep, after filling their bellies, when the sun got hot, would seek the shade of the nearest trees and coil till the cool of the evening, standing up with their heads under each others bellies.

On these occasions, the old professional shepherds would seek oblivion in sleep, which I never could do, my mind was ever active, thinking, doing or planning something, books were very scarce, the most interesting book I had was the Bible. The most entertaining of which I read till it got too stale.

One part of my run adjoined a neighbouring squatter's run, a creek was the boundary. I often saw Payne's (the neighbour's name) shepherd, but feeling a bit shy I never ventured to cross the creek to go to him. However one day he crossed the creek and came towards me. As he approached, I noticed he was a man advanced in years, between fifty and sixty, grey, stout and straight built. "Good day young man," he said cheerily, "as you would not come to see me, I came to see you." "Goodday," I

Payne Street, Caramut - named after the Sprott's neighbour.

answered, "I am glad to have some one to talk to." "I'm Payne's shepherd, my flock is coiling over there." He said: "Yes, I see." Little more was said when we both dropped under a shady honeysuckle. Our conversation was something after this style. "Been long with Sprott?" he enquired.

"A little over twelve months, Mr Sprott hired us, father, mother and brother aboard ship, as soon as we arrived from home."

"Your name is Mundy then, I have heard of your family. You were very unlucky on your first year here getting burnt out and one of you got burnt severely too, who was it, you or your brother?" "It was myself" I said. "Quite alright again now?"

"Yes, alright a good while."

"My name," he said, "is James Quaid, at your service. I am an old sailor, been at sea the greater portion of my life. These last three or four years turned gently shepherd; it is a quiet, easy, leisurely life and being very fond of the arts and sciences, I find this life very congenial to my tastes and elect to pass my latter days in study."

Seeing he had some books in a bag, I enquired if those were the books he studied. He answered in the affirmative. "For several years I was second mate. I had mastered navigation through my own pluck and perseverance, after that I taught myself the rudiments of other sciences, astronomy, geology etc." "Oh," I said, "you could take the sun at sea and tell whereabouts the ship is then." He laughed. "Yes my boy, I could do that." "Is it possible," I asked, "that I could learn this knowledge without a teacher?"

He asked me if I could read and write: "Yes" I said, "I can read and write and I know simple addition, multiplication, subtraction and division. "You have the rudiments of education and with application, pluck and perseverance you can with your leisure, become a learned man, much better than hundreds who have been to college.

"I would like to learn," I said. "Very well, I will tell you what books you ought to get to begin with. Morrell's English grammar, Walker's English pronouncing dictionary, Stewart's geography, and Morrison's arithmetic. Study these books with a will and you will be surprised how you will get on. Make a start and if you like study you will be successful." "But," I replied, "the books you mention are not to be bought here." "No, but the bullock team any time going to Geelong would get them." "Do you like reading?" he asked me. "Yes, but I have no books to read but the Bible, but the most interesting parts I care for I have read them so often they are stale." "All parts of the Bible," he said, "should never get stale to good people." "Well I replied, "I have read little else. I would like a change."

He showed me, at my request, some books he was studying which, of course, I did not understand, but from the recollection of the figures and lines on them must have been books on geometry, algebra or astronomy.

James Quaid, I found out after by his fellow workmen and those who knew him, was nicknamed 'Arts and Science'. He was certainly a better informed and more respectable man than any of his fellows, but as he held himself a little reserved, he was sneered at. We chatted away till the sheep broke from coil and commenced to turn homewards, when we parted promising to meet again soon.

That day's talk with James Quaid put new ideas into my mind, ideas that never left me through life, ideas of improving my mind by self culture. I went home full of it, told father and mother of it. They could not conceive how I could learn without some one to teach me and told me it would be a waste of money buying books on that speculation, and where was I to get the books. I was confident in my inward self that I could succeed and as for the books, I could wait for the opportunity.

A day or two after I met Quaid again, and being very inquisitive, I asked him many questions which amused him much, and was ever ready to answer as well as he could. It was from him I first learned that the earth was round and not flat, that the sun, as far as we were concerned was a fixture. This was a corker. "Why," I said, "don't I see it rise every morning in the east and travel all day till it goes down in the West." "That is only deceptive, my boy," he replied: "It is the earth that turns round, it revolves completely round every twenty-four hours from west to east, which makes day and night. When the sun rises in the east it is daylight, which we call day and when so far advanced as to disappear in the west, darkness comes on, that is what we call night.

"What holds it up?" was my next query, "what's it rest on?" Then he began to explain the principles of attraction centripetal and centrifugal forces etc. which were, for the present, beyond my comprehension, which however, I believed to be all true, as I had no farther doubt after the first shock. I thought James Quaid was a very learned man, like the innocents in Goldsmith's "Deserted Village."

*'and still the wonder grew
That one small head, could carry all he knew"*

"Tomorrow," he said, "I will bring a book with diagrams which will better explain what I have been telling you."

After some more desultory talk, we saw a dozen blacks coming towards us, three black fellows, two lubra's and a young half-cast, one of the lubras had the usual piccaninny slung at her back, the other was loaded with the day's catch of game, native cats, oppossums, bandicoots, a few birds, a kangaroo rat perhaps. "Good morning," was their salutation (always good morning). Each blackfellow carried two or three spears, a waddy, a bangle, a shield and a couple of boomerangs. Old acquaintances of mine, Frying Pan, Tommy Tommy and Milk and Water. I said: "where quambie tonight?" "Oh, along a water hole." To Quaid: "You 'got him baccan?" "No, I don't smoke." "Ah, you too much gammon, you plenty smoke-Borack smoke." He knew it was no good giving one tobacco without giving a bit all round, lubras too. Like all savages, they had a special craving for the Virginian weed. I said to Tommy Tommy: "Where your mate Jimmy Ducks?" At that, they began to yabber among themselves and look angry. After a while Tommy said: "What for you yabber, Jimmy Ducks, him quambie dead." They had the greatest objection to mention the dead.

THE LAST CONVICTS
The last convicts landed in NSW in 1840 on the Eden which carried 270 men. From that time on most convicts were sent to Tasmania.
In 1849 the ship Randolph arrived in Port Phillip Bay carrying Pentonvilles (another name for convict exiles), but the people in Melbourne did not want more convicts and the Governor, Charles La Trobe, would not let the ship land. He ordered it to go on to Sydney and no more convicts were sent to what became Victoria.

The fertility of the ground at Muston's Creek is obvious.

PETER AND MARY McVICAR
Peter was born in 1803, and married to Mary. They had three children - Mary (born in Port Fairy in 1844), Margaret (born in Caramut in 1845, but died in 1862) and Peter (born at Caramut in 1847 and married to Annie Johnson in 1877).
Peter (Senior) died in 1880.
Peter the son also had a son Peter born at the same place in 1879.

ABORIGINAL TERRITORY
Far from being nomads, the aboriginal population of Victoria had distinct boundaries. Caramut is situated exactly on the border of three regions.

(This is the commencement of Book 2 and the first two pages are missing)

The landlord too was generally a hail-fellow well-met, ready to accommodate his customers in every way. Sometimes a newcomer, after he had had a few drinks, would say to the landlord in the trustfulness of his heart: "I have a cheque here, I'll leave with you to take care of, I might get drunk and lose it; when I leave, stop for what I have had and give me the change." "Certainly, to be sure, safest plan 'Bill'. But Bill seldom got any change or wished to travel on, he was steadily and surely lambed down of the lot.

Bill would have a jolly time of it for a while. It depended a good deal on the amount of the cheque, when some morning before he had too much, the landlord seriously would remind Bill, that things were getting to a low ebb, his cheque was nearly exhausted. "I thought I'd tell you, you know Bill, you want time to taper off, or you will not be able to tackle your next job." Nothing unlikely but what Bill would be struck into a heap. "Damn, you, don't mean to say I've spent that cheque already." The landlord, with a placid conciliating smile would bring out the slate saying: "Here it is Bill, every item my boy; you know, you went it too strong Bill for a day or two. I did not like to mention it. If I had, no doubt you would have told me to mind my own business, so what has a man to do?" Whereupon, handing Bill the slate saying: "Look for yourself." Looking over the slate full of items, Bill's fuddled brain could make nothing of it, he would say, I suppose it's alright." Bill would moodily stroll off to his hoon companions, if any left, and say, "Well mates, I'm about flat low. I must soon be thinking of being on the wallaby track. "By God," they would say: "you are not going Bill, we will share and share alike while I've a bob left." Shearers were mostly ex-convicts and generous to a fault. If there was plenty of money stirring and Bill was helping to drink it, it was well, but if the necessary ran low, the landlord would say to Bill: "Now Bill, my boy, you have had a jolly good spree, isn't it time, don't you think, you were looking out for another job? I won't be hard on you, you know I'll give you a bottle of rum to go away with." So Bill forthwith would pack up his dunnage, which consisted of a couple of blankets, same number of coarse shirts, drawers were not of his allure. Socks were seldom worn, if he required anything in his boots, he used toe rags, scraps of blanket or woollen shirt.

With swag on back, he bid his late friends goodbye; when of course some one shouted drinks all round with varied good wishes. Bill picked up his bottle of rum and left the bar. So exit Bill. Whichever way he went, it mattered little, the first hut he came to, he would be made welcome and invited to stay for the night. Next day he would pass on, until he dropped on a job. Shearers seldom turned to shepherding or hut keeping, but splitting, fencing, making hurdles, etc. The same reckless

DEPRESSION
Following the land boom in 1840 when properties bought and sold quickly at rapidly increasing prices, the economy of Melbourne slumped in mid-1841 when too many goods were being imported and could not be paid for.
Wool prices dropped, people rented rather than purchase, insolvency revealed scandals and fraud and the Bank of Australia collapsed.

The stunning homestead on the site of the original pub.

THE HOMESTEAD

This home at Muston's Creek is not the Sprott homestead Henry refers to often. The Sprott site is on the outskirts of the township, while this one lies at the bottom of the hill through Caramut at what is now the junction of the road from Geelong. It was built over the foundations of the second pub. This magnificent house fell into disrepair, but it was saved from extinction, restored, and is today again the finest house in Muston's Creek. It is without comparison to other residences in terms of stature. In the 1860s and '70s many balls were held there and attracted 'Society' from the entire Western District.

life characterised hut-keepers and shepherds, with very few exceptions. After moping out their hired term in the solitary bush of twelve months, lifting their cheque of £20 or £25 (less charges for slops) they made their way to the nearest public house in order to see life and enjoy themselves in their own brutal way. Poor wretches, without a relative on this side of the globe, no one to care for, and nobody caring for them. Their usual boast was: "When my hat's on, my house is thatched."

One evening, as I was nearing home with the flock, there being a stretch of open country between me and the hut, I saw an unusual number of blacks at the hut and father walking backwards and forwards among them before the door. Wondering at such an unusual crowd of blacks, I hurried home. I found about sixty of them, some inside the hut, more outside and some with a fire cooking by the waterhole. I said to father: "Why do you not hunt them out of the hut, mother has not room to stir?" He said: "I told them to go out several times but they take no notice." I ran inside, the smell of the place was awful, I said: "What for too many blackfellow here, clear out you stinking wretches, pull away along a creek." When they saw father and I meant mischief, they sulkily went out and we shut the door. The varmints, Mother said: "I have given them all my bread, now I have to make scones."

After clearing the hut, father went to his hurdleshifting, and I went to the waterhole where the blacks had all collected to have a talk with them. I noticed a good many strangers among them. I said: "Where come barly so many blackfellow?" "Oh, comebarly along a Hopkins. Blackfellow have big one collobolee tomollow, a missah Gibson's." They must have had over twenty dogs. The reader I presume may never have seen a blackfellow's dog - of all the miserable specimens of distorted creation, I think they take the cake. Hairless, mangy skeletons, disagreeable objects to look at. The blacks are very fond of them, they forage for their masters first, then for themselves afterwards; he never thinks of feeding his dog, that is the dog's business. The lubras are very fond of puppies. I have seen them suckle them at the breast.

After I had yarded my flock, I found the blacks had all gone away. It happened this-wise, Ned Kearney, who was still boarding with us and sleeping in the shearer's hut, was occupied, together with another man, in building a new hut (a slab one this time) on Payne's adjacent station, "to be ready for the coming lambing season." Coming home after his day's work he found mother baking scones. The blacks, she told him, had bothered her so for tucker, "that I have given away all the bread I had for fear they would do

Conflict between white setters and aborigines did not always occur, but if it did the consequences were terrible.

us a mischief, there's such a lot of them and there was only George here. We told them to go out of the hut, they were squatted down all over. I couldn't move for them, but they did not take the least notice. Till Henry happened to see so many blacks, came in to see if there was anything the matter and seeing all the varmints inside," said Mother. Why don't you hunt 'em?" "They won't go out," I said; "Oh we'll see." Father was outside where there was a dozen more. I said: "Come father, let us clear the hut, mother can't move." He put on a resolute look and soon sent them flying, but they looked very sulky, and now they are all squatting round our good water hole and nobody knows what nastiness they'll chuck in it. Ned went to the door and looked at them. Now Ned had great respect for mother, I heard him declare she had saved his life.

The way it happened was this. The reader will remember how I have described the process of sheep washing, two men standing in two or three feet of water to do the washing as the sheep passed between them. Ned was one of the two. After the second day, as soon as he got home, he was attacked with horrible cramps, his cries were fearful, mother put him in her own bed and both father and she began to apply hot wet flannels, the cramps commenced at his feet and went slowly upwards and came on at intervals, not going farther than the abdomen. Peter McVicar was sent for from the home station, about two miles, he was soon there. In addition to hot flannels, he advised chafing, or what today is called massage, at which process he set to himself, with a will. My brother and I kept a good fire burning and the water hot. As near as I can remember, it was about twelve o'clock. The cramps seemed to reach higher up the body. Father was wringing out flannels by the fire when Peter ceasing his arduous occupation for the time, he said to father: "Eh George, but the puir buidy is sufferren sair, and the intervals are mair frequent, I'm afraid for the body if the cramp reaches the heart, he will be in great danger, eh, I must hae been daft not to have brought a drap o'speerets along." Turning to me "Wud ye min, laddie, takkin my mare and gang to Gibson's fur a bottle of whisky." I was alert in a moment, on his horse tied just outside the door, and off for all the old mare was worth. The road to Gibson's was in my run, the timber was not very thick. I rode a beeline, only losing my cap in a honeysuckle branch.

I reached Gibson's in less than no time, as the saying goes. All lights were out, I thundered at the door, after waiting a long minute, Mr Gibson opened the door in undress. "What in God's name is up?" he yelled out, "do you mean to knock the house down?" I had dismounted and was standing in the doorway. Holding the light up to my face he exclaimed: "Henry, is that you, and without your cap, what on earth is the matter?" I said: "Please Mr Gibson, Ned Kearney is taken very bad with the cramps. He got them sheepwashing. Peter McVicar and father and mother are with him. Peter sent me for a bottle of whisky." He asked me a few questions which I answered curtly, then I said: "Please sir, let me have the whisky. Ned might die if he does not get it." With that he got the bottle, while I mounted. I put it in the bosom of my shirt next my skin, buckled my broad belt- tight and was off. I soon reached the hut. "God bless the boy" mother cried out, "you haven't been to Gibson's and back by this time, where's yer cap?" "Lost it mother." Then putting my hand into my breast withdrew the whisky. "We'll done laddie," Peter exclaimed, "ye hae dune brawly."

TALLOW - PUTRID BUT A SAVIOUR
While the Yarra River was spoiled by tanneries and boiling down works which operated within its banks, in the 1842-43 Depression it proved a lifesaver for many throughout Port Phillip. While only 50 tons of tallow were exported to Britain in 1843, that rose to a massive 4500 only one year later!

101

Ned had just gone through a severe spasm and lay quiet - supposed to be dozing. Peter touched him and said: "Are ye awake Ned?" who answered, "Yes Peter, but I wish I could sleep. I feel so used up." Peter mixed a small quantity of whisky in water saying: "Here mon, tak this, I daurna give ye cure muckle for fear of inflammation." Ned drank it eagerly, with an injection to try and sleep from Peter.

From that out, the paroxsms became less frequent and less severe till they finally ceased, when Peter gave him twenty drops of laudanum, when he went to sleep like a top. It was nearly daylight

A typical sheep shearing shed and farm of the 1850s and '60s.

CARAMUT LINKS
Most residents in Caramut are unaware of the origins of the names in their small town. However, they include many of the first settlers Henry has introduced us to such as Sprott (spelt incorrectly on the sign at Caramut), Palmer, Gibson and Brown. However, the most recogisable name is 'Hawker'. Harry Hawker was believed born in Caramut and was the originator of Hawker-Siddeley aircraft manufacturing company in Britain. Harry Hawker was a WW1 Sopwith test pilot who bought the assets of Sopwith and formed H.G. Hawker Engineering. The company later purchased Gloster and Armstrong Whitworth Aircraft companies, A.V. Roe and Armstrong Siddeley Motors. Hawker built the Hurricane, Spitfire, the Fury and also the spectacular Harrier Jump Jet. Harry Hawker was born in 1899 and killed in 1921 in an aircraft accident in England, but his name and business survived into the next century.

when Peter left as proud as could be, being sure that his patient was safe. I hope my digressions will be pardoned, when I assure the reader my only object in recording these events is to portray fully, things as they really happened in those days of long ago.

But let us return to our mutons - the blacks. Ned went to the mob of blacks as he told us with intention to hunt them straight away. They were sitting round their little fire of three sticks, roasting opossums etc. some splashing in the water, some lubras dipping their mangy dogs in our drinking water (Oh ye microbe and germs, dreamers of this generation, what do you think of it?) This rose Ned's ire beyond control. Like a mad-headed Irishman as he was on rare occasions, yelling out: "Pull away, pull away out of this, you stinking varmin," kicking one, pushing another, punching them on the head with his fist, kicked their fires about, "Pull away, pull away." The lubras screeched as only a lubra can screech. A real terror seized the mob, they grabbed up their war implements, and stampeded with might and main. Ned said himself, it was a wonder they hadn't turned on him. So abjectly terrorised, they must have thought him the 'Devil Devil' himself or fearing the white man's retaliation.

The monotonous weeks and months have passed on and winter and the winter's rains have come, bringing streams down the shallow gullies and the main creeks, cleaning out all the muddy water holes, leaving us a fresh supply of wholesome water. The other shepherd whose year had expired had left.

The hard working bullock was the primary source of heavy hauling power.

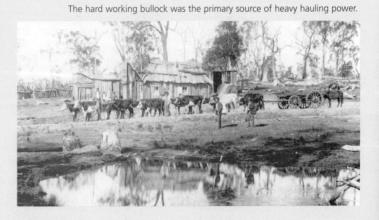

Mr Sprott, who was in Melbourne, had hired a new shepherd to take his place. He was a sailor and a Cockney by birth. He was known afterwards by name of Sam, the sailor. Mr Sprott, while he was in town, bought a splendid looking draught horse, principally for the purpose of taking rations to the out stations in place of Strawberry and Brindle. This horse he entrusted to the care of Sam the sailor to take up to the station, over one hundred and fifty miles. The boss told him he could fix his swag in front and ride, but unfortunately he had not got a saddle to give him, so on the day appointed, Sam made a start, previously endeavouring to fix, with some rope, his swag on the horse's withers, according to some advice he got from an adept in the business, but the horse strongly objected. After persevering for sometime, Sam put the swag on his own back and started leading the horse by the bridle. This suited the horse alright. Sam had a chart of the road and the stopping places. He came to the end of the first day's stage, being a sailor little used to walking, he was very tired. The man where he stopped said: "What a damned fool you must be, to be walking and carrying your own swag and leading a strong brute like that." Next morning the men advised him to get up and hold the swag in front of him, so one gave him a leg up; he got astride alright, when about to hand him his swag the horse reared up, then plunged forward, kicked up his heels and sent Sam flying ahead several yards. That sickened Sam, he never again attempted to mount, but from that out, carried his swag and led the horse. The only things the horse was agreeable to carry were the bridle and his own tether-rope. Sam was never tired of telling us of what he went through and that grey horse. After he arrived on the station he told Tommy the groom about it. Tommy was stockrider and groom in one. Tommy was an excellent horsebreaker without a doubt. He used to blow that never a horse got the best of him, yet Tommy told Sam: "I'll fix him up when I have time."

The subsequent history of the grey horse is as follows. In a day or two Tommy tackled him, using the gentlest and most humane persuasions to induce him to allow the saddle to be put on, but the grey horse was determined to allow no such liberty. So Tommy had to use strategy and compulsion. It took three men to manage it. His front leg was tied up, a twitch put on his nose and a man standing on the off-side, while he manipulated the saddle. The man on the off-side pushed the girth to Tommy with a stick.

The saddle was fixed and the rider with a deft spring, sprang into it. As soon as he was on, picking up the reins, he said, "You can let him go now." Accordingly, he was set free. The groom quietly endeavoured to induce him to start, but no he would not move a leg. At last he received a rather severe application of the spur, at which indignity he commenced to buck, rear on end, dip his head to the ground, throwing up his heels. He carried on this game for a quarter of an hour, till he became streaming with sweat, but never advanced one step.

Tommy kept his seat all right except once, when standing on end, he was afraid of the animal falling backwards, slid to the ground but was on his back again before he could get up, but move on he would not. Some suggested to try the stock whip. The stock whips were powerful flagellators in those days, the handle twenty inches long, the lash eighteen or twenty feet, with a heavy fall terminating with a silk cracker; in the hands of experts, would take a piece of skin off a beast. The stock whip was applied under the belly.

After two or three cuts he made a sudden start for all he was worth and galloped for half a mile, when he suddenly pulled up. He got the spur again pretty liberally and, at last he lay down and would not get up. The oaths and blasphemous words that Tommy made use of on this occasion I was told was terrible, so I had better not record them. Such a sulky obstinate pig of a horse he had never come across before. "Perhaps," Mr Sprott said, "he has been used to the dray. He must have been used for some kind of work." Tommy shook his head and said, "He's been spoilt in the breaking sir, it strikes me he's been used for nothing." "I don't see any marks of work about him." "Alright sir," he replied, "I will give him the breaking bit to champ for a day or two first, for he has a devilish hard mouth. I don't believe he was ever mouthed."

After a couple of days of semi-starvation and mouthing, three or four hands were ready to put the grey into the shafts of the old dray. Fore foot tied up and twitch on nose, the dray was dragged up to the horse, the harness was especially seen to with strong ropes for reins - with strong rope for kicking strap. A man on each side of the horse's head had a short rope in his hand fastened through the ring of the bit. Tommy jumped into the dray taking care to be well back. "Now lads," he said, "set him free," which was done, when the horse began to rear and kick. The rattle of the chains however, started him like magic, stockwhip and spur were not nearly so efficacious as the rattle of the iron links.

The Western District in general has some of the best grazing land in Australia - upon which many dynasties were founded.

STRIPPING THE BUSH

With the onset of the 1841 Depression many people including once highly paid stonemasons turned to finding bark for tanning. It became a major export, but devastated the countryside.
By 1843 every tree from Melbourne to Port Melbourne had been cleared, while the soil was also removed to dig for gravel.
Worse was to come when the Gold Rush broke out.

He made a sudden dart forward and was off at his top-most speed. The men at his head hung on for a short time. The flight was over ground thickly strewn with rocks. One man stumbled, fell and let go, the other man seeing the state of affairs let go too. Tommy held on to the reins for all he was worth, he was only a small man and his strength was totally inadequate, either to stop or guide him, so he slid back to the tail of the dray and dropped off receiving a few scratches on his hands and knees. The grey being a town horse and used to stables and buildings probably thought there was safety inside. The blacksmith's shop was near and the door open, he made for that. The smith, working at his anvil inside, hearing a terrible clatter approaching, hammer in hand, ran to the door only to be met with a horse and dray with all speed coming in. He yelled, held up his hands, threw his hammer at the horse, which, seeing he was not welcome - turned on an obtuse angle and made a bee line for Gibson's pub. But he never got there, colliding with a stump in his mad career, the dray was capsized and horse too, dray wheels up and the horses heels in the air.

The laird, Mr Sprott, was highly annoyed to find he had been so grossly taken with the grey horse. He was such a fine looking animal and the vendor, one whom he thought would not tell him a lie, exaggerated his usefulness so highly, that he gave a pretty good price for him and he seemed good for nothing. Peter McVicar, who knew more about horse dealing than the laird said "what a peety it wus, sir, that ye had na demanded a treel, deelers in horse flesh are a'scoondrels, I wad na trust me ain brither in buying a horse na, na horse deelers are the most trixy cattle in the world." "Excuse me sir, it was only business to have a treel of the beastie ere ye dabbed doon the siller." "Yes, yes Peter, you are right, I know but what are we going to do with the brute, he seems to be unconquerable, quite useless," said the laird.

"Wull," said Peter, "I'm sure I dinna ken what ye can dae we him. If Tommy canna mak something cot o'un, I dinna kna wha can."

For a few days the grey was left to enjoy his liberty in the paddock.

Mr Sprott said to Tommy, the groom, a few days afterwards: "This new horse of our's seems to be a regular failure Tommy, can nothing at all be done with him?" Tommy felt himself disgraced, when he thought of his utter failure to conquer that horse. "Well sir," he said, "I've handled some ugly brutes of horses in my time, but this horse is an hout and houter, I generally managed to make em useful in some way. I've made the worst of buckjumpers into good packhorses when, after a time, they would sometimes become as quiet as sheep in the saddle. If you like sir, I will try and make a packhorse of him, he could take the rations out that way, but Lord sir, he's a hout and houter he's been spoilt sir, in the handling." "All right Tommy, try and make him useful some way."

So next day he made a kind of pannier to place on the horse's back to balance on either side, with receptacles to hold weight. After the usual process of tying up his fore leg and twitching, this was placed on his back, when the pannier was well strapped and fastened on, a pretty good weight of stones was filled in the receptacles. The twitch was taken off, but the foreleg was left tied. In that condition he was left loose in the stockyard for two days, nothing to eat the first day, second day starvation rations. At the end of the second day he seemed very restless from pain, no doubt from standing so long on three legs. So Tommy took pity on him and loosened the leg. The grey did not seem to notice the load on his back. After carrying the swag round the stockyard for two or three days more taking no heed of it in the least Tommy, the groom, confidently assured Mr Sprott that it was safe to pack him with anything, but must not overload him, he was proud too to think he had conquered the grey at last. Accordingly, he was led forth and without any of the former preliminaries he allowed Tommy to load with rations for two outstations consisting mostly of flour with tea, sugar and salt junk. Tommy led him along the track a short distance; the grey going as tractable as any horse could go, giving the leading rope to the man who was to deliver the ration, with this caution: "Don't act rough with him, only coax him, he'll go like an old bullock." The horse went about a hundred yards, then he stopped as if to consider. The man leading him, momentarily forgetting the caution, poked him in the ribs with his stick saying "Get up." He did get up too, both before and behind but not a step in advance. He kicked and plunged that much, that the swag got under his belly. At last, the man, under whose care he was, swore he clawed at the pack with his hind feet and tore it open, flour, meat, tea and sugar were scattered abroad, shameful to see; the horse originally grey became white. Tommy, the groom, did not turn immediately homewards, but stood watching the progress of his newly reclaimed subject, until the stoppage occurred and the subsequent fracas.

When he ran up but could do nothing but swear. The paraphernalia got over the horse's rump, thence on to his legs, then giving the pack a final kick with disgust, made off through the bush, a free horse. The man in charge made an attempt to follow him. Tommy said, "Let the bugger go, if ever he shows his head at the station again I'll shoot him at my own risk." Watching it disappear among the trees, Tommy was heard to ejaculate "Well I'm damned."

I am not exactly sure upon what conditions Ned Kearney worked for Mr Sprott, but Ned claimed four hundred old merino ewes, which Mr Sprott refused to give up at a time appointed. So there was a hot dispute between them. Ned had a run to take them to, somewhere about the Glenelg.

Ned told Sprott he intended to take them away on a certain day (it was from our out station). Before Ned had well started with the sheep, Sprott appeared on horseback and attempted to stop the little flock, but Ned having a good dog drove the sheep under the horse's belly and defied Sprott to stop them. Whereupon Sprott drew from his breast a pistol and deliberately shot Ned's dog.

Ned talked strongly about law that night, about Captain Foster Fyans, the Crown Lands Commissioner, and Blair, a police magistrate at Portland. These two functionaries were considered very just and straight in administering the law, Fyans especially. I have heard often aggrieved working men say: "If I could see old Fyans, I know I would get justice." The J.P.s were all squatters.

Subsequently, however, Ned and Sprott came to an amicable settlement of their grievance, Ned took away his four hundred old ewes and himself. The last I ever saw or heard of him.

Wild dogs were very troublesome that winter. My brother and I slept in a watch box placed between the sheep yards. A large mastiff was tied to one corner; at any unusual sound, he would bark and pull at his chain and jerk us awake, if we had been the seven sleepers. The barking of our dog would mostly frighten dingo, when he would give out one of his short snappy howls, which would start all the dogs around howling for maybe half an hour. Some though, were more daring than others, would spring over the hurdles, grab a sheep, down it, tear out its entrails in a jiffy, when most likely the frightened flock in their alarm would rush to the opposite side of the fold and crush over the hurdles, which were only placed on the ground with prop and tie, and be at large.

The squatters, with a view to pleasure and utility combined, formed a hunting club - in imitation of the fox hunting club in the old country, with the object of either eradicating or ameliorating the wild dog nuisance.

The club had got together a few mongrel fox-hounds and was ready for action. It so happened about this time, there was a female dingo, a notable depredator among the flocks. She carried on her depredations with such impunity in spite of all traps and stratagems lying wait for her. All the coolies of the male kind fell in love with her (it is well known that the dingo and the common dog breed together). Some of the shepherds missed their dogs for days together, much to their helplessness and exasperation to follow lady dingo in her roamings through the bush. I, one day, saw her majesty ambling along, surrounded by half a dozen sheep dogs. In a day or two these delinquents would return humbly and penitently to their masters expecting nothing less than a beating, and in most cases they got it.

This objectionable dingo affected our part mostly. So the new Hunting Club, vowing extermination

FOSTER FYANS
Married Elizabeth Cane at the Melbourne Presbyterian Church in 1843. He died aged 80 in 1870.

THOMAS GIBSON
Thomas Gibson has his name in Caramut still, but historians recognised a later publican as the owner and operator of the first hotel in Muston's Creek.

to this pestiferous brute, and all others of that ilk turned out early one drizzly morning; white and red and white and black spotted dogs, the hunters mounted on all kind of nags. Two wore red coats, one carried a brass instrument which at times he blasted furiously. From information from a shepherd, after considerable dodging round, the hounds picked up the trail, the run was clear, no hedges, ditches, fences or obstacles of any kind to impede progress. Everybody singing out: "Tally ho, Tally ho, Tally ho: and the vociferous yelling of the curs frightened poor dingo to her utmost speed, out-distancing the hounds for a few miles, then she commenced to flag. Finally came upon dingo, when she clapped herself on her tail and set her enemies at bay. No pluck on earth is equal to a wild dog driven into a corner to fight for its life; the jaws seem to be all teeth and the vigorous snaps given at assailants were like the crack of a whip, and whether from canine sympathy or fear, not one of the hounds injured her in the least. The hunters rallied up in great array shouting, egging and encouraging the hounds to tear the varmint to pieces, but it was of no use, some began to sulk away, others seemed utterly indifferent.

Suddenly when dingo saw herself less and less opposed, made a dart and had another run for it, and got scatheless away, much to the disgust of the hunters. Some said the hounds were no good, others said they were badly trained, others pleaded the long run had tired them.

A few more hunts were got up with little or no success. Eventually the club fell to pieces altogether, and became defunct.

One squatter cleverer than his neighbours dropped upon an efficient plan of poisoning the wild dog; in fact, in localities where the plan was carried out, the dingo became totally extinct. The plan adopted was this, when a wild dog surreptitiously worried a sheep, when his hunger returned he would be sure to return for another feed, the shepherd on discovering the dead carcass, would impregnate the body well with strychnine, a second feed would generally settle Mr Dingo, or a lump of mutton so treated and placed in his tracks were mostly effectual. On this occasion the shepherd would muzzle his own dog.

Events worth recording were rare but I must mention stuttering Sam the mailman, he had a round from Mount Rouse to Port Fairy which he compassed once a week on horseback. The delivery of the mail between those places was not very punctual, he seemed to travel at anytime day or night. During that winter, as our hut was in his route, he called various times at two, three, four o'clock in the morning. Father and mother always got up to welcome him, get him a pannikin of tea and something to eat. Sam, he stuttered horribly, was always full of the country's news and his own adventures, narrow escapes, crossing swollen creeks and rivers. Sam certainly had a rough time during the winter months.

Sam, the sailor had been with us about two months, he was hired for twelve. Time went heavily with Sam, he got a stick and each night before supper would cut a notch in it, another day gone he would say. He often wished himself at sea again or in Piccadilly, Pimlico or Hampstead.

The lambing season was approaching again. I had a flock of ewes. My brother a flock of wethers, we got orders to shift to a new slab hut half a mile farther than where Ned and I camped last season, a sheltered country on account of the lambs.

So one lovely spring morning my brother and I with our flocks, keeping well apart, at sunrise started for our new outstation. It was about three miles away, managing to arrive there at sundown. Father and mother with our belongings, with hurdles for the sheepyard had preceded us on the bullock drays, and had all things in order. Our hut was on the edge of a swamp, which intervened between us and the creek (Muston's Creek). The homestead was visible two miles or so away. The grass was magnificent.

My run was west side, my brother's on the east; father bargained with Mr Sprott for a splendid cow, just calved so we had plenty of milk and butter. I never tasted butter to equal it, before nor since. Father also bought a mare, a nice looking beast, something of the racer about her, his object was to breed from her, but she turned out a single failure. He also bought an Arab entire, a very pretty animal, but he had a diseased bumble foot. He didn't pay so much for him, about £5 I think, and it pleased my brother to ride through the bush on him - he was not very lame. The entire was not a good spec. These purchases made a hole in our £55 for the second year. I am not certain but I think we got £60 for the third year, but I had no bonus as scab inspector.

About this time, a young man of the gentleman type visited us, newly out from home, he knew our part and many people that we knew well. He had received a liberal education so he said and

TRADE UNIONS SHAKE THE
ESTABLISHMENT
While trade unions were illegal in Britain, the Masters and Servants Act was passed in Australia in 1845 which declared that employees could not be treated unfairly. From that Act came the first trade union which was formed for tailors.

HERE   AND   THERE;

OR, EMIGRATION A REMEDY.

'BACK HOME'
This cartoon was published in England to encourage emigration to the colonies. It shows starving children in England but their counterparts in Australia with plenty.

spoke of his people as beyond the common sort. He was employed on the adjoining (Sheen's) station. In course of conversation with him, I asked him if he could lend me some books. "Well," he said, "I have only one, a 'Chamber's Edinburgh Journal' which I have read over so many times, you can have that. I'll give it to you." Next evening he brought the book, being one of Chambers old series, but entire. I was delighted. I was never tired of reading it, so amusing and instructive. I read it many times over. Chambers Edinburgh Journal as an educator and pure literature, has held its own to this day.

One day when out near the boundary of my run, the creek, I espied Quaid, my old friend, on the other side with his flock. I made over to him, but he being in a deep study over one of his problems, I suppose did not see me till I got close to him. After mutual explanations as to what had occurred since we last met, and to how we came to be there, I told him what a grand book I had got. He recommended the Journal highly and said I could not have got a better. We met often after that and some evenings he came to see father and mother. The old man affected to be religiously inclined, that pleased father, but I doubted Quaid's sincerity.

Finding time heavy on my hands, I planned a new industry, making imitation cabbage tree hats (scarcely any other hat was worn then, but the cabbage tree). There grew a coarse grass on the banks of the creek, about two feet long and half an inch wide, with edges on it like a saw, would cut one's fingers to the bone, when green, if handled rashly. This I cut and boiled for a time, then spreading out thinly on the grass, exposed to the night dew's and rain, would bleach white in a fortnight. Then nothing more to do but divide it down the middle with the thumbnail and work up into notched plait. About seventy yards would make a hat. With an old cabbage tree for a pattern, I could imitate the pattern fairly well and received as many orders as I could turnout at 5/- each. On an average it took me ten days to complete a hat, a black tape around the rim and a one inch black ribbon round the head with a bit of calico lining completed the head gear.

One day when mother was busy with her household duties, a man appeared at the hut door in great distress of mind and manner. "Whatever is the matter man," Mother asked. The man's story was something like this - "My name missus, is Bill Tattam, I'm shepherding for Sheen (Hopping Sheen) you know, next run, and my wife was hut-keeping for me and another shepherd Jack Lyons, curse him.

BILL TATTAM
Married Caroline Vine in Maryborough in 1860. They had a son Charles.

107

This is a building constructed by an early white settler family. The first farm hands were brought in to help clear and work the land, and when later Selectors purchased their land from the government, it was on the proviso they cleared it of all trees.

Jack's time was up two days ago, so he went Sheen and got his cheque, intending as he said, to go to Port Fairy, so another shepherd was put in his place. Well, what do you think Missus? Yesterday, when I was out with my sheep, Jack the sneaking wretch came to the hut and persuaded my Lizzie to bolt with him, yes Missus, they've bolted, oh Lord; oh Lord, my dear Lizzie has gone and left me, oh dear, oh dear what shall I do?"

Here-upon, Mother said, he began to howl piteous, to hear Mother tell him: "If she was a woman of that sort, she was not worth troubling about, and a good riddance;" and asked him if she was his wife. "No," he said, "but we have been together for two years and I'm sure kinder man could not be to a woman than I was to her. I've called here Missus," he said, "to enquire if any of you saw them pass yesterday. I have an idea they have gone to Gibson's. " Mother had heard nothing nor seen anything of them, she told him. "Ah well," Bill said, "I'm going there and if I find them there, by the lord Harry, as sure as the Devil made little apples I'll be the death of Jack Lyons if I have to swing for it." With that determination, he started.

In about three hours Bill Tattam returned from Gibson's pub, it was hardly two and a half miles distant, to our hut, hatless with a black eye, several cuts on his visage and blood copiously spilled down the front of his blue woollen shirt, one arm of which was nearly torn off. He walked into the hut and plumped down on a stool, the picture of misery and despair. Father happened to be in at the time; mother having told him of his previous visit, said: "Why mate, it looks to me as if you have been fighting." "Yes by God, a man stole my wife and has very near settled me in the bargain. How would you like that mate?" Father said it was a catastrophe not likely to happen him and advised him to get some water and wash the blood off his face. Bill seemed utterly demoralised and said little, but mother made him a pannikin of tea which he drank, offering him food: "No Missus" he said, "my belly's full."

After sitting a while in silence, father said to him: "Where are your sheep mate, is any one looking after them." "They're on the bloody run," he said, "they can go to hell for what I care," but after a time Bill Tattam picked himself up and shuffled off back to his lonely and desolate life, no doubt for many days a broken hearted man.

Some days after mother paid Mrs Gibson a friendly visit, who told her all about the fracas between Bill Tattam and Jack Lyons. Bill arriving at the pub, the first thing that met Bill's enquiring eye was Jack and Liz sitting cosily, close together sitting on a log as happy as two sand boys, both half seas over. They did not twig Bill till close on them, who without more ado, gave Jack a righthander on the jaw, whereupon the fight began with varied success for a time Liz crying out: "Give it him Jack; give it him, the scum."

Jack was the bigger man and besides was fortified within, while poor Bill had nothing but his wrath to support him, moreover, was wasting his breath with foul language, was getting sadly mauled, when a crowd collected (if five or six can be called a crowd) and separated them crying, "Shame, Shame," on Liz and her paramour; who, as the saying goes, sneaked away with their tails between their legs. Liz was very good looking in the face, but she had bumble feet; Bill told how he met her in Hobart Town two years ago, and took her off the street. He had a bit of money at the time, offered to take her over to Port Phillip where they could hire to a squatter as a married couple and go into the bush; to which plan Liz readily agreed. Coming over to Melbourne, Bill and Liz had a jolly time for a while, while Bill's money lasted. Funds getting low they hired as man and wife for a year to Mr Sheen to go and work on his station.

Late one evening Quaid came to our hut bringing the startling news that the other shepherd in his hut, and the hutkeeper had had a quarrel and fight. After the fight was over the hutkeeper was taken very ill and in a short time after died.

Wondering and surmising what the upshot of it would be, Quaid left for home in a very disconsolate state of mind. A few nights later he called again. There had been an inquest held and it was ascertained that he had some internal complaint and a blow over the affected part would be liable to cause death; so as Quaid being present gave evidence that it was a fair fight, the hutkeeper was acquitted.

Blacks were more than usually numerous this year; not in large crowds but in small parties, two or three times a week we received a visit of from one to three or four asking for food, being cunning enough not to come too many at a time; they seemed to be getting careless now of foraging, as hitherto, for themselves, but depended more on the whites to supply them with damper and mutton, which was seldom refused them, and easier to obtain. Sometimes with a deal of coaxing they could be prevailed on to chop a bit of wood. One day, come King John, bearing a brass plate on his breast with his name inscribed thereon, asking mother for food. Mother said: "Yes King John, I give um you tucker, you chop um me wood." At this his Majesty looking her despairingly in the face, said: "Borack, me chop um wood, me (rubbing his stomach) too big one hungry." Mother gave him as much as he could gorge, then he stretched himself in the sun in a state of beatitude. After awhile, not offering to pick up the axe, Mother said: "Come now King John, you've had a good feed, chop um wood"; he looked at her indignantly and said: "What for you yabber, chop um wood me too big one bellyful."

The Australian aboriginal is supposed to be the laziest and the most intractable of the human race; they are expert in some things if it takes their fancy, but any exertion requiring continuous application, is against their nature. Squatters have tried to make them useful on the station, but it lasted for only a very short time. They would soon be off to join the tribe and don the blanket or opossum rug again. I knew one - Tommy. Tommy, a smart looking blackfellow he was, worked as a stockrider for a squatter for two years, then suddenly gave it up and joined his tribe.

In 1842 Captain Dana organised a corps of twenty-five native police from Western Port; after being efficiently drilled they soon made a smart troop. They were utilised not only in suppressing outrages among their country men, but also in capturing white bushrangers, they were engaged in several conflicts and showed both coolness and courage.

Captain Dana and his blacktrackers were thought a deal of for a time, but finally became a signal failure. Six died of drunkenness, two killed while drunk, nine deserted, threw off their clothes, donned the blanket and returned to the bush, eight only remained faithful to the end, and led respectable lives.

Coming home one evening mother said: "There's been a terrible row among the blacks across the creek, I wonder what's up." After supper, my brother and I agreed to go to the camp to ascertain what had occurred. As I have said before, they had a great dread of being alone after dark, under dread of wild blackfellows or that spirit called Boubelcarnie. So no matter how they scattered during the day they always congregated, as many of them as possible, together at night. We made straight for the camp. Approaching near, we noted one sitting by his fire about fifty yards from the rest; coming near we saw it was Milk and Water. "What for, Milk and Water, you no quambie along a other one blackfellow?" my brother asked him. Milk and Water looked straight at his bit of fire, but never opened his mouth.

Passing on to the camp, two or three lubras were howling a sorrowful ditty; one of them said: "Milk and Water bad fellow, he kill um my blackfellow, he want um me." Milk and Water was a noted fighting man and an insatiable bigamist. If he saw a woman he fancied he generally got her. Whether the blackfellow was really killed or Milk and Water claimed his prize, I never knew.

Lambing time came on when I was fairly employed. I would go out a certain direction to the end of my beat in the morning and return the same route in the afternoon, what lambs dropped in the forenoon, would be able to travel with the flock returning. Lambs dropped on the way home, I often

had to carry in my hands, hanging by the fore legs. It would not be safe to leave them out all night on account of wild dogs. Sometimes father would come to meet me, but his time was fully occupied in shifting the two yards every day, chopping wood, carrying water, milking the cow, and looking after and tethering his horses. I slept in the watch box by the sheep by night, but luckily we were not troubled with wild dogs. When lambing was over, the percentage was considered good, but the boss did not allow any bonus.

The next event was the shearing of the two flocks. A temporary shed had been erected and Tom Horton, Tom Fairfield and two inseparable mates, called Peter and Paul, who were called the Apostles, were employed to do the shearing. During the shearing the blacks were more numerous than usual, two of them seemed helpless, scarcely ever moved away, the poor wretches were gradually dying with venereal disease; "broke it" they called it.

There was a black protector stationed at Mount Rouse, fifteen miles away, named Dr Walton, appointed by the Government to relieve any necessary wants of the black, medical or otherwise, but whether they did not believe in him or objected to his psychic, it is hard to say, but very few

It was often considered that killing aborigines was virtually not a crime. Slaughter was rampant.

ever troubled him except for food.

Venereal disease and rum were the white man's legacy and where the white man is fully established, the aborigines are totally extinct, excepting a few black settlements under the protection of the Government and some of them are half-castes.

When the shearing was completed, we had orders to shift six miles away, on to another out-station. Our boss had arranged with Mr Burchett a neighbouring squatter, for a portion of his run. A new hut had been built for us and we were on the nomad again for pastures new. Our second year having expired, father engaged again at the same rate of pay for another year.

Our station was on Burchett's Creek. Peter McVicar, the overseer, was stationed midway between us and the Homestead.

It was about this time, I wrote the first letter from home to Uncle John, my father's half brother.

Boyishlike, I boasted and bragged of how we had got on, told him of our horses, our cow, what wages we were getting, and what a fine country it was, and advising everybody to come. On this occasion I made my first attempt at poetry -

Oh yes, you say I fain would come
To this your beautiful country
But my attachment to my native home
Makes me content to dwell in poverty

110

Uncle John was more intelligent than the common, he had received a little education at a night school; he had also a permanent situation a little above his co-workers, and considered himself fairly well off. He worked at a coal wharf on the canal for Geo Clarke & Co. at Fenny Stratford. He answered the letter in due course to father, saying how glad he was to learn he was doing so well; with other news told him he himself had seen the error of his ways and had been converted in the Baptist chapel, grandfather too was converted, and was now quite a different man.

As to poverty, he said no doubt there was plenty of it about, but as for himself he had no cause to complain, in conclusion wishing us all well and hoping that we should all meet again in that happy land, where there was no more sin nor sorrow.

This is all the correspondence we ever had with our people of our native home.

I liked our new run much better, but it was rather monotonous, few events occurred worth recording, one though was rather startling.

One morning very early father came to the watch box and called me saying, "Henry, get up and go for Mrs McVicar, your mother's very ill," so I roused immediately and set off for Mrs McVicar about twenty-one miles. When I reached there and told her mother was ill, she rose straight away, while Peter went for a horse which he kept on tether. After putting on a man's saddle, he helped her on to it, straddle legged, and I, with the reins in my hands, had to pilot her through the bush. I could not help looking back sometimes to notice what a grotesque figure she looked, with her hands clinging to the pummel of the saddle.

When we arrived it was daylight and mother was crying out fearfully. Father said: "Call John and get your breakfast, then let the sheep out." John and I looked very solemn during the meal; as soon as it was over, we were hustled off.

About midday when the sheep were coiling, I thought I would run home to see how mother was. When I neared the hut I saw father busily shifting his hurdles, I said to myself, mother must be better surely.

On entering the hut I was met by Mrs McVicar all smiles. "What do you think," she said: "you have got a little sister." To say I was astonished would be putting it mildly, I was struck of a heap; as I had no idea of anything like that was going to happen. My brother was the youngest and he was twelve years old.

She went into the bedroom and brought out a bundle of calico with a little face peeping out and said: "Isn't it a little beauty, arna ye glaid." "Yes," I said.

Poor little sister; with the remembrance of her life's career, father dying when she was ten and her mother's foolish training - I almost wish she had never been born.

Time sped on; I have nothing to record till next shearing. Another temporary shearing-shed was erected near Peter McVicar's hut. A rougher set of men could hardly conceived that the shearers in that shed; one in particular, his name was Jack Taylor, one of the most obscene and brutal type I ever came across. The way he hacked the poor sheep was something appalling, often taking pieces of skin off as big as a penny piece. Peter McVicar was going round with a tar brush dabbing the sores after the sheep had been shorn. Peter's ire rose at the way Taylor hacked the poor brutes about and said to him "Mon, we dinna want ye to skin the puir beasties, but jist to tak the woo'o." Jack's retort to this had better not be recorded. A day or two after this I was standing by watching Jack operating, the sheep he was shearing was very restless; he deliberately bent his head to the sheep's mouth and bit a mouthful out of its upper lip and spit it out. I had noted before, sheep wanting the upper lip and easily guessed shearers had done it. I met this Jack Taylor two years later and had to live a month with him, but of this more later on.

Father had shopped away the stallion for another cow and sold the second mare. He bought and purchased an unbroken chestnut filly. We possessed two horses, two cows and three calves.

Our twelve months service was near the end again, when father fell in with a squatter named John Brown who owned an extensive run at Mt. Elephant, and offered us £60 a year for our next year's services, which offer father, after consulting us boys, agreed to accept. So he bought a dray, put a tilt on it and got ready for a shift. The place we were going to was fifty miles from Geelong called Brown's Water Holes, the names of localities were mostly named after the first settlers, though most of them in the latter days have been renamed. Our term having expired, the dray was loaded with our belongings including about fifty fowls, we made a start one morning for our new situation. It was hard parting with our old friends, especially the McVicar's and the Gibson's.

COILING:
When the sheep mill round and lay down, as like a clock spring, to sleep at night or rest during the heat of the day.

111

New South Wales

VICTORIA

Muston's Creek   Ballarat

Geelong   Melbourne

Once on the road from Muston's Creek to Geelong the country is flat, and is very suitable for sheep and cattle.

WALKING TO GEELONG

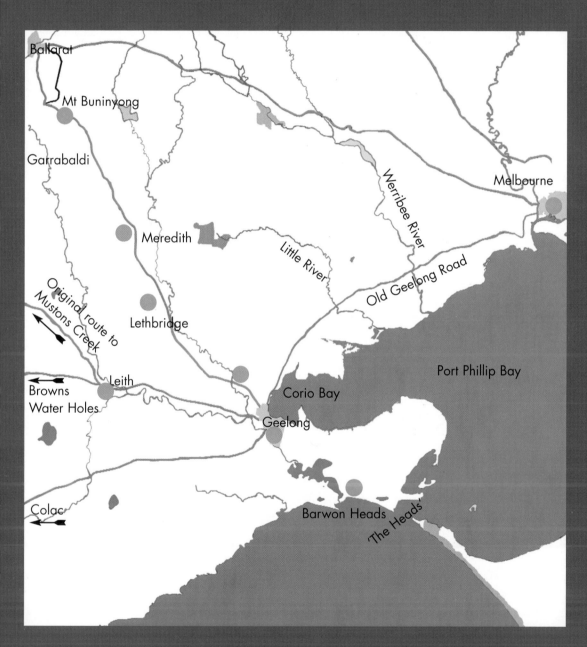

Ballarat
Mt Buninyong
Garrabaldi
Melbourne
Meredith
Werribee River
Little River
Old Geelong Road
Original route to Mustons Creek
Lethbridge
Port Phillip Bay
Leith
Browns Water Holes
Corio Bay
Geelong
Colac
Barwon Heads
'The Heads'

BROWNS WATER HOLES

The Mundy's were offered a new contract for twelve
months shepherding when they reached Browns Water
Holes on the road to Geelong. However, the property
they worked was a long way from the main road, and
not as fertile as where they came from.

Mt Elephant from the road to Caramut.

LIFE AT MT ELEPHANT AND GEELONG

My brother drove the cows and calves, I led the filly, father drove Flower with mother and baby in the dray. At the end of our first day's stage we pulled up at a tumbledown hut on Captain Webster's run at Mt. Shadwell. I remember it turned very cold. There was only room and hardly that, for father, mother and baby to sleep in the dray. John and I had to sit by the fire but the evil of it was, wood was scarce round the hut, so we had to make fire with the slabs of the old Captain's hut to keep our fire going. There was not much of the hut left no doubt previous travellers had utilised the slabs as we were doing. We lay down in front of the fire, it was a very exposed situation, the wind was piercingly cold; we dropped off to sleep many times, but waked up as often to warm the other side by turning over. Daylight was more than welcome, when we had a hasty breakfast and were on the road again.

That day we pulled up at Elephant Bridge.

We had better lodgings that night. There was a public house; father and mother slept in the house, John and I took a good sleep in the dray. We did not start very early next morning, as we had before us a short stage six or eight miles to one of Mr Brown's out stations at the foot of Mt Elephant. There were two flocks at the station tended by two brothers named Carter, one of them was married. They were kind people and made us very welcome.

Mt Elephant, beside being on elevated ground, must be, I should think, eight hundred feet high above the surrounding country, a very old extinct volcano. At a distance it resembles the body of an elephant without legs. The locality is very thinly timbered; the ground was covered with peaked honeycombed rocks; in the interstices, where was a little soil, very rich grass grew which was said to be very fattening. The next day we had twelve miles to go to reach our destination.

The previous day's walking and scrambling over the Mt Elephant rocks had made my feet sore; and

Looking back from the area which the Mundys worked from, to Mt Elephant in the distance.

leading a horse when one has sore feet, I thought ridiculous, so I chanced backing the filly, so pulling a half hitch on the halter, fixing it on the filly's under jaw I asked John to give me a leg up. I expected a spill, but no such thing happened, she went as quietly as a well broken-in horse. We reached Brown's out station, where were stationed two shepherds, the two brothers named Carter.

Although it was early in the afternoon, Mrs Carter prevailed on us to stay for the night. At sundown the shepherds came home. The Carters were Lancashire people and we passed a very pleasant evening.

Next morning we resumed our journey; we had only twelve miles to go. I insisted against father's protests, to ride the filly again. Father had in the old country been all his life among cows and horses, in fact in his younger days had been considered a pretty fair jockey, but he had had so many spills and "busters" that all confidence seems to have oozed out of him. The filly however, was quiet enough.

Very soon after starting we came in with a bit of bad road. Mt. Elephant swamp, of black sticky mud. We, however, reached Mr Brown's homestead about sundown where we were welcomed and stayed that night.

Mr John Brown was a Scotsman, a bachelor aged about fifty-five; the only relation he had with him was his nephew, Thomas, who was about twenty. The overseer's name was Thomas Clayton, two or

Once a fine home with valuable outbuildings, this place has been abandoned.

BUILDING MATERIALS
Timber suitable for building was so scarce in Victoria that it had to be shipped in from Van Dieman's Land, the USA and Asia.

Lime for cement was made locally, firstly from crushed shells then stone. When bricks were produced for the first time in the late 1840s improved lime was produced at Portsea, Point Nepean and at Geelong.

The Mundy's view to Colac remains unchanged.

three general useful men, a married couple and a groom, constituted the inhabitants of the Homestead.

Next morning, we were taken to the out station destined for us, three miles distant. The greater portion of our run was a treeless rocky plain; a flock of sheep each was allotted to my brother and me, father had the hurdle shifting, as formerly, mother doing the hutkeeping business. The water supply was as usual in summer, a string of water holes in place.

My run extended towards the homestead for two miles. The only timber there was about, was there, a few scattered honeysuckles and sheoaks, to which I made in summer, for shade for myself and flock. My brother's run was on the other side of the creek extending Geelongwards, not a tree on it as far as the eye could reach and miles beyond.

To the south was Robinson's near Lake Corangamite, on the north was Chirnside. The lake eight or nine miles distant, on the elevated ground, could be seen plainly on a clear day - a great place for game and waterfowl, on the other side, Colac and the Warren Hills were distinctly visible. Mt. Elephant appeared an immovable hump on the horizon.

If it had not been for the scarcity of trees, the exposure in winter and want of shade in summer, I should have preferred our new home to Muston's Creek, the outlook was so much more interesting but the soil was poorer, not such good grass which is an important object to a shepherd.

The country seems to be of pre-paleozoic or very primary formation, large granite boulders and masses of columnar rocks on the banks of the creek were exposed in places by riparian denudation.

Somewhere about this time, happened the wreck of the ill-fated emigrant ship Cataragui on King's Island bringing to Port Phillip four hundred souls out of which only nine escaped.

For several years the proceeds of land sales had been utilised by the authorities in Melbourne in bringing out from the old country, picked, lusty men and women and. their families to colonise Port Phillip. At various times, shiploads safely arrived, bringing altogether 220,000 safely over without any accident, but the unfortunate Cataragui at last was lost. One of the survivors called at our hut one day and told the sad tale.

After having been at our new place a week or two I prevailed on father, when he went to the homestead for our weekly rations, to ask the boss if he had any books he could lend. When he returned, behold, he produced two Chamber's Edinburgh Journals, these were a Godsend. I read and reread those journals many times, till there was nothing in them, but what I mastered and fully understood. No plates or pictures in them but all solid reading. The leading articles were on useful knowledge, some tales, some poetry, but what claimed my attention most of all were the lives of self taught men from the lower orders who had risen to eminence in science and poetry. It recalled to mind Quaid's advice.

I made up my mind, the first opportunity I got, when the next bullock would be going to Geelong, to send for the necessary books by which I could teach myself some little knowledge. The mantle of ignorance seemed to hang over me like a cloud; I was severely conscious of it. I wanted light.

The next book I got from Mr Brown was Tom Jones, which interested me much, especially 'The Old Man of the Hill'. The last I got for a time was one volume of Hume's 'History of England'. A travelling hawker called at our hut carrying a little of everything suitable for sale in the bush. He had a few books; I bought two or three novels off him and the 'Pilgrim's Progress'; also some moleskin to make myself a pair of trousers the hawker cut them out, I put them together myself. Ned Kearney had taught me the art of backstitching.

The scab disease here had been stamped out, but there was plenty of foot rot. Two men occasionally were sent out to pare the cripple's hoofs and apply the vitriol remedy. The two men were named Paddy Malony and Bill Jones, alias Curly Bill. Whether Paddy had served his time or not I never knew; if he had he kept it, wisely, to himself. But Curly Bill had and boasted of it, he was born in London; the first trade he became proficient in was picking pockets, then he made a tour through England calling at most of the big towns exercising his profession, intermixed occasionally with a little burglary till he got nabbed and was transported to Van Dieman's land; what his sentence was I do not know, but by his own confession, by his own irritability, it was considerably lengthened. He was about forty when I knew him, a wild unscrupulous character.

One morning, we had just finished breakfast, father said something to him he did not like. Curly Bill whipped out his footrotting knife and holding it open backhanded rushed up to father saying: "What would you say if I stuck this into you." Father stood still and with a laugh said: "Bill, you are a queer fellow, that can't take a joke." With that he dropped the knife and said no more. Paddy turned as white as a ghost, mother looked paralysed. I was looking round for something to floor the wretch with, when father's soft answer turned away his wrath. Curly Bill had a peculiarly shaped head, the heaviest was behind his ears and very large.

A year or two after I studied phrenology, which came out as a new science. I thought of the shape of Bill I s head and was convinced that it was of the extreme criminal type; but since that phrenology as a science has been condemned; nevertheless, I feel convinced there is something in it. It is often said, let a man or woman be ever so bad, there is always found some good traits in their character. Bill often spoke of his mother with great feeling, his conscience no doubt smote him for the misery and trouble he had caused her; perhaps she was weeping in the court, while he in the dock was having sentence passed upon him.

Mr Brown when in Geelong hired a boy of fourteen and sent him up to work on the station; he was a well-behaved, bright, intelligent lad, and was taken to by everyone. He said his mother was a widow and he had hired to work on the station so as to be better able to help her.

Four months passed when he asked Mr Brown to oblige him with a cheque for what was due to him to send to his mother, to which request he readily assented. Just at this time, Curly Bill was leaving Brown's and was going to Geelong; the boy innocently enough thought it a good chance to send his cheque to his mother, asked Bill to oblige him. Some, when they heard of it, shook their heads in doubt for the poor boy's cheque, but Bill proud of being trusted, honestly and truly, fulfilled his mission.

Two years after there was a report that one Bill Jones alias Curly Bill and others were captured as bushrangers and had received severe sentences. That was the last I ever heard of Curly Bill.

The time, the opportunity had come. The bullock team was going to Geelong. I took advantage of the chance to send for three books, namely English grammar, geography and arithmetic. In a fortnight's time the treasures arrived. I set myself for all I was worth to study. The work I had to do did not interfere in the least.

I took lessons in each, once in the forenoon, then a couple of hours spell with the same lessons again in the afternoon. In a year I had mastered the grammar, acquired a general knowledge of geography and had gone through arithmetic up to cube root where I stopped. I then began to think of learning more but I had no one to advise me. I felt at a lose end what to do. At last I concluded to learn the dead languages, Latin and Greek. The next opportunity I had, I sent for a Latin and Greek grammar. Goldsmith's History of Greece and Rome which thoroughly took up my time.

Our first year had passed and father engaged again for another year for the same money £60. We had increased in stock another foal and two more calves, father had sold the chestnut filly.

Blacks were not very numerous, occasionally they paid us a visit, the scarcity of timber, no doubt, was the reason, as they had no material to build their mia-mias with, wild dogs were seldom seen, but bandicoots and kangaroo rats were plentiful, native cats were a perfect nuisance, a plague; they would

EARLIEST GEELONG AND PORTLAND
Geelong, 45 miles to the west at the other end of Port Phillip Bay to Melbourne, was first settled by whites in 1836. By 1838 there were over 300,000 sheep grazing in the Geelong district.
Further west on the coast Portland had been established many years before by whalers and principally the Henty brothers who came over from Van Dieman's Land looking for suitable farming properties.

SINGAPORE TERRACE
The precise address of the old Singapore Terrace was 50-52 Eastern Beach, on the Geelong foreshore.

make their way into the hut by night and turn things topsy-turvy. It was the greatest place for black and diamond snakes I ever knew. I carried a stick with me on purpose for killing them. In the warm weather I scarcely missed a day without killing one, sometimes three or four.

One moonlight night in March, I nearly trod on one; the only time I ever saw a snake out of his hole in the night time. The stumped tailed iguanas too were plentiful, but these although they would bite hard, were not venomous. I never saw a kangaroo the two years I was there, in fact I only saw one while at Muston's Creek.

Of the feathered creation there was no great number in comparison with forest country. Wild turkeys, which is a bird of the plains, and black swans in the small swamps, often paid us a visit.

This fine house is built on what was 'Singapore Terrace'. The view is seen left.

About this time someone, I forget his name, imported a ship load of Singapore cedar as a cheap valuable timber for house building, cabinet making etc. The Singapore Terrace in Geelong was built of it. With the cargo of timber came out a number of Singapore natives, some of these stayed in Geelong, a few ranged the colony in search of employment; one day one of them ran into our hut in a wild, frightened, distracted state and fairly dropped on the floor with exhaustion. "Missus, missus," he cried out, "blackfellow kill me." According to his account, two of them were travelling together when some natives saw them. Even at the then stage of civilisation, any blacks not aborigines, were wild blacks and they considered they were justified in killing them, which they would do if caught, without any hesitation.

Mother ran out, expecting to see a lot of blackfellows coming, but none were to be seen, they must have been on the tracks of the other fellow. Whether they caught him or not I never knew.

I have nothing of any consequence to record till the end of our second year, when father having accumulated a little money was ambitious enough to think of buying a small block of land and with his two boys, to start farming. He was advised to go to Geelong and buy land on the Barrabool Hills. So giving Mr Brown notice at the end of our engagement that he was going to leave, Mr Brown bought our two cows and what progeny they had. That left us with only the draught mare, the dray and two foals.

So one fine morning we hitched up Flower to the dray, well tilted, containing all our belongings. We all rode comfortably Geelongwards, the foals following; after five years service in the bush.

FRED DUVERNEY
The Frenchman's Run (May 1844-March 1847) was a hotel operated under Fred Duverney. This is the only reminder of the place.

This was Forbes' hotel in Geelong.

The first night we reached the Frenchman's, a public house kept from the earliest days by a Frenchman named de Varney. Very few Port Phillipans, who had not seen or heard of the tricks of Mr and Mrs de Varney. At this time the de Varney's had left three years ago after making their fortune

Henry's favourite view of Geelong - from Bell Post Hill.

and gone home to France. It was reported after that de Varney was seen over by a railway train and killed. de Varney's successor was named Forbes, who afterwards kept a public house at the corner of Pakington and Spring Streets, Geelong.

The next day's stage reached the Leigh. The next day about four o'clock we were on Bell Post Hill, overlooking Corio Bay, the sea again. There was not much to be seen of Geelong in the distance, as it was very small from our point of view. I did not dream then of the happy and sad future that lay therein for me.

Coming into the flat among a few sheoaks and many sheoak stumps for about two miles, we stopped in a thinly populated suburb in Gertrude street in Newtown. There happened to be plenty of grass for the foals, while the mare was fed at the dray.

Nothing was done that night, but in the morning father was looking round and making enquires about land, when

The Mundy's own first permanent home was here in Gertrude Street, Geelong.

he came in contact with a man named George Gutteridge, who offered him a two roomed weatherboard house, newly built, on a piece of land sixty-six feet by one hundred and twenty feet, for £25. After some haggling father bought it and forthwith shifted into the house. Two sides of the ground were fenced.

Our first thing was to fence the front and one side. It was agreed also to build a three stalled stable which I volunteered to take in hand, while father and John were to do the fencing; of course, they were to assist me when I wanted help. So father went into the town to order the necessary timber.

The stable was to be twenty-four feet by twelve, skillion roof ten feet in front and eight feet at back. They borrowed tools to do the fencing, but I, being the carpenter, demanded proper tools. There were some small houses being built close by so I went to watch the carpenters working and what tools they used. I watched them till I thought I had the hang of the whole business telling father to get two boxes,. a saw, hammer, chisel, square and an inch auger, a big pencil, a marker (gauge) and a strong fishing line. He opened his eyes and said, "Whatever do you want all them things for, what are you going to do with a fishing line to build a stable?" I said: "No matter, you'll see." In due course the materials were delivered and I commenced work. I mortised all the plates, then tackled the studs, taking it for granted that every piece was exactly ten feet in length.

Typical stables of the period and the type Henry, John and their father built.

I measured two inches from each end, squared it round and gauged it, I cut the shoulder of the tenon with the saw but thought it waste of time and trouble to saw it down. I split it off with the chisel. The blocks were the next thing, but I had no level to get the level with; a neighbour named Curly Smith came to see me often. I told him my fix, when he went and borrowed a spirit level, so that was alright. John and I borrowed a crosscut saw, cut the blocks and soon had them placed level with our level and straight edge and fishing line. "There," I said to father: "You can see now what the fishing line is for." "Pooh," he said, "any bit of strong string would have done as well." I could not but admit that, but my idea of a strong string was centred in a fishing line. The next thing to do was to put the studs and plates together, they were all three by two. The studs fitted into the bottom nicely, but on fitting the top plate some studs went into the mortices alright, but some went only half way home and others would not reach at all. Curly Smith and father had been summoned to give us a lift up with half the front. When father saw how the thing fitted: "Why boy," he said, "you've cut some of the uprights too short." I saw where I had blundered, in a minute. Curly laughed - "You know all these sticks are not exactly of one length, you should have cut one first, then cut all the rest by it."

One end of course was alright, so I took out the shortest one and cut all the rest by that. After that the stable went on like a house on fire. I have dwelt long on the building of this simple stable because it was my first assay in the building trade. I was always fond of woodwork. In my younger days I took advantage of every chance I had to practise. I bought books and studied building and all trades connected with it. It was not till I was thirty-five that I ventured to proclaim myself a carpenter; when I received the regular wages 10/- a day and was second in skill to very few.

From that my son became a carpenter who I must admit excelled me in skill, for a good reason he started young and scarcely ever did anything else, his two sons are also carpenters as good tradesmen as one could meet. Thus from small things, greater spring.

Father being a devoted Wesleyan fell in with some of his co-religionants, of whom he asked advice as to buying land and starting farming. They advised him to have nothing to do with land, as agriculture was not paying at all well. A bag of flour could be bought at the mill for a pound, hay was cheap and oats 2/- a bushel. They told him there were several ways in laying out his money than taking up land, and as he understood dairy work, they advised him to buy cows and sell milk, which he ultimately made up his mind to do. He told us boys what conclusion he had come to. "Well," I said, "father, you can do as you like, but I'm not going to milk cows, nor hawk milk about." "That's alright," he said, "I'll see to that, you can work the mare, cart wood, water or anything you can get to do. John can take out and bring in the cows." Be it known there was plenty of open country and grass and no commonage to pay.

Full of this new idea, father had not started the fence, but was buzzing round looking after cows. Ultimately he secured three first class ones, for he was a good judge of a cow. John and I had to knock off our work at the stable and rig a cowbail. All things being in order, father was up early in the morning to milk and then with wooden yoke on his shoulders a can of milk swinging at each end, he

WESLEY

This is the grand Wesleyan Chapel built in Geelong in the 1860s.

This house at Ballarat's Sovereign Hill is almost identical to the first Mundy home described by Henry.

sallied forth crying out: "Milk-oh, milk-oh." He succeeded fairly well the first morning, but did not sell quite out, but after a few days he had more applicants than he could serve - his milk was the genuine article and the people had come to know it. He bought more cows as his customers increased and sold milk from the house during the day, so I had to fix up a small dairy at the back of the house.

JOHN ROBBINS
Died in 1885 aged 76.

The stable being finished, I had to do the fencing, the neighbour adjoining helped me, as far as his side was concerned. His name was Robbins. Johnny Robbins became very familiar with our family. I met him and his wife now and again for many years. He died in Shepparton, his widow married a man named McIntyre.

The fencing being finished, we bought a large water tank, but which fixed in the dray made a water cart. All water at that time had to be brought from the Barwon River a mile and half. So I started water carting, but the demand was not sufficient to keep me going. I commenced carting fire wood at 5/a load, two loads of water at 1/6 made 8/- a day. But I did other kinds of carting, stone, bricks etc. I had one good contract carting bricks from Newtown to Moorabool Street at 3/- per 1,000. I carted 6,000 a day.

Our neighbours were quiet, decent people, ever ready to oblige. Our closest neighbours were an old couple; both ex-convicts, they took their beer very regular, but not to any excess. A little way from us was a brickmaker named Hyatt; the old man, his wife and all the family

'Irish Murphy's' in Aberdeen Street, the place which was Little Scotland but now is Newtown, is in the next block to the Mundy home. It is believed to have been 'Arthur's', but was originally named 'The Argyle' in the best Scottish tradition.

boys and girls were all brick makers, and terrible grafters. For material they had excavated a large cavern in their allotment.

Hyatt and his wife were early immigrants and had settled in Geelong from their first arrival. The mother and sons were sober enough folks, but the old man would have a burst now and again, well pretty often, and was liable to attacks of D.T's.

During these attacks, according to his talk, he had great tussles with the devil, he would talk about these unpleasant contests with his Satanic Majesty as long as you had patience to listen to him or mother would pounce on him abruptly and drag him home. Poor old Moses, he had taken the pledge, as often as he had toes and fingers, but if ever he went into Little Scotland, he found it impossible to pass Arthur's pub unless mother was with him. Three retired squatters lived in Newtown namely Armitage, James Austin and Captain Adder who bought land at the first Geelong auction sales; and procured large slices.

Things went on smoothly enough with us, until my brother met with an accident. One evening I brought home a barrel of water in the dray which I could not sell. Whenever this happened for safety's sake we lowered the shafts onto the ground. In the morning father and I went to lift at the shafts and my brother sat on the tail of the dray to help. When the load came to a balance father lifted more than he ought to have done. When the load got overbalanced and up backwards it went; the barrel of water slid out on top of John, the end caught him and broke one of his legs. The well-known (in afterdays) Dr Bayley was sent for, who set the broken limb saying at the time the ankle was split too and it would be sometime before he would be able to work again.

A fortnight after my brother's accident I took ill myself. Dr Bayley called it the low fever. I suspect it was what is called typhoid now, I suffered no pain but felt low and exhausted, lost all desire for food, had no care or wish for anything. Father took his misfortunes very much to heart. "Here I am," he said, "two big boys both laid up in bed and no one to help me to do anything."

After two weeks or so I broke out in to a profuse perspiration and from that began to mend, the fever brought me down to a very weak condition. When myself again, I started work again but had lost some of my custom. Father had bought an acre of land off Paddy Welch, a well known character at that time, for £25. The agreement was he could either pay cash or work it out. Paddy was a busy man and owned a quantity of land. So all the spare time I had was taken up paying for this land.

It must not be forgotten that I had not ceased persevering in Latin and Greek. Latin was my especial favourite, I carried the grammar in the breast of my shirt and at leisure times had a look at the lesson on hand; but Sundays were my principal days for study, much to father's annoyance. He wanted me badly to go to chapel. "Do you more good boy, than studying Latin, what's the good of that to you. It's only doctors and lawyers that require to learn Latin." He even went so far as to bring to me one of his favourite parsons, to try to convince me of the error of my ways. The parson said, "What's the good of Latin to you my boy, if you lose your own soul." I said: "Mr —- my soul is my own, the Creator gave me a mind to think and reason with, the same as every other human being and I tell this, although I am young I have passed five solitary years in the bush and have seriously and conscientiously thought about the faith father taught me, and believe some of it is unreasonable and false." "Um, oh I see," he said, "you are a free thinker, I advise you to read the latter hours of Tom Paine, David Hume and Voltaire." I said I had never heard of the trio.

Yarra Street in the 1850s.

After giving me what he considered his best advice, no doubt with the very best intentions, he left me to my fate. In after years I read a horrible account of the agonies of these dying men, depicting them suffering the torments of hell in their dying bed, till they went in despair to a dreadful fate. These writings were afterwards condemned as pious frauds, attempting no doubt with the best, enthusiastic intentions to bolster up the Puritan faith.

In the course of many weeks, my brother recovered from his injuries and was able to work again, taking out the cows and bringing them in at night, but father and John did not seem to hit it very well. Neither of us ever got any money and we never had what could be called a respectable suit of clothes since we landed in the colony. I got a few books now and again which father considered wasted money, but mother often secretly helped me to a few shillings for that purpose.

Father often attended the horse sales and did a bit of horse dealing, but I do not think he made much profit out of it, he was not rogue enough. He sold the draught mare and the youngest foal and bought a grey horse for the dray, a lively little horse, as staunch as a bullock, but was apt to bolt, father did not like him for that. So he said to me: "Let's break in the filly, she is three years old it's time she was broken in." "Very well," I said, "we'll tackle her tomorrow." "Alright then."

The filly had been amongst us ever since she was foaled and was as quiet as a sheep. While father was doing his milking in the morning and taking it round, I got in the filly and had her harnessed. Unshipping the water barrel, we took the dray into the road. We got her into the shafts alright. With a short rope fastened to the bit on each side, father on the off side and I on the near, bid her proceed; moving on a bit she heard the rattle of the dray behind, made a plunge for all she was worth

1880
Old Geelong in 1880 was little changed from the 1850s.

122

forward at full gallop. We hung on for another fifty yards gradually pulling her round till I brought up against the road fence, full butt. Father came up as soon as he had got his breath, saying: "Take her out, take her out, I'm not strong enough to hold her." I felt greatly disappointed for I had been hoping to have her to work in the dray. John of course was there, but his leg was still weak from the accident. In a few days father sold her at auction, she fetched a fair price, but I do not remember what it was. She was a splendid beast for a three year old. Two or three years after in the digging times, I heard she fetched at auction £90.

Our house had only two rooms and it was too small. John and I built two skillion rooms at the back, one of which was reserved for a dairy; but John and father could not hit it at all. The state of things did not suit John, he wanted to make a little money for himself, so he made up his mind to go back to the bush again, and get a job of shepherding or hut-keeping. Father had picked up an acquaintance with a man who pretended to be very religious who was going to the bush to look for work. As John was determined to go, father recommended my brother to the care of this friend; who turned out nothing but a rank hypocrite. They travelled three days together when this friend said: "I don't see any good of two of us going together; you better go your way and I'll go mine." So they parted.

Work was scarce, or John was hard to please. He tramped three weeks from station to station till the soles of his boots began to drop off, which he tied on with bullock hide; gradually making for Muston's Creek where he arrived at last, and met some people who knew him.

Since the time we left, the station had changed hands. Mr Sprott had sold it to Dr James Palmer, a man well known in Melbourne in those days. He was the third Mayor of Melbourne; he laid the foundation of Melbourne Hospital; he was elected speaker in the first Legislative Council under the Lieutenant Governorship of La Trobe.

John interviewed by Mr Findley, Palmer's overseer, told him he had worked on the station before for Mr Sprott, that he knew Mr Gibson the publican and some others, whom he named who were still on the station. After a few enquires Mr Findley came to the men's hut where he was staying and hired him for six months, as a shepherd. The wages I think at that time was about £25 a year, of course with rations. John was stationed at the hut on Burchetts Creek, where our sister was born.

Father continued buying and selling a horse or a cow now and again. The piece of land he had bought in Newtown he exchanged for two acres on what is now called Hearn Hill. The same land is now included in the Geelong New Cemetery; he bought a hack and saddle to fetch in the cows after John left.

The cows generally wandered as far as Bell Post Hill. If I happened to be at home that was my lot to fetch them. One afternoon I went for them and saw they were in McLeod's paddock. I had found them there once or twice before. I passed some men in a paddock harvesting. When I reached the entrance to the paddock where the cows were, I found the panels up; taking them down, I drove the cows out, and as I was driving them down the hill, past the harvest men working, they suddenly rushed through the fence, hooting and yelling, trying to intercept my cows. I saw their intention, cracking my whip and

Another view of Geelong as it was in 1880.

DR PALMER
So successful was Henry's one time employer Dr Palmer that he became a major land holder including a parcel of 50 acres which he purchased for £240 - it became the suburb of Hawthorn.

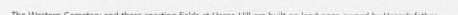
The Western Cemetery and these sporting fields at Herne Hill are built on land once owned by Henry's father.

123

The land on what was McLeod's Paddock, looking towards the road which leads to Batesford.

hunting them forward, and it being down hill, I got them travelling at full swing, they took no notice of the men, but rushed past them, as if they did not see them. The ground was thickly strewn with loose stones; not able to stop the cows and being a mob of half savage Irish, one and all commenced to fire at me with stones, trying to knock me off the horse; but in their savage fury they must have forgot to take aim; for not one of the stones hit me, though the missiles flew fast and furious. One stone thumped on the horse's ribs, which accelerated his speed considerably. When I had got without the range of fire, I looked back to see the mad devils shaking their fists at me. When I reached home I told my story to father and a neighbour, who had three among the rescued. The neighbour laughed, but father took it very seriously, he said: "You rescued the cows from their possession with intention to pound them. I must see Mr McLeod tomorrow morning," but he had no occasion, for McLeod came that evening. He said I had no right to drive away the cows when he had them in possession with the intention to pound them for trespassing on his land. He said: "I did tell the men to intercept and stop the cattle," but he had not the least idea they would be mad enough to throw stones at the boy, adding these wild Irish when they become exasperated seem to have no reason. Father agreed with what McLeod said, so with mutual apologies, as I had suffered no harm, they agreed to let the matter drop.

At the auction sale father bought a splendid-looking saddle horse; he said he got him dirt-cheap, and so I thought myself, if he was as good as he looked. He was put in the stable that night, well-fed and groomed, next morning was saddled and bridled and taken into the road; I was anxious to have the first ride, father not having the least objection. I pulled the reins together, put my foot in the stirrup and was astride him in a jiffy. No sooner was I seated, than up he sprang on his hind legs, nearly bolt upright. The shock was so sudden, I let go the reins and fell a buster on my back on the hard road, I lost some wind for awhile, but was not hurt, but I got into what is called now-a-days, a thundering rage and used some very unfilial talk to my parent. I said: "You have gone and bought a buckjumper; why the devil didn't you get a trial of him before you bid for him, you are old enough to have better sense." "A trial, a trial," he said; "Why, while the sale was going on, he came galloping in with a rider on his back. The horse was all of a muck sweat. The man said held ridden him fifty miles that morning to be in time for the sale. I thought that was trial enough, you are not good rider enough Henry, you must have pulled too strong on the reins or something." "Well," I said, "you often talk about your having been a jockey and the horses you have broken in, you get on him and see how you can manage him." He shook his head and replied: "No, no Henry, I'm not so young as I was." I had a faint notion how father had been got at. The horse being an intractable brute, some clever jockey had backed him and sat him till he got him to go, galloped him till he was dog-tired, then ran him in to the sale yard. As likely as not, the auctioneer was privy to the dodge.

On the next sale-day father took the new horse to the sale-yard and sold him. In the evening at supper, I asked him what he had got for him, he said, as much as I expected. I did not put the matter straight to him to ask him what he did get, as I knew he would not tell me a lie, he looked very glum

The original pub which Henry and thousands of others frequented at Batesford, is now a fine home mostly hidden from view.

over it, not wishing to hurt his feelings any farther, I said no more about it.

Two or three weeks later, we both went to Fyan's Ford for a load of straw off a farmer named Jakes, down a steep hill to a flat on the Moorabool River. We put on a small load as we had only one horse, the little grey. The ascent of the hill from the river being so steep, the road went slantwise, one side was much higher than the other. The wheel on the high side struck a stone and over went the load, horse and all sliding three or four yards down hill. Jakes below in the valley saw the mishap, and with two men came to our assistance. We got the horse free of the shafts unhurt, pushed the dray onto the road again and reloaded the straw.

Jakes was a Scotsman, and as we were ready to start again he remarked to father,: "The grey is a grand little beastie, nae doot, but he's owre sma' fur yer kin o'wark; now I have the noo in the stable you a beastie that wad suit ye till a. The's ane o'twa wha dune a ma ploughing this season, he's as staunch as a bullock, but the pair hae bin owre warked and air dog puir I sold the ither one becas he was old, but this yane I have the noo is a young beastie, I'm gaun to feed him up. I'll sell him to ye noo cheap becas I ken it'll tak a little to bring him back into good flesh again. Come ye noo and have a leuk at him, there be nae harm dune."

Father looked at me, said: "What do you think?" I said: "I'm going home with the load." Father went back with Jakes and when he came home he told me he had bought the black horse. I answered nothing. He said: "I gave only £10 for him."

Next day he took the money with him and fetched home the black horse. I was startled when I saw the animal; one could count every rib, high ragged hip bones, long legs and pinched belly. He looked as if he hadn't had a good feed for a month. "In the name of goodness, father," I said, "you don't mean to say you gave £10 for that bag of bones." "Chut, chut," he returned, "he's poor I must say, but plenty of good feed will put him right in a fortnight, you won't know him."

So the black horse was stabled and duly and plentifully fed, morning, noon and night. He ate, ate, and ate, in fact he was a real glutton. As father said, he's a good feeder, a good feeder is always a good doer. He had as much oats, bran and hay as he could stuff in; but at the end of a fortnight he had not improved one bit. Father said he must have worms, I'll have to give him a few balls. So balls were administered without any good effect. After another two weeks feeding's without any good, he said, perhaps he wants exercise, you'd better take him out for a load of wood or two and give Captain a spell. "No," I said, "you don't catch me driving that skeleton about." Nevertheless I took him for a few loads of water without any good result. Some said he was strained in the kidneys, others, he must have worms, or a bad digestion.

However, I got full up of Geelong and longed again for the bush. I had been working and earning money for the six previous years and all I had gained was a few books. I told father I was tired of town and intended to go again to the bush to make some money for myself, as I was nineteen years old and asked him what he was going to give me for what I had done.

He was struck with surprise at the idea that I expected anything. He said what I had earned was his till I was twenty. His views and mine did not coincide. I got vexed and told him it was very unjust to John and me to help him make the money he did and give us nothing. He said when I sell that two acres of land I'll give you something or I tell you what I'll do for you. I'll give you the cob with saddle and bridle and you'll have this also and think yourself well off. "No," I said, "you can keep the old cob, I'm going to work on the station to make some money for myself, and buy a horse if I want one of my own," adding, "I would not care so much if you had made better use of the money you had; it strikes me you are just fooling it away in buying, selling and chopping in horses; stick to the cows and milk, what you understand, and leave horses alone."

My words I thought were strictly justifiable, but whether he thought I was too severe, or whether he thought my words were true, I do not know, but he suddenly burst into tears. That was more than I could stand, I ran out and left him, I regret being the cause of those tears to this hour.

However, I was determined to go to the bush again, to make my way to Muston's Creek to my brother. In a day or two I had my swag made up containing a couple of blankets, a rug, a pair of pants, and a shirt. Books were the heaviest item comprehending a Latin dictionary, and grammar, a Virgil Caesar's De Bells Gallico, Quintus Curtain's De Gestus Alexandri Magni and Sallust's de Bello Africano, Goldsmith's History of Rome and a French Primer, also a Greek grammar.

Victoria Valley

Victoria Valley provides a surprise for the unaware. From a distance it appears to be simply two large hills a good distance apart. However, once the track is taken north between the hills it gradually narrows over a long distance, and eventually funnels into the hills of the rugged Grampians. It has been home to many families who have owned land there for many generations, and some of the groups which Henry and John approached for jobs still have their later generations working their farms.

Henry and John Leave Home

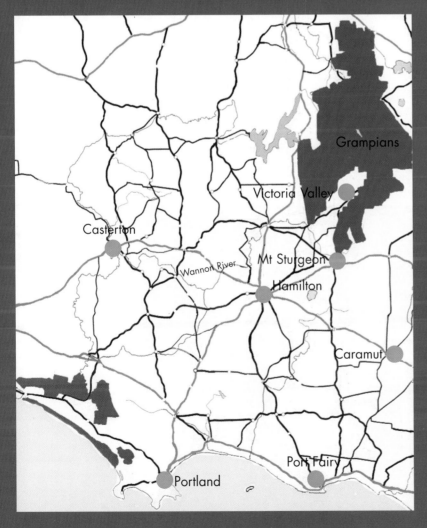

This map gives an indication of the amount of walking Henry and John undertook to find satisfactory jobs. They had already walked over 100 miles to reach Caramut from Geelong, and later went on to Hamilton, the Wannon River to the west, then to the Victoria Valley before eventually finding jobs deep inside it.

John soon went on to Horsham which is north of the Grampians.

RETURNING TO MUSTONS CREEK
THEN ON TO VICTORIA VALLEY

So one fine morning I bid mother and father and little sister goodbye, little Jane cried bitterly; we were very fond of one another. Mother slipped a few shillings into my hand. I shouldered my swag and was off on the wallaby track.

I little dreamed that morning of the events that occurred during my absence of fifteen months before my return, events that materially affected my future life.

I took the road over Fyan's Ford following the Barwon along by the way of Wardy Yallock, crossed the Leigh, reached Austin's Station that night where I stayed. Then a long weary journey over the plains, taking it leisurely always reaching a station before sundown, where I was always made welcome.

At length reaching Russell's Station on the Hopkins, where I met Tom Horton, whom I have mentioned before, as a shearer one year in Sprott's shed, in company of Peter and Paul, the apostles. "Hullo, young Mundy," he said, "where are you off to?" I told him I was going to Muston's Creek, my brother was there. I stayed there that night. Being an easy stage to Sprott's, I went to John's hut that night, much to his surprise. We had a long conflab that night, John said: "I believe Findley wants a hutkeeper for this hut, our present hut-keeper, O'Donahue, is a Catholic, the other shepherd is an Orangeman and they are always quarreling. We will take a walk into the home station tomorrow night and see the overseer," which was agreed on.

Going to the homestead next evening, we saw Mr Findley. John introduced me to him as his

The bridge over the Hopkins River leading overland to Muston's Creek.

brother. I asked him if he had a vacancy for a shepherd or hut-keeper, I told our family had been with Mr Sprott for three years, and had left three year ago, that I knew every inch of the run. Looking at us both he said: "You would like to be together?" "Yes," we answered. Mr Findley replied: "If you like to take the hutkeeper's place, I will employ you for twelve months at the wages going, £25 a year." "Alright sir," I gladly said. So I signed the agreement then and there. He said to John, "How are O'Donohue and Baxter hitting it no?" "Worse than ever," John said: "Ah well, tell O'Donohue to come in tomorrow. I'll find him something to do at the homestead." Then we left and went to see the Gibsons.

They were surprised to see us and made us welcome. After staying there an hour John said: "We'd better make tracks." "All right John, but I'm going to get a bottle of porter to drink on the way home." So getting the bottle with the cork drawn and paying half a crown for it, we started taking a pull at the bottle alternatively on our way. Thus we celebrated our meeting, and I can truthfully say that that was the first money I spent in alcoholic drink since I had been in Australia, and further, since I was born.

Arriving at the hut, John told O'Donohue that Findley wanted him at the home station and that I was to take his place, both he and Baxter seemed pleased with the arrangement, and so I was settled down as hutkeeper. I knew my duties alright, to fry or boil a bit of meat, make tea and occasionally bake a damper, in which art Ned Kearney had made me perfect. I had to shift two sheepyards every day, which took me about two hours, and sleep in the watch box by night.

In the course of a few days, the overseer came to pay me a visit to see how things were progressing. I was inside at my books then he pulled up his horse at the door, coming in, he noted the books on the table took them up and examined them,

"What" he said,"are you a Latin scholar?" "Trying to be sir," I said, "but I am only self taught." Taking Virgil he looked at it a while then said: "I could read Virgil pretty well at school but it does not seem so easy now for want of practice." He then took Caesar's De Bello Gallico and commenced "Omnis Gallia in trees partis dividitur." "Ah," he said, "this is easier," and kept on reading while I slung the billy, or rather the kettle, trotted out the damper and salt junk, a tin plate knife and fork and a clean pannikin, invited him to a feed. "Well I never," he said, "and you have had no teacher." I assured him I had never been to a school of any kind since I was eight years old, except on board ship, by a voluntary teacher.

After partaking of his rough and ready meal Mr Findley rose to go farther on his round, saying: "I am pleased to meet a young man like you aspiring after knowledge, but I cannot see what benefit dead languages will be to you. I had a smattering of it at school, but any further than a help to understand my mother tongue, I do not know what benefit it has been to me, in fact I have forgotten one half of it. To study a line of science might bring you to eminence, but then you require instruments and many facilities to be able to study any science, whatever which to you are not procurable. The best advice I can give you is to study history or perhaps geology." Bidding me goodday, he galloped off. Notwithstanding what Mr Findley had said I still continued studying Latin, just for the love of it, I thought it such a beautiful language.

Three months of my time had passed when we were told that Mr Palmer had sold the station to a man

The spectacular peak of Mt Sturgeon.

VIOLET CREEK
On September 9, 1839 the government granted approval for the site of a village at Violet Creek.

CAMERONS

These are members of the Violet Creek Cameron family gathered in the 1880s for a special occasion. They are members of the family of John and Jessie Janet Cameron who married at Violet Creek in 1856. John Cameron lived from 1816 to 1890.

named De Little. Mr Findley told John and me the station had changed hands, that we could stop our time out with the new comer or, if we preferred it, we were at liberty to leave.

John and I, as we were both free at one time said we would leave. So went to the home station and lifted our cheques off Dr Palmer and started on the wallaby track together for fresh fields and pastures new.

Starting, we made tracks for Mt. Sturgeon, when we reached it, just for curiosity's sake and to get a good view round, but we saw little but tops of trees. The mount itself was rocky and bare except for plenty of grass, trees and a few stunted trees. There was a pub at the foot, where we stopped all night and until dinner next day, then we set off towards the Grange (today called Hamilton). We made three stages of it before we reached the Grange. The most remarkable event to remember of that part of the tramp was the disgusting water we were compelled to drink; tea made from it left a coat of red paint on the inside of the pannikin, and had the most disagreeable taste. In places there were small swamps which were then dry and crusted thinly over with salt. When we reached the Grange we called on a squatter, on Violet Creek, named Angus Cameron.

Going to the working men's hut, we found a young man busily engaged preparing supper. We enquired if this was Mr Cameron's station: "Yes" he answered, "it is; are you looking for work?" In answering in the affirmative, he said: "There's the old buffer, you can see in the paddock yonder making hay by himself." After a few more words we went straight to the squatter, he was busy cocking oaten hay. We noted also a double barrelled gun leaning on one of the stooks of hay.

Bidding him good evening, I enquired if he was Mr Cameron; he said he was; casting a look round, I said: "Your hay is nearly fit to stack Mr Cameron." "Yes," he said, "another day it'll be ready, do you know anything about haymaking?" "Oh yes," I said, "my brother and I came from a part of England where there is nothing else but farming." Then he remarked: "You did not come from London?" "No sir," I said, "we were born in Bucks forty-four miles from London, we only saw it once six years ago, when we were, father, mother and we two brothers, hired aboard ship by Mr Sprott with whom we lived for three years, his station on Muston's Creek."

Telling him our movements after that, he said: "I knew Mr Sprott. Are you looking for work? But I suppose you are." "Yes," I said, "either shepherding or hutkeeping, but we would have to have a job together." "Well, I'll see" he said, "you can stay at the men's hut tonight, come to me in the morning. I will see then what I can do, but do not take any notice of those fellows at the hut, they are a rough

Mt Sturgeon from the old pub at what is today known as Dunkeld.

rowdy lot." Thanking him we lifted our swag's and returned to the hut. The first question the hutkeeper put to us was: "What did old Cameron say?" We told him the purport of our conversation. "Don't you have anything to do with him, he is the most deceitful, cantankerous old wretch ever a man worked for, there's no possibility of doing anything to please him. There are three of us shipmates, we told him we would like to be together so he hired us all three, the other two are shepherding, we wish we'd never seen him."

In the evening, the two shepherds came in full of fun and frolic, especially over our prospect of a job with the old villain. They all three gave poor Cameron a frightful name. By their conversation and Cockney slang, I knew what they were, Pentonville exiles, a shipload of which was imported, as I have mentioned before, in 1845.

We all had breakfast together before sunrise, the three of them advised us strongly not to go near the old bugger; if we had anything to do with him we'd regret it. John and I picked up our swags, thanking them and bidding good morning, left. I said to John: "I do not believe Cameron is the devil they paint him, but I do not like these young fellows, they are no good, they are not our sort, let us go straight off and look for work farther on." So instead of going to see Cameron we started the contrary direction and was soon out of sight.

In about two hours walking, we came in sight of a hut, for which we made. When nearing the hut three very large savage dogs came barking and yelling at us. I said to John: "Let us keep on towards the hut and pretend to take no notice of them." They met us as if they were going to eat us, but did not touch us. Expecting someone to appear out of the hut, but no one was forthcoming and knocking, no one opened the door, so we sat on our swags in expecting somebody to be about; the dogs went away for a short distance, then all of a sudden made a rush upon us like so many tigers yelling and showing their horrid white fangs. They repeated this manoeuvre three or four times. It seemed to be getting dangerous.

I said to John: "There seems to be no one about, we had better make tracks before we are ate up." We picked up our swags, just about to start. I was putting my arm through the loop that went over my shoulder, when the most ferocious one of the three grabbed me on the arm, the other two furies were making for John. The axe happened to be lying handy, which he grabbed and kept off his assailants, then came to my assistance and made the brute let go his hold on my arm. With the axe he kept the brutes at bay, till I burst open the hut door, when we both rushed in and slammed it tight, thanking our stars that we were safe. As far as I could guess, we sat there two hours and no one came. At last a woman opened the door, followed by two children - a boy and a girl; by seeing the swag's outside, she expected to find someone inside, she looked a bit scared on entering, but only for a moment.

We explained the reason we had taken the liberty of bursting open the door and showing her where the dog had bitten me and torn my shirt, she was all sympathy and proved herself the good Samaritan. She bound up my arm and mended my shirt sleeve, saying she was very sorry for what had happened, adding she did not know why Mr Cameron kept such brutes for. "This is Angus Cameron's out station"?

131

"Yes," she replied. I then told her we had stopped there last night and all about it. "Ah," she said, "those Pentonvilles are a bad lot, you did right in leaving, though Mr Cameron himself, is not a bad man at all." "That is a nasty bite you got on your arm, no doubt you will carry the marks to your grave (she was right for I have the mark of one tooth now). These are what are called wolf dogs, bred from a pair imported by Mr Winters from Germany some years ago."

I said to John: "Hadn't we better be going, it will be well to get out of this lion's den." "No" the woman said: "you shall have a pannikin of tea and something to eat first. I'll see the dogs do not molest you, they're awfully afraid of me." We could not refuse her pressing invitation although we were not hungry, not long having had breakfast. After the snack was over we were ready to start, she said: "I'll hold the one that bit you and the children will hold the other two." They went out and got hold of the dogs; the woman said, "You can come now." We went to pick up our swag's when the dogs set up a ferocious yell, feeling twice as vicious by being held back, we had not got many yards when all three were loose. The stockyard was close handy, we made a straight line for it and was on the top rail in a jiffy. "Oh, the wretches," the woman sang out, "but I'll fix 'em"; so she called them all three into the hut and shut the door. "Now" she said, "you can safely go," and we went thanking her for her kindness.

Fairly on the track again we had previously intended to visit Winter's station on the Wannon; but fearing to encounter more of his wolf dogs, we sheered off to the right towards the Smoky River.

We travelled several days and called at many stations without success. We went along the Glenelg River, making for Rose's Gap, at length we reached Pig Carter's station, the entrance to the Victoria Valley. A wide valley between the Victoria and Grampian Mountains. It was about noon when we arrived there. We found the hutkeeper, the squatter's son, busily employed making scones, on which he invited us to dine (being hungry) with aid of beef dripping and salt- the scones went high.

Mr Carter said their's was only a small station, they only had two flocks and did not require any fresh hands at the present, but there were two big stations in the valley and very few men seeking employment ever went

The only water hole in the Victoria Valley - where Henry and John were disturbed by cattle in the night.

through, most likely one or both of us would get a job. He asked us to stay the night, he said: "You will not get to Robinson's homestead tonight, but Robinson has an out station five miles out this way, you may reach that. We decided, however, to travel on.

We went on till sun down, when a water hole came in sight, the only water we had seen since leaving Carters, being a hot day it was a welcome sight, for we were very thirsty, so lying down

The Victoria Valley is surprisingly long and wide.

we had a good drink. John had a blister on his heel, found it painful to walk. I was tired too, so we agreed to camp for the night.

As the night was warm we stretched out on the ground in our blankets, were soon fast asleep. Some time in the night I heard a sniffing, blowing noise and the sound of many footsteps, looking up, I saw lights like a thousand stars, and starting up, there was a sudden stampede and a thundering roar. A mob of cattle had come to drink; this adventure gave me a bit of a shock, but I think the cattle and I could cry quits, as they didn't come back.

We were not in the habit of carrying anything to eat with us. We had to start without breakfast; but it did not matter as Robinson's outstation could not be far off, we could tell by the sheep tracks. After a while we espied a man on horseback and a flock of sheep. Getting closer, "Good Lord," John gasped, "what a picture." A man on a horse, no one on earth could tell which was the leanest, whether he was a black or white man, it was hard to say, for dirt; his hat was brimless, his upper portions were covered with a ragged woollen shirt, tied round the waist with a strip of bullock hide for a belt, and his pants they were like Joseph's coat of many colours. His saddle, what was left of it had seen better days, the stirrups and stirrup leathers had been replaced with hide, and the stuffing round the seat had parted company with the saddle long ago. His bridle was of hide also.

Today even the sealed road in the Victoria Valley fades to a dirt track.

This apparition rode jauntily to meet us. "Good morning mates," was his cheery salute, "you couldn't have come from Carter's this morning." Returning his salutation, "No," we said, "we camped at the water hole away back." Then he said, "Yelve had no breakfast, come to our hut, it is close handy and my old woman will make you welcome." So saying, turned round and stalked on before us. "Follow me," he said; John and I both recently had read Don Quixote, I remarked to John this is Don Quixote on his steed Rozinante, Sancho his squire is only wanting, to complete the picture. After half a mile's walk we reached the hut where two small children came out; to say "Like the Dutchman they had nodings on" would not be literally true, but nearly, made up of rags and patches. "Hi, Betty," he sung out, "here's two men who've slept at the water hole twixt here and Carter's and have had no breakfast, look alive gal and sling the kettle."

At his call, a spectacle appeared in the doorway that eclipsed all the surprises that we had had for the last twelve hours. A short squat woman, her long hair, at least the most of it, was tied behind the back of her head; the ends hanging down her back, from her waist upwards, she had not a scrap of clothing, with the exception of a coat of dirt, she looked as if she never had had a wash since she was born. Her naked breasts hung down to the waist band of her skirt which was as dirty as her skin, her feet were bootless.

"Lawks a massy," she cried, "we are so glad to see you, it is such a treat to see anyone travelling in this

133

outlandish hole, come in, I'll soon get you something to eat," the man too, was just as pressing and fussy. We thanked them but said we were not at all hungry, we would rather wait till we got to the home station, but it was no use they would take no denial. It was with a feeling of disgust we sat down to the table. Poor souls, they were so anxious to feed us. I whispered to John, "Let us take a bite and a drink of tea, it won't poison us."

Another hut of the type common then.

After all, the meal did not look so bad, we ate some of the damper and drank a pannikin of tea each. They pressed us not to be afraid, till we rose from the table ready for a start. I said to the man: "What makes your horse so poor, with all this good grass about?" He said: "He's got the lampas very bad, besides he's as old as the Grampians," pointing over to the mountains. "I'm a bit shaky on my legs," he continued. "I bought him to ride after the sheep, I got him dirt cheap." After giving us minute directions to find Robinson's home station - thanking them for their kindness we made tracks.

Trudging along the road, we discussed our late adventure, wondering what the Robinson's would be like. It was a dismal outlook, high mountains on each side, forming a valley from fifteen to twenty miles wide. Early in the day we reached Robinson's home station. A young man met us and made us welcome, made some tea for us and set before us the usual fare, damper and salt beef, then enquired where we had come from. Then we told him the story of our travels and our calling at his outstation but that morning, and what a queer dirty couple they were. He laughed. "Yes," he said, "they are perfectly horrid. Nearly two years ago when we hired them, they were pretty decent looking people, but since they have been living in that quiet out-of-the-way place, they have deteriorated into almost wild beasts. Their time will be up in two months, we will have to get rid of them then, for they are a disgrace to any place, although I must say Jack is as good shepherd as we ever had."

"This is only a small station, we can only run two flocks, we have about twelve miles along the Valley there is plenty of room towards the mountains but is too barren for anything, our principal station is at Horsham where father lives. My brother Jack and I manage this one, my name is Tom. If you are looking for work which I suppose you are, we want a shepherd but we can only employ one of you. Our other shepherd left last week and Jack and I have to take his place, we take it day and day about, you had better both stay here tonight. We can employ one of you and I'm almost sure Mr Dwyer the next squatter fifteen miles farther on wants a shepherd."

An original sheep hut in the Western District.

In the evening Jack came home with his flock. They were two decent young men Tom and Jack, there were no women on the station but everything was clean and decent. The brothers agreed to hire one of us, so John and I had a consultation. As he was nearly knocked out I advised him to take the job for ten months so as we both could meet at home next Christmas, and if I got a job I would arrange for the same; to which he agreed. The cheques we held we agreed to send to the old people, mine was about £8 but John's was considerably more. We had no use for money, if we wanted any clothes we could mostly get them out of the slop chest off the squatter we were working for.

So John hired for ten months to Robinson brothers. In undoing our swags previous to turning in, I put my books on the table. Tom, who seemed to be fond of books asked leave to look at them. "Of course," I said, "and welcome." Picking up one he laid it down, then another. He enquired: "Are you brothers English?" "Yes," I answered, "thorough-bred." "What language is this then?" "It is classic Latin, written about 2000 years ago, the language of the old Romans, the conquerors of the

Cattle and sheep are still the major income earners in the Victoria Valley.

world, as far as it was known at that time." "Yes," he said, "I have read of the Romans and Greeks of the olden time, it must be nice to be able to read the books just as they were written at the time. I suppose you have been in a high class school." "No," I told him, "it was only a fad of mine, I was only self-taught." Picking up Goldsmith's History of Rome, he exclaimed: This is English, how much I would like to read it; but of course can't spare it, if you could, I would take the greatest care of it, and would not fail to give it to your brother when he left us." It was sore against my will, but I did not like to refuse him, so I lent it to him and like most lent books, as lenders of books only know, it was never returned to its owner.

Next morning, solitary and alone after bidding all goodbye, I started for Dwyer's station fifteen miles distant. I felt a little melancholy at first, but my spirits soon rose. I was young then and never said die.

Little did I know or dream of the fate which befell me eventually at Dwyer's station, where I met the little maid who was destined to be my wife and mother of all my children. My darling, loving Ann, but we must not stop to moralise, life must tell its own tale.

It was a lonely road I traversed that day, little wider than an opossum track. I saw neither man nor beast except half dozen kangaroos, that stopped a moment to look at me, then continued their journey at a quicker pace. It was near sundown when I reached Dwyer's.

Going to the men's hut, the first man met was Jack Taylor, whom the reader will remember I have mentioned before as a shearer in Sprott's shed, who bit off a sheep's upper lip because it was restless. Jack had just knocked off work, he stared hard at me and said: "Ain't your name Mundy? "Yes," I answered, "and your name is Taylor." "Yes, that's right. Looking for work?" "Yes," I said, "I wonder if there is any chance of a job here?" "Well," he said, "I heard 'um talking the other day about wanting a shepherd." After a little more talk Mr Dwyer himself came up and Jack turned to me when he asked: "Where's your father and mother?" I told him: "In Geelong keeping cows and selling milk." Mr Dwyer came up to me bidding me good evening, and asking me where I came from. I told him I had come from Robinson's that morning, that my brother and I had been travelling together looking for work, that Mr Robinson had hired my brother and I was looking for a job for myself.

He said: "It seems you are acquainted with Taylor?" "Yes," I said, "I knew him three years ago at Muston's Creek as a shearer where I was shepherd." After a little more talk he said: "I want a shepherd, go to the men's hut tonight and we will talk matters over in the morning." Going into the hut I found a small woman and two children. I told her Mr Dwyer had sent me in and probably would hire me in the morning as shepherd. "Alright lad," she said, "sit thee down. My husband is not home yet, he is out with the bullocks he'll likely be in, in half an hour, you don't mind waiting that long for your supper do you? I'm sure you had no dinner." "Yes, ma'm," I said, "I can wait longer if need be." As she was inclined to be talkative I told her about the extraordinary man and woman we had come across at Robinson's. She laughed heartily at that. "I've heard of them," she said. "They call the man dirty Jack and the woman dirty Bet, and by all accounts they do not belie their names."

Soon after a tall, well-made man entered the hut. "Good day mate," he said, "looking for a job?" "Yes," I said: "I think I'll get on with Dwyer in the morning. Decent man he seems?" "Oh, yes - very. There's a big family of them altogether. There's Mr and Mrs Dwyer, and two young children. There's old Mr Nash, the wife's father and his two other daughters Maria and Luch. Then there's old Nash's son, William. Nash who is the overseer, and a cousin named Mason and my little woman has to wash for the lot of them, besides looking after her own domestic affairs and cooking for a shepherd. It's too much for her. I'm going to leave when our time is up and that will not be long. Though they are very nice people

TOM DWYER
Was married to Kate (Catherine) and had children all born in the Victoria Valley - John Henry (1846), Edmund (1850), Fanny (1850), Phillip Doyen (1851) and Elizabeth (1853).

I must say." "Who cooks for the house?" I enquired. "Oh," he replied, "they have a man cook in the hut next door, who cooks for the house and two or three rouse-abouts." "Jack Taylor has his meals with you then?" "No he don't. Do you know Jack Taylor?" "Yes," I said, "I've met him before." "Did you know any good of him?" "Well," I said, "I can't say I did." "No," he said, "I'll bet you didn't. He has a job of piece work here, fencing, he comes in here to boil his billy and cook what he wants to, then takes his food into his little shanty to have his meals; of course he is welcome to that, my woman likes to be obliging when she can. One evening he came in and the fire was low, he went on shamefully, abused her with the most beastly foul-mouthed language one ever heard. His wife was crying when I came in and told me what had happened. My word didn't I pounce on him; I said: 'You foul-mouthed, loathsome imp of hell, what have you been saying to my wife?' He was still at the fire. 'I've half a mind to double you up and chuck you behind the fire for a back log as sure as my name is Dick Bell. You mean, beastly hound.' I never saw a cowardly cur look more frightened."

RICHARD BELL
Born in Cumbria.
Died in 1868 aged 33.

Bell was a big strong man, and very hot-tempered when put out, as was testified many months after, as I was told kicked his wife on the result of which she died. Bell was tried for manslaughter but acquitted.

At length Mrs Bell sang out: "Come on you men and get your supper; never mind Jack Taylor, he is not worth talking about." After supper and considerable more talk, they made me a bed on the floor by laying down some sheep skins, the best bed I had had for many a night.

In the morning, Mr Dwyer hired me for ten months. It was in the early part of January, 1851. I was to sleep in my old domicile - the watch box, and Mrs Bell would cook for me. But he added you had better have a day's rest and fix things up shipshape.

On the morrow I commenced my new duties as shepherd. I had a fine flock of steady old ewes, things went on steadily enough. On the first opportunity I sent word to John where I was. The summer was exceptionally hot. I do not remember a hotter time. At last came that never to be forgotten day. Black Thursday on the 6th February. On that day I had got about a mile from home, coming to a waterhole I stripped off and had a good long roll in the wet, head and all. The heat was suffocating.

An hour after that, I happened to cast my eye on the Grampians about 8 miles away, one part was brown and the other black, I could not discern either smoke or fire, but I knew it was the mountain on fire. A little after midday the wind got stronger and I saw odd burnt leaves floating in the air. "A burnt child," it is said, "always dreads the fire," so I sent my dog to head the flock back; by the time he had them at my foot, the floating leaves were much thicker. We, the dog and I, hurried the sheep on at the greatest speed we could. The heat was intense and the charred leaves became thicker, and thicker; the grass too was high. If I could only reach a quarter of a mile nearer home, I would be pretty safe as there was much less grass; and once at home station, it was perfectly safe. I had not gone much farther when I was met by William Nash on horseback, riding as if the devil was behind him, coming up. "Well done Mundy, you have done well by coming home, all the hands on the station are coming looking for you. I'm going to look for poor old George; he may be in danger, but there's not the grass there, as there is here. By the Lord," he said: "it is hot," turning round to continue his journey. I said: "You'll meet fire on the road, pick out the place where there is the least blaze and rush through with all speed you can and then if you know of water handy, make for it and get a drink."

S.T. Gill's view of an 1850s shepherd.

A few minutes later, I saw half a dozen men, headed by Mr Dwyer, coming to meet me. "My word Henry," Mr Dwyer said (he always called me 'Henry' and I always addressed him and old Mr Nash as 'Sir') "you did well hastening the sheep home, there is a terrible fire not far off." "Yes, sir," I said, "I'm sure of it; look at the Grampians how black they are behind." In a very short time, we had the sheep in safety and I and my poor old dog and all hands, made for the water barrel and got a good blow out.

It was not long after, when I heard the well known crackling and roar of the fiery demon approaching. Mrs Dwyer and all the women folk were rushing about in great excitement, fearing, as they said, of being burnt to death. I said to Mrs Dwyer: "Don't be afraid ma'am, the fire can't come here." "Why?" she enquired. "Because there is nothing for it to burn." "God help us," she said.

As it neared the station, the roar of the flames died gradually down and passed down into longer grass. On the other side of the station was a swamp of thirty or forty acres, as level as level could make it, covered with water six or seven inches deep; where we obtained our drinking water by cutting drains into a deep hole sunk for the purpose. The swamp was covered all over with almost impenetrable reeds six or seven feet high; as green as they could possibly be. No one ever dreamt it would burn but the heat of the atmosphere and the approaching fire and the wind behind it, dried the reeds to such an extent that the conflagration scoffed the whole swamp down to the water's edge, and dried up a considerable amount of the water.

The fire passed on towards Robinson's. I was thinking of John, but as Mr Dwyer remarked, there was not so much grass on Robinson's run, being more taken up with ferns and grass tree; besides, I did not think that John would be caught napping; he knew his way about under such circumstances; at least to take care of himself.

Mr Dwyer and the ladies stood back and let the men have their fill first, the smoke was suffocating, everyone was continuously sipping and swallowing water to moisten his parched lips and to keep the throat from drying up.

A little after sundown, William Nash made his appearance, coming slowly up to the station with a wild distressed look on him, he came up to us, slid off his horse and staggered like a drunken man. Of course, we were all at him for news. He put his fingers to his open mouth, as much as to say: "Give me a drink for God's sake, before I choke." One of his sisters, Maria handed him a quart dipper of water; while he was drinking, we noticed his previously long brown beard had disappeared within an inch of his skin. After a ravenous hearty drink he said: "Give the horse a drink," then finished the dipper-full. "Well," he said," I thought I'd never reach home, the smoke is thick enough to cut it with a knife, and poor old Jack was nearly done." His married sister, Mrs Dwyer brought him out a chair; considerably refreshed, Bill sat down and briefly told his tale.

"John," he said to his brother in-law, "to begin with, the whole flock is unharmed. Old George and his wife are safe but the hut is burnt to ashes." "Good Lord," the women exclaimed, "how did poor old Mary escape?" "Hold on, hold on, don't bother, I'll tell you all in good time, but give me another drink," the drink was brought. Old Mr Nash said to Mrs Dwyer: "Put a gill of brandy in it Kate, but drink as little of that water as possible William."

With renewed energy, Bill continued: "After leaving Mundy, seeing that he was nearly out of danger, I rode on for about two miles, when I saw flames amid the thick smoke (looking at me), I did not see any weak place anywhere; so I made a bull rush at it straight, but oh Lord it was hot, the hottest part I think was just before you came to it. The blaze was yards above my head; such a width it was too, it must have been forty yards, I had pulled my hat well-down over my face to save my eyes, but from the smell of burnt hair, which told me my beard had suffered and Jack's coat. After we had passed through the fire, the burning timber and smoke for a while made the place like hell. I did not know where to look for a water hole, but, as luck would have it, I very nearly ran into one. Jack and I enjoyed the luxury of that God-send, I can tell you. I discovered my moleskin pants were on fire in several places so I went into the water and sat down. I was

Victoria Valley herd.

lucky I wore a woollen shirt. I mounted Jack again and rode him into the hole up to the saddle flaps; feeling much refreshed, I started to look for old George. I had an idea where I was likely to find him, but seeing nothing of either man or sheep, I made for the hut which I found - only a flaming mass of sticks and slabs.

"My first thought was to look for a sign of old Mary among the ruins. After careful scrutiny, I came to the conclusion that neither she nor her bed were caught in the fire. I began to look round for any place where the old girl might have gone for safety. Do you recollect John, a great ledge of rocks about a hundred yards from the hut up the banks of the creek?" "Yes, yes, sure I do, its as bare of grass as the palm of your hand and about half an acre big."

"That's where I found poor old Mary with a few of her poor belongings near her, her head in her hands, resting on her knees, crying and praying for her husband George. She did not notice me till I was close to her before she saw me." "Merciful heaven, Master William, where did ye come from? oh, have you seen my man, my poor George, oh if he is dead, I shall die too; for forty years we have worshipped our God together and now to be parted like this. I'm sure we always did our best to please him. Surely this has been a day of wrath, oh, my poor George." "Hush, hush," I said, "we must not blame God for things, for all we know, are not true. Look at me, I've been through the thickest of it." "And a narry escape you've had by the looks of yer. In heaven's name Master William," she said: "will ye take the dipper to the water hole and fill it, I'm ready to shake."

"Taking Jack by the rein with the billy in the other hand, I went for the water. To my surprise when I arrived at the water hole, there was George's dog up to his ears in the water taking a cooler, looking round expecting to see old George, but he was nowhere in sight. After giving Jack a drink and treating myself I hastened back and told Mary who broke out afresh: "Ah," she shrieked, "he's burnt to death." "Nonsense," I said, "George is coming home to look after you. The dog would not wait for him, George will be here in a few minutes." "Praised be the Lord, William, there is some hope then?" "Can you tell me the direction he started this morning?" I asked. "No, no, not for the life of me, but didn't you see which way the dog came?" "No," I said, "I only saw him in the waterhole," but she queried: "Which way was his tail pointing, no doubt he ran straight in." "That may be," I said, "but dogs generally move about a bit when they rush into the water to cool themselves."

However, I jumped on Jack and made for the direction the dog's tail indicated, thinking it very likely, too, he might have gone in that direction. And sure I was right. I had not gone a quarter of a mile when, through the smoke I spied George, I shouted out and rode towards him. The poor old chap looked fagged enough. He spoke hardly above a whisper. "Oh Master Willum, is that 'e?" "Where's the sheep George?" "The sheep is alright," he said, "up among the rocks. And my poor old gal have you been to the hut?" "Mary is alright George, only breaking her heart about you." "Thanks be to the Lord," he fervently whispered. "I was terrible affeared about she, oh but Master Willum I am terribly dry." "The hut, George," I said, "is burnt down." He looked at me wistfully, but said nothing. I pointed to his wife sitting on the rocks; and then pretended to examine the smoking remains of the hut, not wishing to witness the scene of their meeting.

After a time I went to them, George had had two or three drinks and moistened his soul and was able to talk; told how he saw the fire coming. "The wind was not very strong or we'd a'been catched alright, for the rocks was half a mile off. Bob and I worked hard to get there with 'em. When we had got 'em fairly on, Master William, I knowed they was safe for there is not a blade excepten wher' there a handful of dirt here and there. I was thinking of my poor old gal all the while. As soon as I knew the sheep was safe I moved for home, quite two miles and half. I thought I'd never get here. And Mary has saved our bed, blankets and the best of our clothes, such as they are, and the best of all besides her own self, my old Bible. God bless her dear old plucky heart."

When George had had a short spell, I proposed to go in search of the flock; so with a bottle of water each we started. We soon met them, but, no longer on the rocks, they were making homewards slowly, no doubt for water, there was not one of them injured as far as I could see. I said to George: "I'll away home to assure Mr Dwyer that you and Mary are alive and safe and not one of the flock is injured; and be sure we will be here as early as possible in the morning with rations and men to build you another hut, and whatever you have lost by the fire, Mr Dwyer will make good." "Aye that I will," said Mr Dwyer. Mrs Dwyer asked: "Haven't the poor souls anything to eat?" "I don't think they have."

There was little use going to bed that night, the heat was so intense. The station was on elevated ground. I sat on a log and watched the blazing forest along the Valley, the slope of the mountains seemed to be all afire, there was no darkness neither in heaven or earth that night; as I sat on the log, I saw a snake now and again pass by. Towards morning I felt sleepy but was afraid to lie down to sleep on account of the snakes. I had often heard of snakes crawling up one's pants for warmth. I argued with myself, it is not warm to night, but a cool place, so I lay down and slept safe enough.

In the morning, as soon as the bullocks could be yoked, two tarpaulins, rations, all the available slabs, and timber that could be found useful for building a hut, were loaded on the dray. Jack Taylor as head carpenter in the post and rail and hut building trade, with two assistants, were sent off to build a new hut for George and Mary.

We got our mails once a week, every Saturday from Mt Sturgeon, fifteen miles distant. The papers of the sixth, designated Black Thursday, a record day of heat, fire and disaster. It was said that Melbourne, being chiefly built of wood, that if it had caught fire, very little of it could have been saved, fires had broken all over the colony, as it were, simultaneously.

A large number of stock had been destroyed, homesteads swept away, shepherds and others burnt to death. Some had saved their lives by rolling in the nearest waterholes, some had died of exhaustion and thirst. Many had saved stock and their own lives by setting fire to the grass in front and following on to the burnt ground. But when night came on it was said the spectacle was scarcely describable. Mount Macedon was simply a hill on fire, whichever way one looked, anywhere the country seemed to be burning. The Portland District was reported to be all in flames.

The profits of squatocracy had been decreasing for several years through so many dry seasons. The loss of stock was enormous. The weaker ones wanted to sell but who would buy, in face of the late experienced droughts. It was the cause of an enormous fall in prices. Sheep bought by the first pioneers cost two pounds a head, were offered for 12/-, afterwards for 8/- down and down to 2/6. It is authentically asserted that some were sold for sixpence a head. Very few old colonists have not heard the song of 'Billy Barlow' who sold his sheep "At sixpence a head and the station give in."

A squatter of Yass named O'Brien found an expedient, he calculated that the mere tallow in a sheep when boiled down would realise six shillings and that the skin and fleece ought to realise a total value of eight shillings. The scheme was a God send; practised by many privately. Then, establishments in various places were established, for boiling down poor jumbuck for his fat. Mutton was cheap, a sheep's leg for sixpence and the head for carrying away.

Boiling down for the fat was a great relief generally; but many were so involved with the banks, were compelled to realise and sell to their richer neighbours, and then came that disastrous year of Black Thursday leaving so little grass to tide over the summer, the outlook was disheartening enough; those who had sold thought they had done the right thing, and those who had bought regretted it, but it so happened, copious rains fell nearly all over the colony. In a week or two after the green grass sprang up from the heated soil like magic, there was soon grass enough for all stock. Those who had means and had bought heavily at prices, then at the prices then going, are the great landholders of today. The gold diggings broke out that year, and many thousands of the picked men, of the earth, came rushing to Victoria to make their fortunes. There was a plentiful sale for beef and mutton and land was still one pound an acre to the

Deplorably foul boiling down works were a life saver for many.

squatters, who bought up the best of the land and made sheep runs of their own and fenced them in. But we must not anticipate.

Four weeks had passed since Black Thursday. Bell, the bullock driver's time had expired, and he, wife and family were leaving. As Mr Dwyer was wanting stores from Geelong, it was arranged for Bill to drive the team down and Dwyer would hire another driver to bring it back. Seeing my opportunity, I gave him a letter to my people asking them to send me a shepherd's overcoat and a woollen comforter for my neck, by giving the parcel to the new bullock driver to bring back to the station.

In the meantime Mr Dwyer asked me if I would mind cooking for myself; it would only be until the team returned. I told him I had no objection. Jack Taylor was still making use of the hut to cook his food, he being on piece work, was supposed to do for himself. The rations in the hut were common to us both. Jack one night baked a damper; I had been living on scones sent in by Mrs Dwyer but in the morning seeing the damper Jack had made, I cut a hunk off it. In the evening, thinking to tickle his vanity about his cooking, I said: "That was a grand damper you made last night Jack!" "Look here," he snarled, "I'm not here to cook bread for bloody shepherds and a bloody jimigrant in the bargain." His beastly abusive tongue went on till I could not stand it any longer, so I retorted: "An immigrant is as good as an old lag anyhow." At that, his face grew livid with rage; the language he blessed me with, I would not like to stain paper to repeat; picking up a long handled fire shovel he cried out: "You young imp of hell; if you don't apologize I'll split your bloody brain pan open" - apologise to him, a man I loved as the devil likes holy water - "the idea." He stood in front of me with shovel lifted ready to strike. I saw my opportunity. I made a quick dash and caught him round the waist, gave him a smart kick with my heel behind the bend of the knee and backwards he went on the broad of his back, and I on top of him. For a minute he lay as if wondering what had happened, falling, the back of his head struck the earthen floor heavily and must have struck a projecting stone, as his head was cut, as I could see by the blood on the ground. He looked very pale. I got up and asked him if he was hurt, he did not answer for a time.

I began to be afraid that he was mortally injured, when he yelled out: "My God, my skull is smashed in." I felt the back of his head, the hair was wet with blood but I did not discern any bones grating together. "Get out," I said, "you must have fallen on a stone." I gave him a drink of water, he looked pale, I thought he was going to faint. I got him into a sitting posture and bathed the hurt. By and bye he said: "I wonder if the blokes in Blake's kitchen heard the row?" "It isn't likely or they would have come in," I said, "Why?" "Well," he said, "it would be as well to keep it quiet and not to let them know we quarrelled over a bit of bloody damper." "Alright," I said, "if we are to be friends, I'm agreeable; nobody will hear of it, unless you tell them, but to say you acted more like a wild beast than a man." "Ah," he said, "it's my beastly hot temper, I've been often told I was only born to be hung, and I believe it is true." Jack seemed penitent and quite cowed down, but I trusted him not.

I did not see him in the morning, as I had to have the sheep out by sunrise. I left the kettle boiling for him, in the evening he was home before me and had lit the fire. I enquired how his head was. "It's been aching all the bloody day and my neck's that bloody stiff, I can't turn my head round." "Jack," I said, "why do you spoil your good English by mixing it with such useless dirty words?" "I don't know," he said, "it's the bloody habit a man gets into." If I had been a reforming parson then I might have made a convert of Jack for twenty-four hours, but I was not.

Two misfortunes happened to me, soon after, I went out one night to get some firewood, the shortest piece I could find was too long; the red gum in the Valley is very short in the grain, and brittle; our usual way of shortening such pieces was to bang them down on a low stump, but this time the plan did not succeed, it bounded off and hit me across the shin. In a day or two it swelled and became so painful, I could not put my foot to the ground. I had to lay up for several days. Mrs Dwyer, being the station doctor, was very kind and attentive to me in the way of ointment, bandages and advice, so that I soon got right with all the fuss my leg was around.

These short and knotted red gums Henry mentions are at the entrance to the Valley.

Shortly after, I had a violent attack of dysentery, which, in a fortnight's time brought me so weak, I could scarcely crawl after the sheep. Jack Taylor advised me to chew wattle gum which I did but without any or very little good. I must have been delirious one night, all alone in my watch box. I woke myself often by talking in my sleep and had a great craving for a bottle of porter. In the morning of that night I told William how bad I was and requested him to ask Mrs Dwyer for a dose of castor oil and fifteen drops of laudnum (Peter McVicar's cure). "Why Mundy," he said, "you do look bad, how long have you had dysentery?" I told him. "Alright," he said, "I'll see Kate and tell her what you want, but perhaps she has something better, doctors, you know, do not like patients to know more than themselves." In the evening Mrs Dwyer came to the hut and said: "Mundy, William tells me you have dysentery badly." "Yes Ma'am," I said, "Taylor advised me to take wattle gum for it, but it does not seem to do me any good." "Dysentery," she said: "is so common in the bush I was advised before I left Melbourne, by a doctor, to secure a plentiful supply of medicine he prescribed himself, he said it was infallible as a cure for dysentery, so here's a small bottle from it. Take a tablespoonful when you go to bed, and the same when you get up." In a day or two I felt the beneficial effects of the medicine, and every night she told the cook to send me in some warm soup. I was not to eat any meat. In a few days I was myself again, with an appetite insatiable.

Coming home one evening, I saw the loaded bullock dray standing near the house. Going into the hut I saw a woman at the fire preparing supper. "Good evening ma'am," I said. "Good evening," she replied, "are you the shepherd?" "Yes, I'm the shepherd, are you the new laundress?" "Yes," she answered, "is your name Mundy?" "Yes that's my name." "Oh," she said, "we have a parcel for 'e, your mother brought it to us the day afore we left. Bell gave your people your letter and told them where to find us." "Were they all quite well, do you know?" "Yes, I only saw your mother and sister - a little maid about five." At that point of our talk a pleasant looking inquisitive girl who I supposed to be about fourteen, but as I learnt was only twelve. "This is Mundy, Ann," the woman said, "the young man we brought the parcel for from Geelong." Looking at me, she said, "This is my maid, she has come to be nursemaid." "I am very glad you've come," I said: "I've had to cook for myself since the Bells left, though Mrs Dwyer was very kind, she often sent me in some scones and cooked meat." The girl had sat down on a long form, shaped out of a slab. She looked hard at me but didn't speak till she said to her mother: "The missus does not want me tonight mother, she says I must be tired, I'd better take a rest." "That's kind of her, how many chiels is there?" "Only two mother." "I'll have the supper ready soon," the woman said. "Gribble has gone to put the bullocks into the paddock he'll be back soon." "Gribble who is he?" "Well, my husband William. Our name is Gribble." "Oh, I see, your husband is William Gribble, you are Mrs Gribble and the daughter is Ann Gribble. We're getting on alright," I said, when the girl laughed softly. Gribble came in shortly after, a man about thirty-

Wool being hauled to port for export to England.

five, five feet ten inches in height, fresh and florid looking with a pleasant countenance. "This is Mundy," Mrs Gribble said, "the young man we brought the parcel for." "Oh," he said, "how are you? Glad to see you, have you been long in this outlandish place; it seems to be all mountains and rocks?" "About four months," I said. "Supper," Mrs Gribble said, "is read. Come on, we can talk after supper." Gribble said, "I must get in the bedding, old woman. Hold on a bit, there's a big bunk in the bedroom, I want to see if there's any bugs." The bunk was covered with sheets of stringy bark, lifting the edges of the bark, were seen, bugs. The bark was forthwith pulled off and put on the fire, the bugs were a sight enough to make one creep, millions of them, there was little talked about that night but bugs, till bed time, when they made their beds on the floor.

I undid my parcel and found an overcoat, a comforter, a lump of cake, a bag of lollies and some needles and thread; feeling in the pockets of the coat were ten shillings wrapped up in paper. I supposed that was all the change I was to get from my £8 cheque. I was satisfied. I distributed some of the lollies among the Gribbles and retired to my watch box on the hill side.

Things went on smoothly. Jack Taylor had finished his contract and was gone, I never saw him after. John hearing I was sick came to see me after I had got well, he had been shifted to a hut half way between Robinson's and Dwyer's, my run too was in that direction so we often managed to meet.

We met one day too many, busily talking and not thinking of the sheep meeting, the two flocks came in sight of each other behind a hill and began to run together, before we could cut them a number of John's got mixed with mine. Here was an annoying misfortune, it meant a day of drafting. There was nothing for it but tell the bosses. One consolation, both flocks were clean of scab. In the evening, putting as long a face as I knew how, I said to the overseer: "William, we have met with a misfortune today, my brother's flock and mine got mixed." "Oh," he said, "too busy reading." "No," I said, "too busy talking." He laughed. "Well, I have to see the Robinson's and have a draughting match, our yards are the best." Two days after, the drafting took place and the two flocks were separate again. All the reprimand we got, was to be more careful for the future.

When the Gribbles had been there about a fortnight Mrs Gribble said to me one evening: "Mundy I'll do your washing for 'e, if you'll give my maid some lessons in the evening, after she's done her work. She's very backward in her schooling. She went to a school in Geelong sometimes, but I had so much trouble to get her to go she didn't like it, perhaps she'll get on with you." I expressed myself quite agreeable to the bargain, in fact I felt secretly delighted to think I should have that little girl for company every night.

My pupil was very backward indeed; but she was anxious to learn. Every night I gave her a lesson in writing, reading and simple sums, she got on remarkably well for the time I was teaching her. I told her when she was tired not to do any more. Then we talked about our experiences in Geelong and elsewhere. Black Thursday, our recollections of England, our voyage over the sea etc. In fact we became quite chummy, speaking for myself, by day I longed for that hour of sweet intercourse by night.

John and I met occasionally in the middle of the day. One day he told me our Don Quixote was dead and buried. I asked him the cause of his death. "People say," he said, "the hot weather dried all his marrow up." So poor old Jack, the shepherd was dead and buried. Buried in the usual bushman's coffin, a sheet of bark, tied around with hide; without service or ceremony, on the side of

All properties were isolated and had to be self sufficient.

the range.

Robinson's having no further need of Bet's services, packed her off on a bullock dray to Port Fairy. The first stage, the dray stopped at Dwyer's for the night. Bet came into our hut, she seemed transformed into an almost respectable woman, her two children too were clean, the poor beggars must have undergone a severe scrubbing down. Bet talked of her poor John incessantly, what a good husband he had been and what she intended doing etc. Poor Bet.

Time passed on till my twentieth birthday arrived, 25th June. I mentioned it to Gribble at breakfast, he said you have forty more years to live Mundy before you are an old man.

I often think now of his remark. This year I am eighty.

Lake Wendouree was a milky coloured swamp when Henry first sighted it. In 1956 it hosted Olympic rowing.

THE GOLDRUSH AND MORE ...

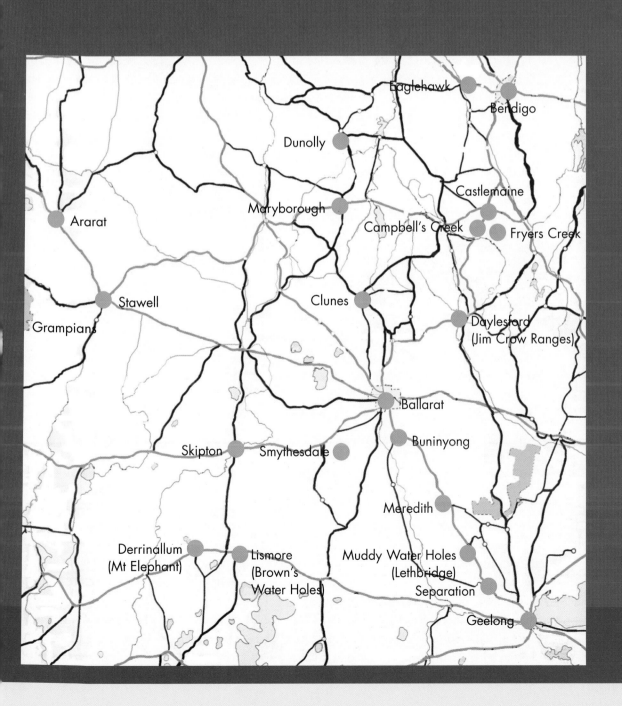

How S.T. Gill saw a family digging for gold in the early 1850s.

That year Port Phillip became Victoria, and was the exciting time of the discovery of gold.

The talk of the world, the last two or three years was of the rich finds of gold in California. Smitten with the gold fever, thousands had left Australia for San Francisco to seek their fortunes. A few were lucky, but many were disappointed. Among the lucky ones was one named Hargraves from New South Wales, where he remembered country similar to auriferous ground in California. He came back, went prospecting in the early part of 1851, found gold on the Turon. Another find shortly after by a blackfellow; a very large nugget which was magnified to an enormous weight. Another disappointed Californian digger returned and discovered gold at Clunes. His name was Esmond. This was in July. Another prospector named Hiscock, a month later found gold at Buninyong; but neither of these finds paid little more than common day's wages.

The indisputable fact that gold had been discovered was enough to set the Geelong people and those of the surrounding district crazy. Mother Jamieson's pub at Buninyong was thronged with gold

Coopers (here) and Mother Jamieson's were the most important pubs at Buninyong.

seekers. They hunted along the gullies and grassy flats of the River Leigh till Esmond and his mate Kavanah came to the site of the present city of Ballarat and agreed to sink a hole on a flat, which for what reason I do not know, was called Poverty Flat; after sinking six feet, they struck wash; it is said the gold was as plentiful as the dirt. In two days the two men netted half a hundred weight of gold, £3,000 worth. Near to Poverty Flat was the celebrated Golden Point where some made, each, a hundred pound a day.

The reports in the papers drove every one mad. Quartz was said to be an indication of gold; every shepherd, hutkeeper, stockrider, every man, woman and child. All the world and his wife were looking for and examining quartz. Vessels arriving in the bay, in spite of all precautions, lost all or nearly all their crews, the sailors with a small convenient bundle tied in a handkerchief, leaving chest and pay behind, by hook or by crook, sneaked off and made for the diggings. One captain took a wise course; he called his men together and said: "Now men, I wish to deal fair with you and I expect you to deal fair with me, and not leave me stranded here, like other vessels for want of a crew. I propose that we all go to the diggings together for three months; if you all promise me faithfully to return at the end of that time; you will not sacrifice your kit and your pay, for the time you have worked will be forthcoming when we reach home. The captain's proposition was unanimously agreed to and they all went to the diggings, some did fairly well and some but little, but they all turned up at the appointed time, and were soon homeward bound.

We had the loan, every week, of the papers and read the exciting accounts of the gold discoveries. The Gribbles and I discussed the wonderful turn our fortunes had taken, if we could only get away to have our chances of making a pile before all the gold was gone. Not that I had any great craving for riches, nor ever have had, but I knew the Gribbles were bent on going to the diggings when their time of service was expired. I was anxious to go too, but we could not leave till our time was up and got our cheques; so we had to bide our time. My time was up in October, the Gribbles a fortnight after. Their intention was to go to Geelong first.

The day arrived that set me free. I would rather have waited for the Gribbles, but having no plausible excuse for doing so, I had to set out by myself. My brother had been transferred two months before to old man Robinson's station at Horsham. So one bright October morning, with my cheque in my pocket, I shouldered my swag and bid goodbye to the Gribbles, not without a little throb at my heart for my little pupil. Hoping soon to see them all again, I set off at a four mile an hour walk for Mt. Sturgeon.

The journey before me was one hundred and fifty miles to Geelong which I intended to accomplish in three days. About eleven o'clock I reached the pub at Mt Sturgeon, and on to the Geelong road. I did not stop. Very soon I came to the Wannon River, which had risen considerably from a late rain. Not liking the usual crossing place for fear of bog holes, I went up stream, where it was widened out to one hundred and fifty yards, where I could see the tips of the long grass in the deepest places. The middle reached my waist. I thought it a fearfully long distance and freezingly cold, and rough walking, however, I got over without mishap. The smart walking and the sun being pretty warm, I soon got bearably warm and dry, for I was thinly clad. About two o'clock I came to a pub. (I cannot remember the name of the place) where I stopped and had a good meal. The people there persuaded me to stay for the night. one thing, I did not like the looks of the crowd, at the place, who were there, and another thing, the thought of losing so much precious daylight was intolerable so away I started again. I travelled on till it was dark, it was only a bush track, and rough from cattle tracks and ruts; by daylight it did not matter much, one could pick his way, but after dark I had many a stumble; so I had to walk slowly. In the middle of the night I saw a fire ahead. Coming up to the fire I found it was a bullock dray camp, tarpaulins spread over the poles, all was quiet. I hullooed to one of the drays, someone sung out "Who's that?" I answered: "A traveller going to Geelong." "Where did ye come from?" Mt. Sturgeon." "Why did you not stop at the pub on the road?" I said I was in a hurry and asked them how far it was to the next public house. "What you mean, Gardener's Creek?" "Yes." "About fifteen miles." I thanked them. I thought they might have asked me to shake down under the tarpaulin (as I heard them muttering together) but they did not. Making for the fire to see if I could find anything to eat, I saw a camp oven, lifting the lid there was a solitary mutton chop which I appropriated and started again. Onward, onward, "immer vorwarts." I was glad when day broke. At ten o'clock I pulled up at the Gardener's Creek public house. If it had been today, the first thing I should have asked for would be a drink of stimulant, but such a thing then never entered my head. My greatest want was a good solid feed and a rest. So I concluded to stay the remainder of the day and all night and make the Leigh the next day, which I did.

It was a pretty good day's travel but the road was good. I had a jolly nice bed at the Leigh, white sheets and everything up to the handle. The night before, afraid of bugs, I slept in my clothes, but here I ventured to doff my pants. What a ghastly contrast, my legs were the colour of the dirt I had travelled over. It seemed a sin to pollute such a bed with my dirty carcass; nevertheless I sprang in and had a glorious sleep, the sleep of the just, till daylight did appear.

My next day's stage by Bates Ford to Geelong, was a short one, only twenty-five miles. As I had passed Bates Ford and had reached the top of the bank, a man with a horse and dray caught up to me and offered me a lift. He had come from Ballarat and told me of the heavy finds of gold that had taken place and the thousands of people there living in tents. And other diggings too had broken out at Mt. Alexander he told me. When we reached Bell Post Hill, that glorious scene which I had, before and since so often admired, the full view of Corio Bay, the ocean beyond, the North Shore, the open plains and the You Yangs. The shipping and boats in the Bay, the little town of Geelong sloping down to a bold shore, I, being in a hopeful mood, seemed to be particularly grand to me then.

The view to the You Yangs.

On reaching Ashby, I bade my friend with the dray goodbye, and made for Newtown. As I approached home, I saw my sister Jane standing just outside the gate; she looked around towards me when I held up my hand, she gave a screech and bounded for me like a deer, threw her arms round my neck and cried with joy. "Where's John? Isn't he home?" "No." "Oh he'll be home perhaps tomorrow." Jane and I loved each other in those days. My poor unfortunate

GOLD - BEFORE THE RUSH
Gold was first discovered in Australia in February 1823 when James McBrien found it in the Bathurst district. It is thought that it may have also been found before but people were unwilling to report it. McBrien's report was suppressed by the government. According to the law, gold would be owned by the government, not the finders. Little was known about gold mining methods, business owners were afraid of the population abandoning their jobs and there was a fear of unsavoury types emigrating. When W.B. Clarke showed Governor George Gipps his nuggets found at Hartley, NSW in 1842, it is reported that Gipps told him: 'Put it away Mr Clarke, or we shall all have our throats cut'.

TOWNS DESERTED
'It is quite impossible for me to describe to your lordship the effect these discoveries have had on the whole community ... Cottages are deserted, houses to let, businesses at a standstill, and even schools deserted. In some suburbs not a man is left and the women are, for self-protection, to forget neighbourhood jars (fights) and group together to keep house ... The price of provisions has naturally, increased.'

Charles Joseph La Trobe writing to Lord Grey.

147

A long lost section of the original road to Ballarat from Geelong.

sister. Mother had heard the screech and came out to look for the cause. We shook hands, mother was never demonstrative. I never knew her to kiss me. "Oh Henry," she said, "so you have come home again. I am so glad to see you, do you know anything of John?" I said: "He ought to have been home by this time, his time was up a day before mine, besides, he hadn't so far to come." "Father isn't in, he's gone for the cows out Fyan's Ford way, he be home soon," mother said. Father turned up after a while. We shook hands, he said: "I'm rejoiced to see you home again Henry." And he looked it. Poor old father; he would have killed the proverbial fatted calf, but as it happened, he had not one then. Mutual explanations and enquires, how things had gone on since we parted, ensued. After supper the great discussion was the diggings. I urged: "When John comes, we will all go to the gold fields and make our fortunes." Father looked thoughtful and said: "Well, a half of my customers have left for the diggings, I can't sell the milk I used to, but what am I to do with the cows." "Dry the milkers off," I said, "and turn them out on the You Yangs and take the good ones to the sale yard and sell them." "Sell them," he replied, "who'll buy cows in these topsy turvy times?"

The morrow came but John did not make his appearance. Father and mother wondered why he had not come, but I knew John well enough to know he would not bustle or inconvenience himself if it was to be avoided. John, not like me, had a habit of taking the world easy. The second day, however, John made his appearance, dusty and travel worn, but I understand he got a lift some part of the road. There were more rejoicings; we were all together once more.

There was nothing for it but to follow the goldseekers. The next cattle sale day, father took his full milking cows to the sale and sold them for what he could get, which was very little, for who wanted milking cows; it grieved him to his heart. He said: "they were given away." In a week or so the other cows were driven out to grass towards the plains. Some, he afterwards found again and some he never did. John and I had a cheque each, each amounting to about £20, the greater part of which was spent in providing a fit-out for the diggings. Implements required for gold digging were an outrageous price. We purchased a pretty large tent, a cradle of the most approved make, a puddling tub, a long handled dipper, tin dishes, picks and shovels, rope and buckets and various other things, besides a plentiful supply of provisions and to make our outfit complete, as nothing like stimulants were suffered to be sold on the diggings, father provided a two-gallon keg of rum. He liked a drop now and then, but I can say with truth, that he never drank to excess. It took about three weeks to get in readiness for a start. Our dray had on it a good tilt and father possessed then the best horse he ever had, he was a real plum. I was expecting to see the Gribbles before we left, but they made no appearance, so we made a start for Ballarat, where we arrived early the third day. We passed Golden Point which was covered with innumerable wooden windlasses with awkwardly devised wooden handles.

ONE WAY TO BALLARAT
Unless the new digger was prepared to walk north and then follow cattle trails to find Ballarat, the only other way was to pay for a £1 steamer passage from Melbourne to Geelong and then walk 50 miles to the Ballarat fields.

Over 150 years after the place was over-run by prospectors, Ballarat still shows all the signs of its earlier life.

The claims then were only eight feet square, the depths ranged from six to twelve feet. Not far from the Point was water, where men were employed extracting the gold from the washdirt; four bucketfuls were tipped into a tub, the water scooped on to it; then stirred about with a spade till the water became thick; the tub was then canted, till the dirty water ran off and fresh water supplied, and so on till the dirt was all dissolved and nothing left but gravel and what gold there might be. The last tilting of

Ballarat as it was when the early stages of the gold rush were in full swing.

GOLDEN POINT
Golden Point was one of the first goldfields in Ballarat and yeilded fabulous riches. It remains mostly unbuilt on.

DAYLESFORD
The pretty town of Daylesford in the Jim Crow Ranges was originally Wombat Creek. That changed when gold was found in August 1851. A new rush occurred there in 1856 and 1857.

the tub showed the richness of the dirt by forming a golden streak on the upper edge. The contents of the tub was by degrees transferred to the hopper of the cradle. A man rocked the cradle with one hand, with the other ladled water from a long handled dipper into the hopper, till all the fine dirt had passed through; overhauling the stones; for mayhap, any nugget might be there, the rest was pitched out. The fine dirt that passed through, passed over three or four ripples about an inch high, which caught the gold and heavy sand. When the tubful had gone through, the ripples were swilled into a tin dish and panned off, leaving only the gold and small particles such as chips of iron, and emery.

We stayed looking on for about three hours then proceeded to look for a camping place. The best place we could find for water and grass was Wendouree swamp, where we elected to stay for the night. Wendouree swamp was grown all over with long wire grass and had, as far as I can recollect, from eight to ten inches of water of a whitish colour. The next day we had a tour of inspection to look for a spot to stick in and sink a hole (John and I). It seemed very perplexing; it seemed that all the golden ground had been worked out. All round, the locality where gold had been so good, were sunk innumerable shicers (blanks)- it was the opinion of the majority that Ballarat was worked out for good and all, but there were reports of two other gold fields. Fryers Creek and Forest Creek reported to be enormously rich. Crowds were leaving Ballarat daily for these new Eldorados. So we concluded to go to the new rush and left Ballarat after the third day. To the new diggings was about fifty miles.

The original road through the Jim Crow Ranges

We passed Captain Hepburn's station; over the Jim Crow Ranges (now Daylesford) then crossed the Loddon and finally reached Fryar's Creek; where we camped only about a mile distant from the Loddon, where a gold commissioner's camp was fixed.

Diggers were swarming from all parts, many passed five miles farther on to Forest Creek. Looking round next day, we found a surface diggings, that is where gold is found on the surface just under the grass. Someone had taken away a few loads and left it most likely to look for something better. We picked up a load and washed it in a slovenly way, putting it into the cradle dry; it did not require puddling; if a lump of dirt was too hard to dissolve, a crack with a stick or shovel was sufficient. The first load we obtained three of a woman's thimbleful, a full thimbleful was supposed to be an ounce. We put through several loads of that, but hearing of much better things John and I resolved to sink a hole at a new rush called 'Windlass Hill.' Father objected strongly against this. A few had bottomed on gold at twenty-five or thirty feet. Father thought that was a ghastly depth, he said one would not catch him down one of them deep holes for anything. But John and I were bent on trying our luck and sunk a round hole; we could not get father to take a spell of sinking; he would handle the windlass as long as you like. We bottomed, at length, at twenty-two feet. It was a rank duffer.

A few days, after walking up the creek looking about, I noticed a girl squatted down by a pool of water with a tin dish in her hands trying a prospect, now shaking round the dirt then swilling it off; peeping closely now and again for signs of the precious metal. On hearing my footsteps she looked round, then

GETTING TO THE GOLD DIGGINGS
A camp stretcher bed in a pub en route to the diggings cost £1 per night, while taking a coach instead of walking could cost between £10 and £30 - a fortune then.
If a potential digger wanted to walk, only two routes were available. One was north to Seymour and then across the Goulburn River at £1 for the punt, or head north via Flemington Road and the Black Forest.
There were no true roads in the earliest days of the gold rush, only stock routes.

stood straight up. "Good Heavens," there was my dear little pupil of Victoria Valley, Annie Gribble. We looked at each other in mute astonishment, she dropped the dish and ran up the bank to a tent close by and cried out: "Mother, Mother, here's Mundy." Mrs Gribble ran out saying: "Lawks Mundy, when did 'e come? When did 'e come?" There was great shaking of hands and mutual

Excited residents left Melbourne by any means available.

questions and answers on both sides. I told them how I had got there. They told me how they had arrived at Fryar's Creek. Dwyer's had taken them to the pub at Mt. Sturgeon on the Geelong Road, where they would have to wait their chance of a bullock team passing into town.

It happened then, that many parties were coming overland from Adelaide to the Victorian diggings. (It must be remembered that 1st July, 1851 Port Phillip was made a separate colony, and had a Governor of its own, and was called Victoria).

Gribble happened to drop in with one of these parties of three or four men whose horse was nearly knocked out. They offered to sell the horse and dray to Gribble cheap, on condition that he would take their swags on to the diggings, so he bought the turn-out and by easy stages, reached Fryar's Creek.

In course of an hour Gribble himself made his appearance all smile and wonder to see me. He told the tale over again of how they got there, a few days ago. He said he had met two Geelong men he knew well and they had made a party and were going to try their luck, as soon as they could find a promising spot.

After a lengthy conversation I left, promising to call again in a day or two. Two days after, I called, but they were gone and left no sign. It was no good enquiring where they had gone for nobody knew any one else's business; the only thing I could ascertain was, they had left early that morning. A few days after was Christmas Day. After dinner mother and my sister went out for a stroll into the ranges and got lost. Being away longer than was expected, father got anxious, after a further time, we all three went in search of them. We got news that a woman leading a little girl as fast as she could walk going along a road directly away from home. Father and I put the horse into the dray and started off in pursuit. We had not gone far before we heard of them again, going full haste towards Ballarat; again we received news of them. At last we espied them ahead, going as if their very life depended on getting home, and going away at every step. At full trot we neared them. Mother was dragging and Jane was howling, until I let out a yell that startled them, looking round, Mother recognised us. Father let out: "Wherever are you going woman?" "Going home," she said. "Going home woman, you're going to Ballarat." We bundled them

FRYERS CREEK GOLD STRIKE
Henry speaks modestly of his finds at Fryers Creek, but in fact it was one of the most successful and famous alluvial gold fields of all.
It is likely he did very well indeed, and for years after any alluvial find was compared with that one.

into the dray, in doing so, having on a pair of woollen cord pants, split them from the fork down to the knee and had to hold the tear together with my hands till I got home. That was our Christmas day on Fryar's Creek diggings in 1851.

The licence fee at that time was 30/- a month or half an ounce of gold. Gold was selling then for £3 an ounce while its legitimate value as was after ascertained was £4/4/6. Police were hunting up and down the workings continually asking diggers to show their licenses. If he happened to be risking it with no license, and caught, he was marched with other delinquents to the Commissioner's camp, and fined £5 and compelled to take out a licence or go to jail for a month.

The gold got in Fryer's Creek was a very narrow streak. The slaty rocks ran across the bed and had acted as ripples in a stream to intercept the gold in pockets, some pockets were very rich. The gold was about six feet from the surface, consequently the bed rocks were all laid considerable width where the gold was so scattered that it did not pay. The lower end ran into the Lodden and there the gold ran out. The payable part of the Creek was all occupied when we arrived, but there was a little gully about one hundred and fifty yards long between two hills, running into the main creek where a few claims were quietly being worked. It struck us, this little gully might be a likely spot, so John and I pegged out a claim and commenced to sink. At night we told father who enquired how deep it would be, I said the holes next were about eighteen feet. "What nonsense," he said. "I told you before to have nothing to do with them deep holes." However, we went at it on the morrow and sunk it eight feet. in two days more we bottomed on a broad flat stone. It happened to be my shift down. I sent up about half a bucket of dirt asking John to wash it. After washing it he whispered to me down the shaft, "There was half an ounce of gold in it." "Bravo." I selected about six or eight inches deep of the earth of the stone which sloped considerably. Fearing I had not taken the wash high enough, I asked him to try some headings, which he did and got a pennyweight so the wash was a foot thick after cleaning the bottom well off, which was sent up and put carefully on one side. I was heaved up and John went down and commenced a drive in the headings leaving a foot of wash dirt underneath. By night we had a load of wash dirt. At night, reaching home we told father of our good luck; he was pleased enough. "Tomorrow I will take it to the creek and wash it." Next day he took it to Campbell's Creek, washed and got six ounces of coarse gold. Father, in fact the whole of us were in great glee that night.

The early bridge over Fryers Creek from Campbell's Creek.

GOLD FEVER

'Gold, gold gold. My dear A. we are all gone mad with gold, and what will be the end of it nobody knows.'

Frances Perry, wife of the first Anglican bishop of Melbourne, writing to her sister Amelia in 1851.

Almost every piece of ground was turned over.

Henry's father took their gold to nearby Campbell's Creek.

We got a load every day and father washed it and brought home an average five ounces daily. As we were out of sight below, no one on the surface could tell which way we were driving. We were working up the gully where no one as yet had pegged off.

We were asked many questions, what we were getting and direction we were working. Our careless answers were: 'Up the gully was nothing, the only ground worth working was between us and the claims already occupied.' But as we kept on working someone got suspicious and went down our hole by night; it was easy to do, as there were alternate steps to climb up and down.

One morning we noticed tracks of night invaders, lollies and raisins were here and there scattered about, and plain evidence that fossicking had been carried on by night thieves. The same day two fellows pegged out a claim about us, and before the day was over, the whole little gully was occupied.

The greatest colonial artist of the goldrush era was S.T. Gill, born at Perriton in Devonshire in 1819. His father was a Baptist minister and schoolmaster. Gill initially attended his father's school and then Dr Seabrook's Academy in Plymouth. In 1839 he and his family emigrated to Adelaide and in March 1840 he placed an advertisement as an artist in the South Australian Register.

Gill joined the Horrocks Expedition into the interior of South Australia as an unpaid draughtsman in 1846. In January 1847 sixty-two of his works were displayed in the Exhibition of Pictures. Financial success did not follow, his drinking increased, and in 1851 he was declared bankrupt.

In 1852 he travelled to the Victorian goldfields, where he produced his most enduring and best known works recording the boisterous life of the gold digger. Lively and informative with masses of detail of daily life: dogs, children, women, the optimistic in search of riches. His sketches immortalised one of the most romantic periods in Australian history. All aspects of humanity, the greedy, the sly, the opulent and the miserly, were captured by his quick eye and expert brush. In 1853 the Argus waxed lyrical:

'One of the pleasantest friends we have is a gentleman signing himself S.T.G. Personally, he is an entire stranger, for instead of boring us by the occupation of that very scarce commodity, editorial time, he sends us incessantly specimens of his industry, which are of such high merit, that we find ourselves constantly plunged into that delightful ecstasy, a complete speech-lessness of admiration. We have before us, at this moment, a series of lithographed sketches of stirring events in Australian life, in which the correctness and animation of a 'Phiz' blend in happy union with humour worthy of a Cruikshank.'

Gill returned from the goldfields, unsuccessful like so many others, and began to record the life and events of the rapidly expanding city.

Before leaving for Sydney in 1856, he was on tour in Western Victoria.

Gill's depictions of human foibles and failings followed the English tradition of illustrative comedy. The disparity between high and low life was reflected in Gill's series of lithographs and watercolours of successful and provident diggers, who are contrasted with their successful and improvident counterparts.

It is hard to reconcile the civilised world depicted in many of Gill's watercolours with the depths to which Gill sank prior to his tragic death. The circumstances can be pieced together from the brief reports in the press and the report of the inquest. On Wednesday 27 October 1880, Gill collapsed on the steps of the General Post Office and died. The following day the *Argus*, which in earlier times had referred to

We did our utmost to gouge out what we could before they bottomed. They were cunning enough to leave a good wall between us, otherwise they would have found some portion of their claim with the bottom out. We turned then to the other side of our claim which was the richest. John struck dirt one afternoon, it was nearly half gold. I said: "We'll have a lark with father when he comes to load for the 'morrow," so we put by half a tin dish full.

When he sang out and made known that he was back and whispered to us what the last load turned, we asked him to try the dirt we sent him up, to see if it was any good. "All right," he answered. He was gone a considerable time.

At last he sung "Below there." I crawled and looked up; father was lying down on the flat of his belly with his head as far down the hole as he could put it; his eyes shining like two stars, whispering: "There was nearly a pound weight in it." "Alright," I said. John and I had a good laugh over it. The gold was weighed at a store we passed going home, it was eight ounces.

The remaining part of our claim was soon worked out, though it was richer than anything we had previously got. The bottom was different to anything I ever met with after. In my long experience, it was covered over with unevenly placed flat stones from eighteen inches to three feet across, bedded in very stiff blue clay. We thought there might possibly be gold underneath; we laboured a considerable time to lift one of the stones two feet across and four inches thick, under was the cleanest stiffest clay I have ever come across, as John said, it required an adze to work it.

We bored down for two feet, but nothing but clay. I have often thought since, the best gold might have been below. However, we left it to look for something new. We had done fairly well that hit, the gold we had got sold for about £350. John and I agreed to allow mother half a share. Father, John and I had a full share.

The water now on Fryer's Creek became undrinkable; what was left was merely mud pools. The thousands of tents on the Creek shifted down to the Loddon River on to the flats. We shifted too. The population was extremely crowded, especially at the junction of the Creek and the river, tents were close together all facing a passage some fourteen feet wide, where they boiled their billies, did their cooking etc.

Here and there, were large tents called stores, who professed to sell everything from a needle to an anchor, also with great caution, rum, brandy, gin and old tom. Doctors chemists, dentists tents were plentiful enough. Such an homogeneous mixed population the world had never seen or possibly would see again. Bush furniture weavers, watchmakers, shoemakers, carpenters, bricklayers, tinkers, tailors and candlestick makers; every trade and profession was represented; all dressed in rough diggery's clothes, ready, looking for their fortune.

In the daytime the calico town was quiet enough, those who had payable claims were out working and those who had not been successful were out among the ranges and gullies on the "Qui vive" armed with tin dish, pick or shovel. Oft-times, a report would spread of a new find five, ten or twenty miles away, which had been worked for sometime on the quiet. It might be true or it might

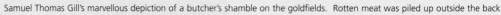

Samuel Thomas Gill's marvellous depiction of a butcher's shamble on the goldfields. Rotten meat was piled up outside the back.

not be, but the report was enough to cause a stampede to the new rush; each one enquiring of his travelling neighbour, for the exact locality and more information of the new find. If the report was genuine, they mostly all found it eventually, but if it was a hoax, after some miles, coming back with disappointed looks, some unwilling to believe, searched farther.

At night-time, when all were in camp, the noises and scenes were indescribable. I regret my inability to do them adequate justice. During arrivals home, and cooking supper, the talking and yelling was incessant. After supper, nearly everyone owned a gun or pistol and they commenced firing and kept perhaps, a full hour. What with firing of guns and barking of dogs, it was deafening. After the firing

As Henry writes - brawls were part of life on the goldfields.

slackened, accordions, concertinas, fiddles, flutes, clarionettes, cornets, bugles, all were set going, each with a tune of his own. One individual, after the noise had subsided a little, he was a good player on the cornet no doubt, pretended to be only learning. he would play a few notes of a tune fairly, then a false note would slip in. He would stop and try again, got on better next time, failing several times. At last he started and played splendidly till all at once he let go such a ridiculous noise that would make a donkey laugh. Another wag, one night, played a trick of beating an erring wife; thumping something, it might have been a bag of flour, a man's voice yelling out: "You call yourself a wife, you beggarly brute. I'll stop your gallop or my name's not Tom." Then an imitation of a woman's voice: "You wretch, you wretch, you brute, do you call yerself a man." Thump went the blows again, fell thick and heavy. "Oh, oh," in a wailing woman's voice. "Oh Tom, Tom, I'll never do it again." Nevertheless, Tom thinking she hadn't got enough gave her a few bangs more. Many people round thought the farce was real, rushed to the spot to save the woman from further ill-treatment, only to be laughed at.

Although the sale of intoxicating liquor was forbidden, drunkenness was rife. Thieves were everywhere, robberies were of frequent occurrence, not only by night but in open daylight. I heard of a man, one day, of what he witnessed on Fryer's Creek. He was at the Windlass, saw a strange man approach, the man on the next claim saying: "Here you bugger, hand me over my share said: "Who? I do not know the gold." The man accosted said: "Ware you? I do not know you." "I'll bloody soon let you know me," then with that, he tripped the man up, slipped his hand into his pocket and pulled out, not gold, but a roll of notes and made leisurely off. A number of men standing round saw what happened, thought it a quarrel between mates and did not interfere; it was no concern of

Gill's depiction of a grog shanty.

their's; but after the thief had got clean off everyone was convinced it was a daylight robbery. Very few old diggers but what have not heard of the notorious thief Black Douglas; he was a well known pest about Fryer's Creek at that time, whose depredations were well known, yet he managed to evade the police for a long time.

The police force was so small, and inadequate to cope with the many outrages committed, that it was difficult to get them to interfere, unless something very unusual happened. There was no patrol. If the police were wanted they had to be sought, but what they did do was arbitrary and drastic. For instance, there was a notorious grog shanty on a bend of Fryer's Creek, well known to be the resort of thieves and the worst scum of the community; many complaints had been made to the Commissioner about it. One day, he marched up his police force, set a light to this shanty and burnt it to the ground. After the burning, I saw the smoking remains myself. The way they treated the unlicensed captives taken during the day was to ram them into a lock up, built of heavy logs, as long as there was standing room, to remain there all night, till the court opened in the morning.

Intoxicating drinks were sold nearly in every store. Then there were regular grog shanties; these were conspicuous by having a large square shutter hung on hinges at the top, on one side of the gable end of the tent facing the road; by day this shutter was either hung or propped up; inside was a rough counter

Gill's work in the most glowing terms and hailed him as 'one of the notables of the land of gold,' reported the death of an unknown. The *Daily Telegraph* provided much more detail including a description of Gill's appearance: 'A fearfully sudden death occurred yesterday afternoon. About half-past four a man, name unknown, about forty years of age, of slender build, 5 ft. 8 in. in height, with reddish beard, was observed to fall down on the Post-office steps. Constable Connolly, who was on duty, at once had him placed in a cab for the purpose of having him taken to the hospital, but he expired almost immediately. In his pockets were found a purse, key, and a book on which was written the name of Davies and Co., chemists, and several bills on which the name 'Gill' was written. The body now lies at the hospital dead-house awaiting identification and an inquest.' By Thursday the *Herald* was able to confirm that it was artist S. T. Gill: 'who once occupied an opulent position, but has of late been in reduced circumstances'.

Brief reports from the inquest appeared in the Age and the Argus on the following day, both referring to his drinking habits. The cause of death was given as the rupture of an aneurism of the aorta. On the day of his death Gill had been to the office of the architect Arthur Peck, who had given him a drafting job, but his hand was so shaky that Peck sent him home. Constable Connolly saw Gill stagger against one of the pillars and collapse. Dressed like one of the unforgettable caricatures from his watercolours in an old brown sack coat, brown striped vest, dark grey trousers, striped shirt, elastic-sided shoes and a soft white hat, he was 'in the most filthy state and crawled with vermin.' Also giving evidence at the Inquest was George Parker who had an interest in art and had befriended Gill and other artists. He described Gill as 'an habitual drunkard' who had 'lived upon him for the last few months.'

Gill's life may have been miserable and his death tragic, but his work is known and admired by many for its lively and amusing depiction of a society evolving in a new country made rich by gold.

A true democrat, Gill remains Australia's best known and most loved artist of the early colonial period.

Mary Lewis with Christine Downer

where were placed five or ten gallon kegs of hop beer, ginger beer, lemonade, cider etc. which were retailed out at 6d. a pint pannikin. All the shanties sold grog at I/- a glass that was an egg cup mostly. The most noticeable twang about the grog was cayenne pepper, so I was told; I did not taste it myself.

Sunday was washing day, scores of men could be seen in front of their tents with tin dish or bucket washing their weekly shirt and flannel. As a rule Sunday morning was fairly quiet. In the afternoon, some preachers would elevate themselves on the trunk of a fallen tree, or in a dray, with two or three of his own persuasion and commence to sing a hymn which soon attracted a crowd. If no drunks happened to interfere, the service would pass off alright, but as likely as not, one or two or more would join the crowd and with their ribaldry and beastly talk, would upset the service, some would laugh and some, the more seriously inclined, would talk to them quietly and perhaps induce them to leave.

Surprisingly, there was some formal order in the goldfields settlements, and generally Sunday was taken off from digging for rest and domestic duties.

Every store or shanty had a commodious tent at the back for the accommodation of customers, where gambling and drinking were continuously carried on, where it would not be safe for a single policeman to enter. The police never interfered, unless they were urged on by some aggrieved informer. Informer - an informer was looked upon as one of the blackest of Satan's crew. If he happened to be found out, his life was in danger.

Late one Sunday afternoon three drunken Irishmen came lurching against our tent, where a savage mastiff was tied up very short, father's favourite dog, he had reared him from a pup when we lived on Muston's Creek. He was a quiet enough dog when loose, but when tied he knew he was on duty. One of these Irish men ran right on top of him, though he did not bite him, startled him nearly out of his senses. Starting back "By Jesus," he yelled, "I'll kill that brute and looking round found a lump of firewood, picked it up, made for poor Spot with intention to annihilate him. I sprang before the dog and said: "Leave the dog alone, he's safely chained, he cannot touch you if you keep away from the tent." "Stand out o' me road, stand out o' me road," he yelled, "or I'll smash yer own brains in, ye bloody Saxon." With that he made a determined swipe at me, which I dexterously dodged or it would have been bad for me. I whipped into the tent, picked up the gun, saying to the ruffian: "If you touch me or the dog with that log I'll shoot you dead." No sooner were the words out of my mouth than the gun was snatched from my hands and I was lifted up and passed over the crowd that had assembled. I should think about twenty yards, when I was lowered softly on the ground and kept there for about a minute. When I had been disposed of, Sam Yates, a shipmate of our's took my place in defence of the dog.

The Irishman had lost his weapon the same way as I had lost the gun, so he struck at Sam with his fist. Sam was a strong young Wiltshire man, gave him such a terrible lift on the jaw that felled him down. His two mates came forward and placed a hand under each of his arms, lifted him up and slowly walked him away. The police camp was about two hundred yards away. Ten minutes after a policeman with a horse pistol in his holster, and a carbine slung over his shoulder, walked slowly up saying: "What's the row here?" All that anyone could tell him: "They went in that direction." After waiting, looking round officially for about ten minutes, he stalked unconcernedly back to camp again.

For three or four weeks after we had finished our successful strike, John and I were trying for another payable claim we sunk several holes, but without success. I was suffering with sore eyes, and so was father. It was a common complaint at the time, called the sandy or gravelly blight. The inside of the eyelids became inflamed and covered over with small white pustules the size of a pin head; when the eye was closed it seemed like a lot of needles pricking and unbearable when you laid your head down to sleep. I passed a considerable part of some nights walking to and fro in the tent. At last I went to a doctor, who after examination told me to lay down on my back on the ground; he poured some horrible liquid into my eyes which I thought must burn them out, the anguish was terrible. After I had paid him, he said, "Go home now and lie quiet for awhile, I think that will fix you up, if it does not, call in again," which I resolved there and then I never would. However my eyes improved after, but were very weak.

Father began to get very fidgety and wanted to go home, he had had enough gold digging, if he got home a little silver would do him. Mother had rheumatics in her knee and wanted to go too. So as our third months licence was nearly run out, we resolved to sell our digging turnout, and start for home. In two days, we had disposed of everything we had to sell at satisfactory prices, and were on the road for Geelong. The first day we passed through the Black Forest, on the road going from

Fryers Creek at its height when Gill captured the activity there. Today the bush has grown back over the diggings left behind by thousands of fleeting miners.

154

Melbourne to Forrest Creek, where we picked up a 70 lbs bag of sugar; next day we turned to the right and made for the Three Sisters, three hills just visible in Geelong. In four days we reached home. Everything was inside the house, just as we had left it, only covered with a coat of dust.

The next day I took a stroll into the town and could not but notice how deserted and quiet it was, business places were, some of them, busy loading for the diggings, but general work was at a standstill. Coming along Malop Street towards the Union Hotel, who should I see coming out of the hotel but William Gribble. He did not notice me till I spoke; when he turned round and greeted me with all the welcome he knew. "Mundy is that you! I had not the least idea of meeting you, how are you my boy?" shaking hands with a grip of vice. "Come in and have a drink," he insisted, turning back to the Union. "All right," I said, I could see he was three sheets in the wind. He called for a glass of rum and I for ginger beer. "Oh," he said, "take a drop of rum, that's better," but I declined. We sat down in the bar parlour and he told me about his good fortune.

The Geelong water tank in the very early 1850s.

SLOW HAUL
William Howitt reached the Bendigo gold rush via McIvor in a wagon - covering 40 miles in 30 days. Such were the appalling conditions.

"The day we last saw you on Fryer's Creek in the evening, news reached us of a new diggings at Bendigo, so we had everything packed up and were ready to start by daylight. When we reached Bendigo and saw people washing on the creek we camped. Next morning the four of us went in different ways to scrutinise round. We all met again at dinner time and Jack Lincoln, you know Jack Lincoln don't you?" "No." "Well," Jack said, "not far from here I came across half a dozen men working at the top of a little gully running down from the top of a hill. I asked a few questions in a careless sort of way, but none of them gave me any satisfaction." "Look here mates," Jack said, "these men are on gold, let us all four go this afternoon and peg out a claim each, it is only six feet to bottom."

"So that afternoon, each man pegged out his eight feet square and sunk about two feet so as to show the ground was taken possession of. Next day the all four of us bottomed on good gold. Well, Mundy, to cut the story short we each of us collared £400 to our share in six weeks. Some wanted to look out for other claims, but the old woman and me and Ann were bound for Corio (Gribble always called Geelong Corio, its primitive name) so, as I owned the dray we all came down together. I had not been here more than two or three days, when I found out that houses and land were going almost for a song, people wanted to sell to raise the wind to be off for the diggings. A man who knew I had just come from the diggings and had a bit of money, offered me three brick houses in Hope Street, Ashby, they were built together, one was a chemist's shop; the next two rooms, the next four rooms all in splendid order. He offered the lot for £400. I had a talk with the old woman about it and she said offer him £300. Well I could scarcely sleep all night, thinking about it. Take £300 out of £400 there's only one hundred left. And what if all the people all left what good would be the houses? In the morning I told the old woman and Ann about what I had been thinking, but they said the people would all be sure to come back

The other Gribble buildings have been demolished, but the four roomed house survives.

sometime. So I went to the man and offered him £300, and damn me, Mundy if he did not snap the £300 there and then.

Of course I got it all fixed up properly with Gregory, the lawyer, and everything about the title made straight; but come along let us go home; won't they be glad to see you. We will have another drink first, talking has made me dry." "Yes," I said, "but I'm going to pay." "No, no, Mundy," he said, "not if I know it,' not if I know it, you're as welcome as the flowers, you're as

A typical police barracks in the goldfieds is faithfully reproduced here at Sovereign Hill. Note the policeman asleep with his feet poking out from the tent!

The sons of Donald McLarty from
Argyleshire in Scotland. A surprising
number of McLartys came to Australia
in the 1840s and settled in Melbourne
and Geelong.

Alexander was known as 'Sandy' and
both were popular publicans in
Geelong in the mid-1840s through
into the 1850s. They married sisters
Catherine and Anne Walker, Catherine
to Sandy in 1845, and Anne to
Donald in 1849.

Sandy and Catherine had Ivor
McDonald in 1846 but he died when
two months old. They then had Mary
(1848), Donald (1850) and Ann in
(1852).

Donald and Anne had Anne (1850),
Duncan (1851) and Jean (1853) before
Anne became pregnant again in 1859
and had Sarah Jane. Tragically, Anne
died aged 29 while giving birth, and
their baby died in 1860 aged only four
months. Donald remarried to Annie
Smith in 1860.

Equally tragically, Sandy was declared
insane in 1854 and died the same
year. Asylums were a major part of
life in all larger towns and cities in
that era, and people with brain
tumours or other medical conditions
were all sent to those institutions
where they often died.

Catherine was remarried to Hugh
Dodd in 1857.

DICK RUFFINS AND
AUTUMN STREET

Autumn Street was originally known
as Fyansford Road. This is believed to
have been Dick Ruffin's hotel.

welcome as the flowers in May." We started, crossed the dam and up the gully towards Ashby coming to Sandy McLarty's hotel, the bottom of Autumn Street. "Come in here," he said, "I want to see old Sandy"; I strongly objected but he insisted that I had to go. But Sandy did not happen to be in, so we did not see him.

Leaving, we passed into Hope Street, nearly up to Pakington Street, when he stopped me, pointing to some brick houses. "There," he said, "that's 'em." "Well," I returned, "and you bought that lot of houses for £300. If I am any judge they are as cheap as dirt. "Fact," he said, "we live in the four rooms, the shop is let to a chemist for £2 a week, the two rooms are empty."

Walking up to the front door Gribble turned the knob and we passed in. There was another hearty welcome, much shaking of hands, and more enquires as to where Gribble had found me and when I had come down and what luck I had had, than I could answer for a while. And Ann, the little maid of the mountains, seemed to have shot up into a woman. She was dressed so neat and comely, she had on a flowered muslin frock with bell sleeves, white openworked stockings and sandals fastened daintily round her ankles with elastic bands, a small white collar round her neck, a plait of her black hair dexterously arranged, crossed her forehead, she looked, I thought, a little queen.

I stayed till pretty late that night. They were all free and open with me about their affairs. Gribble had a bottle of rum in the house to which he applied frequently. Sometime after tea Gribble wanted Ann to go to Dick Ruffin's in Autumn Street for a quart of half and half. "I know mother would like some." "Indeed, I don't want any," she said, "and unless Mundy would like some, the maid shan't go a step for 'e." I added, I did not want any, and Ann refused to go. A few angry words ensued when Mrs Gribble said: "Look here Mundy, every night nearly, since we came from the diggings, he's gone to bed drunk, if he means to carry on like this, I shall be sorry we ever got that gold." Gribble seemed used up and lay down on the sofa and was soon snoring.

We three, commenting on the change affairs had taken, I casually addressed "Ann Gribble." "That's not my name at all," she said, "I should be sorry if it was." From conversations I had inferred as much before. "No," Mrs Gribble added, "Ann's true name is Ann Gillingham. I'll tell 'e how it was. I have been married twice; my first husband I married in England whose name was William Masters; after being married four or five years and having no children, as my brother Jack had as many or more than he could well provide for, we offered to adopt a little girl about eighteen months old, who is Ann here now; Jack and Betsy were agreeable and so the thing was settled. My maiden name was Gillingham.

In 1847 we emigrated for Port Phillip in the ship Tasmund. After a long and tedious voyage we landed in Geelong, where we were hired by a squatter for twelve months, to go to work on a station. On the station we met Gribble and became intimate. When our time was up, we came back to Geelong. After a time Gribble came here to see us and was a constant visitor. My husband took of fever of which he died. Gribble was uncommonly kind to the maid and me and well, to cut it short I married him. A kinder man there could not be only for the cursed drink, if he is where it is, and starts drinking, he never knows when he has had enough."

When I left that night, they invited me to visit them often, of which invitation, I took the advantage of seeing them at least once a day. This went on for a fortnight, when I began to get fidgety about trying my luck again on the gold diggings. My brother was all on for it too, but father could not be moved a peg, he said he had had enough of the diggings. If he could make a little silver at home, it was enough for him; he would do a bit of carting, get in the cows that were out and sell a little milk, that would keep them right enough.

So John, I and a neighbour, a married man named Hearn, in conjunction with another party, started again for Fryer's Creek. When we arrived there, it seemed as lively as ever, several offshoots were working, and Wattle Flat, where the Creek had widened out, was being sunk upon with the hopes of striking a rich lead in some part. We struck in on the Flat and sunk a hole forty feet, but without success. We sunk several shallow holes with the same result. Robberies and stealing of wash dirt by night were incessant.

No man known to be on gold felt safe in his tent at night. Of course, everyone had firearms. John had a good pistol, I had a large horse pistol, about as long as your arm, an old fashioned thing with a flint lock; sometimes it missed fire. One night it was very windy and the door of the tent being fastened with string blew open. John seeing it open got up to fasten it, just then I woke up and saw a man standing in the doorway. I sprang up, levelled my old gun straight at him and cried out "Who's there?" John faltered out: "It's me." Mercy on us. What a shock I got, for my intention was to fire, if it had been a thief. Talking about it afterwards John remarked: "The old thing mightn't have gone off."

One morning, a little after sunrise, as I was out in the front of the tent frying some chops, there was a great hullabulloo in the flat. "Stop thief, stop thief, stop him, stop him." Our tent was on the hillside commanding a full view of the diggings below, I saw a man running for his bare life, a crowd running after him yelling, "Stop thief, stop thief." Before the fugitive were several tents through which he would have to run the gauntlet, before he could reach the range.

A crowd ran out in front of him and blocked his hasty career, wanting to know what it was all about; leaving the chops alongside the fire John and I ran and joined the mob; surrounded by a ring of diggers, stood a tall, gaunt-looking man of about thirty-five, of dark complexion, with a very black beard, by his broken English I judged him to be a foreigner, probably an Italian. He said: "Why you run after me and stop me when I haven't done a thing?" A bag that he had dropped a hundred yards back before he had been blocked, someone had brought to hand. "Here's the bag," a man sang out, "let's see what's in it." "Yes, yes let us see what's in it," cried many voices. But the man who had started the hue and cry spoke: "Look here mates," he said, "that man's a gold thief, I caught him fossicking in my claim a few nights ago, but he got away. Now look here mates, I just tell ye exactly how it was; it was this way, I had a pretty good claim in the creek below; there I noted several times, some one had been down fossicking by night, so, to be able to watch it better, I shifted my tent as near as convenient to the hole. A few nights ago, I thought I heard an unusual noise, so I got up and looking down the shaft I saw a light and with that I sang out: "What thief is that below there?" Immediately the light went out. There were some tents about a hundred yards away. It was two o'clock as near as could guess. I thought at first of rousing some of the men to catch the thief, then again I thought to myself, by the time I have roused them and get back the man will be gone. I knew he could not escape to any other claim, I shouted out: "You had better come up at once I'll stop here till daylight. If you don't and then if a mob gets to know what's up you'll stand a very poor show to escape with your life."

"After a time I heard him stepping up, as his head reached the surface I struck a match and looked him full in the face. "When landed, I made a rush and grabbed him, trying to put the crooked maginnis on him, but he slewed too quick. We had a tough tussle for it, but in the end, he wriggled out of my clutch and bolted. Going to the butcher's this morning for a bit of meat for breakfast, who should I see there but me nabs, on the same business. I could swear to him at once, both from his features and his voice." "Hullo matey," I said, "we meet again, you are the cove that robbed my claim the other night, I'll swear ti you among a thousand." "Vat, vat, you say, me rob your claim, you big lie, you bad man, me honest man, sell jewelry to digger, you make one big mistake." There were others at the butcher's standing at the time waiting to be served. They said to me: "Are you quite sure?" "Quite positive," I said. "Well then," they replied, "let us seize him." When the fellow saw we were determined to grab him he made tracks and we after him crying out, "Stop thief." He did not go far before he was blocked, and that's him I saw coming out of my claim I'll swear it if I was on my dying bed."

There was silence for a while, when someone spoke. "What are we going to do with him, there are no police near here to give him in charge. " A voice came out of the crowd which unmistakably from its nasal drawl, proclaimed itself to be Yankee: "Do as we do in California, lynch him." There was silence for half a minute, the accused man turned green. Then a man, a noble, earnest-looking fellow he was, enquired: "Where is the man who spoke last." Then a tall, lean-looking fellow stepped forward: "Here I am gov. It was me I reckon, Hiram Jones late of Californy, and California born." The previous speaker said in a quiet earnest way: "Look here, Hiram Jones, late of California, Califor-nian-born, we are law-abiding subjects of the British Queen Victoria. If a man is accused of breaking the laws of the Realm, if caught, he is handed over to proper judicial authorities to have a fair trial, if found guilty he has to suffer the penalty. We have no sympathy with mob law in the Queen's dominions, nor do we,

A rare photograph of the scenes Henry lived through. This photograph of prospectors was taken in the mid-1850s when people were still arriving from all parts of the world to seek their fortune. Many died trying, others gave up and stayed, while others moved on to new fields in Australia and elsewhere.

Hiram Jones, tolerate Californian ruffianism in this land."

To this speech, the majority agreed, but all wanted to know what was in the bag. So the bag was opened. On the top was a small collection of shining Breemidgeham jewellery, in pockets beneath were a chamois leather bag containing about a pound weight of roughly cleaned gold, in another pocket, a thick roll of bank notes, in another a number of watches, gold rings etc. These were all spread out for everyone to see, on the ground. One man identified one of the watches as his. "It had," he said, "been stolen from his tent in the daytime."

The man who had spoken last spoke again. "Appearances," he said, "are against this man, tie him to a tree and let some one go for the police. Who will go?" "I will," said the man's first accuser. "Very good." The accused man protesting his innocence was run up to a sapling, his hands tied together by the wrists on the other side, everything put in its place again into the bag, which was placed beside him. The crowd then dispersed, except a few who were desirous to see the finale. John and I went home to breakfast to find that a thief of a dog had scoffed the chops and licked out the pan. The police arrived shortly after and took the man away prisoner. How he got on, and what was his fate, I never heard a syllable.

We had no success this time at Fryer's Creek. After having been there a month we thought it best to try some other place. We shifted our tents - our mate's Hearn's and our own, to Campbell's Creek, as near as we could get to Forrest Creek diggings. We sunk a very hard hole on Montgomery's Hill. It took us three weeks and turned out a duffer.

There were then great rumours of the rich gullies at Bendigo. John and I resolved to go there. We did not invite our mate to go with us, as he was not much account at his best. So we tied up our swags one morning, leaving what we could not carry with Hearn, and off for Bendigo. We arrived there the second day, passed by the Commissioner's camp, where were stationed some English soldiers, passed Long Gully, California Gully, American Gully - all studded with a row of tents on each side and working in full swing.

Not a shadow of a chance to edge in, as we could see. Then onward to Eagle Hawk gully, the richest run of gold ever found in the world I believe, all from six to eight feet sinking, every one busy, quietly and earnestly working. No chance there. We went farther on to a gully named Peg Leg, so called after the man who opened it, who had a wooden leg. This gully had been recently opened. Several duffers had been sunk in it and some were seemingly on payable dirt, as they were steadily working on, but they all had the same tale to tell. The prospect they had got was very poor, they were piling up a few loads to take to water to wash, to give it a fair trial.

Peg Leg was a bit of a problem, as it was wide. However, we pitched our tent there, bought picks and shovels, tin dish etc. and stuck in at random. The first day we sunk seven feet, next day was Sunday, which we devoted in manufacturing a windlass; we borrowed a saw and chisel off a neighbour and finding a prostrate tree just the size we wanted sawed off a windlass barrel.

The next thing we wanted was a crank naturally grown in one piece. We walked about a long time when we espied a beauty in a lightwood tree, but had to climb to get it, which we trimmed and dovetailed into a projecting end of the windlass, cutting a shouldered groove to about three inches thick, six inches from the handle and the same at the extreme other end, to form the bearings; then two cross legs for it to work on - the windlass was complete. Next morning we took to the claim. I

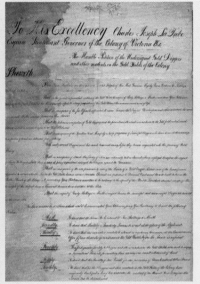

THE GOLDFIELDS PETITION AND JOHN MUNDY

The first formal signs of unrest from gold miners came in 1853 when the Goldfields Petition was sent to La Trobe. It was signed by between 5000 and 6000 - not including the Heathcote signatures which were lost when the Gold Escort was held up and robbed. It is thirteen metres long and bound in green silk. It was rediscovered in the late 1980s after being thought lost, and took over two years to transcribe all of the names. One of the signatories was believed to have been John Mundy.

There were 60,000 gold diggers plus their families in Victoria then, 23,000 of whom were in the Bendigo region.

In June 1853 the Anti-Licence-Gold-Association was formed in Bendigo to give voice to the miners' many grievances including the 30/- per month licence fee. It was presented to La Trobe on August 1, 1853 but mostly ignored, and so the protests continued - culminating in the Eureka Stockade.

Bendigo, here in its earliest days, was one of the richest goldfields in the world and the city today shows the wealth brought to it with some of the grandest buildings and thoroughfares in Australia. Eaglehawk was five miles from Bendigo and also one of the best fields of all.

left John to rig it while I went to buy a rope and bucket and procure a lump of fat to oil the bearings with, to make it go easy and keep the machine from squeaking.

Shift about, we worked like navies, sinking to bottom that night. We were down fourteen feet, as deep, or deeper than any hole near us. We went home in great hopes that night as we were fourteen feet and no signs of bottom, we might be on a golden gutter. We were up and at it early next morning, but others were there before us. The ground above and below us was pegged out for a hundred yards each way. I took the first shift down, sunk two feet but no signs of bottom or gravel wash, only raw coarse sand. John then took a spell below, and after he had sunk six inches sung out I have come to pipe clay. "No gravel?" I asked. "No, only coarse sand." I told him to skim a prospect of the pipe clay and would try it. The crowd heard we had bottomed, crowded round the shaft to know the result. I tried the prospect at a pool near by and only got a few fine specks. "Oh," cried the crowd, watching me pan off, "it's a shicer of the worst kind." It was nearly dinner time. I hauled John up.

Of course, we were disappointed but not disheartened, we went home to cook our dinner. As we were passing along, I happened to go and look down a hole that had been bottomed the day before, I saw a man on the bottom with a knife picking out gold from the side of the shaft, and putting it in a pannikin. He did not see or hear me, his mate had probably gone to the tent to prepare dinner, so there was no one to warn him of strangers being about. Pulling up to John, I told him what I had seen. We then had a look round for the nearest unclaimed ground to the hole I had been looking down both up and down the gully and selecting a spot, securing four sticks pegged out claims for two 16 X 8. While discussing dinner we determined to leave the claim we had bottomed as a duffer and start to sink again that afternoon on the new claim; which we did and sank three feet before night. Others around us, seeing us working, enquired if we had heard or seen anything. "No, we were just sinking on spec, what was the good of shepherding a twelve feet claim."

The dodge of shepherding was this, one man would make out three or four claims and dodge round during the day looking for signs, watching prospects being washed etc. and where they thought was the

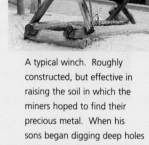

A typical winch. Roughly constructed, but effective in raising the soil in which the miners hoped to find their precious metal. When his sons began digging deep holes rather than looking for alluvial gold, George Mundy turned away from that pursuit and went back to his cows and carrying.

best spot would sink. Shepherding was excusable in one hundred or a hundred and fifty sinking but I could never shepherd a twelve feet hole.

The next day we sunk to seven feet and rigged the windlass. The day after, we bottomed at ten feet and got a very fair prospect in the tin dish, which was considered payable. The next thing to procure was a cradle and puddling tub; the cradle cost us £4/10/- and the tub (half a beer barrel) 30/-, which was very cheap, but we happened to drop on some diggers who were leaving for town.

We did fairly well out of that claim. I

Shepherding holes - if unattended for 24 hours they were legally free to take.

think we cleared about £80 a piece.

Provisions and everything brought from Melbourne, principally by bullock teams, were an enormous price. Carriage was £200 a ton. Teams coming through the Black Forest were often two months on the road. A bag of flour was £25 at the store, sugar 2/6, salt 2/- a pound and everything else in proportion. Butchers meat bought from the surrounding squatters was comparatively cheap, and sold at the butchers stalls, beef 1/6, mutton, hind quarters 8/-, fore quarters 7/-.

After having worked out our claim in Peg Leg, wandering round one day, looking for a likely spot to make another venture, I fell in with William Gribble. "Hullo Mundy," he cried out, "how are you? Had any luck?" After I had told him all particulars. "Well," he said, "you have got a little, but I and my three mates came six weeks ago and have not done a thing." "Who are your mates?" I asked, "do I know them." "Yes, you know three at least, John Charlton, Fred Green and old John Crosby, and another man. Green has been laid up with rheumatics, he's crawling about a bit now but is useless. I think, Mundy, I'll be going home again soon. Charlton is sick of it too."

"Oh," I said, "try on a bit longer there's plenty of chances yet." "I don't know," he replied, "it seems to me, all the good ground is taken up, those who are on it are all right. Eagle Hawk is a very rich gully, if

Sovereign Hill's version of a genuine rough shop built to supply the temporary inhabitants at their diggings. It is easy to see why so many small settlements disappeared as quickly as they were built.

we had only been in time for that." "Where are you camping?" I asked him. "Among a crowd of tents on a rise just at top of Peg Leg." "My brother and I are camped there," I told him, "it is a wonder we had not met before." On locating our camping places we were only about three hundred yards apart, and often after, visited each other. Another fortnight passed, sinking hole after hole averaging from six to fifteen feet.

At the top of Peg Leg where the run of gold started from the surface, the surface had all been taken away to the depth of six inches, underneath was a bed of red, tough clay, about two feet thick, which carried gold but difficult to puddle. A few had been working this clay till water getting scarce, left it. A good downpour had fallen and filled the shallow holes which had been worked out, and left. Having water handy, we pegged out a claim on it. A few others followed our example. We did not get more than ounce a day, which was considered poor enough, but we had our ears and eyes open, watching for any new find or report of a new rush.

In the meantime Gribble and his party broke up, disgusted with their want of success. Three of them decided to go back to Geelong, but John Crosby wished to stay on.

He was a man about sixty-three, but as active and alert as a much younger man, a jolly, goodtempered old chap. We asked him to join us, which he willingly did. Crosby was a broad, Yorkshire man, and the stories he used to tell us in his native dialect, were highly amusing. The three sold what they had, I bought a feather pillow off Gribble, I thought perhaps the little girl I had left in Geelong, who had occupied my thoughts very much since I had left, might have slept on the same pillow. We were obliged to stop puddling the clay for want of water.

We heard a report of a rush at the bottom end of Back Creek, near where it ran into Bendigo Creek, ten feet sinking, the three of us set in there, and bottomed a hole a piece for three days, without any success. So we gave Back Creek a rest and loitered round for a day or two.

One morning as I was lighting a fire to cook breakfast, I saw two men with pick and shovel, crossing over the range. Bye and bye, three more, all bound in the same direction, over which event we consulted together during the meal, and decided to cross the range in the same direction. After we had gone about half a mile; we came to a small gully, almost hidden with whipstick scrub. There were half a dozen holes in working, and each had a little pile of wash dirt piled up. It was evident enough they were on gold. The sinking was on an average twelve feet.

We pegged out each his eight feet square, leaving two feet wall between, as close as we could get to those already bottomed. No questions were asked of the neighbours because we knew it was useless, but we started to work right off, taking shifts about. We bottomed the second day, after carrying over the windlass and fixing things in order. A dishful off the bottom yielded two dwts, which was satisfactory. After taking off the bottom, we sank in the pipeclay and were ready for driving.

The first load of wash dirt we got was carted to the nearest water and old John was appointed to put it through. He came to the tent at night, all smiles, he had over two ounces. That was John's job thenceforth, to wash what my brother and I rose during the day. It suited him better as one of his legs had been broken in his younger days and remained stiff.

BACK CREEK
There were four places known as 'Back Creek' within the goldfields. The Back Creek Henry mentions became Talbot, and it was surrounded by many other nearby gold areas including Amhurst and Mt Greenock where Henry and his family would spend many years.

Old John objected to the thought that he was not able to do his share in the hole. He said: "If I can't do ma shar in t'hole, I'll brussen ma sehn but al'll da the washing if tha loiks." We managed to raise a load every day for him. Somedays he got three ounces, one day he reckoned he brought home four, didn't he chuckle over that. The gully was soon rushed from end to end, and was named Napoleon Gully. After we had been working a week, there happened a digger hunt. I have not described one yet, though I witnessed two in Fryer's Creek.

Old John's job was to haul the dirt from the hole - to which he objected.

Half a dozen police, accompanied by two troopers, all armed, the police carried muskets, bayonet fixed, the troopers rode well-groomed, spirited horses, in their holsters were large deadly horse pistols, they travelled one each side of the gully. They came with their horses from the direction of Peg Leg, driving four or five unlicensed diggers before them, whom they had caught in Peg Leg. The troopers darted one to each side of the gully, to intercept any fugitive who might be making for the ranges, while the police demanded off each one he met: "Show yer licence." All were prepared till they came to our neighbours above us, two Irishmen, and very Irish at that. "Sure sor," one said, "our mate has gone to the camp this marning for licenses for the three 'av us, an he isn't back yet." "Oh that'll do," the police snapped in. "That'll do, you have no licence, fall in," letting the butt of his musket fall with a thud on the ground, and they had to join the other delinquents from Peg Leg. And so it went on, all down the gully.

The hunters returned back with about twenty men driven before them like so many cattle, the diggers savagely hooting the police as they passed, no doubt the spirit that brought on the Eureka Stockade had begun to brew. They passed on to visit Eagle Hawk and other diggings on their way back to the camp and would have a big haul before they arrived there.

Our two neighbours who were driven off did not appear again for a week, in the while the adjoining claims had been encroaching on their ground, one drove nearly up to their shaft. We were not innocent of a bit of gouging; when they went below and saw how they had been encroached upon, they went outrageously mad. I thought someone would be murdered. One fellow, prancing round with a pick whirling in his hand, looked awfully dangerous. I was on top at the time hauling up some dirt. One of the men in the claim above was helping to load a dray, he looked a bit scared, and so did I. "I suppose if I could have seen myself," he said. "Why didn't you get your licence like other men, then you would have been safe." "Licence is it," he roared, "sure we hadn't the means to pay for it, we had been unlucky a long while and as soon as we dropped on a bit of gold the blasted police must come and snatch us away from it, the devil take 'em. We've been locked in the logs while ye, ye damn thieves that ye are, have been gutting our claim out, thieves that ye are, the likes to ye would rob Jesus of his shoe strings." "Now look here," I said, "if it had not been for me and my mate, and that man and his mate, and others, your claim would have been jumped two or three times, because we told them how it was." "Jumped, how the devil cud it be jumped, when our tools are below, an the rope an' the windlass in the hole." The man loading the dray spoke again, and said: "You know yourself, it's a common dodge, if people have more payable holes than they can work at once, is to leave a windlass and rope on the hole to hold it for the time; besides tools cannot hold a claim without some one to use them. I'll tell you what it is , you're jolly lucky your claim wasn't jumped. If it had been, you'd have lost that big pile of wash dirt too, you could not have claimed it, as in getting it, you had no licence." The two men scowled ominously, but said no more.

After working our new claim a couple of weeks, we began to accumulate a little lump of gold, first one carried it and the other, during the day; gold is a disagreeable thing to carry in your pocket, even a few ounces owing to its lumpy dragging weight; we were at our wits end to know how to keep it. Thieves were ever on the alert, watching those who were known to be on golden claims.

I thought Fryer's Creek was bad enough, but Bendigo at that time beat it hollow. Rumours of robberies, murders, and missing men were heard of every day. The police force was totally inadequate to protect the many thousands spread over hill and dale. The police never left the camp, except they were fetched or on a diggers hunt, or to parade with the Gold Commissioner, when he was called upon to settle disputes about claims. A few English soldiers were stationed at the camp, who kept sentry over the safe or stronghold, where diggers lodged their gold for escort to the Treasury in Melbourne; thieves were prowling about at all hours of day or night, and the protection inside was a wall of calico. It was a nerve straining problem. Everyone slept with a loaded gun or pistol by his side.

As to our gold, being tired of carrying it about, we concluded to put it in a pickle jar and bury it in the ground, beneath one of the bunks. Our tent was still at Peg Leg, as we thought it was the safest place, the distance to work was only half a mile. One Sunday as we were all sitting in the tent, I was trying to torture a tune out of an accordion which I had recently purchased for £6, a man stepped to the door and said: "Ah, you have got an accordion, and a nice tone it has too, having a tune eh?" "Oh," I said, "I can't play, I'm only trying." At that, without any ceremony he stepped into the tent and sat himself on the bunk saying: "Let me have a try." He played several tunes very nicely.

He was smartly dressed, his delicate hands I could see were not used to handling the pick and shovel; and he had a clean shaven face, another indication of a thief. After he had gone, old John said: "Na, luik ye here lads , if yons na a spying thief I'm mistaken, did na ye see how he turned aboot his cen, while he war playing; we'll hae to look out o' neets arter this." John and I laughed it off, remarking; "If he did enter the tent by night, he would get what he did not come for." Two nights passed and nothing happened, on the third night, something waked me, I had no idea what it was, but when one's nerves are on the stretch, a small thing will wake him. After, I lay very much awake, listening with all the ears I had. I felt the tent shake, but heard nothing. My brother's bunk was on one side and mine on the other and old John's was across the end. Without doubt, I heard some one quietly moving near old John's bed. I put out my hand and gave it a wide swoop round and came in contact with a man's hand picking up my old pistol; crying out: "There's a thief in the tent, if you stir I'll shoot you." Old John sang out: "It's me, it's me, I was just feeling fort'gun, yes I know there's some one prowling about for I felt the tent shake as if some "yan" had got against the strings, 'ah, ony wish I could get a seet on him I'd gie him the contents o' ma gun." The dogs were barking all round; but that was nothing unusual, they scarcely ever ceased barking by night.

We had a good laugh over our scare in the morning. I remarked they're not likely to trouble us again as they found us so watchful. Old John shook his head, and said: "Ah dinna know. Ah dinna know lad, they know we've got gold in the tent and happen come some neet and cut our throats, who knows, we canna always be watching." My brother remarked: "That's not a pleasant prospect to go to sleep on."

We were getting well on with our claim, another week would finish it. Nothing very particular happened after, except an encroaching dispute to settle, which the Commissioner and his police were called. A great mob, as usual, surrounded the Commissioner, to hear and see what was going on. The case took over an hour; after the departure of the Commissioners, the crowd dispersed and some of the diggers declared they had been robbed, their pockets had been picked in the crowd. It was afterwards reported that the Commissioner's own pocket had been ransacked, whether this be true or not, there was little doubt of the digger's grievances being true, the way they carried on.

A trifling incident happened to us which is hardly worth recording yet to illustrate the state of the times I will mention it. In cooking the meals we took turns week about. It was my week, and I was cooking Sunday's dinner at a fire twenty yards or so from the front of the tent. I was boiling a leg of mutton; going from the tent at intervals to watch how it was progressing. The last time I went to look, the boiler was there but the leg of mutton was gone; I called to the tent and told them what had occurred. John ran one way and I another along the row of tents. I enquired as I went if anyone had seen a man passing carrying a leg of mutton? "Yes," one man said, "A man passed a minute ago, carrying a leg of mutton by the shank, look there he is now just see, going over the rise." I ran after him, soon caught up to him, snatching the mutton out of his hand. I said: "You mean, lousy thief, would you steal a man's dinner out of the pot while it was cooking." "Oh, oh I found it just back there," he stammered. I saw the fellow was the worse for drink, it was useless to say much. Some diggers standing near enquired what was up, I told them. There was a general laugh.

We finished our claim at last. The last load Old John washed only went half an ounce, so we left it at that, it was not good enough.

We borrowed scales and a magnet from the storekeeper we dealt with; cleaned our gold and divided it into three parts, something over thirty ounces each, took it to the camp and booked it for escort to the Melbourne Treasury.

The Post Office was at the camp, so as we had not enquired before in Bendigo for a letter, neither

THE ORIGINAL TREASURY
The first Gold Escort arrives at the Treasury in William Street, Melbourne. Gold brought from the Victorian goldfields was originally stored in various bank vaults around the city. Yet as the finds flourished and quantities increased, there was little available room to keep it securely. The first Treasury was constructed under the orders of Governor La Trobe. From 1851 gold was deposited at this building.

LIFE WAS CHEAP
So many people died, particularly babies and small children, that it was considered human tragedies were 'two a penny'.

The gold escort coming through the Black Forest heading to Melbourne.

of us, we wished to know if by chance there might be one. Enquiring for a letter was a tedious business. A long line of saplings extending for a hundred yards supported on forked posts led to the Post Office. Applicants for letters had to pass down this fence in order as they arrived. The last comer had to go to the far end. After waiting two hours we had the satisfaction of knowing there was nothing for us.

Passing back home through Eagle Hawk we saw a crowd collected. Wanting to see what was the cause, pushing through the crowd we saw the body of a man lying on the ground, who had just been extricated from a fall of earth. He was dead. A little farther on in front of a shanty were two men stripped to the buff fighting like two demons and a mob in various stages of intoxication enjoying the fun and encouraging them on. The fighters seemed to have no regard to time, but slogged away till they became exhausted. Ultimately one dropped down and said: "Look here Bill, I give you best, shake hands." But Bill was not much of a second-best as it seemed to me.

Arriving home, we felt as if we had left a great trouble behind, our gold was safe. The next thing to do was to look for another patch. We sunk a few shallow holes without any success. In our travels round we noticed for the first time grog-hawkers going round among the diggers at work, carrying tea kettles with a pannikin slung on the spout, singing out, jump-up, jump-up, the kettle contained grog which was doled out at 2/- an egg cup. Old John and my brother, on one occasion, took a drink of jump-up. John declared it was so hot it nearly choked him, which was pretty evident by the way he gasped. Old John said it "burnt his wizzen dahn to't seet."

One day a fearful thing happened at the head of Peg Leg. Whereas I have mentioned we worked the red clay till, for want of water, we had to stop. After a heavy rainfall, others took up the clay puddling and to prevent their sludge from running into other diggers workings, they were compelled to dam it to five or six feet high, a young man below the embankment was throwing up more dirt to raise it a little to prevent the slum from trickling over, when two feet of the top of the dam burst upon him. It left him over his knees in the slime; he made haste to run out of it as quickly as he could, but he could not move his feet, the suction under his boots held him fast.

There were plenty there to help him, if possible, but no one under the circumstances would venture to walk in. The whole embankment was seen to be moving. Someone suggested a rope: "We'll pull him out." A feasible plan. A rope was sought for, off the nearest windlass, but before it was secured, the whole bank collapsed, and smothered the poor fellow over with the horrid sludge. In an hour he was dragged out with a rope - dead. I was not an eye witness to this sad catastrophe, and glad I was not; our tent being near the spot, we heard all about it when we came home in the evening.

Reports were rife of three new discoveries of gold, one was the Whipstick, but no one seemed to know where it was, several went out in search but came back disappointed. Another report about a new diggings called Mount Hope, numbers set out in search of it, but came back as they went - could not find it and gave it the name of Mount Hoax.

Whipstick, I believe turned out a reality, but as far as I ever learned Mount Hope was altogether illusionary. The other rush, Daisy Hill, was substantial enough; stated to be forty miles from Ballarat and seventy miles from Bendigo.

We resolved to go to Daisy Hill. No sooner was it resolved, than it was to act. We disposed of our digger's appliances, with the exception of a pick, shovel and tin dish to a Johnny Allsorts, and asked a carter what he would take us to Daisy Hill for; he said £60. "Saxty pund" old John cried out in indignation. "Saxty pund, why mun, there's ony oor three swags and t'tent we cud carry it a for the matter o't." "Carry it then," the man said, "I'll not go for less. Another thing I don't know the road well enough."

So there was nothing for it but shank's pony, as other carters we asked would have nothing to do with it. Next morning we tied up our swags, and swags they were too, without a doubt, for weight; I had the tent, some books, my blankets and the feather pillow, John had his blankets, a pick and shovel, some tucker, tea and sugar, etc. Old John had, besides a pretty heavy swag of his own, a tin

Water was the most important and valuable asset in the diggers' efforts to find their gold. It was also very difficult to procure.

Today the entire 'Golden Triangle' area, which makes up the old goldfields from Ballarat to Bendigo and beyond, is hauntingly littered with the ruins of boom-time constructions and gaping holes.

Old Eaglehawk still has all the hallmarks of an old gold town.

dish, a billy and three pannikins tied behind, so that he rattled as he went.

One great grievance troubled us, we were leaving a large lump of damper behind, which was hard to accommodate in any of our swags. Before leaving Old John said: "Looks tha here lads, ah na gahn talief that good damper a hind, I'll carry it mesehn, unter ma airm." With that he picked up the damper and putting it under his arm, we marched, took the way of Eagle Hawk through Long Gully, California Gully and American Gully by the Warden's camp and on to Porcupine Creek.

We travelled on till about midday, when we came to some large round granite rocks; the day was warm, and we had lost a considerable amount of perspiration; coming to a larger rock than usual, I dumped down my swag on the rock and said: "Let us have a spell here and some dinner. I'm as hungry as if I hadn't any breakfast or supper last night." Which proposition was unanimously agreed to. The billy boiled and tea made, I said to Old John; "Now we're going to lighten your load of half of your damper." "Aye, aye lads," he said, "pitch in, tha art welcome to the whole o't." During the boiling of the billy, I had unfolded the tent to dry in the sun, as it was wet with dew when I rolled it up. We all three felt that we were heavily loaded, I was the worst off as I had the tent ten by twelve to carry, besides I had several books and I made up my mind to leave some of them behind. I looked them over. Some were dear old friends. I could not find it in my heart to part with them. I had a volume of nearly all Shakespeare's works weighing seven or eight pounds which I resolved to sacrifice. So when we left I laid it on the granite boulder for someone to pick up. Old John declared his load was lighter, but steadily refused to leave the remaining part of the damper behind him.

We travelled on that afternoon till nearly sundown and coming to some water we concluded to camp for the night. We slung our tent between two trees, spread out our blankets after supper on the grass and slept the sleep of the just.

The early morning found us on the tramp again. We made a good stage that day; stopping only to get a dry snack about noon, as we could find no water to make tea. Towards evening, we came to plains with only a clump of trees here and there, crossing a creek and coming to a patch of timber, we concluded to camp for the night. As I was unloading my swag and happening to look over the creek we had passed I saw a big wild turkey behind some rocks. After pointing it out to my mates, I said to Old John: "Lend me your gun John, I'll have a shot at that fellow." "Aw reet," he said, "pit anither charge o' shot in her an tap o' the ain that's in and happen she might get some o't; I'owd gun scatters sae." Doing as I was told, I crossed the creek where I was unseen by the turkey, and peering over the rocks I saw the bird within shot, picking round, unconscious of danger. I waited till I could get a broadsider, and taking a steady careful aim, let fly. I did not know where I was for a few seconds, one thing was sure, I was lying on the broad of my back and my right shoulder felt out of joint; ruminating a bit, I sat up, looked at the old carbine to see if it was entire, it was all right, then looking to where the turkey had been, I could not see a sign of it, probably the noise had frightened it away. But getting on to my feet I discerned a heap of brown feathers lying motionless. I walked up and found the turkey was dead, not a kick left in it, just one shot had passed through its head. Proud I was, carrying back the large bird, it was a fat one too. The two John's were surprised at my luck. Old John commenced to pluck it and my brother made up a roasting fire and fixed a frame to lay it on to roast. So we had turkey that night, for a rather late supper.

Old John suggested as tomorrow was Sunday, with such a plentiful supply of meat we should rest there on the morrow and to start again early on Monday morning, which was agreed to. We took it out Sunday morning, we did not stir till ten o'clock according to Old John's watch, which he assured us had been owned by his grandfather. Damper and cold turkey for breakfast, washed down with strong tea. During the day old John told us some very stiff stories of his escapades in Yorkshire. According to his own accounts he had been a bit of a bad boy in his time. His wife and he could not hit it very well, so he hired as a servant to a gentleman coming to Australia, leaving wife and family behind.

We were uncertain as to our whereabouts on our track to Daisy Hill, we had passed to the right of Forrest Creek and were making considerably to the right of Ballarat, as we supposed. There was no track or road to guide us, and, going through the country only guided by the sun and not knowing the

One of the most difficult jobs was securing valuables in huts.

point of our destination, we were a bit puzzled. We had only met a very few and none of them had ever heard of Daisy Hill.

In the afternoon a man rode up to us asking if we had seen any stray cattle about there? No we had not. "On the tramp?" he enquired. "Yes," we told him, we were bound for Daisy Hill and asked him if he could direct us, and put us on the direction. "Daisy Hill, Daisy Hill," he pondered, "I never heard the name before." "It is a name of a new gold diggings," we told him. "Ah, that accounts for it," he said, "that will be the name given to the new diggings, no I cannot direct you mates." With that he rode off.

Wandering about the country with our heavy swags, without being sure of where we were, was disheartening; when Old John with a roll of his wise old head opened his mouth and said: "Look hyar lads, its brussening wark humping these heavy swags arand t'country wid aht knowing T'road, Ballarat can na be far frae here, let's turn to t'left and make forlt; when we get to Ballarat, twill be easy to learn road or happen can hire a dray." "Good on you John" we said, "we'll start for Ballarat in the morning." So it was agreed on. After a turkey supper, a good sleep and picking the turkey's bones for breakfast we rolled up our dunnage, and started to look for Ballarat. We had not gone far when we struck a beaten track, which we followed for five or six miles when a man on horseback caught up to us. We enquired of him if we were going right for Ballarat. "Well nearly," he said, "this track will meet the road, it goes within two miles of Ballarat, when you will be sure to see people about, to enquire of. Ballarat is about fifteen miles from here straight.

We asked him if he knew where Daisy Hill was, he said he had heard of a new rush to a place of that name but could not direct us where to find it. Coming to some water, we boiled the billy and had our dinner. We came in sight, or rather sound of Ballarat after it was dark; it was too late to go in that night, so we made a fire and rigged the tent roughly; not knowing where to find water, we ate our supper dry, spread out our blankets and were soon asleep.

I had a good sound sleep, but whether from the dry supper I had had, or anxiety, I cannot say, but I awoke long before day and, like the Yankee, got a-thinking. My thoughts reverted to that little maid in Geelong, wondering if since I had been away she had seen anyone she liked better than me, this thought gave me an irrepressible anxiety to see her again. Here was I only sixty miles from her, and thinking of going farther, why could not I go to see her now. My mind was full of uncertainty and dread of something I could not tell what. I did not feel as if I had pluck enough to go straight to her before I had ascertained how things lay.

About day break I heard Old John moving. "Getting up John?" I asked him. "Yes lad," he said, "ma hugging bones ak frae liggin." My brother awoke then, and the three of us rose and commenced to put swags together and make for Ballarat. We went to a store not far from the Commissioner's Camp, bought some baker's bread and tinned salmon, went to a fire burning, boiled the billy and discussed over breakfast. We made enquires about Daisy Hill, but could not get any very satisfactory information about it, only that a good many had gone there, and that it was forty miles away towards the Pyrenees.

Old John, my brother and I, in a halfhearted way enquired if there were any chance of getting a lift there but without any satisfaction. At last I said: "I am sick of this Daisy Hill, let us sell the tent etc. and go home for a while and have a rest. You two must be tired of the heavy swags you are carrying. I'll not carry this confounded tent any farther, my ankles are giving way" (which was true). I do not think any proposition could be more heartily seconded; it was agreed to unanimously. So we disposed of the tent, pick, shovel, tin dish etc. and made ready for departure, only stipulating with the purchaser of our tent to have the use of what we required for one night more.

I told my brother and Old John, instead of going to Geelong I was intending to travel on foot to Melbourne and go to Geelong after. They could not see through that, but strongly tried to persuade me to go with them, as empty drays were going back to Geelong, we could get a ride cheap; whereas to Melbourne there was not even a track to Ballarat; but I must have my own way.

"Well then," Old John said, "if yuh gae t'Melbourne gae to t'Devonshire Arm's i' Newtown and we'll meet tha this day week and we can tak oot ahr gowd frae the Treasury the gether." So it was agreed.

Bendigo later became a company town when the alluvial gold all but dried up.

When it came time to leave, miners nearly always sold their equipment rather than carry it. An impromtu auction was a source of amusement as well as profit.

Typical accommodation used by miners is recreated at Sovereign Hill.

Henry walked from Ballarat to Melbourne through country which had no tracks and crossed through these hills onto the flat plains beyond Geelong.

FINDING GOLD AND LOVE...

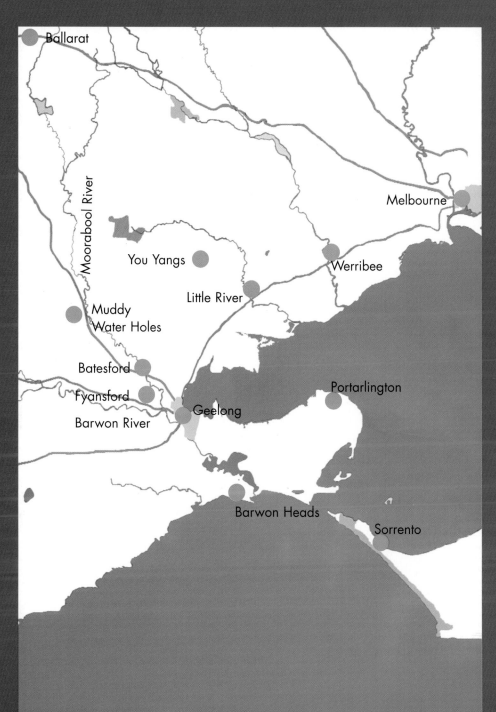

Ballarat

Moorabool River

You Yangs

Little River

Muddy
Water Holes

Melbourne

Werribee

Batesford

Fyansford

Barwon River

Geelong

Portarlington

Barwon Heads

Sorrento

HENRY'S DESTINATIONS

All of these areas are just a few that were familiar to Henry as a young man. To sell the group's gold, which had been sent ahead to Melbourne, Henry, John and Old John walked south to Ballarat from as far north as Bendigo. The others returned to Geelong, while Henry walked from Ballarat, across land to near Little River, then on to Melbourne across the dry plains.

'THE SWAMP'

The swamp area which Henry describes and which once was so obvious in what became New Footscray and Dynon Roads, was used as a domestic and industrial waste rubbish dump in the 1950s and 60s and is now almost completely built over with factories. The Yarra River was also widened and straightened by Lennox in 1847, but the area which is now occupied by Victoria Dock was once a different place.

George McCrae wrote of the area as it was in 1841: It was: "One of the chief beauty spots of Melbourne. It was a real lake, intensely blue, nearly oval and full of the cleanest water. Numerous waterfowl waded in its waters, and the air was heavy with the mingled odours of the golden myrnong flowers and purple fringed lillies."

However, to allow for ships over 200 tons to enter Melbourne and be cleared through Customs House in Flinders Street, rocks and mudbanks were all removed.

The old hotel near the banks of the Salt Water River is believed to have been built by the operator of the punt.

morning I started off and left them. I had a good idea of the direction for Melbourne. My swag seemed like a feather, to what it had been, I reached a sheep station on the Moorabool that night, where they were shearing. I was made welcome there and stayed all night. After breakfast I was on the track again. About noon I saw the You Yangs, a long way to the right. It was all plains now, and just before sundown I crossed the Werribee, taking a drink as I passed.

When I had mounted the bank on the other side, the sun was just disappearing. Undoing my swag, I spread out my blankets, rolled myself in them, the night was warm, I slept without once waking till the dawn. As soon as I could well see, I tied up my swag and was off again.

After a couple of hours travelling I struck the Geelong to Melbourne road, when I had traversed my way along a bit, I came across an old camp site where someone had discarded a piece of biscuit, it looked like someone had been striking matches, I snatched this up and after scraping off the sulphur, greedily ate it. I had had no dinner or supper yesterday, no breakfast that morning nor any prospect of a dinner that day, as yet. By the Lord though, I was hungry. I had money in my pocket and £30 sewn in the lining of my cap, and starving. I thought what a wretched place the world was to live in, if one happens to be in the wrong place, and those endless wearisome plains; every mile you travel, is like the one left behind.

At last the old public house on the Salt Water River came in sight, the same old inn we passed eight years ago with the bullock teams when we were going to Muston's Creek. I anticipated the meal of chops or steak I was going to put away; one thought gave me a bit of a shock, it was late in the day, maybe dinner was all over and I would have to wait for supper. Well I might get a snack of some kind, till supper was ready.

As I neared the house it appeared to have a dismal and uninviting appearance. No one was to be seen, not even a dog; there were neither doors nor windows in it, the house was a desolation and a wreck, empty. A little farther was the punt and the puntman who told me the house had been closed for years.

I then enquired of him how far it was to Newtown and the Devonshire Arms. About a couple of miles, he told me, across the swamp, pointing with his finger towards some buildings. I was in no humour to have a talk with the man, but started in the direction shown, over a dry, black-clay, crabholey swamp. I soon arrived at the Devonshire Arms. The first thing I asked for was a glass of wine, the first wine I had tasted since long before I left England, when I stole a pint bottle of Parson Winter's port.

There were two hours to wait for supper, no meals at all hours then, so I took a stroll outside, where I met Peter McVicar. I spoke to him, calling him by name, he did not recognise me. I asked him if he did not remember the boy Mundy, who got burnt in a bush fire at Muston's Creek, and you were his doctor. "Eh laddie," he said, "is that yersel, I wadna hae kenned frae Adam, ye hae aae grown, wahrare ye gaun the noo." "I am just come from Bendigo," I told, "and am now going to Geelong - to father and mother, who have been living there these three years ." "Did ye hae any luck at Bendigo?" he asked. "Oh," I said, "we got a little gold, but nothing to boast about." He told me he had settled on a piece of land at Port Fairy, he had been at Ballarat and Forrest Creek but "hadna dane muckle," he

The tiny historic Devonshire Arms remains very much 'as was' in Fitzroy - or 'Newtown'.

was on his way home now and thought he would stay there. For some reason or other I did not see Peter again.

A bullock bell rattled at six o'clock and the cry was supper. Oh, a motley crowd rushed into the dining room, jostling each other for seats. I managed to get a seat myself, but there was not room for all; others had to wait. It was Irish stew, potatoes, bread and butter and green stuff. When I had put away a pretty good feed, rose from the table with others, to make room for those who were waiting. The Devonshire Arms was two or three miles from Melbourne proper, but owing to the number of new arrivals, accommodation was not to be had in the City, so that every house of accommodation in all the townships for miles round to their extremity and beyond were busy. A rough meal was 2/6 and a bed, of the best they could give you, the same. My bed in a large barn of a room was upstairs, stretchers arranged head to foot, close to the wall, and a double row down the centre. I slept soundly for a while, but whether from the hearty supper I had made, or something I could not say, I lay awake some time, when the occupant of the next stretcher got up and lit a stump of candle which he held to the wall exclaiming: "Good heavens, look at that, thousands and millions." I lifted my head and said: "What's up mate?" "Oh," he said, "look at the bugs." I looked, and truly it was a sight, enough to make one feel creepy all over. I jumped out of bed and drew my stretcher from the wall, he did the same. "Did ever you see the like." We took our blankets off and shook them, the bugs were all over the floor. "I wish it was morning," the young man said, "I shan't sleep another wink after this, I'm itching all over." The stump of candle collapsed, and we had to turn in again.

In bed we began talking about the diggings. He told me he had just left Ballarat and had done fairly well, he was now going home to Adelaide by the boat in the morning. After some further talk he asked: "What part of England did you come from?" "Buckinghamshire." "Why that's where I come from," he said, "What part?" "Bow Brickhill," I answered. He started up. "What, where the church stands on a hill?" "Yes." "You will know Fenny Stratford and Simpson then?" "I know them both very well indeed," I said, "I went to school at Simpson to a master with one leg named Dick Bodily." "Good gracious," he exclaimed, "I went there too. "What's yer name?" "Mundy," I told him, "Yes, by jove," he said, "You are Jack Mundy then?" "No," I replied, "that's my brother, he went to that school after I left and what is your name?" "My name," he said, "Poole, Tom Poole, my father kept the lock and canal between Fenny and Simpson." "I know the locks and the name too," I said, "I have often stopped on the tow path, to watch the boats pass through. Tom Poole, yes, I often heard John talk about you." "I should not wonder. Jack and I were great chums, where is he now?" "He will be here in four days time if you could wait." "I can't," he said, "I must be off on tomorrow's boat." "I really would like to ..." "Stash that Jabber," someone growled out, from the centre beds, "and let honest people sleep, if ye can't sleep yourselves." "All right," Tom said to me, "we'd better not talk more now, we'll have a further talk in the morning."

We rose some time before breakfast and had a long pitch. After breakfast Tom tied up his swag, and squaring with the landlord, made ready to go, inviting me to have a drink with him before leaving I took a glass of ginger beer, he took the same. We shook hands, hoping to

DEVONSHIRE ARMS
The Devonshire Arms is the oldest surviving hotel in Melbourne. Only eight pre-1851 buildings survive in Melbourne. The Devonshire Arms was built in 1843 and licensed to Joseph Cowell Passmore.

meet again, but we never did.

That was Saturday. I had thought of going into the City but thought again, a rest would be better. I had four days before me before my brother would come. On Sunday I was told there was not so much to be seen, however, I made up my mind to go after dinner.

We sat down to our Sunday's dinner in a quietly, good-humoured manner. Some did not answer the bullock bell, who were quietly sleeping on their bunks or on the green grass around the hotel, having imbibed over much. Things went on quietly and orderly for a short time, when one at the table made a deprecatory remark about the food and the way it was served out, when the waiter took it up, telling the complainant he would either eat that or none, if he did not like it, he could leave the table. When the dissatisfied man said something to the waiter in return, whereupon the waiter sprang forward and dealing him a "schlogging" blow with his fist on the face, knocking him backwards off his seat, upsetting the seat and two or three with him. The struck man scrambled up and made straight for the waiter. There was a fight there and then. The landlord hearing the fracas, came in roaring out: "If you want to fight, go outside you're not going to fight in my dining room."

Everyone sprang up from their dinner, some saying: "Yes, yes, landlord, that's right, let them go outside and have it out, the cur, to stand behind a man's back and strike him sitting eating his dinner, you miserable cur." All marched outside leaving their meal. Nothing is so pleasing to a digger as a fight. The abused man had a mate there, whom he chose as his second. There was sometime before the waiter could get a second, at last a man of the hotel volunteered. Two sponges and two bottles of water were brought and the fight began.

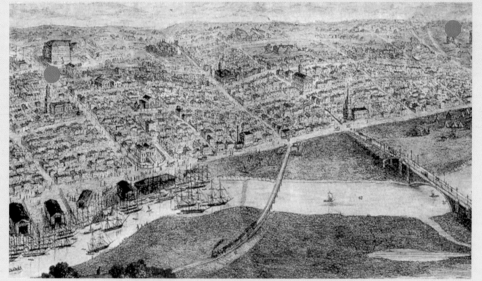

Melbourne in the mid-1850s with the new steam train running though what was Canvas Town. The train bridge is now known as the Queen Street Bridge and the other is Princes Bridge. The dot on the right marks the spot where the Devonshire Arms stands. The one on the left is the area of the Treasury where Henry, his brother and John Crossley picked up their gold for sale in the city.

The waiter, an ex-convict had the best science, his opponent a little heavier man understood little of pugilism, attempted some fierce swinging blows but they mostly landed in air, but at length he got a twister in, right on the nose. "That's a guid ane Jim, that tickled his smelter, ah know Jim." Jim, every one now had got his name and began to barrack. "Jim, give him one in the lug," "Jim, thump the devil," "Jim, give the rotter back that smack on the shonk," "Do na brussen yer sehn." Urged on by his seconder, Jim received one or two under the jaw. He was a plucky one and being so much encouraged by the crowd, held on bravely. The waiter receiving nothing but hisses and groans seemed to collapse and get stupid, when Jim gave him a swinger on the left eye that settled the business; the waiter caved in amid the jeers and taunts of the crowd. Jim was the hero, for the time being. He had fought for the cause of freedom and won. Some one expostulated with the landlord for keeping such a waiter; he answered: "What can I do, if I sack him, I cannot get another, I am sorry to tell you boys, I cannot help myself."

The conversation dwelt for some time on the late fight, some told stories of the rare fights they had witnessed on the diggings till the assembled gradually dispersed. I still had thoughts of going into the city, but did not relish the walk much. There did not happen to be a cab or omnibus in sight, so I postponed it till the morrow. There were no trams nor even railways in those days.

About four o'clock, a strange procession hove in sight, coming from the city - six open carriages, each drawn by two splendid horses; the bridles profusely ornamented with rosettes and flowing ribbons of all colours, likewise the other harness and the carriages were decorated with ribbons which streamed in the wind as they came along at a rattling pace towards the Devonshire Arms. "A digger's wedding, by jove," someone called out, "and coming here. Now mates we'll see some fun."

They drove up to the hotel in brilliant style, there were six carriages and every one accommodated five persons. In the front carriage were the bridesmaid and best man with the driver. In each of the other carriages were the driver and two couples. The bridegroom and the bride in the first carriage were lolling in aristocratic ease in the back seat. As they drove up, the bridegroom rose up and said: "Landlord, I believe?" who was standing ready to receive the company. "Yes," the landlord said, "and

The corner of Bourke and Spring Streets, Melbourne in the early 1850s. The 'Old White Hart' is now the famous Windsor Hotel.

very much at your service." "That's all right, the bridegroom answered, "this is my wedding day and I am giving my friends here, behind, a bit of a treat, by driving them round for a bit of fresh air like." "Just so, just so," joined in Boniface. "This," continued the bridegroom, "is my bonnie little wife, the best girl in all God's world - barring none." At that the imperial goddess lifted her white veil and smiled, whereupon the bridegroom gave her a resounding kiss. "Oh, Jim," she said, "don't be after making an ass of yerself." "Now landlord," Jim said, "these with me are all my friends, I have invited them out to get a little fresh air and amusement. We came here to have a wet, I wish everyone to name his own drink even if it is champagne, and I'm the man to stand, Sam." The landlady was standing behind her spouse when they both said: "Certainly, of course, of course. Tell all your friends to alight, and come into the parlour; the drivers perhaps cannot leave their horses, we'll attend to them, and to you all, to the best of our humble ability." At that Jim stepped down and handed out his precious bride; the landlady kissed her rapturously. Both landlord and landlady wishing them all the good things and happiness the earth could give them. The landlady took possession of Mrs Jim, while Jim and the landlord went to all the other carriages, inviting all to a wet; some were wet enough already, not excepting the ladies for one would have turned a somersault if it had not been for the timely assistance of her attentive swain.

Amid the jocularity and noisy laughter, the host and hostess conducted the new arrivals into the rough, but spacious parlour and with two assistants began to supply orders. Jim sang out: "Now mates, don't be backwards, order your drinks, it is not every day we kill a pig, nor does a man get married every day. I feel very happy myself, and it is my sincerest wish that all my friends should be happy too." After this short speech Jim sat down alongside of his girl on the best sofa, when someone proposed drinking to the health of the bride and bridegroom which was received with vociferous cheers. The fun grew fast and furious; what with the laughing and screeching of the women and the loud talking of the men the situation became uproarious, a pandemonium. One got up to make a speech to congratulate the bride and bridegroom on the happy occasion, but it was no use, he could not be heard. After half an hour of this riot Jim got on his feet, held up his hand when sudden silence prevailed. "Look here, mates," he said, "let's have one more glass round, and then skedaddle. The wedding dinner (pulling out a gold watch) will be ready for us in an hour's time and our friends at home will be expecting us, and it'll make a mess of things if we cause the dinner to be spoiled." Chorus - "Hear,- hear,- hear, another glass and we make tracks sharp." A few minutes after the drinks had been discussed, Jim roared out: "All aboard."

The ladies hurried to the large pier glass, to put in order, in some cases, their much dishevelled hair and put straight their little bonnets, perhaps very much awry. The men marched out, though some of them not very straight and waited at their respective carriages for their lady-loves, who mostly walked demurely up to their waiting lovers. They all boarded without mishap, though a little trouble was experienced in getting on deck, the lady who nearly turned topsy turvy on alighting. Her gentle lover met her, she took his arm and walked up to her carriage. He put her foot on the step, lifted her and pushed her all he knew, but her foot slipped. He tried twice more with the same result; she was too limp to handle. A man standing by said: "Look tha here mate, gets thee up into t'wagan and tak baith her hands, and ah'll put her feet on t'step and give her a shove." And that's the way the difficulty was got

STREETS FORMED
As mentioned by Henry, the first Melbourne streets were formed and metalled in 1843/44 which provided some drainage. Small bridges were necessary to cross the roads without stepping into the deep gutters, but the paths were described as looking like porridge.
In 1844 Alexander Sutherland was paid £413 by the council to build a large timber drain down Elizabeth Street to try to prevent flooding.

171

over. With vociferous hurrahs, waving of handkerchiefs, laughing and screeching of the ladies, they started citywards, singing: "He's a jolly good fellow, which nobody can deny."

It is customary to take note of the dresses worn by the bride, bridesmaid and other guests. The above wedding was celebrated fifty-nine years ago, in the latter end of 1852. I will try as far as my memory serves me, to describe the get-up on the occasion of both sexes. Mrs Jim was decked out in the most costly garments. White silk gown, trimmed with many tucks, bordered with broad white lace. A long train, tight sleeves all much laced. Her dainty little head hung round with short curls, surmounted with what the ladies called, a duck of a little white bonnet, profusely covered with orange blossoms. On her hands, or rather one hand, was a white silk glove, the other was ungloved, to show how many rings she wore, holding the glove. Her little feet were finished with silk flowered stockings, encased in white silk sandals, fastened with elastic bands. She had long pendant ear drops in her ears. A gold watch - guard hung round her neck, to which was attached a tiny gold watch. The bridesmaid was similarly got up. Bye-the-bye, I had almost forgotten the gossamer shawls and veils, which enveloped the two goddesses. The dresses of the other ladies were also rich and rare, but varied as to colours. Streaming, long, wide ribbons loud and conspicuous, especially on their bonnets (hats had not come into fashion among the ladies in those days), all wore ear-rings or drops. Their hair was dressed in various fashions, some had it fastened in nets, all wore costly shawls and either gold or silver watches with guard around their necks, and as many gold rings on their fingers as they could muster.

The dress of the bridegroom, Jim, approached the aristocratic, with a few exception. He wore a swallow-tailed coat which he designated as his claw hammer, with open front, white-silk, open vest, which showed an elaborately pleated white shirt front, wellington boots, a wide shirt collar, a white silk handkerchief round his neck, knotted after the fashion of the day, fastened by a gold pin to his shirt front; his long hair was well oiled and dressed. His spouse had ventured to advise him to don a belltopper but Jim considered, by so doing, would be making a laughing stock of himself, declined. There was not. in those days, an article of wearing apparel, and even at the present day, among the lower classes, so much ridiculed and despised as the chimney pot hat. Jim wore a soft white felt.

The rest of the male guests were variously dressed. All had white gloves either on or in their hands. The most conspicuous thing among them was jewellery, gold or silver watches and rings. It cannot be said that the digger of that day was a dandy in clothes, except on the occasion of his own proper self getting spliced; wellington boots, felt or cabbage tree hats, tweed trousers, coat and vest, a broad leather belt round his waist, in lieu of braces, to keep his pants up; his long hair and whiskers well greased or oiled, a regatta shirt, a loud-coloured silk bandanna folded round his neck drawn through a gold ring, the points fastened to the breast of his regatta with a gold pin. These furnished the rigout of the digger of the day.

On Monday morning, the waiter made his appearance at the breakfast table with sticking plaster on his nose and his eye in a sling. He looked fierce and savage, as if he would like to hurt somebody, but no one took the least notice of him. He had been guilty of a cowardly trick, and had paid the penalty. That was enough, no one hinted of the affair after.

At nine o'clock I made my way into the city.

I had not been in Melbourne since we had first landed; the first place I looked for was Elizabeth Street; I was best acquainted with that locality. I found it much altered, but in what way I could scarcely tell, except that Collins and Bourke Streets were made traversable for vehicles, and pedestrians.

The population was enormously increased, and everybody seemed up to their eyes in business; the noise, roaring, screeching and rattle of vehicles was incessant. The most conspicuous thing that drew my attention was the number of people running around with articles to sell. These I could tell were mostly new chums, at least as far as their dress and appearance went. One accosted me in a very humble way, holding out a watch guard, saying: "Can I sell you this sir, real genuine gold sir, I'm one of the unfortunates, just arrived in Melbourne with wife and three young children, where there is no place

to put our heads, but a miserable shed and provisions are so awfully dear; what little money I have will soon be done, unless I can get some work, but there are so many in my position, work is hard to get. I wish I could get to the diggings, I am trying to sell what few things we brought from home with the object of getting there. When we left home we thought the diggings were in Melbourne, instead of a hundred miles away. Have you been to them?" he asked, "Yes," I replied, "I have just left them." "You have made some gold then?" "Yes a little," I said. "Oh," he said, "do buy this guard, I assure you I gave £3/10 for it in London." It did without a doubt look a very pretty trinket. As I never had possessed a watch I

Left: The bustling business end of Bourke Street looking down to Elizabeth Street.

Above: Flagstaff Hill is today a beautiful garden opposite the Victoria Market, but when it was established it had a flagstaff which was used by the captains of ships in the river to set their clocks, and for the conveyance of messages.

intended buying one. "Three pounds," he said. "Oh," I said, "I do not want the guard, but I will give you 30/- for it." He looked as if he felt shocked at my hard heartedness. "Gimme £2," he said, "and its your's." I turned to walk away: "No," I said, "30/-." "Alright," he said, "here you are," giving me the guard and I him the money. "If that is not a sacrifice," he said, "there never was one."

Carrying the guard in my hand as I walked towards the Yarra it struck me it felt light for gold, and the first jeweller's shop I came to I went in, and asked him if that chain was genuine gold. I told him I had just bought it for gold and would be obliged to him if he would test it and tell me if it was genuine. He took it, looked it over, then applied the test. "How much might you have given for it?" he asked. I said 30/~. "Well," he said, "it is not worth more than 30 pence, its gilded brass." "That thieving new chum had taken me just like a new chum." "That's their dodge," he replied. "Do you know, the city is full of thieves and swindlers of all kinds, men and women, the scum of Tasmania and Sydney and they are reaping harvest just now in Melbourne. God knows there are plenty of new arrivals in this congested city, who are honest and without money, going round trying to sell their valuables, even their clothes, to raise money to keep themselves, wives and children from starving, and to pay for any kind of shelter to cover their heads by night, until they can see a chance to get employment, so that they can raise enough to walk to the diggings."

It is a strange state of affairs just now, some are throwing wealth about like dirt and some, owing to the high price of food, are in want of bread. The real professional thief, who has never seen the diggings, is making as much gold in Melbourne, as the man who has been there and honestly gained it. "Have you been to the diggings?" he enquired. "Yes," I said, "I left Bendigo a few days since." "And were you not interrupted on the road?" "No," I said, "I came on a very unusual track from Bendigo, except through Ballarat, my gold I sent down by escort and now's in the Melbourne Treasury."

"You did right," he said. "Do you know," he continued, "there are bushrangers infesting every road from the diggings, waylaying every poor, unfortunate, unprotected traveller they happen to meet and stripping him of all he has, money or gold. You being on the diggings, did not see much of the papers." "Very little," I replied. "Well," he said, in parting, "be cautious young man, trust no stranger in Melbourne." I thanked him and bid him good day.

I next made my way to the Yarra, where a strange spectacle met my view on the southern side of Flinders Street (if it could be called a street, for there were no buildings on the Yarra side), a long row of

The original Treasury building was leased by the government and stored all of the gold brought in by escort until the late 1850s. It was robbed in the mid-1850s and the gold never recovered. It was situated near the old Mint.

173

CANVAS TOWN INTO EMERALD HILL

The southern side of the Yarra Yarra River bank was to become known as Canvas Town during the gold rush, but the first permanent part of what is now South Melbourne was 'Emerald Hill' which is where this lower photograph was taken from. It is looking north to the Crown Casino and western part of the city.

Collins Street as it was in the early 1850s.

RAG FAIR

'Rag Fair' was the area between Flinders Street and Flinders Lane most noted for Customs House. However, it was then, and has forever since, been occupied largely by the Jewish clothing industry, and while the name may have been lost, the trade certainly wasn't.

people standing with a long row of articles spread out on the ground, clothing, bedding, guns, pistols, watches, jewellery, and all sorts of things one could mention, for sale for any price they might fetch.

These were new arrivals from all parts of the earth, who had to sacrifice their precious belongings to buy food. Sitting down on the planking on the landing of the Yarra, next to another idler like myself watching proceedings: "This is a strange state of affairs," he said, "up till lately, Melbourne was the quietest place on earth and now it seems to have gone entirely mad, and all for the sake of gold; people are rushing here from all parts of the earth, headlong, thinking, if they can only land in Melbourne they can pick up gold straight away and return home with a fortune; and here are hundreds selling their blessed rags to get food to eat."

"Are they still coming?" I asked. "Coming in thousands," he replied, "10,000 have arrived this last month, and still they come. There is not accommodation for the half of them." "See," he said, pointing across the river to Emerald Hill, "that town of calico and canvas, 4,000 people are stowed away there. They pay 5/- a week for permission to put up a tent, while, black and yellow, rich and poor people, all living side by side; some landed here without a pound of ready money and are obliged to sacrifice their goods to buy bread and a little to help them to walk to the diggings. Those who have the means start off at once, but the crowds are not going out of Melbourne as fast as they are coming in by a long way." "Why are these heaps of merchandise stacked here," I asked him, "not claimed and taken to the warehouse?" "These," he answered, "are haphazard consignments sent out by merchants from the old country, who have been accustomed to make Australia a dumping ground for all inferior goods they could not dispose of at home. Hearing of the high prices given here, they have consigned goods to any merchant they happen to know or have heard of." "These are the goods with which the squatter furnished his slop chest," I enjoined. "Just so," he said, "but they do not take now. Consequently, the Melbourne merchant ignores uninvited consignments and leaves them there. They will be sold by auction some day for a mere trifle, to clear them out of the way. Why, I read in the Argus the other day, that there were enough boots consigned to Melbourne lately as would supply each inhabitant of Victoria with a dozen pairs each."

"Have you been to the diggings yourself?" I asked him. "Yes," he said, "I left Bendigo a fortnight ago, I had a fairly good claim on Eagle Hawk. You have been on the diggings too I presume?" "Yes," I said, "I have been twice and made a little each time. I am on my way home now to my parents in Geelong, and shall be going there in a day or two." He said: "Do you drink," No," I said "nothing stronger than ginger beer." "Same here," he put in, "but we can have a ginger together in a friendly way as others can take brandy cobblers." I agreed. "Come along," he said, "over to the Sydney, we'll see a little fun there."

As we passed the row of saleable articles lying on the ground, a pretty fair business was doing. "Do you know," my new acquaintance asked, "what they call this mart?" "No," I said. "This is 'Rag Fair'." "Not a bad name either," I replied, "from the heaps of clothes displayed." Arriving at the public house, we found the bar full of noisy men and women, all either drinking or talking.

The landlord, a skinny little fellow, and the landlady just the opposite, with two waitresses, were serving out drinks for all they were worth; men and and women pledging one another in brandy spiders, cocktails, gin slings etc. wishing long and happy days etc. The women were mostly Hobart towners, I could tell by their coarse language, two or three men stood like statues, propped up against the counter, too drunk to move for fear they would fall.

Two men were loudly disputing about some private grievance of their own, one was pulling off his shirt preparatory to taking it out of the other fellow's hide. When the landlord called out "Sam!" Sam made his appearance, a broad set, though not tall, strong muscled man. "Sam," the landlord said decisively, "turn those fellows out, I'm going to have no fighting in my bar." Sam was what was called the Chucker-Out, he carried a quiet persuasive smile on his face, not at all inclined to offend customers if it could be helped. "Come now," he said, "You two fellows if you intend to kick up a row and fight, go on to the Yarra bank and have it out there, you can't fight here." The one who had his shirt on said: "I said nothing about fighting," and looking the "chucker-out" up and down, taking his measure: "I'm not going out for you or two like you," whereupon the chucker out with a smile, before all the crowd, caught him up round the waist and trailed him out into the middle of the road, where his mate followed him. They there became friendly and shook hands so the threatened fight ended.

The next disturbance was between two girls, Hobart Town Sal and Lanky Jenny. Hobart Town accused Lanky Jenny of trying to coax her man away from her. Hobart swore it was a lie. I should not like this clean paper to be fouled with the language they used to each other, and it would be incredible to decent people to believe it; at last like two tigresses, as they were, began to tear at each other's hair, and scratch faces, when the landlord opened the flap of the bar counter and took Hobart by the arm and said: "Sally we can't allow this in this respectable license house, you know that yourself, if you want to quarrel go away an quarrel. I believe it's all a misunderstanding, Jenny would not do such a mean thing as you accuse her of." "But she called me a who could stand that, to think that I want her white livered squint eyed cow of a man - oh." "If you insist on making any more disturbance here I will send for the police, and have you both locked up, which I should be very sorry to be obliged to do, and you both know that." That settled the dispute for the time, but the belligerents looked daggers at each other, as if intending to end their dispute at some future time.

Having nothing more to watch and my glass being empty, I looked round for my new friend to return the compliment of his shout, but finding him busily engaged talking to one of the girls, I did not like to disturb him. I sneaked off quietly, made for the nearest restaurant and got my dinner. After having had my dinner, and some quiet talk with some very decent fellows about the abnormal state of things in Melbourne, I made my way back to Newtown. In these latter days there is no such place known as Newtown; I have enquired of several old residents, but have only met one who remembered both Newtown and the Devonshire Arms. He told me it formed a part of Collingwood.

Next morning after breakfast, I started again for the city, intending to inspect Canvas Town and to walk on to Sandridge, to see the salt water again. As I approached the corner of Swanston and Bourke Streets, a man, decently dressed, met me full bat. "Beg your pardon," he said, pulling out of his pocket, to all appearances, a splendid looking gold watch, "do you want to buy a gold watch, I'm one of the unfortunates who have come to Victoria looking for gold, thinking, when I reached Melbourne, I should be on the diggings, but I understand the nearest gold finds are a hundred miles away and I had very little money when I came, which is now all spent. To get to the diggings, I am obliged to sell the only valuable thing I have, this watch, a present my poor old father made on leaving the old home, it's real genuine, gold jewelled in eight holes, a splendid time keeper, my father paid £20 for it in Birmingham. I will sell it for £10. Look here, I'll show you the inside." Opening the case he showed the inside; it seemed to be going alright, then he said: "See for yourself. I'll guarantee what I've said, about its quite O.K., just suit you to a tee and only £10, cheap as dirt." From some words he had dropped, I knew my man, but wishing to have a bit of revenge on his class, I pretended to be inclined to buy the watch. I said: "I never had a watch yet and do not understand much about them. I tell what I will do, let us go to a watchmaker and have it examined and tested, if it is all you say, I will

Collins Street from the new Treasury building.

CANVAS TOWN
The so called 'Canvas Town' stretching from St Kilda Road on the south side of the Yarra River was a tragic and desperate place where many poor souls perished with no hope.
Often husbands would leave their families with nothing but the promise to return. They never did, and it became Melbourne's first slum area despite the New South Wales government charging rent for a piece of land on which to pitch a temporary canvas home.
It was also dubbed 'Little Adelaide', and the notorious area eventually became so desperate it was cleared in 1853 when crime became rife.

give you £7/10/- for it." "What's the good, going to a watchmaker, he has watches of his own to sell," he answered, "and would not tell you the truth to two parties bargaining for a watch, he would charge for that and I would not pay for a test I could not rely on."

Opposite Top: Melbourne in the early 1840s from the south bank at later Swanston Street. Above: The same scene in the mid-1970s.

"Why can't you take my word for it, I assure you on the honour of a man, that all I have told you about the watch, is as true as gospel. I would cut off my right hand, than deceive a decent young man as you appear to be. I know there are plenty of swindlers in this beast of a city." Then I said: "You will not." He sullenly replied: "If you like to call on a watchmaker. Now take my honest word for it, there it is, at your own price. I would not let anyone else have it for that."

"Look here," I said, "you mentioned swindlers, I believe you are one of them, you are one of the gang of the five hundred and forty thieves that now infest Melbourne. You are a Vandemonian, no doubt from Launceston or Hobart Town, where all the scum of the British Kingdom have been dumped, that is where you have learned your nefarious trade. I am a young man, but I have been in Victoria eight years, almost continuously mixed up with ex-convicts and old lags, who have enlightened me a little, take your Brummagem watch and yourself off, before I give you in charge." The fellow looked thunderstruck at this sudden turn of affairs; brazening up he

said: "I'm a honest man, this is more than I can stand, I'll have the law on you, strike me blind if I don't, I'll make you prove yer words, I'll give you in charge for insulting me in the street." "All right," I said. He then bustled off in a great hurry to do something, what I never knew. Crossing Flinders Street, a man met me with a suit of black cloth to sell. "Just fit you," he said. "Where did you steal it?" I asked him. "I'm an honest man and no thief," he retorted. "Well then," I said, "take your suit and go to blazes."

I took another look at 'Rag Fair', then gave a boatman a shilling to ferry me over the Yarra, and proceeded to look over Canvas Town. It much resembled a digging township, only the streets were straight and allotments were marked off in an orderly way, but the people looked different. One could tell the recent arrivals from Europe, the men by their velveteen coats, corduroy pants, billy cock hats, or fustian jackets and trousers and red healthy looking faces. The women were dressed all fashions, from silks to common cotton, ladies living next tent to common slattern no distinction of classes there, arrivals from California, America and all parts of the earth; white, brown, black and yellow, although the main flood of Chinese had not yet commenced. At intervals were stores, bakers shops, butchers stalls, restaurants, drink shops, barbers shops etc. It was a motley assembly, all cooking, washing etc. done out in the open. Water carts, drays, loaded with firewood continuously passing to and fro what with children, squalling women screeching and men shouting, the noise was uproarious. I was told eight thousand souls lived in Canvas Town.

'Canvas Town' was recorded by S.T. Gill who showed just how large and busy it was.

After traversing it from one end to the other I made, as I thought, for Sandridge, but I kept too much to the left. On reaching the sea coast, not far from where the Esplanade is now, the last quarter of a mile was thickly covered with ti-tree scrub almost impenetrable. Several boats were fishing a little out on the bay, two or three were baiting their lines preparing to go.

I accosted one, thinking to have a talk with him, but he seemed to be too busy with his work and not in a talkative mood. I bade him "Good day," and remarked: "what a number of ships are anchored at Williamstown." "Yes," he answered, "there is a lot, and I reckon they'll have to stop anchored a long time yet, before they lifts anchor." "How is that?" I asked, "Why, because," he said, "all the crews, leastwise most of them, have run away to the diggings leaving the captain and the mates to look after the ship."

The scene in 2003 from the St Kilda end of Port Melbourne beach looking to Williamstown in the distant left.

"Perhaps," I said, "some of the crew will come back after a while." "Yes," he said, "they may all come back, those who have made a little gold may and those who have had no luck will be disgusted like I was." "You have had experience on the diggings then," I said. "Yes" he replied, "but I had no luck, I came back to my old trade, fishing, if I am lucky I can make a pound a day now." He pushed his boat into deeper water, giving a push with the boat hook, manned his oars. "Good day mate" he said, and was off.

I made straight back to Melbourne, I bethought myself, going along, of buying a new suit of clothes when I came to Collins street. Arriving there, I stopped at the front of a Jew's shop, was feeling the texture of a pair of trousers, when the Jew came out. "You vant a pair of trousers?" he queried. "Oh no," I said, "I was only looking." "Come inside, come inside," pulling me by the arm, "dere ish no ding to buy. I sell sheep, very sheep, yo get noding so sheep in anoder shop." "Very well let's see. show me a decent suit of dark cloth." "I vill," he quickly replied, "mit pleasure, vat your size?" "Five's" I said.

The 1853 coach to Sandridge leaving from the Albion Hotel in Bourke Street, Melbourne.

An early drapery in Collins Street.

With that he pulled out a dozen suits. "Ah, here is von number five vich I recommend, real honest wool, vill wear to the last tred" . "All shoddy," I said. "Shoddy, I keep no shoddy, by Got no." "Show me something better." He pulled out more. "Now here," he said, "is the best I got, dese are dear, dese are vat de gentlemen's in the city wear, the newest style-just out from London." Holding up a pair of pants: "Look at that now vor style, dis ish, number five too." I looked over them and the coat and vest for a time, the Jew praising up his goods all the while. "How much for this suit?" I asked. "Vell," he said, "as I told you, I alvays sells sheep, I'll let you have dot suit for £7/10/-, de lowest." "What," I said, in feigned astonishment, "you are thinking you have a greenhorn to deal with, I know the value of clothes, I served in a draper's shop for sometime,

The Queens Wharf in Flinders Street where Henry, his brother and Old John Crossley sailed for Geelong in the Vesta.

I will allow, clothes, on account of the times, are higher than they used to be, a short time ago that suit could be bought for £5. I tell you what I'll do, I'll give you £6 for it's not worth more." "Oh no, no, I can't let it go for £6, ridiculous, £6 for that splendid suit, look at it again." Holding up the coat: "I've looked enough," I replied, "and I'll not give you more, however I'll take a hat if you are reasonable, but none of your tricks or I'll not take the suit at £6." "Vat kind hat you vant?" "Soft brown felt," I said. He produced a hat that suited me. "How much?" "De hat, de hat, ish 10/-, oh mine Got, dat is zu sheep, but vat can I do, I must sell, I have von big bill to meet to my merchant. Don't ye vant to buy some new boots too, dat nice suit vill besser look mit Vellington boots?" "Yes," I said, "let me try on a pair of Wellingtons." I got a pair to fit and asked him the price. "£3/10/-" he said, "I cannot charge you less, so help me. Don't you vant some shirt, some handkerchiefs?" "No," I said, "that's all, make up the account." "No socks, no flannels?" "No." He wrapped up the bargains, excepting the hat, which I put on, leaving my old cap on the counter. I paid him the bill, £10. "You vill not take de ole cap?" he remarked, "I'll put him on the fire." I started, as if I had received an electric shock. "No," I quickly said, "I'll put that in my pocket, it will come in handy to wear at home at odd times." There were £20 in notes in the lining of that old cap.

I then, with my bundle under my arm, made away for Newtown. As I neared the Devonshire Arms, I heard the bullock bell ring its welcome call. It sounded pleasantly to my ears, as I had had nothing since breakfast, but a bun and cup of coffee.

Next morning was the day on which I expected to meet my brother and John Crosby from Geelong. I donned my new suit, hat and boots, and as I could not see myself in the cracked mirror in the barracks, I went down-stairs to comment upon my figure, before the large pier glass in the parlour. I was astonished at my transformation, quite a dandy. "I wonder what Ann will think when she sees me?" was my first thought. One thing in my get-up was wanting, my hair was too long, it turned up like drake's tails over my coat collar behind, so on my way to the city, I called on a barber, who duly operated on my cranium, trimmed, shampooed, scented and oiled it to perfection, I arrived at the steamboat's landing place on the Yarra about twelve, but the boat was not due till one o'clock, but I saw plenty to amuse me during the hour's waiting.

At last the Geelong boat, the Vesta, was announced, coming slowly in. The first man I saw that I knew, was old John, then my brother. There was a crowd on the wharf; they kept looking round, not recognising me, till they landed and spoke. Old John looked me over, wagged his old head. "Lad," he said: "A sudent hae knowed thah, if ye hadna spoke, what's thah being doin to thee sehn." "Oh,' only got a new suit and got my hair cut. You look spruce too, from what you did, when I left you at Ballarat, and John, I see, has been to the draper's too. How are the

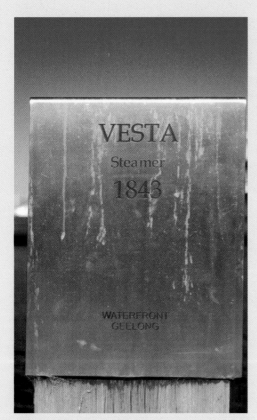

VESTA
Steamer
1843

WATERFRONT
GEELONG

In Geelong the old boats and ships which regularly sailed in and from the port, are honoured with monuments on the pier. Included is the Vesta.

people in Geelong?" "Mother, Father and Jane are all right and thought it very strange you did not come with us." "The Gribbles," Old John put in, "too, are all reet and wanted to know the reason yuh had gaed t' Melbourne afore ye came hame. Ann said: 'Isn't Mundy coming back we ye when ye gae there.' Ah said, 'Yes, ma lass mak sure ol that, ther's somebody in Geelong he's ban to see. Ah know I'lass'. She sat a little, thinking, and then said,'"Who is that I wonder,' and ah said: 'does not pertend tha dae not know.' 'How am I to know,' she said sharp, and lifted her sehn and went oot."

John told me father had sold the block of land near Manifold's vineyard, which he bought three years ago for £25, which I partly worked out with horse and dray, for £400, and he was intending to give John and I £100 each, and keep £200 himself. Old John told me Gribble had been offered £1,700 for the houses, which he had paid £300 for. Things appeared to be booming in Geelong.

Old John asked me if I had found the Devonshire Arms. "Yes," I said, "I arrived there; it took me nearly three days and all I had to eat was two meals, excepting a bit of biscuit I picked up on the road." "Sarved tha reet" , he said, "why could na ye hae kam wie us." "Well lads," he said, "ah'm gaen to shoot, coming up to a pub, ye can do what ye like I'm on for a drop of rum. After we had taken our rest in Geelong ahem for the town." I told them all about the cowardly waiter, the digger's wedding, Rag Fair and Canvas Town, and meeting with sharpers etc. "See thee, old John, see, thee lads, tomorrow we'll gae to t'Treasury and tak out ahr gowd, and sell it to l'bank, and sell it and leave t'Devonshire Arms and stay one neet t'taen and gae home on Saturday, and ah'll bet Mrs Gribble and Ann'll be at t'jetty tae meet us."

Arriving at the hotel, supper was nearly over, however, we got a good meal. After supper, I told my brother about meeting Tom Poole, and how it came about. "Tom Poole, yes," John said, "I remember him, we went to Dick Bodily's school together, I should so like to have seen him, but as he lives in Adelaide, perhaps I never shall." "What is father doing now?" I asked him. "Oh," he said, "he does a bit of water carting and odd jobs, he has the same horse yet, as fat as a mole."

After breakfast, we started for the city, went to the Treasury, lifted our gold and sold it at a bank, I think we got £4 an ounce for it. I had been thinking a good deal about buying a present for Ann; what should it be, a watch, a brooch or what? So the three of us called on the jeweller, who tested my brass chain. He knew me again. "Ah, young man," he said, "have you allowed yourself to be done by the sharpers since." "No," I answered, "thanks to your advice. I've come off scot free that way since." I told him I wanted to buy a present for a friend, a nice dainty little brooch or something of that sort. "Ah, I understand, a little present for your sweetheart." "Perhaps so," I said. He showed me several. "Here is one," he said, at last, "a real beauty and quite the fashion now." It was an oblong, jet ground, filigreed with flowers in gold, edged with a rim of gold and set with several small rubies in the centre; it looked superb in its nest of cotton wool. "How much?" I asked, "£6/10/-" he replied. "Is that the lowest?" I asked. "Yes," he said, "that's the lowest." "Very well, I will take it." (My daughter Emma has this brooch at this present day). "Anything else?" he asked. "I was thinking of buying her a watch too," but then I thought it would be overdoing the thing; so I said: "I want a watch for myself." He showed me several silver watches. I said: "These are too large, show me some smaller ones." "Here is a dainty little lady's silver hunting watch," which took my fancy. "How much?" "£5," he replied. "All right I'll take it, and I want a silver chain to correspond with the watch." The chain was 30/-. "That's all," I said. John was looking on earnestly, while I was doing business with the jeweller. After it was over, he asked to see a gold watch, the size of mine, he was shown several. One at last took his fancy, a neat little gold ladies watch, open faced, it was a little beauty. Asking the price, the jeweller told him it was £10 including a hair guard. John bought it.

It struck me John had a girl in his mind's eye somewhere too, but who she was, I had not the least idea, however, I know this much, she never got the watch for two years, later it was missed from off the mantle piece, when a strange woman slept at our house with whom father had engaged to take to Ballarat. Mother and a neighbour searched the woman, but could not find the gold watch. It was not seen after.

On leaving the watchmakers, we repaired to a restaurant and had dinner, then crossing the Yarra, inspected Canvas Town, the small vessels and boats on the river. Not wishing to be out late, on account of the money we had on us, we made our way back early, to our lodgings in Newtown. When dinner was over, next day, after settling with our host, we prepared for a start to the city, intending to get beds there, so as to be ready for the Geelong boat, at nine in the morning. We put up at the Sydney Hotel, so as to be handy to the boat in the morning.

It was a noisy uproarious shop, women and men all at the bar drinking. We did not go to bed till one o'clock and to sleep in different rooms. We wanted to be in the same room but it could not be managed. I was shown into a room, a bed was pointed out to me into which I slipped, putting my swag under the

THE VESTA

Frederick Manton, later to own a major department store at 200 Bourke Street known as Mantons, latterly occupied by Coles, owned two small steamships brought from England.

The Fairy Queen was brought out in parts in 1840 and assembled on the south side of the Yarra River opposite Customs House. It was launched on April 3, 1841 and did the run from Williamstown to Melbourne.

The Vesta was his second ship and arrived in cases in January 1842. It was not landed at Queens Wharf and therefore avoided wharfage fees. It was completed in March 1842 and launched on the 'Canvas Town' shore in front of nearly all the population to 'reiterated cheers of the admiring multitude'. It was an iron hulled ship of 109 feet in length and powered by 70hp steam engine. its maiden voyage was from Melbourne to Williamstown which took 66 minutes to get there and 60 to return.

In June 1842 Manton won the government contract to transport officials in the Vesta to and from Williamstown at 1/6 per head, and goods for 8/- a ton.

A third ship, known as the Governor Arthur, was added to the Manton fleet in September 1843 and it took over the Melbourne to Williamstown run while the Vesta then plied the route between Melbourne and Geelong.

In the summer of 1843-44 it was popular for 'Sunday holiday excursions' which departed from the Wharf Steam Mills at 6.00am for the three hour run to Geelong. The return voyage cost 8/- in the cabin, or 12/- in the saloon.

Manton's business operated from South Melbourne and in 1842 he installed one of only two stationary steam engines in Melbourne for grinding flour and sawing timber. The mill was operated by Allison and Knight on the land bordered by Collins Street and Flinders Lane.

stretcher and my pants and valuables under the pillow for safe keeping, so that if there was any movement of them I would know. How long I was asleep I could not tell when someone gave me a poke in the ribs. I started up saying: "Who's that, what do you want?" A fellow stood leering over me with a candle in his hand, said: "Get out of this, you are in my bed." A bit taken by surprise I said: What?" "You're in my bed, get out." "Not if I know it," I told him, "this bed was given to me and I paid for it." "Ah, well, we'll see whose bed it is." With that, he began to pull the bed clothes off me. I could see the man was drunk. I gave him a pretty smart blow in the stomach and sprawling backwards, he tumbled. I happened to have caught him on the wind-bag, as pugilists call it, and he lay gasping on the floor for fully a minute. There were several beds in the room, the fracas woke two or three, wanting to know what the hell was up.

The candle, of course, was out as soon as the man went over, and the room was in darkness, but no one seemed much concerned about what was up and all was soon quiet again. The man on the floor picked himself up and staggered off. I slept but little after and welcomed, with satisfaction, the breaking of day. As soon as I could observe properly, I looked round for my would-be ejector and saw him at the far end of the room fast asleep, on his back, on the floor.

About seven o'clock, I got up, had a wash and spruced up, lifting my swag, went down stairs, where I met Old John and my brother, astir before me, awaiting breakfast. I told them of my night's adventure. Old John made this remark: "See tha lads, ah wadna live in this cussed Melbourne gin I wus paid fur't. We'll bein Geelong t'neet thank guidness." After breakfast we made for the wharf.

The Vesta was getting steam up and we went aboard. Promptly at nine the hawser was let go and we passed slowly down the Yarra. The passage then, in the saloon to Geelong, was a pound (now it is 3/6 return). I had never been between Melbourne and Geelong by boat before, so I enjoyed the trip and felt quite happy with everything and everybody. The boat was pretty well crowded, only one or two drunks who were quite peaceable. After two hours steaming, I sighted the You Yangs, the dear old You Yangs and the north shore of Corio Bay. There was no stoppage at Port Arlington then. In due course the gong sounded for dinner, a nice dinner it was too, which only cost 3/- with tea or wine as you chose. Coming on deck, yes there was Point Henry, that long pointed promontory which I had looked at from the other side so many times; and then the Bar, which Geelong had been scraping and dredging for years. The sandy bottom could be seen, dangerously near to the boat's keel, as plain as the clouds in the sky. Next came

The old port in Corio Bay - with Singapore Terrace in the middle distance on the hill and Limeburner's Point on the horizon.

into view, Limeburner's Point, the vessels and boats at the wharves. We were making for the Moorabool wharf, where a crowd could be seen waiting the arrival of our boat. Slowing up to the pier, I looked anxiously for those I was wishing to meet. As the hawser was thrown out, I saw them. My girl and Mrs Gribble peering among the crowd on the boat. I was standing near the rail, not near John Crosby and my brother. I saw signs of recognition with them, but me, they did not notice. It struck me, they had never seen me before wearing a hat, so I pulled it off and waved it to them. Ann saw the signal first, and drew her mother's attention, when they both waved their parasols in token of recognition. The boat and the gangway were soon fixed and passengers filing ashore. I, with swag on my arm, was soon on the jetty shaking hands with Mrs Gribble and Ann, whose hand I gave a significant squeeze, at which I thought she blushed a little. "Oh Mundy, how are you?" was Mrs Gribble's salute, "what a swell you are," "Yes," I said, "a swell carrying a swag." "That's nothing," she replied, "everybody carries a swag now-a-day, at times." My little girl said nothing for a while, but looked very coy, and pleased.

Mrs Gribble, Old John and my brother walked on, Ann and I dropped behind, after a time she said: "Why did you go to Melbourne before coming home, why did you not come down with your brother and John Crosby." "Oh," I said, "it was just a fancy I took to see Melbourne, my gold was there and another thing I did it all with one trip in the boat, my brother and old John paid £3 for trips and I only paid £1. She thought my excuse strange. After a silence of a minute she said: "Do you like Melbourne?" "No," I said, "it's a dreadful place, everybody seems to be going mad, either with too much money or too little, and people are coming there so fast, there is not accommodation enough to stow them away." I told her then about the Digger's wedding, Rag Fair and Canvas Town.

Geelong remains a busy port. This is Yarra Pier.

When we had reached Pakington Street, I said: "I'll go home now Ann and get rid of this swag." "Oh no," she replied, "you must come to our place and have tea." "So I will, as soon as I have seen my people, plenty of time," I remarked, pulling out my silver watch, "it's only half past four." "Oh," she observed, "what a dear little watch, did you buy that in Melbourne?" "Yes," I said, "and look here sweetheart," I whispered, "I have in my pocket a present for you." She said never a word, but ran after the others to tell them I was going home first, then coming to their place to tea. I made my way through Little Scotland into Gertrude Street. I was soon home, where I met mother and Jane, they were overjoyed to see me, assailing me with half a dozen questions at once. Where was John? Why did I not come home before I went to Melbourne etc.? I told them Mrs Gribble and Ann had met us at the wharf and we had promised to stay for tea; only I wanted to see them first and get rid of my swag. Mother sniffed and said: "We would have met you too,

Looking from Limeburner's Point towards Portarlington at the entrance to Corio Bay.

but did not know when you were coming. I suppose you want to be with that gal." "Where's father," I intercepted. "He's just gone for a load of water. I suppose John told you he had sold the ground?" "Yes," I said, "and he got a good price for it too. John and I got a little gold but did not make a pile." "I suppose you had enough of the diggings for a while," she said, "and going to stay home now." "I do not know mother," I returned, "what I'm going to do yet, but I'm not going to be idle. "

After some more desultory talk, I went to Gribble's. The first I met at the gate was William Gribble. "Hullo Mundy," he cried out, giving me a hearty shake, "how are you? Got some gold I hear. We were out of luck when I saw you in Bendigo, we never got a pennyweight of course you know. I've been loafing at home ever since. Did Old John tell you what I have been offered for the houses, £1,700." "Yes," I said, "it's an astonishing good profit, as you only gave £300 for them." "It's luck Mundy, all luck." "Are you inclined to sell?" I asked. "Well," he answered, "I'm getting short of money, I'm only getting £3/10/- for the shop and £1/10/- for the two roomed house and we are living on this." "Why, that," I said, "is £5 a week, that ought to keep you three, perhaps you are too much on the beer?" "Ah well, Mundy," he said, "a man going out, you know, he is sure to meet somebody he knows, when we are bound to have a glass together, but whether I have much or little, and as sober as I am now (he was three sheets in the wind then) the old woman flies at me like a bulldog and says, here you are drunk again, and goes on with her nasty tongue, till it's more than I can put up with, so I goes out then and gets real tight.

"One day, I'd have settled her, only for Ann, she kept putting herself between us. There is a young fellow not so old as you, I knew him before I knew you, his name is Fred Tite, he is inside now, he is a downright little swiper, no matter where I go, he is sure to find me and we have drinks together. The little fool has been to the diggings and done pretty well and insists on shouting every time, and when I come home, he will come with me mostly drunk. The old woman says it's my fault in encouraging him to drink, why, if he did not drink with me, he'd drink with someone else. It's enough to drive a man mad." It seems Gribble," I said, "your good luck has not made you happier." "No Mundy," he replied, "I wish gold had never been found and I was on a station, bullock driving. I do, so help me God. Come inside," I followed him inside.

I was introduced to Fred Tite, quite a young fellow, one would be inclined to call him a boy, full of giggle and good humour. Old John was just telling of our journey from Bendigo to Ballarat, having turkey for Sunday's dinner, instead of nothing but "t'oud damper." Fred was three parts tight and very talkative, told me he was an orphan, had neither father nor mother, how he had been brought up in an orphan asylum

DICK RUFFIN
There were many members of the Ruffin family in Geelong from the mid-1840s, but publican Richard Ruffin married Ann Turner at the Geelong Presbyterian Church in 1851. He remarried London-born Sarah Harris in 1867.
They had Grace Elizabeth (1867), George Edward (1869), Isabella Elsely (1872 - died at two), Sarah Emma (1873), Amy Elsely (1875) and Minnie Ethel (1877).
Richard Ruffin had a hotel in Yarra Street, Geelong in 1848.

181

The Geelong region and much of the south western parts of Victoria were home to a large tribe of Australian natives called the Wathaurong. With the arrival of the first Europeans in 1802, the numbers of full blooded original inhabitants began to decline. Today a large number of words and names from the original Wathaurung aboriginal language are preserved in the place names and street names within the Geelong region. Anglicised though they may be, we now treasure names such as Moorabool, Gheringhap, Malop, Moolap, Corio, Geelong, Barwon, You Yangs, Bellarine, Colac, Beeac and Birregurra.

Although there has been some proof of Dutch visitors before him, Matthew Flinders was the first known European to visit the Geelong region back in 1802. He came ashore and explored parts of the region including the You Yangs.

The next visitors were explorers Hume and Hovell crossing overland from NSW in December 1824. Local natives told Hume that the bay was called "Jillong" and the land "Corayo". Somehow, over the years, the names have been reversed.

In 1838, the 'Town of Geelong' was pronounced with a population of 545, the survey showed a hotel, general store, church and a wool store.

By 1841, Geelong was sending wool to England, it had its own newspaper (the Geelong Advertiser - still going today) and a regular steamer service to Melbourne. By 1851, it was the fifth largest town in the colony and a busier port than Melbourne.

In 1852 the gold rush started which dramatically expanded Geelong's importance. Its population increased twenty fold. However, the restrictive sand bar at the entrance to Geelong's harbour, and the publishing of a 'false map' by the merchants of Melbourne to show its closeness to the Ballarat gold fields, eventually saw it fall behind.

Geelong became the wool capital of Australia, with its busy ports and waterfront woolstores. Major manufacturing companies came to the region, such as the Ford Motor Company, which commenced on Geelong's waterfront in 1925 before building its first Australian

till he was sent out to work. Told me a lot in a short time. Old John at last sprung up and said: "Look ye here lads, ah'm gaen tae skoot, ah havna wet ma wis, and sin ah left t'boat, I'll gang to Dick Ruffin's for t'". To Mrs Gribble: "gie us a jug lass, ut'll haud half gallon of haef and haef." Fred jumped up and said: "No John, you won't, I'm going to shout at that." There was a long altercation, about who was going to pay for it, but Fred won, and was off with the jug, without another word and was soon back. When it was doled out, I declined any, and the women folk did the same. "Look's tha here Fred," Old John broke in, "Ah cud hae told thee, he wadna drink but soft drink, but tha gaed cot in sic a blazing hurry, I hadna a chance. I havna seen him drink owt but ginger beer. " Off shot Fred again and was back again in a brace of shakes, carrying half a dozen of ginger pop. The women folk and I drank the soft stuff, while the others discussed their half and half.

In the noise of the conversation that followed, I motioned Ann into the front room. There I drew out my pocket the case containing the brooch, opening the cover, showed her the jewel nested neatly in cotton wool. "Ann," I said, "this is a present I bought for you in Melbourne." Her eyes glistening, she coyly said, "Oh Mundy, whatever did you do that for, that must have cost a lot of money, how much did you pay for it?" "No matter," I replied, "what it cost, if you will only accept it, wear it and think of me." She blushed as she took it, thanking me, but said no more, young as she was, she understood.

After tea was over, we had a game of cards 'all fours', a game very popular at that time, but quite out of date now; we did not stop late, John and I went home. Father sat up to meet us. He was pleased to see us, he said, altogether under his roof again, and hoped we would stay and have a good rest, and naturally enquired what we thought of doing next. "For my part," I said, "I had had enough of the diggings for a while, at least." "I've got a hundred pounds for each of you," he went on, "with what money you have, you might try something else; there are many things you can make money at, if you're careful. Some do well buying and selling at the auction sales, excepting cattle and horse sales. You want to be pretty smart and understand well what you are doing to succeed in that line." I broke in here and said: "Father, what benefit have you derived in dealing in horses?" "Well Henry," he said, "to tell the truth, I should have been better off, if I had let it alone, there are so many swindlers and rogues among horse-dealers, that an honest man stands no chance. Don't have anything to do with horse-dealing. Then there is farming and market gardening, but the worst of it, is land is so awfully dear now. Then there is carting about town and what is better - carrying to Ballarat." "Ah," I said, turning to John, "that's the best, don't you think so John?" He thought it was.

I paid the Gribbles a visit nearly every day. Mrs Gribble said to me: "That was a nice brooch you gave Nance; I knew you had a liking for my maid and I think she likes you. I'm not going to interfere, but you must remember she is so young she does not know her own mind yet. Somebody might come along she would like better, don't set your mind on her too much, for there is no knowing what may happen. I'm not going to interfere; the maid shall please herself; she is as good a girl as ever breathed." "Yes," I added,

A primitive means of crossing the Barwon River.

"I know that, and I mean to gain her. I don't care how long I will have to wait." "The only thing," she continued, "I regret is, she has not a more peaceable home. Gribble is always drinking and I can't put up with it, it makes him look sottish and bloated. I like a man to take a glass and be jolly, but it's sickening to see your husband make such a beast of himself. "Perhaps," I ventured to say, "if you had more patience with him, and instead of abusing him when he comes home, and show a little more forbearance, he would not be so quarrelsome." She got angry at this and said: "He always comes home ready for a row, you can see it in his face." "Perhaps," I answered, "he is expecting a row, and is prepared for the first shot." But feeling I was on dangerous ground, by taking Gribble's part I put in: "Why don't you pack him off to the diggings or get him to do some work? He kept sober enough when I saw him in Bendigo." "But he won't go," she retorted, "he wants to sell the shop and two roomed house, but I'll not consent. If he did, he'd only squander the money."

For several days I strolled about the town. I tried buying things at auction rooms and then selling them in another room, but I found there was nothing in it, partly from my inexperience, but mostly from a clique of half a dozen sharp men who made it their sole business. They worked together to draw strangers on, to bid for their goods. Any fresh things put up, one of the clique would get them cheap, at his own price.

One day I dropped into an auction in Yarra Street where a government land sale was going on. I bid for an allotment up to £90 which was knocked down to me, for which I had to put down a deposit of ten per cent. The land was situated near the Three Sisters, twenty miles from Geelong. The next day I hired a saddle horse; gave a pound for the day for him. He went all right for four or five miles, when, cantering along at a merry pace. On a clear track, his legs got twisted together somehow, and down he went, and I over his head. The change was so sudden that I had to lie and think for a few seconds before I could realise what had happened. The horse was standing there, the bridle reins hanging down. As luck would have it, I was not hurt, only got a shaking up. I examined the horse, to see if there were any fresh wounds on his knees. There were none, but some old abrasions carefully blackened over. Did I not bless that man who lent me the horse, knowing he stumbled and did not warn me. After the spill I proceeded cautiously. I found the allotment by the survey marks. It was sold as land, but it was half rock, large smooth granite boulders, some of them big enough to turn a wagon and team of horses on; a real useless piece of country, unless for growing a little grass in patches about enough to feed one sheep to ten acres; a downright sell. I made up my mind to forfeit my deposit, to have nothing to do with it.

Enquiring about prices of carriage to Ballarat and the prices of goods bought in Geelong and the profits when sold in Ballarat, I made up my mind what I would do. I would go into the trading and carrying business to Ballarat, the first thing I did was to order a two horse dray to be built, which I considered suitable for the occasion. While the dray was being built, I looked out in the horsesale yards, for two good horses. One day at auction, I dropped across a good looking upstanding grey which I fancied would suit me. He was guaranteed to any trial. Father was with me, he was of my opinion (father was never so happy as when dealing in horses). The grey was knocked down to me for £60, he stood the trial satisfactorily.

Gribble had become much steadier of late, except when he happened to meet Fred Tite, when they often came in boozey. Fred was a very lively fellow when in drink, and good company, as some thought in his boyish way, he delighted in making the women folk laugh at his comical gestures and tricks; isn't he a funny fellow, they would say. Fred, poor fellow, came to a sad end a week after I saw him for the last time. He was drinking in South Geelong and one night, after dark he strayed down to the bank of the Barwon, fell in and was drowned. Some say he committed suicide. It was hard to say. He was seen floating next day near the bank. When the tidings of Fred's tragic death reached Gribbles next day, there was not one but was deeply sorry for the poor, erratic, misguided orphan boy. Gribble was visibly affected and kept straight for a long time.

About this time, Mrs Gribble's brother, Nathan Gillingham, with his wife and family, arrived from England. The family consisted only of two boys, Edwin about seventeen and Nathan, fifteen years of age. Edwin was destined to be my life-long friend. He died at Castlemaine seven years ago. They were a family of hand weavers from Somersetshire. Nathan and his wife Fanny were a jolly pleasant couple. It was most amusing to me, to hear them all talking the Somersetshire dialect together.

Nathan Gillingham had come to Victoria with the hope of making his fortune and as it had taken most of his capital to pay for their passage, he was naturally anxious to get to the gold diggings. A little over a week after their arrival Gribble, John Crosby, Nathan and another man, who owned a horse and dray made

factory in North Geelong. In later years, Alcoa, vehicle component manufactures and Shell Oil Refinery boosted Geelong's economy. Its long forgotten waterfront has been transformed into a fine precinct.

Moorabool Street, Geelong in 1857.

The Yarra Yarra River, and Melbourne city which was vastly developed from the place Henry knew when Nathan Gillingham arrived in Australia with his family.
The paddock on the right is the now flattened Batman Hill. This photograph was taken from near Spencer Street, but there was no bridge there then.

183

GRAPES AT BERRAMONGO - BELPERROUD

In the last days of 1839 the ship 'Mary' brought Swiss brothers Jean and Alexandre Belperroud to Sydney Heads. Lieutenant Governor La Trobe's wife, Sophie de Montmollin, was Swiss, and when visiting his wife's country La Trobe - himself of Swiss descent - had spoken much of the British colony in Australia, so the Belperroud brothers decided to emigrate to Port Phillip. They had no idea of the size of the country, and found they were in Sydney, over five hundred miles from their destination. Eventually they made their way overland to Melbourne's shanty-town, where they took temporary jobs while they looked for suitable country. By 1841 their names had become John and Alick, with John marrying an Irish girl who had arrived from Galway Bay. Early in 1842 the brothers went to Geelong, but the colony had been hit by its first depression. In 1842 Alick Belperroud took up fourteen acres on Fisher's Hill near Highton; John, some land above the Barwon between Pollocksford and Fyansford, thereafter known as 'famed Berramongo.' By the time the necessary land acts were formulated, John Belperroud, who had started out by renting ten acres for £20 a year, was the owner of Berramongo and more land besides. At first he could not afford to buy a horse or plough, so every inch of soil was turned by hand to loosen up for the vines. The land was cultivated for the first two years for root crops and vegetables, and a nursery of fruit trees established. The sale of these to British orchardists enabled Belperroud to plant most of his land with vines under conditions as

Lethbridge town is now off the main Midland Highway between Geelong and Ballarat. It is now very quiet.

up a party to go to the Oven's River diggings where a rush had lately broken out. So all things settled, they started on their long journey.

My new dray having been finished, I bought a one-horse load of various commodities, bran oats, butter, cheese and other things and started for Ballarat. I paid John to go with me, for it was necessary to watch the horse, by night, against horse thieves. The first night we reached the Muddy Waterholes, the second, Watson's public house (now Meredith), the third day we arrived in Ballarat and sold a portion of the goods. Next morning I was soon cleared out and got halfway home that day. I had a better idea after the first trip what would pay best. John bought a horse so that we could carry bigger loads and we went into partnership according to our ventures; as I had had many enquires for fruit, when in Ballarat, I resolved to procure some for the next trip. Fruit was scarce and dear.

The best place I could think was Belperude's vineyard on the Barrabool hills, where I made for one afternoon, with the dray and an empty barrel that bottled beer had been packed in, intending to get as many peaches as I could, as I thought that would be the best kind to sell. Arriving at the vineyard I was offered plenty of peaches at four a pound. I agreed to take as much as the barrel would hold. I was a complete novice those days, in packing fruit. When the barrel was three parts full, he remarked (he was a Frenchman): "I tink you put more, dey smash one in de oder so much." "All right," I said, "perhaps you are right." When I paid him he said: "You must come look my cellaire and see de vines." I said, "I'll have a look at the cellar, but I don't drink wine." "Ha vel," he said, "you pleeze yourself." When down the cellar he drew a glass of wine from a cask and holding up to the light saying: "You see dat now, isn't he look splendeed, you taste dat." I tasted it and drank it. "I have some vite vine here," drawing from another cask, "noting beat dat it is de dry vine, you taste him." I did taste and swallowed "him" and so he invited me on, tasting from one cask to another, till I felt my head going round and felt I was getting too much and declined any farther tasting. I bought two bottles to take home. Lashing the barrel well to the guard irons I started for home. I felt in high spirits and, not content to go a walking pace, I urged the horse on to a trot. The road was pretty rocky in places which made the barrel dance about to such a tune, that if I had not had the precaution to lash it; it would have pirouetted out of the dray. I noticed, moreover, the peaches were sinking considerably and slackened speed.

Before I reached the Barwon bridge, I began to feel very sick and queer. The mixtures of the different samples I had tasted began to disagree. However, I got home alright. Mother came out when I was putting the horse into the stable. "Well," she said, "did you get - whatever is the matter Henry? You look as white as a sheet." I said, "I feel white mother." Then I told her. "Come in" she said, "and lie down. You'll be better soon and I'll make you a cup of tea." A cup of tea - I did lie down in a short time in the stable, but o'lord, as Mark Twain once said, I nearly threw up my immortal soul. I had had no dinner which made it worse.

After a couple of hours I felt better and selected some of the best peaches and went to see my sweetheart Ann. Mrs Gribble and Fanny Gillingham were there, all three looked hard at me and almost simultaneously said: "You are not well, been eating too many peaches." When I told them what had

happened, didn't they laugh, I thought they would never stop. Fanny said: "Why didn't e' bring us a drop and not put it a'in thy own belly." "I did bring a couple of bottles," I said. "I'll bring you one tomorrow, you are welcome to it, I'll never touch another drop of Bellparoud's wine while the stars shine." Next morning John and I had the disagreeable task of sorting the peaches, separating the sound from the broken ones. They panned out about half and half. Mother made jam. Mrs Gribble and Fanny made jam, plenty of it.

On the following day, we purchased such goods as we considered would pay best, ready for a start on the morrow. Arriving in Ballarat, our things sold satisfactorily. The peaches we sold by the dozen and realised just about what I paid for them at the vineyard.

Not grape production now, but a cement works.

Some of the shanty keepers advised me to venture in spirits and bottled beer and stout, but I considered the game too risky. Governor La Trobe, being a military man, and believing in harsh compulsory measures was determined to stop the sale of all intoxicating drinks on the goldfields. A man was allowed to hold two gallons of spirits for his own use and no more. If a carter was caught with more it was looked upon as contraband and smuggled in for sale. To make things doubly sure if caught the team was confiscated, all the liquor in bottles or in casks was spilt by knocking the heads off casks and smashing the bottles.

Rum, gin, brandy, beer and stout have been known to run down Camp Hill from Lydiard Street in streams. What was more, the carrier was fined fifty pounds, half of which was given to the police who caught the offender.

An unfortunate bullock driver, a carrier between Geelong and Ballarat knowing the great profits in smuggling stuff to Ballarat, having made small ventures before, rashly loaded a whole cargo of it. Arriving in Ballarat, the police got scent of what his load consisted of, surrounded his dray and marched him up to the camp, where the whole lot was emptied out, his team of bullocks seized and he was fined £50 or six months imprisonment.

In face of these cautions, I thought it best to leave drink alone. But still, in spite of all the danger and restrictions the supply did not decrease one bit.

Flour fetched off the dray £7/10/- a bag, in Geelong it could be bought for £2/10/-. We loaded with twelve bags of flour but there was a heavy rain just then, especially about Buninyong, which made the roads heavy. We reached, with difficulty, within twelve miles of our destination by keeping well in the bush off the main track. We got stuck twice and John's horse, in a bog was a real duffer. When we got out and on solid ground we camped for the night. In the morning I said to John: "Let us take off six bags and I'll go to Ballarat and sell them, while you can stay and mind the other bags and keep your horse too, I'll go in with mine." Everything being fixed, I started alone, keeping clear of the main road on an old track past Buninyong, a track I had been three years before, before Ballarat was thought of, as far as Jock Winter's crossing of the Leigh. I turned off then to the right and had not gone half a mile when the off wheel went down to the bed, I tried the horse once or twice, but I saw it was no use.

Here was a pretty fix, considerably off the main track, and by myself and had to unload bags of flour in a bog hole there was no help to be got. I took out the horse and viewed the situation; about twenty yards away was sound ground. I took a bag in my arms, I could not get it on my back, and struggled through the mud to the hard ground and so on with the whole six. Then to get the dray out, I always carried an axe and spade in case of such emergencies. I got a log of wood as fulcrum, close to the nave of the wheel, cut a stout sapling for a lever, clearing the dirt from the spokes, lifted the wheel nearly a foot.

favourable as any he had known in Switzerland.

In three years the vines were yielding grapes for sale - in five he was selling his own colonial wine. He had purchased vines from Hobart and from MacArthur at Camden, but now he decided to try vine grafts from Europe. These were duly sent out by relatives but the ship came no nearer than Williamstown, so he walked the fifty miles from Berramongo.

The fifties saw a stone house rise, from blocks quarried and cut on the land. Above the architrave of the cellar door was carved the cross of Switzerland, from whence he had returned after a brief holiday, setting the seal on his happiness with the report: "This colony is the finest country in the world."

Bullockies made a long, thirst quenching pause at Berramongo before flailing their teams up heart-bursting Fyansford Hill. The selection of wines - all matured on the vineyards - was truly staggering. Burgundies, clarets, muscats and ports. There were German riesling

A dramatic example of the difficulties encountered in moving goods through the bush in the pioneering era.

wines, cabernet, frontignac, tokay, and a very ordinary unrefined wooden-casked type known as 'colonial wine.'

The discovery brought thousands of people, and Berramongo lay close to the Great Western Road to Ballarat diggings, and the vineyards were nearing their prime. There were also cherries, grapes, apples, pears, plums, peaches, strawberries, mulberries, apricots and figs, all for a few pence a half pound. This activity was second to wine-making. Even for those hard drinking days, the amounts spent were astonishing. As often as not the drinks were paid for in gold dust and small slugs.

One October night the Belperrouds were sitting over a fire in the large parlour with Auguste Hinke, their cook, and Jean Willener, a vine-dresser. Seated with them at the table was Louis Kowald, giving news of the diggings, for he had just returned from Ballarat. They were interrupted by a loud knocking so John Belperroud rose and challenged the callers in French and English. Suddenly the door was forced open by two intruders, who brandished pistols and ordered the company to face the wall while they searched the house. Hinke expostulated in broken English and was immediately shot dead. The Belperrouds had been trained as cavalry men, and had fought in the Austrian army. John took a few pieces of silver from his pocket and suggested he take the candle to get more money. As he moved back he threw the candle though the doorway, while Alick smashed the shoulder of one man with his chair. John snatched his sabre from the

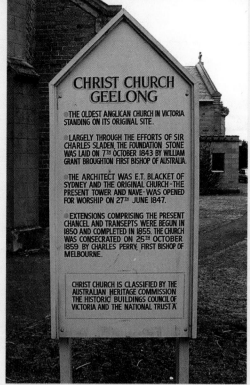

The goldfieds in the east of Victoria were extremely rugged.

Next thing was to block it there. I had plenty of material ready, but I could not let go the lever to put it under, so I got another lump of wood, heavy enough to keep the lever down and raised the wheel by degrees in that fashion. Making the road good with wood laid crosswise, I put the horse in and prepared to load again. This was a feat of strength beyond my ability. I could lift a bag within six inches of the tail of the dray, but to save my life, no higher. So I cut another sapling, same length as the lever and rolled the bags up. This bit of exercise took me about two hours. I got into Ballarat without further mishap and sold every bag of flour for £7/10/- before it was dark and camped there for the night.

I was off early next morning to where I had left John. On the way counting the money I had taken, I found out I had taken a useless £20 note for which I had given change for a bag of flour. It was a custom in those days in sending notes by letter to cut the note into two and send one half in one letter and the other half in another which the recipient could paste together. This note I had taken, strange to say, was two half notes of two different banks.

The Mundys and Gillinghams had many happy and sad reasons to visit Christ Church. The first was for Nathan Gillingham's funeral.

Loading the other six bags, we got into Ballarat by one o'clock. The first thing I did was to look for the man who gave me the bogus note. I happened to catch him leaving his tent for his work. The man seemed to be honest enough, he told me he had taken the note as alright. "I received it at the store for gold I sold, and if it is not good he'll have to make it right." With that, he gave me four £5 notes in exchange for the doubtful £20. We sold all our flour and camped at Buninyong that night.

On arriving in Geelong I found Gribble and his party were back home from the Oven's diggings. They had been away over two months. They had had no luck and what was worse Nathan Gillingham had been taken bad with dysentery and came home very ill. He lived only a few days after reaching home and Fanny was a widow.

During our last trip, father had been attending the horse sales and had bought another horse, a likely looking black mare. "Just the thing for a leader for you Henry," he said, "quick in her action, a little faster than your horse, suit you out and out. She is staunch too, she had a good trial. "What kind of trial?" I asked. "Oh, the usual trial, locked wheels, staunch as a brick; you can have her for what I gave for her £50." I liked the appearance of the mare and as I wanted a good leader, the roads too every week were getting worse, so I said: "All right father, I'll give you the £50."

John and I loaded again for Ballarat. We did not take flour this time, but chose goods more easily handled, and arranged to have double leading horses, one hooked on to each shaft. The black mare proved to be a good one, but John's horse did not prove himself at all up to the mark, by hanging back when it came to hard pulling, and checking the black mare. The team had hard tugs now and again. At last we got stuck in mud. We eased the wheels with the shovel, but could not get out, because John's horse wouldn't pull at all, so I took him out, and with a little more easing of the wheels my two horses took the load out. John was disgusted with his horse. "The first chance I get," he said, "I'll sell him or take him to the saleyard and let him go for what he will fetch." However we landed safely in Ballarat and soon got rid of our load.

While there, I was repeatedly requested to bring liquor, promising to take it off me as soon as I came to the tent, barring any police being in sight. "Bran, chaff, oats will serve to hide the stuff (grog). You have been here several trips and the police know the goods you always bring, they will not suspect you." The extra profits were tempting and the danger and the risk stimulated me into daring anything, so I promised to think over it.

On our way back, we met a man with a team of two horses, he was pretty heavily loaded. He complained of the roads, said he had been stuck twice and had to partly unload, he only wished he had another horse. John said: "I'll sell you this one," pointing out his horse. "What do you want to sell him for?" enquired the man. "Well," John said, "he has not the quick step as the black one, they do not keep well together, it makes it hard on the other horse, otherwise he is alright. I intend to either chop him or sell him in Geelong." John made a satisfactory bargain with the man for the horse and leading harness, and we proceeded on our way.

When at home I was pondering over the advisability of taking a few cases of brandy and Holland gin next trip. I told father about it. He shook his head: "No Henry," he said, "it's too dangerous, leave grog alone, you are doing fairly well as you are doing, have nothing to do with grog; suppose you got caught, what then?"

John did not buy another horse, so I paid him to go with me next trip. I was all on my own. I could do as I liked. In loading, I bought two gallons of over-proof rum. In the evening, with the aid of a little water. made it into thirteen bottles. Next morning we were on the road again, stopping at the Muddy Water Holes the first night.

It is difficult to know why the track to Ballarat went through the Stoney Rises when there is flat land around it. The modern highway is located several kilometres away.

We reached the Stoney Rises the second night. The night was very cold, I said to John: "What do you say if we have some rum hot?" He was agreeable, so we drank one lot. After a while he suggested we might as well have another rum to keep out the cold, which we did, and two or three more after that. We talked of big things and built stupendous castles in the air that night by the fire; till I felt unbearably sleepy. I asked John to take first watch of the horses, I crawled up to the top of the load under the tarpaulin, and was soon oblivious to the world. When, perhaps after four or five hours, John called me, I tried to sit up, but the heavy tarpaulin over me made me think I was buried alive, and began to sing out pretty loudly. When John lifted the tarpaulin off me, saying: "It's one o'clock Henry." "One o'clock?" I sat up, looked round, yes. there were the stars, the tops of trees plain enough, but what part of the universe I was in, or who I was, or how I got there I could not realise, till after some heavy thinking it dawned on my muddled brain that I had been fool enough to have taken an over-dose of rum.

The Stoney Rises are on the original road to Ballarat.

bedroom wall, jumped through the window and raced round the house to cut down the murderers. They had already fled and were shooting, but Alick pursued them with a reaping hook. Next day a police search of the Barrabool Hills yielded no clues.

Auguste Hinke was buried on Berramongo on that part of the property known as the 'the wilderness.'

A reward of £100 was offered for the apprehension of the murderers. The reward was increased to £300, but the murder remained unsolved. A fortnight later Jean Willener, died by his own hand at Batesford, and Willener's distress after Hinke's death was said to be the reason.

In the 1860's the vineyards prospered. John Belperroud won a prize of one hundred and fifty guineas for treatises on vine cultivation and wine-making in Australia. The quality of local wines improved greatly, vintage wines sent overseas taking first prizes at the Bordeaux and Paris exhibitions, and the Belperrouds passed to tranquil old age when the dreaded

John had been asleep too, I knew, but said he hadn't, then crept up under the tarpaulin. The horses were not far away, it was a still night. I could hear the bell and even at times, the clink of the hobbles, so I sat down on a bag of chaff by the fire. Though feeling dozy, I resolved not to go to sleep. A little before daylight, I was suddenly startled by hearing a horse galloping through the bush. It came nearer, but at a slower pace. I got up and went to the horses, making sure they were all right. As the stranger rode closer I said: "Good morning." "Oh" he answered, "are these your horses"? "Yes," I replied, "they are." "I'm camped a couple of miles on," he said, "and missed my horses about an hour ago and hearing your bell which sounds very like mine, I made sure I had found them. Botheration, I can't make out where they could have got to, I heard the bell about three hours before I missed them." "Did you hunt well around the camp?" I asked him. "Well, I made a circuit round," he replied, "till I heard your bell, when I thought I had found them." Then, bidding me "good morning" rode off. Whether the man was a horse thief or not it was impossible to say, but I put him down as one. Every trip I made to Ballarat I heard of cases of horse stealing. It was a very easy matter for a thief, if he stole a horse, to sell it. The plan was to run him into Melbourne and sell him next day at auction, and no questions asked. There were no telegraphs in those days.

The next stage, we reached Ballarat about one o clock and stopped at the foot of Prince Regent, on the slope of a rise, to have dinner and feed the horses, I with an eye to probable business afterwards, as there were a considerable number of stores and tents on Prince Regent and Canadian Gullies; the jeweller's shops as they were called. A small distance from our stopping place were several men idling about, shepherding for a chance of the lead coming their way.

After the horses had finished their feed, the black mare was anxious for a bit of grass, which was plentiful just there. I tethered her to a stump, as I thought clear of the holes, several of which had been sunk various depths by shepherds, but proving to be off the line, had been abandoned. The mare, as it proved, had not been accustomed to the tether-rope, got it behind one of her hind heels and kept backing on to the rope and tightening on to

Sovereign Hill utilised many original buildings.

it till she threw herself down. There was a hole twelve feet deep close to her, in rolling over her hind-part went in to the hole, and down she went as tight as a cork in a bottle, for the hole was round, and there she sat on her tail, her hind legs buckled up over her belly, and her head about six feet from the surface. The only part of her body she could move was the head, the back of which she kept pounding against the side of the shaft, and I believe if it had been hard, she would have knocked her brains out, but it happened to be soft clay.

"Holy Moses," here was a fix. How was it possible to get her out of that? The diggers came rushing round. Some proposed one plan, some another. At last one man going down the slope a bit said: "Boys, let us dig a sloping trench, so that she can walk out." That struck the crowd as the best plan. There were more volunteers than could find room to work, and at it they went. After they had been working a while, I thought of the rum, bringing out a bottle and a pannikin, I gave each of the workers a stiff dose. There was no such rum like it on Ballarat they declared. Then Jemima! Didn't the dirt fly. In three quarters of an hour they had brought the trench to within three feet of the bottom of the shaft, when, twisting the mare round a little by aid of a rope on her fore legs, she fell into the trench and scrambled up quick-and-lively, and out she walked, little the worse except a few abrasions. To say that I was pleased at the restoration of my £50 mare to her feet, is putting it too mildly. Out came two more bottles of rum. I treated those who had worked and some who looked on, for I knew they would all have been willing to help, if there had been room. As rough a lot as diggers were, they were always ready to help and ever risk their lives for a fellowman in distress.

Seeing I had grog I was asked if I had any for sale. "A few bottles," I told them. I sold five or six bottles in a jiffy when a crowd began to muster round the dray. I took out another bottle and said: "This is the last, this is all I have got and please do not crowd round my dray, the police might come along and smell a rat." With that, they cleared off, hiding the bottles where best they could.

After all things got straight again, we yoked up again and visited the stores to dispose of the load I had, bran, oats, cork butter, cheese, two or three bags of cabbages etc. I disposed of a good quantity. Several of the stores and shanties asked me for hard stuff. I told them perhaps next trip I might bring some. That was not much satisfaction, they wanted it then. One storekeeper ordered me to bring him three cases of Holland gin, two gallons brandy, and five of rum. A shanty man wanted five gallons rum and two cases of Old Tom.

OLD BALLARAT

This view is from the top of the mullock heap at Ballarat's Sovereign Hill. It is a genuine old mine at Golden Point, and looks down to the 1850s main road leading into the city from Geelong. Henry often camped at this location while he sold his goods in the centre of what was the old town at the end of this road. The large hill in the background is the ever-present Mt. Warrenheip.

Having no contraband aboard, we camped in the heart of Ballarat that night. What goods I had, were easily disposed of before dinner-time. I came in contact with another party wanting hard stuff, two noted shanty keepers in partnership, I will not give their real names, I had known in Geelong. I will call them Lanky and Squat - one was a very tall thin man, the other quite the reverse. They wanted some cases of Holland gin, brandy and I think some bottled beer and stout, I promised to bring it. In the afternoon we started on our journey. John was not well, he was taken with an attack of dysentery and was glad to get back home.

After I had loaded up for the next trip, he was not able to go with me. Not being able to get anyone to accompany me I started alone. I kept the horses tied, and fed them at the dray by night, and did not hobble them out for safety. Having a light load, the grog that had been ordered, a few other articles with bran, oats, vegetables etc. I got on without mishap. When nearing Ballarat, I met the man John sold his horse to. When carriers of acquaintance met on the road, they generally stopped a few minutes to have a pitch. I remarked the roads were getting worse and very much cut up, and looking at his team I did not see the horse John had sold him, so I said "Where is the horse you bought off my mate?" "Oh," he said, "I shot him." "Shot him?" "Yes," he said: "I got stuck coming up a little on this side of Watson's. He gave one pull and after that refused to pull another ounce. I tried him all manner of ways, but it was no use. I was that mad I took the gun out of the dray and blew his brains out." "What a silly thing to do," I said, "why did you not put him in the saleyard and sell him? It astonishes me, he always pulled fairly well with us." "Oh," he answered, "I was a fool I know, but I have such a beastly hot temper."

We then, each went his way. I arrived late in the afternoon at the Prince Regent and Canadian Gullies; the coast being clear, I delivered my orders and sold a little besides and got the cash. When I came near to Lanky and Squat's I left the team standing, it was just getting dusk, till I went over to the shanty, looking about me to see how the land lay. Entering the tent I saw a stranger behind the counter talking very loudly to some other fellows behind a calico partition. I asked to see the bosses, or one of them. "What about?" he enquired. "Business," I told him. He laughed and said: "If you want to do business with Lanky and Squat, you will have to come early in the morning, at this time o'day they're always dead drunk." I ventured to tell the man I had some stuff for them which they had ordered last week. "All right," he said, "I'll tell 'em, but you come early in the morning, they'll be sober enough then." After asking for a drop of Old Tom for myself, shouting for the man in charge and three or four more who happened to come in, I took the team a little on from the shanty among the tents.

I took out the horses and fed them and myself too, boiling my billy at one of the numerous fires. Several diggers stuck me up for a yarn, wanting to know what I had for sale. I sold some vegetables after dark and a few other small things; some asked me for spirits, I told them I didn't deal in it. I talked about the town, in turn they informed me of the finds of gold, new rushes, accidents, digger hunts, police doings etc. till I daresay it was eleven o'clock, when I spread my blankets under the dray and lay down as usual in my clothes. All noises ceased about twelve o'clock. The silence seemed oppressive after the uproarious din of the fore part of the night. I felt lonesome, having no one with me. All I could hear was the constant champ, champing of the horses over the feedbag. Between the shafts and an occasional growl of my little dog Prin, lying at my feet on the blankets.

It must have been three o'clock before I dozed off into a sound sleep. I had been sleeping an hour when Prin gave a ferocious yell and darted through the spokes of the wheel. Starting up, I saw a part of a man, just his legs, standing close to the wheel. "Hullo," I sang out, "what do you want?" The figure then drew back when I saw the outline of a man. "Can y-ye tell me the r-right way t-to Gol-golden Poinsh?" "Golden Point is just straight behind you," I told him. "How f-far isht?" "A quarter of a mile." "I-I'm losht," he said, and tumbled and staggered about. "I-I don't know where I am." He went on: "if-if you'd only get get up mate and show, show me the way." "I told you the way," I said, "and clear out of this before the dog nips your shins." Then he tried to make friends with the dog, but Prin would have none of him and kept snapping and growling at him for all she was worth. At last he staggered off. I watched his outline till he crossed the light of a dying fire. He was walking straight and steadily then.

I did not sleep after. Daylight soon broke and as soon as the sun rose I was alert watching for Lanky and Squat. I had not to wait long before Squat made his appearance, then Lanky, both looking seedy enough. "Hullo," they almost together cried out, "is that you?" "Yes," I said. "The top of the morning to ye. You have brought the stuff?" Lanky enquired. "Yes," I answered, 'it is close handy and I would like to get it in before the police are about." "The police," Squat exclaimed, "they won't be about for two hours yet, the lazy beggars are too fond of sleeping in." The three of us carried the stuff from the dray to the shanty. They paid me without a murmur, in fact they got it from me cheaper than they had ever got any before, but I was satisfied with 100% for a week's turnover, with the cash in my pocket and all safe. On receiving the money from Lanky, half a dozen revived drunks shuffled into the room; of course I had to shout for them, together with the two landlords.

After my horses had finished their morning's feed and I, my breakfast, I yoked up and proceeded to dispose of what articles I had left, which did not take long. When I was on my way homeward, I saw two suspicious looking characters on horseback who passed me with a "goodday." I had my money, excepting about a pound's worth of silver, rammed well down in a chaff bag, a hiding place I often made use of.

When I reached home John did not seem much better, he was too weak to go with me the next trip. In fact he did not seem inclined to go at all for the present. I did not care to go again alone. Going, as usual when home, to see my little girl. Edwin Gillingham, with his mother and brother Nathan, were still staying with the Gribbles. As I was talking to Ann and telling her about John being sick, and had to go by myself the last trip, I asked her if she thought Edwin would go with me? "Oh yes," she said, "I'm sure he would, he'd go anywhere with you. You ought to have someone with you," she added, "if some of these bushrangers thought you had money about you and all by yourself, they might kill you for it."

"Not likely," I answered, "that anyone will get up on me at night. Not while Prin is with me. Anyway

it would not matter if I was killed, I'm only one in the world, I should not be missed." Ann looked hard at me then said; "What nonsense, wouldn't your father, mother, John and your little sister miss you?" I looked into her sweet little face for a second or two, then whispered, significantly. "I wonder if there is anyone else who would miss me?" Suddenly she sprang up from her chair. "Oh," she cried, "here's Old John coming, I know," and rushed to open the door for him, and John moving his head from side to side with a merry twinkle in his eye, bade us all "guid e'en." I felt annoyed with Old John for the first time, for breaking up our tete-a-tete so inopportunely.

Ever since Nathan Gillingham's death, Old John had been Fanny's most assiduous and devoted friend. It was very apparent to all that John, the old rogue, had his eye on Fanny, but according to account, he had left a wife in Yorkshire. He had come to Australia as a servant several years before, but it did not matter, she might be dead, or at any rate she was a long way off and he was never likely to see her again, so he made up his mind to capture Fanny although he was sixty-four years old.

Gribble was only idling about, but kept what was called steady, only got drunk occasionally. He talked of going to the diggings again, if he did he would go to Ballarat with me. Late in the evening I said to Edwin: "What wages are you getting at the place where you are working?" "35/-" he said. I asked him if he would like to come on the road with me. "Oh wouldn't I," he replied, "I should like it." I told him I would give him 50/- a week and his food, but he would have to share with me in watching the horses by night, when turned out. When in town, I told him he would have nothing to do but look after the horses sometimes, and help me load. That was all splendid, he was in great glee. He told his mother, she was pleased too.

About this time a new order of things was introduced on the diggings with regard to the supervision of the police. The policy of La Trobe and his government became, like themselves, very unpopular. The carriers and storekeepers, the suppliers of food and necessaries for the population greatly resented the too often unnecessary interference of the police in ransacking drays for the discovery of contraband goods, often breaking and destroying other goods; so eager were they to secure convictions for the sake of the fine. The police were no longer to receive any part of the fine, instead, a party of spies, detectives they were called, were to roam at will over the diggings to spy out and bring to punishment, all offenders against the law in any shape, but principally against sly grog sellers.

The drink traffic, instead of being stamped out as La Trobe intended it should be, was no doubt on the increase. Some of the shanties were kept by old ex-convicts and the down they had against these detectives was intense. They designated them as informers and placed them in the category as government flagellators, that is, men whose duty it was to flog recalcitrant prisoners when serving their time. This spy system was almost a failure, very few arrests were made. The detectives received only their common pay, the sole incentive to seek out offenders, was their duty, which did not count for much. In fact, some of them fraternised with storekeepers and shanty-keepers and had a fine rosy time and all the grog they could drink; while those who did actually do their duty, were in danger of losing their lives, and were quickly changed to other quarters.

The day on which I engaged Edwin was Friday, and he had not finished his week where he worked till next night. I loaded the dray myself on Saturday in order to be ready for a start on Monday. I had

190

got no special orders but loaded with goods I knew would be the best for sale, principally spirits and bottled malt liquors, and some bags of chaff, bran etc. to finish the top of the load, taking especial care no sharp edges showed under the tarpaulin which covered the whole. We arrived in Ballarat Wednesday evening, and camped a mile from the diggings. I had an idea, on the road, of trying Eureka next. I had heard a favourable account of it for my line of business. So I rose pretty early next morning, leaving Edwin in charge of the dray and horses to try my luck in Eureka, which was two miles beyond Ballarat.

The first store I called at, the man asked me where my dray was. I told him on the road. "Well," he said, "I don't mind taking some sugar, butter and a case of Holland gin." I then went further on into the heart of Eureka diggings and called at a large store situated a considerable distance from any other store. The man who owned the store, though not his real name, I will call Eakin. Several men were there at a counter, I supposed enjoying themselves. I asked if I could see the storekeeper, looking at me suspiciously, a man on the opposite side of the counter replied: "Yes, here I am at your service. What is it?" I said, "I want to speak to you privately." "Alright," he answered, "come

Eureka Street leading to the site of the rebellion.

On the old main road into Ballarat, and close to the centre of the original hub of the town, lies an anonymous roundabout whose turn to the right was once the major road known as Eureka Street. Surprisingly, Ballarat seems to place little significance on its masses of historic areas. Most travellers pass by without realising what dramatic things happened in the surroundings, eventhough they may be familiar with the events.

this way," leading me into a back partition, then said: "Alright, we can talk here." I told him I was a carrier from Geelong and what goods I had for sale and the prices. "Good," he said, "I am in want of some of the things you mention. Bring up your dray, we will most likely be able to do business." "I said: "I usually deliver hard stuff early in the morning before the police are about." "No doubt," he said, "you are right there, in other places; but I have no reason to fear the police myself; they are my friends, if they caught you at my store you would be perfectly safe." "Yes, I answered him, "but there is running the gauntlet from my camping place to get here." "No doubt you are right," he said, "you will be here early tomorrow morning then?" "Yes, without fail." "Will you have a wet?" he asked. "Don't mind." I took a drink of Byass's stout. After talking a while of things in general I said: "Let us have another drink. What'll you lads take," I said, turning to half a dozen standing by, "name yer poisin." A short time after, I left, inwardly chafing at the necessity of having to wait till the morrow, for it was not more than twelve o'clock. I wanted to get home by Saturday night to go to the play. However there was nothing else for it.

At break of day we were yoked up, and started, arriving at the first store the man was not yet up. "Who's that?" he sang out. I told him, he was soon out. "You are early men of business," he said. "Yes," I answered, "we aim to be earlier than the traps you know." I showed him the things he had asked for. He was satisfied with the gin from its brand and the soundness of the case, the sugar he tested and something else. "All right," he said, we took them into the store. When he paid me I asked him to have a drink. "No," he said, "its too early"; then considering a second, "oh, well," he said, "I'll take a drop of wine." I and Edwin had wine too. All settled, I made for Eakin's. Eakin was up and looking out. He examined my loading, agreed, after looking at the brands of brandy, gin, Old Tom ale and stout, to take it all.

There were then some mats of sugar, two casks of Cork butter, a few bags of oats and bran and a few other light things. He noted these in his pocket book and the prices. The sugar was seventy pound guaranteed, the oats and bran were so much a bag. After he had added up the whole amount, he said: "Look here. I'll take all you have got, clear you out in fact, if you will knock off £2." I replied: "you know very well I am letting you have these things considerably below what you have been paying for them, it's too bad to want to stop £2." "You will make a thundering good profit if you do knock off £2," he said. "Look at the risk I have to run", I answered. "No risk at all my dear boy," he replied, "in dealing with me."

Then he told me he had been a member of the police force, he had a mate, his partner, in it yet. They had agreed to start a store between them and he (Eakin) was to leave the force and run it while his mate should still retain his position in the force. "What with the police and the diggers, I am doing a very good business. I can see you know what goes off best and if you bring a load of assorted goods principally hard stuff, most likely I will be able to take the principal part of it or perhaps the whole of it every trip, as you say, you generally make a trip a week." Looking at the chance of partial protection and also the quick sale of my stuff I said "very well, I will abate the £2."

MASSES OF GOLD
Between 1851 and 1860 the USA produced 41% of the world's gold, most of it from California where it had been discovered in 1849.
Australia then produced 39% of the world's gold, most of it from Victoria.
Between 1851 and 1861 Ballarat and Bendigo produced £124,000,000 of gold or over 56,000 tonnes. That was over half of the world's gold.

While Edwin and I were unloading, about a dozen seedy looking fellows came to the store. When I was paid, of course I was expected to shout for all present. Eakin, no doubt had signalised that cheap drinks were most likely forthcoming. There was no other thing expected of me but to shout for all round; it cost me 14/-.

Bidding them goodbye we started homewards. On passing Golden Point a man I knew met me and seeing I was empty asked me to take a load of sheepskins for him to Ryrie Street in Geelong.

I asked him if they were all at one place and ready and how much he considered it was worth. I will give you £5, he said, to take them down. They are all ready here at the butcher's shop. We soon loaded the skins and were soon on the road again. The roll of notes I had, I pushed among the skins for safety.

We arrived home in good time on Saturday. After supper I hastened to visit my girl and the Gribbles. Edwin told how he enjoyed the road and his new billet; his tongue never stopped telling of what he had seen. Gribble had been boozing rather much lately. Mrs Gribble wanted him to have another try on the diggings, to try his luck at Ballarat. "So I will old woman," he said, "if you'll go too. We'll pack up right away and go with Mundy next trip, if he'll take us." "Oh I'll take you," I said, "if you have not too much luggage." "Only the bedding, a few clothes and a few cooking things and a tent," he answered. "What do you say old woman?" "I am quite agreeable," she replied. "Is Ann going too?" I enquired. "No," her mother answered, "Ann and Fanny must stay and mind the house."

So it was agreed that they should go to Ballarat with me on Monday. After this affair was settled I said I was going to the theatre, and asked Edwin to go with me, he was overjoyed at the idea. I looked at Ann but not daring to ask her mother for her consent to let her go too for fear of a refusal. Edwin and I went.

These were happy times and nothing delighted me more than to see George Coppin, the great comic actor on the stage, whose popularity at that time was at its height; then there were Holloway, the tragedian, Chambers the villain of the plot and Webster in all capacities, and Mrs Webster the sweet singer and others, the quarter of an hour of interval, then the after-piece.

I never enjoyed myself more in my life more than at that time; except, after a time, when I used to take Ann with me.

The theatre came out about eleven o'clock. When Edwin and I arrived Gribble's they were still busy in conversation. I gave Ann some little nicknacks I had brought her. There was Old John sitting very close to and a-courting of Fanny who shifted a little away, but it was no use John sidled up. "Well lads." John said, "hoo did ye enjoy yersens." "First-rate John," I said, "you ought to have been there and taken Fanny." John chuckled at that, and got a little closer and said: "I'd tak thee lass. Willin, if tha woulds't gae." "Gets thee out," Fanny retorted, "think's I'd be sen going to a theatre we an auld frump like thee." John, nothing abashed said: "Tha'rt going to be the owd man's darling, masin "Does ent e' make a fool of thee self, John Crosby," Fanny apparently cross replied. "Na na," John put in: "Ah'm na fuile, it's the bonniest little woman in the world and I mun hae her," with that he hitched another inch nearer and tried to take her hand, when she got up and sat in another chair.

I paid them another visit next day, Sunday, and as usual had tea there. They had been busy packing for their intended trip to Ballarat. Gribble was about half on and swore he was going to be lucky this time. He was acquainted with a man named Grace who had a wife and child. He was going to Ballarat too and had agreed to be mates. Grace had agreed with a man to start on Tuesday. He said he had a tent to buy, and other small things which he had intended to get, while I was loading on Monday morning. He added too, we cannot go far at any rate on Monday so I agreed to wait till Tuesday, when both drays could start together and be in company; besides I would have another night with my sweetheart.

Monday morning found us early on the road. There were a few tears between Ann and mother but the latter assuring Ann if they were not lucky soon, she would be home again, or if they were prosperous she would bring her a big nugget. The roads were anything but good. The men walked over bad places and rode on favourable occasions. Horse drays having light loads could best pick their way by shunning the main bullock track by taking to the bush for it. There was a dreadful slough of despond called 'Scott's Swamp', near the foot of Mount Buninyong about three hundred yards across of black sticky mud. Many a bullock lost the number of his mess there; one team by itself never attempted to cross it. Two teams and sometimes three would yoke together and take over a load at a time. Sometimes a bullock would fall, but no stopping to get him up again. The poor brute was dragged along by the neck to the other side dead or alive, very often choked. Horses could not travel

Mt Buninyong to the north as the road heads down to the former Scott's Swamp.

Bakery Hill is now only a name. Once it was buzzing with diggers.

'Scott's Swamp' as it was. It is now known as Scotsburn.

at all through the sticky mud on account of their flat feet, bullocks had the only chance. On the third day we arrived at Ballarat. Gribble and his mate Grace selected Bakery Hill for a camping place, pitching their tents temporarily for the night intending next day to go into the bush, get saplings and fix them permanently.

I had not seen Lanky and Squat for over a fortnight, so took it into my head, after supper, to pay them another visit. I found the same man attending to the business as before. He knew me of course. "Hullo," he cried out, "where have you been? The old uns have been looking out for you." "What's the matter," I asked, "are you in want of stuff?" "Run out of everything but rum," he replied, "where's your dray?" he said. "I'm camped on Bakery Hill." "Ah, too far, or I'd take on myself to take a couple of dozen of ale and stout. What made you camp on Bakery Hill right in view of the camp?" I told him I had brought a man and woman from Geelong and that was where they wanted to camp. "Can't you" , I asked him, "wake the old men up, if I got their order, I could be here by daylight." "No," he replied, "I'm not going to try, if they are awakened out of their drunken sleep they're so horrid cross and perhaps tell me to go to hell. They are first rate fellows when sober, but as intractable as pigs when in liquor. Come down early in the morning," the man said, "the same as you did before, they are sure to take some off you." "Very well," I said, "I will," and left.

Yoking before breakfast I called on Lanky and Squat who appeared to be lively enough and ready to do business. They took bottled ale, stout, two or three cases of brandy, and some gin, a fairly good bill altogether. After being paid and shouting several drinks, I started on a back road to Eakin's place. Young Edwin asked: "When are we going to have breakfast?" he felt hungry. "Oh," I said, "take a lump in your fist for the present, we'll have breakfast when we get to Eakin's."

We reached Eakin's alright, and seeing us he came and said: "What have you got for us this time Mundy?" I replied: "Butter, bacon, cheese, tea, sugar and some stuff - I'll show you bye-and-bye, we've had no breakfast yet," I continued, unhooking the horses, "and the horses have not had half a feed." "Had no breakfast? We've had our's, but if you and your mate will come in, Mrs Eakin will prepare you some in a jiffy." I thanked him, and when we were ready, followed him inside.

Mrs Eakin received us cordially and when she ascertained what was required of her had the frying pan on and steaks frizzling in less than no time. She was a tall, pleasant looking woman with very engaging manners, a real lady. While we were breakfasting, Eakin was overhauling the dray, and when we returned said, "I think I can take all you have got, except all the bacon, two sides are enough for me for the present." "Alright," I said, "perhaps the next store may take it as we go back, I have not called on him yet." After a little apparent cogitation, "Oh well," he said, "I'll take the lot, clear you out, but you must allow me a little discount. When you come next time," Eakin said, "I wish you would bring some potatoes, I have not seen any for a long time and am often asked for them. I do not mind what I pay for them in reason you know." "Potatoes and flour," I answered, "I leave to the bullockies, considering the state of the roads, they are a too heavy loading for horse teams." "The bullock teams seldom come as far as Eureka," he replied. "If you could bring only a couple of hundred weight, it would be obliging me, if only for our own use." So I promised to bring them next trip.

HER MAJESTY'S THEATRE
BALLARAT

Theatre was part of Ballarat life from the early years of the gold rushes. The earliest theatres were associated with the hotels along Main Road, the commercial hub of the Ballarat Flat, in the midst of the diggings. The best known were the Victoria, the Charlie Napier and the Montezuma. These goldfields theatres were wooden structures, very susceptible to fire, and were regularly destroyed in major conflagrations along Main Road and rebuilt.

Ballarat's first permanent theatre, the Theatre Royal, was built in 1858 in the new township on the hill, away from the crowded conditions on the Flat. The Royal, in Sturt Street, was a part of the shift in the centre of business activity away from Main Road to the Township.

Her Majesty's founder was Sir William Clarke, Baronet, and it was known as The Academy of Music. In 1898 the Theatre was sold to James Coghlan JP, Harry Davies and Johannes (John) Heinz. Davies was a draper, Coghlan a brewer, and Heinz a butcher - known as "Rags, Bottles and Bones."

193

BALLARAT

Ballaarat (original spelling) began in April 1837 when Thomas Livingstone Learmonth climbed Mount Buninyong. Next year William Cross Yuille and Henry Anderson formed a sheep station at what is now Lake Wendouree. Learmonth and Scott took up land near Buninyong. For the next thirteen years this district was like any out-back of Australia. Twice every year their bullock wagons travelled to Geelong for supplies for seventy families living in bark huts and mud cabins.

Buninyong was the centre of the district. Here was Mrs Jamieson's Inn, Campbell and Woolley's General store, and the only church in the district. In August 1851, Dunlop and Regan discovered gold at Poverty Point in Ballarat East. In a fortnight there were 400 digging for gold around Golden Point, at the foot of Black Hill, and on both sides of the Yarrowee - and finding plenty.

In 1853 - 319,154 ounces of gold worth more than a million pounds, went to Melbourne under Police Escort. During the

four following years, 1854 - 1858, more than 2,500,000 ounces, worth about 10 million pounds, was taken from Ballaarat in this way, and probably much more was taken away by lucky diggers in their boxes and bags. The total amount of gold secured in the Ballaarat district from 1851 until 2000 was more than 21,000,000 ounces, or 643 tons. The block between Eureka and Esmond (now York) Streets, was the original centre of Ballarat. In that one block were sixty shops, twelve hotels, and four large well equipped theatres. Shops and hotels did not close till midnight and the roadway was always crowded with laughing noisy people. Early in 1852, the Government

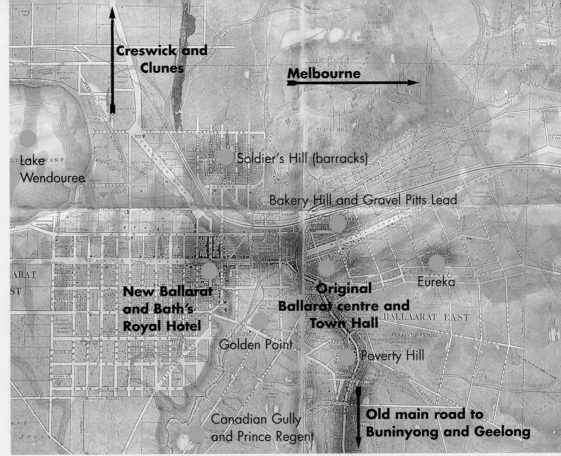

An 1860s map of Ballarat.

Left: The mail coach from Ballarat bursts into Geelong.

When I reached Bakery Hill, Gribble and Grace had just come in from the bush. I had promised them if they had cut the sticks for putting up their tents I would let them have a horse and dray to bring them in. They had all they wanted ready they told me, so both of them with Edwin, went with the dray to bring them in, while I waited with the women.

While I was waiting, a man passed by whom I knew very well. He was a local preacher in father's chapel named Burrows. He saw me, came to me saying: "Good day Mr Mundy, how are you?" "Pretty well thank you," I replied, "how's yourself?" "All right and thank God, but not lucky in the digging business. I and my two mates have been on Ballarat now three months and have done nothing and not the shadow of a show yet. We are full up of it and are going to return home. I was just looking about for a dray going to Geelong to get a lift down with our swags." I told him I was going to start for Geelong that afternoon, I was only waiting for my dray, I had landed a party there yesterday and had lent them the dray and horse to get sticks for fixing their tent. "What a pity," he said, "I do not know exactly where my mates are just now and probably will not see them till the evening. Can't you stay till the morning." "I think I can." "I think I can find you a couple more who want a ride down. How much do you charge?" "A pound each," I told him. "That's not unreasonable for a man and his swag to be conveyed 60 miles." I said, "It will take two days to go down, we will camp one night at Watson's, half way, you could get your meals and sleep there." "That would do very well," he replied, "if you will wait till tomorrow and I will try and hunt up the other two men." I told him I would wait till tomorrow.

Late in the evening Burrows came and told me there were five men beside himself who wanted a lift to Geelong, if I could accommodate them. "Yes," I said, "I can take you all. You can sit on your swags riding, but you will have to get lodgings at Watson's for the night." "That's all right, what time will we have to be here?" "After early breakfast," I told him.

When we were yoking up, the six men were there. After bidding the Gribbles "Goodbye" we started. When ten miles on the road, one of the men produced from his swag a square bottle of Holland gin and passed nobblers round in a pannikin; all had a drink, but Edwin, who did not care for drink at that, and I never pressed him.

Passing Burnt Bridge a couple of miles, we stopped for dinner and another dose of gin. Two miles on the road the man with the gin bottle proposed emptying it. Burrows declined any more, nevertheless the bottle was emptied and pitched overboard. When we arrived at Watson's there was, as usual, a pretty good crowd. It was then the only public house between Bates Ford and Mother Jamieson's at Buninyong.

My six passengers went in for supper which was bread, salt-junk and tea in pannikins. This feed was charged 2/6 for. Beds were full many times over, if they had had them. Each traveller had to use his own swag if he had one, and doss on the dining table or under it or on whatever part of the dirt floor he chose to select for his night's rest under the roof; for this sleeping accommodation was charged 2/6. Burrows being sober, had his eye to business, was fortunate enough to secure a spread for his blankets on the table. Edwin and I of course slept in the dray. The horses I kept tied up to the feed bag, all the night.

Burrows in the morning had a fearful tale to tell about his night's lodging. He sat up till one o'clock, among, as he termed it, the drunk blasphemous crowd. When it appeared to be somewhat quiet, he turned in to try to get a little sleep. Next to him on the table, a man had been sleeping and snoring, like a pig, in his drunken sleep for sometime. "Just as I had dropped into a doze," Burrows said, "the fellow put his arm round me and hugged and pulled me about, called me his dear Jenny and protested how he loved me and tried to kiss me. As soon as I could get free of the brute, disgusted, I sprang off the table, dragging my blankets with me. I rolled them into a heap and sat on them till I saw day breaking, when I rolled them up and left the wretched den. They call it the Devil's Hotel don't they?" "Yes," I said "that's what it is called." "Rightly named too," he replied, "I hope, please God, I will never enter such a house again."

The newer hotel at Meredith replacing Watson's.

But the days of Watson's Hotel were numbered. A road from Geelong to Ballarat was then being surveyed, coming from Geelong leaving Watson's a quarter of a mile to the right, and the nucleus of the township of Meredith was formed half a mile from Watson's by Richard Gosling formerly of the Union Inn in Malop Street, Geelong, building a decent hotel. The doom of the Devil's Hotel was sealed.

Edwin was making ready breakfast. I said: "Mr Burrows, breakfast will soon be ready, you had better join us, we have plenty," which he did and was very thankful.

My passengers being all aboard we made an early start. We stopped halfway to have dinner, and feed the horses, when I hauled out of a chaff bag a bottle of Martell's brandy and giving each one a good nip, and then, on the road again, another, which emptied the bottle. All were as merry as sandboys. At Bates Ford two or three insisted on shouting, in which case I was urged to pull up. I had to sing out to them to come on or I would leave them behind. Bell Post Hill at last. Everyone expressed their pleasure on seeing again the beautiful Corio Bay with the ships and boats, and houses nestling down to the receding shore. We reached Geelong in good time, when each one went his way.

After supper Edwin went to see his mother and I to see Ann. They were both busily employed washing up tea things. We had to answer many questions as to our trip, how did mother like Ballarat and how did Gribble behave himself, had they pitched there nicely, did I think there were good chances of dropping on gold? Which queries I answered to the best of my ability. Then I asked Fanny had she seen my old friend, her sweetheart John Crosby lately, "Drat him" she said, "he be here every night, the auld fuil, I be right sick o' um, I'm june blunt you know, I tell un what I think o' un." But Fanny took it all in good part, seemed more pleased than vexed, laughing all the time she's talking. She was an excellent mimic, took off old John to a nicety. John halted a little on one leg. Having been broken in his youth, one limb was a little shorter than the other. She would limp up and down the floor and imitate him to perfection.

After an hour's chat Edwin and I left to go to the theatre, promising to call in on going home. The play was grand as usual, Coppin in the after-piece excelled himself as Uriah Heap 'I hope I don't intrude'. On returning, I took Ann I recollect, a bag of Barcellona nuts and gingerbread. We cracked nuts and threw the shells at each other, and thoroughly enjoyed ourselves till it was half past twelve; when Fanny said: "It is time fur young men out courting to go whum." "All right Fanny," I said, "I'm off." Going to the door and bidding them good night Fanny said to Ann: "Why doesn't go to the gate we 'un?" Ann came out and just went through the gateway when an overpowerful longing seized me to kiss her. I suddenly took her round the neck and pressed a fervent kiss on her lips. She tore herself away, ran inside the gate and shut it saying: "What did you do that for?" "Oh," I said, "Ann, because I couldn't help it." We looked at each other over the top of the gate for about half a minute in silence, she pretending to be angry, and I to

sent Surveyor W H Urquhart to lay out a formal township, and he quickly saw that low-lying Main Road was an unsuitable spot. He decided to get out of the population areas, and lay his township upon the plateau. He meant the new township to go north and south.

Lydiard Street was to be the main official street, with public offices, churches, banks and hotels; Armstrong Street was to be the main business street; Doveton Street, the residential street, while cross streets were named Dana, Sturt and Mair Streets.

On 5th May 1857, the first municipal Council met at the Golden Fleece Hotel in Lydiard Street. An underground pipe was laid from the Lake, the spot where the Burke and Wills Monument stands today.

The 'Welcome Nugget' was found on 10th June 1858, at the corner of Mair and Humffray Streets, at a depth of 180 feet. It was 1/2 cwt. of pure gold.

Several big disastrous fires destroyed both sides of the business block between Eureka and York Streets - and frequent destructive floods that inundated Main Road forced the merchants to seek safer areas. Main Road lost its importance as the shopping centre, and Sturt Street gradually became the place where business was done.

1869 was when mining reached its most prosperous point. There were more than 300 mining companies with extensive plants around Ballaarat, giving employment to thousands of miners and supporting some seventy sharebrokers, buying and selling shares for their speculating clients. The population of Ballarat was more than 60,000.

In 1870 the bottom fell out of the mining industry. The drop in the value of Ballaarat mining shares was equal to half of all the revenue of the Government of Victoria.

In 1871, Ballaarat was gazetted a City, and the City Hall was commissioned, though it took ten years to finish.

Early in 1858, the Municipal Council engaged George Longley to make a Botanical Gardens on the west side of Lake Wendouree. Till 1887, the centre of wide Sturt Street was

195

occupied by two lines of tall blue gums, but making the street dark, dull and damp in winter time. In that year, Mayor T H Thompson, despite much opposition, had the gums uprooted and replaced by oaks and elms. Then in 1896, Mayor C C Shoppee made a flower garden in the centre of the street between Armstrong and Doveton Streets. The people owning shops in other parts of Sturt Street got to work and with the help of Mr Arthur Farrer, gradually built up the 'floral way' of which Ballaarat folk are so proud.

In 1857, a rival Municipal Council was formed in Ballaarat East, and it took until 1921 for enmity between the 'Township' and the 'Flat' to die away and the city councils to be amalgamated.

be penitent, till I whispered "good night Ann," to which she replied just audibly "good night."

Oh but these were happy days, little did we dream of what fate had in store for us in the years that were coming.

As Gribble had settled at Ballarat for the time, I conceived the idea of erecting a tent alongside of his; I could reach Ballarat after dark, and unload any goods that were seizable and place them safely undercover, while I could cart them out as occasion required. So I made up my mind when I would be loading on Monday to purchase a tent about 20 X 12, take it with me next trip and pitch it at once. I was telling my brother John what I intended doing. "Much the safest plan," he agreed, "but you will have to get someone to look after it and live in it or you will find if any grog is left in it, it will be cleared out on your return and what can you say?" I said: "As you have nothing in hand just now, will you undertake to look after it and sell what you can wholesale by the gallon or bottle, but do no trade retail?" "Yes," he said, "I'm willing to do that, as I do not see anything better sticking out just now." So it was arranged, and he was to receive his share of the profits according to his venture.

On the Sunday afternoon I went to see Ann and Fanny and had tea with them. Old John was there too, quite at home, he had brought Fanny a large nosegay, pointing it out to me: "Isn't it a beauty," he chuckled. "My word yes," I said, "flowers must be plentiful where you got that." The most remarkable feature about it was its size. "Oh flowers, there is plenty o'em to fettle aw Geelong, I bowt them frae a market garden and gave half a croon for them." "More fuil you," Fanny joined in, "to spend half a crown for a posy for I." But John took no notice of this ungrateful reply to his generosity. John had an axe to grind and meant to carry his point.

On Monday morning, Edwin and I, and my brother John was with us, we loaded up ready for the morrow, not forgetting Eakin's potatoes and a tent for ourselves. I was lucky enough to find a good duck tent and fly. We arrived in Ballarat Thursday evening. Next morning I left John and Edwin with the dray and went to Eureka, to see Eakin to get his orders, so as to be able to deliver them early in the morning. I received a pretty fair order off him, with a likelihood of his taking more things if they suited. On returning to the dray, when just in sight of it, I saw a sight that made my heart go down an inch. Four troopers one on each side, one at the front, another at the back of the dray, sitting straight up with drawn glittering swords leaning back over their shoulders. A commanding officer talking to John and Edwin.

I was afraid of very little those days. I put on a bold front and walked inquiringly up. "Oh," Edwin said, "here's the owner of the dray." Facing me the officer said: "Are you the owner of this dray?" "Yes," I answered, "what's up?" Without replying to my question he said; "What's your name?" Pointing to the plate on the dray, I said: "There it is, you can read - Henry Mundy, carrier to and from Geelong and Ballarat." "Hum." He then went to the other side of the dray and talked to one of the troopers for about a minute, then returning to me, said: "It's a mistake, we thought the dray belonged to some other man." I answered him never a word. He gave command then to the troopers, who forthwith sheathed their swords and went jingling off.

In the early morning we arrived at Eakin's, I told him about the scare I got on returning to the dray yesterday. "What kind of man was the one in charge of the troopers?" he asked. I described him as

Eugene von Guerard came to the Victorian goldfields in 1853, and in the same year painted old Ballarat from the site of the later Bath's Royal Hotel in Lydiard Street South. The large tent is J.A. Rowe's Travelling Circus.

well as I could. He laughed and said: "I suppose you thought you were nabbed alright that time Mundy." "Yes," I said, "it looked very much like it."

At this point of our talk another man came up, and Eakin repeated what I had told him and he laughed too. What they could see to laugh at I could not very well understand, nor did they give me any explanation. Then Eakin turning to the other man: "This is my partner, Mr Amber, Mr Mundy." Shaking hands, we expressed our mutual pleasure on the occasion.

"Now, Mundy, let's see what you've got for us," Eakin said. "It was good of you not to forget the spuds." Looking over the load, he said: "I think we'll take the lot, Charley, eh, what do you say?" "Oh please yourself," Charley replied, "you know best what is wanting."

"Oh," Eakin said, "there are four bags of oats, we don't want them particularly." "Oh," I said, "take the oats and clear me out right, I'll let you have them 3/- a bag cheaper than usual." "Alright," Eakin replied, and then commenced to unload.

The Gravel Pitts lead had just been started, a few holes had been bottomed and proved pretty good. Gribble and Grace had pegged out a claim each, and were now doing a bit of shepherding in great hopes that one of them would be right. They had fixed their tents snug enough on Bakery Hill. The women were settled and content, John and Edwin took the dray to get tent poles, while I chatted with Mrs Gribble, for a time, then went to choose the best spot to fix the tent. When they arrived with the poles I suggested to John the digging of a small cellar after the tent was up, and to spread the dirt that came out over the floor, and to strip some bark by the time I returned, to cover the floor all over, so we could put contraband goods out of sight.

In a short time Edwin and I were on the road home again. We reached Geelong on Sunday night; picking up two travellers on the way. Too late to go out that night. I paid Ann and Fanny a visit next morning. They were both busy sewing. Fanny got her living with the help of her two boys, by making shirts, jumpers and other clothing for the shops. Ann was doing a bit of the kind too, for pocket money. "Lawks," Fanny said, "only whum last night, we expected e' Saturday night, Ann and I expected e' to tea didn't us Ann?" "We had some delay this time," I said, "we lost Saturday nights play by it." "Oh thee art fond of that awled Coppin, I don't know what ye ken zee in un; you and Edwin." "You'd like to see him too if you would like a bit of fun and have a good laugh. Old John, I'm sure, would be proud to take you if ou only gave him a hint." This tickled Ann's fancy some. She did laugh. "I go to the theatre we awld John Crosby," Fanny screeched. "I wudna be sin in a ten acre field we un." "Oh, do aunt, get him to take you and I'll go with you, John will pay for me too I know." "Nay, nay chiel, if thee never goes to the theatre till thee goest we auld John and I, thee ult never go maid." "How is Gribble keeping," Fanny enquired. "Quite good," I answered, "at least as far as I could tell and Mrs Gribble seemed quite content. Gribble thinks he is on the lead this time." At last I said: "I cannot stay any longer, I have to load this afternoon ready for the road tomorrow. I'll call again this evening." Then I left.

After dinner Edwin took one horse and dray and went into the town to load up. Oats, bran, pollard, bacon, hams, cheese and butter from the grocer, from the wine and spirit merchant a cask of Jamaica rum - forty-five gallons, ten gallons dark brandy, the same of pale, some cases of pale brandy, and Holland gin, with a good few dozen of bottled ale and porter. The biggest load I had taken yet as far as value went. The wine and spirit merchants giving me their usual caution to mind and not get "cotched." We returned home and made everything ready for an early start in the morning.

Mother had not been well lately, she got an attack of erysipelas, and had to engage a servant girl to wait on her and the house. Father had plenty to do carting about town carting water etc. He had not the least desire to go to the diggings again.

Another section of the original dirt track to Ballarat from Geelong.

Deep Sinking Ballarat

James. I. Blundell & Co
Melbourne 185

S.T. Gill's lithograph of deep sink mining at Ballarat - probably the Gravel Pitts where this type of ventilation was a characteristic sight.

PROFITS – BUT GAOL TOO!

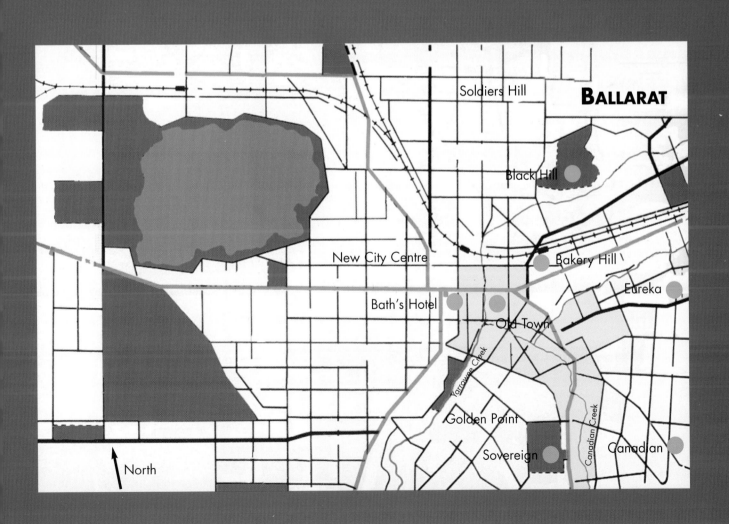

Soldiers Hill

BALLARAT

Black Hill

New City Centre

Bakery Hill

Eureka

Bath's Hotel

Old Town

Yarrowee Creek

Golden Point

Canadian Creek

Sovereign

Canadian

North

BUSY TRADING ILLEGAL GROG ...
HENRY WORKS AT A VERY PROFITABLE BUSINESS,
THEN BUYS LAND IN GEELONG AND LANDS IN GAOL

Edwin

and I reached Ballarat on Thursday afternoon. We found the Gribbles and John alright. John with Gribble's help had dug the cellar as agreed on, but was waiting for the dray to bring in the bark which he and Gribble had got in readiness. Gribble was very sanguine of one of their claims. A hole was going down in a line with him and the claims on gold which would prove, he said, if he had a show or not.

As it was not late, I resolved to see Eakin that night, requesting Gribble to help Edwin to unload the liquors after dark, excepting the rum, which I would help them with when I returned. Arriving at Eakin's, he took me into a canvas compartment where were two mounted troopers enjoying themselves. I looked hard at them wondering if all was right as they looked at me, when Eakin said: "This is a friend of mine who is a carrier from Geelong and supplies me with the greater part of my goods. Allow me to introduce him, Mr H. Mundy." Then signifying them to me, Mr A—, Mr B—- of the Colonial Police Force Mounted Troopers. They both rose, shook hands, saying: "Glad to make your acquaintance, Mr Mundy." One of them, added: "As you are a friend of Eakin's, you are also a friend of our's." "Thank you," I said, "and as we are to be friends, let's have a drink to clinch the compact." They were both agreeable to that.

Naming our drinks Eakin fetched them in with one for himself, then Ambler came in, and had one too. Trooper A. gave a toast: "Here's to our sweethearts and friends and the Devil confound our enemies." This toast was drunk, as the saying goes, with enthusiasm. The troopers were getting pretty well on. They told me that they were sent to arrest a man who was wanted for robbing his mate of eight ounces of gold, but had failed to drop on him, he had probably made tracks for some other diggings, and other confidential talk of little import. One of them at last said: "Well Sam we'd better skedaddle." "Oh," I said, "if you can't stay longer, you must have another drink before you go." "All right," B. said, "just one, that stuff you supply Eakin with is so tempting, there is no refusing it." So all had drinks round again, when after shaking hands and bidding us a hearty good night, unhitched their horses in calico stable, mounted and went rattling off.

I looked out of the tent flap and saw it was getting dark. I said to Ambler: "I must go too or I will not be able to find my way among the holes. Tell me what goods you want." He called Eakin and I told them what I had on the dray. "We can't take all that", he replied, "we want a good portion of it," a list of which he gave me.

Just as I was going to leave three men came in. One of them was a man who had ridden to Geelong the trip I took Burrows down. He recognised me and said: "is that you young fellow? Got the dray here?" "No, I am camping on Bakery Hill. You did not stay long in town," I said. "Just

This scrap of neglected land seen in 2000 was once the very important gathering place on Bakery Hill. Thousands of hopefuls camped on it once it had been turned over for alluvial gold, and many meetings were held here in the lead up to the Eureka rebellion. A few years later a large mining company set up and found the enormously valuable 'Welcome Nugget' in this place.

long enough," he answered, "time enough to have a good spree. It's a dull place Geelong, they may well call it the Sleepy Hollow. Well we came in to have a drink, going to join us?" Landlords I knew objected to taking a shingle off. Though I had had enough, I said: "Don't mind." After his shout, one of the other men shouted and I had to join in that. While we were having the second drink, half a dozen men came in on the same lay. One told about a digger hunt on the Prince Regent and Canadian Gully and other places. What a crowd the traps had caught, the logs were not big enough to hold them standing up, and what the logs could not take in were fastened to trees. One man asked how long would they have to wait in that position. The first speaker replied: "Until either their friends came to release them by paying the fine of two pounds and taking out a licence." Those not so released would have to wait the Commissioner's pleasure in the morning. The most of us knew what the man said was the truth. One man said La Trobe, his Legislative Council and his Proclamations ought to be cast into the bottomless pit, to which fate we most of us heartily agreed.

It was now quite dark and I felt a little timid of crossing over many holes that lay in my track, and I said so. Eakin said: "I'll make a lantern for you Mundy." Taking an Old Tom bottle, he put half an inch of water into it and holding it over the fire the bottom flew off, and dropping a piece of lighted candle into the neck, the lantern was complete.

Passing among the holes, I called to mind many accounts I had heard of men falling down abandoned shafts. Some were killed, some after vainly struggling to get up for days were rescued at the last extremity, others were missed, the only evidence left to tell the tale was their tent and belongings left unowned. Many had no friends nearer than the old country. The police might be informed of it, but what business was it of their's to hunt for missing men. A digger hunt was for some purpose. If a man got crushed under a fall of earth, as soon as it was known, a crowd would muster round the shaft and plenty of volunteers would be ready to the rescue. Brave fellows often carrying their lives in their hands, heeding not the risk, would extricate the buried man, if by any possible means it could be done.

Perhaps he would be dead, and in that case the police were made acquainted with it. After a time, a solitary policeman would appear on the scene, look at the body, examine him. "Yes" , he would say, "he's dead right enough", then thrust his hand into the dead man's pockets and extract what money or valuables and keep possession of it, saying: "Has this man any mates or friends who will undertake to bury him? " If he had mates, they were always ready and willing to place their lost comrade in his coffin, bury him, and when asked who was to be a hatter, some of the crowd round would guarantee to do it. If the dead man was a stranger among them, his papers and letters would be searched to find out the address of his friends so as to inform them of his death.

I arrived at Bakery Hill safely and found John, Gribble and Grace sitting at the improvised table John had made, on some bags of chaff with a bottle of rum and a cup before them, evidently enjoying themselves. John had waited for me to help unload the rum cask, but as I was so long absent, he got Gribble and Grace to help him. They eased it on to the ground onto a bag of chaff, rolled it in, got it into the cellar into its place and to finish the job complete, put the tap in. The next thing to do was to taste it. I was ready for a drink too, after walking from Eureka, so we all had a drink round. After that, we retired to rest.

We rose early and Edwin and I started for Eakin's. Our business there was soon over, but as early as it was, nearly a dozen seedy looking characters dropped in as I was being paid and of course I had to shout for the lot. After that we made for Bakery Hill, calling at the store where I had dealt before. The storekeeper asked me what I had. I told him I had nothing left but hard stuff, and that was at Bakery Hill. I told him what I had. I could bring it up in the evening.

He ordered five gallons of rum, two of dark brandy and a case of cognac. When we got back, John and Gribble were ready to go for the bark. Edwin went with them and I took a stroll over the diggings, Golden Point, Poverty Flat and Black Hill and also by the Commissioner's Camp. What a lively busy hive it seemed, tents and stores in the flats, on the hills, in the gullies, everywhere one cast his eyes; every store had two or three flags flying, flags of all nations but principally the Union Jack. The Australian was

BLACK HILL
Left and above is Black Hill as it was in the gold era and in 2003. Black Hill is just a very short walk from Bakery Hill and on the opposite side of the later rail line to Melbourne.

A fine example at Sovereign Hill of the many different forms of mining employed to crush rock and generally help miners find their fortunes with gold.

common too, bearing the Southern Cross. At the camp was floating the Union Jack only. Even some of the shanties where hop beer, cider, lemonade, ginger beer etc. sold at 6d. a pint, had their flag.

On returning from my ramble, they were back with the dray and were placing the bark on the floor of the tent, covering the cellar over. We made a very neat job of it. John would put his stretcher over the cellar and no one could imagine anything contraband in the tent, unless they were told.

About dusk Edwin and I yoked up one horse and took up Bradshaw's order. There were only two or three people in the store at the time whom I shouted for, pleading the necessity of haste to get back before it was too dark. We were soon returning to Bakery Hill.

Leaving Edwin to look after the horse, I took another stroll among the tents. All were busy cooking their evening meal. It was the repetition of Bendigo over again, everyone seemed in high spirits, laughing, joking and yelling to one another. A stranger would think it bedlam let loose; surely that was the happy land.

Those who were on good gold had reason for their hilarity, but a great many had laboured long and patiently, without as yet, any show; some not knowing how to raise the next meal, except the storekeepers would give them tick, which was seldom refused. If this man struck gold, he knew he would gain a lasting customer. And no one would see a brother digger in want of tucker if he knew it, because were they not all cosmopolitans, hence strong comradeship existed among them.

The present, unlucky ones, were ever hopeful. If they thought there was a show in a likely spot, perhaps it might be fifty feet or more, their party of two or maybe four would start to sink full of hopes of the gold they would find on the bottom. After a week, or may be a month's toil, if they met hard ground they would bottom a rank duffer, alas, all their sanguine hopes dashed to the ground. They would feel dispirited for a day or two, but hope would soon revive and they would laugh and be hopeful with the rest again, their luck would come sooner or later.

In my nocturnal stroll I found myself near Lanky's and Squat's shanty, and went in. The man I had seen there in the evenings before was not there, but Squat himself attending to business. "Hullo," he said recognising me, "Where did you spring from?" "Just having a stroll," I said, "to see what's up." "Got any stuff?" he enquired. There was, I noticed, a very suspicious looking card sitting on a five gallon keg in a corner, very like a policeman I thought. Not answering straight away, Squat noticing the man on the keg: "Oh, he's a friend of mine, one of La Trobe's detectives, he's all square." At this the man on the keg replied, "Square as a brick mate, Mr Squat's a particular friend of mine, he's a jolly good fellow and so's his mate. I wouldn't do 'em the least injury in the world, if I knew it. Of course, you know its my duty to hunt out sly grog sellers to arrest them and bring 'em before the Commissioner. I have been in the police force for some years and this billet was offered as a chance for promotion in a better way than worming my way into a man's confidence, and then betraying him by turning informer. I'll never get it, but I shall not have the honour of being Charlie Joe's detective long if I make no arrests. I shall be appointed in some different quarter."

"You talk like a genuine honest fellow," I said, "let's have a drink of Lanky and Squat's best." "Agreed," he replied, "I have had several already. I'll take one more with you. I have to be careful you know as I have got to report myself."

Speaking of the digger hunt of yesterday, "Is it not a shame," he added "that these young jackanapes, newly imported gentlemen's sons, La Trobe's pets, should be allowed the licence they take before the unfortunate diggers, who perhaps from no fault of their own happen to have no licence, and the new assisting Commissioner's portionless lord's and dukes' sons, friends of La Trobe, mincing round with their gold epaulettes and lace on their coats, who know nothing of the country or people either, "dressed in a little brief authority" play such fantastic tricks before high Heaven as would make the angels weep. Things will not remain long as they are, the British are a loyal law abiding people, but they expect what they have been accustomed to, British Justice. Besides there are a number of foreigners, revolutionisers mostly, who are bound to make strife if occasion occurs. La Trobe at this time is very unpopular."

"Well," at length I said, "I will be going back unless you like to have another wet." "No," he said. "I've had enough mate, thank you, which way are you going?" he asked. "Bakery Hill way I told him. "Alright, he said, "do your business with Squat and I'll go with you part of the way. So telling Squat what I had in the tent, he said: "I've plenty of that just now, but next trip I'll take some ale and stout." "Alright," I replied, "good night" , and we started.

It was about an hour after dark, the evening meal being over the diggers were having their night's enjoyment. Guns, pistols and crackers were going off with yelling, shouting and singing, music was everywhere, bugles, some near, some far away, fiddles were heard in some tents, accordions in others; while that universal instrument, the concertina, seemed to be everywhere. "My word," my friend remarked, "the diggers are still around." "Yes," I said, "and perhaps some of them haven't the patience to wait, mostly they make sure to drop on gold in the long run." Coming to the Geelong road opposite Bakery Hill, I said: "I must leave you now, unless you like to come to my tent and have a taste." "No thank you," he replied, "some other time. I'll call upon you." So saying, he dislodged his revolver from his belt, and fired off three barrels into the air. "That," he said, "is a parting salute. Goodnight." I saw him but once after, I met him in company with other police as I was coming from Geelong. He nodded, that was all.

I made my way to Gribble's tent, they were having a game of cards, all fours, a popular game at the time. Mrs Gribble asked me if I'd had tea which I had not, she soon bustled round and prepared me a meal. After that, I was invited to join in the game. "Alright, but haven't you got anything to drink?" Gribble's eyes twinkled: "No, Mundy," he replied, "not a drop." I went into our tent and brought a bottle of cognac and two bottles of Whitbreads Ale. We passed a pleasant evening. Mrs Gribble was a very moderate drinker, but Mrs Grace could take her tot whenever her turn came. Gribble and Grace were in high glee, very sanguine and jubilant over their prospects on the Gravel Pitt. "Don't make too sure," I said, "it is not known yet whether the Gravel Pitts is a lead or not. There are only two or three claims getting gold yet. It might be only a patch. "That would not go down at all, it was a lead right enough.

In the morning Edwin and I started for Geelong and arrived there Sunday evening. As soon as I had had supper I went to see my little girl who was all smiles, and welcome, anxiously enquiring about mother and Gribble. After answering all her questions I told her of Gribble's and Grace's great expectations, making sure they were on the Gravel Pitt lead with one or the other of the claims they were shepherding. I asked her how much pocket money she had made the last week making flannel shirts. "Oh, not much," she answered. "I have to do the cooking and look after the house, so that Fanny can keep at her work, because she has her living to get, you know." "Yes," Fanny joined in, "she is very thoughtful of her poor auld Aunt." "Oh, get out Aunt, you are not old." "Well," Fanny said, "I be getting on I'm vorty vour." "But John Crosby is sixty five, he does not think himself old, not too old to come courting thee Aunt." "Get's thee along maid, he be only an auld fuile with one leg in the grave and t'other out, he may court I as long as he likes, he'll never get me."

Ann sat quietly thinking for a while and, then suddenly said: "Aunt did Uncle Nat ever kiss thee before you were married?" "Larks chiel, yes hundred o'times. And I kissed he too," Fanny replied. "Oh Aunt," Ann cried, seemingly shocked, "you never." "Why not?" Fanny replied, "Doest know kisses before marriage are sweeter than those after." Fanny, after standing this bit of banter, turned to retaliate: "Does't mean to say," Fanny said, "that Mundy never kissed thee?" "No," Ann answered, "never." Then looking at me, blushed at the lie. The kissing subject dropped then.

Ann asked me if mother had said anything about sending her any money, as she was collecting the rents of the chemist's shop and the other house. Her mother had told her if they should run short she would send word by me and I could fetch it to them. "No Ann, she said nothing to me about money. Anyhow if they do want any, I can let them have some, and you can give it to me when I come back."

I resolved to have a day in town this time, and load on Tuesday. On Monday, I went into town to look round, went to different shops prying such kind of goods I required and into the auction rooms looking for

As the holes became deeper, the need for ventilation became a major consideration. At the very wet and boggy Gravel Pitts Lead beside Bakery Hill these sail like fixtures were to be seen everywhere. They were a successful implement to trap fresh air and vent it into the musty and foul smelling holes. Without them many holes were lethal.

bargains etc. When I went home to dinner Margaret, the servant girl, informed me that a man had called looking for me. I could not guess who it might be. After dinner who should make his appearance but Ambler, Eakin's partner. "Hullo Ambler," I said, "I did not expect to see you down in Geelong." "Well," he replied, "Eakin and I are thinking of going a little into the drapery business, and I have picked out of what I consider a suitable stock, which I think will go well in our store,

With little else to do but work and sleep, alcohol became a major commodity on the goldfields - especially since it was banned!

considering the connection we have; but I have not the money with me within forty pounds. If you would kindly accommodate me with that amount till you call at our store again, I should be so much obliged." "Forty pounds," I hesitated a little. He added: "I'll give you a pro (promissory) note, payable on demand. You'll get the money the next time you call." I thought to myself, they are good customers and they have great influence with the police, also seem to always have plenty of money. So I said: "All right Ambler," and gave him a cheque for £40. Nevertheless that £40 cropped up now and again in my mind, and made me feel uneasy. But later on I argued to myself, I do not see how I could have acted otherwise under the circumstances.

On Wednesday we started again for Ballarat. When we got as far as the Green tents, there was a bullock dray camped on the roadside with loading for Ballarat, which I had noticed the last time coming down. A man pretty well drunk stepped from the dray out to meet us. "Good morning mates," he said, "hold on a bit, there's no great hurry is there come over to the dray and have a drink of English porter. I got a spile in a cask and the drink is leaking out, I can't stop it. Come both of you and have as much as you like, we might just as well drink it as let it run away." Going over to his dray he had his tea kettle full with a pannikin alongside. "Help yourselves mates," he said, "there's plenty of it," which we did, pouring it out of the kettle spout. I said: "Didn't I see you here last week?" "Perhaps you did, I've been here over a week as bad luck would have it, we lost the bullocks and either me or my mate have been out from light till dark looking for them; and devil a sight we can get or hear of them. Come, have another pannikin." "No thanks," I said. "Can't you get another spile and stop that waste?" "I can't stop it," he muttered. I took out my knife and made a fresh spile which stopped the leakage. "Thankee, thankee, mate," he said, "take another pannikin out of the kettle." "No?" "Well, well alright there's plenty of it you know, and you're welcome."

This pretence among the bullockies of losing their bullocks was very common at the time, if they happened to have contraband stuff in their loading. Various devices were resorted to in order to deceive the assignee. The most common plan was to drive back a hoop on a barrel and bore two spile holes, one for air and another for the liquor. When enough had been drawn off, the spiles were driven in tight, cut off close to the wood, and the hoop driven back to its place again. In broaching cases, a portion of the cover was lifted enough to insert a strong butcher's knife and feeling for the most tender part of a bottle with a smart blow on the handle of the knife the bottle was broken. Holding the case over a bucket all the liquor would drain out. No sign was left to show how the bottle was broken, by accident of course.

There was another plan of tapping a cask with two knives, back to back driven into the joint of two staves about an inch apart, the interstice would open and let the liquor out. Some would punish a cask so severely, that when moved would swash and swish about, that it would tell the tale of the quantity that had been extracted. Often in a case of this sort, they would take out the bung and replace what had been taken out with clean sand. Gribble, a professional bullock driver, told me of a trick of taking alcohol out of a spirit cask without leaving any trace whatever. The barrel must be full, stood on end and boiling water poured on to fill up the chines; he said the spirit would come into the top of the barrel as the water went inside. There may be some loss with this method.

Notwithstanding the depredations of the bullockies on their loading, they were generally more patronised than horse teams with regard to common merchandise, except in cases of despatch, or the carriage of alcoholic drinks. Almost all the big storekeepers went to town, bought off the merchants and employed bullock teams to carry their goods to the diggings, the carriage being less. I soon found out the horse team carrier or trader had seen his best days, besides, the drink-traffic had not abated one bit, in spite of all the restrictions and penalties La Trobe and his Legislative Council had passed against it. It was resolved at length to grant a licence to one public house in Lydiard Street, near the Commissioner's Camp, by way of experiment. It was said and wisely too, if the drink traffic cannot be stopped, why not legalise the sale of it and raise a revenue out of it.

The man who built the first hotel in Ballarat was named Bath, who came from Geelong. In a few years he made his fortune, and sold the house to one named Craig, a great racing man. The hotel was greatly improved afterwards and has always been the leading hotel in Ballarat.

Friday afternoon we reached our destination at Ballarat. I found both Gribble and Grace down in the dumps, they had both been duffered out. They did not think the Gravel Pitts was a lead at all only a patch. "Oh," I said, "it's no good being down on your luck, there's plenty of gold elsewhere." John had done a little business in rum and brandy. As soon as it was dark, we unloaded the drink and stowed it away. Lanky and Squat wanted some bottled ale and porter, which I promised to deliver in the morning. After delivering Lanky and Squat's order, I went on up to Eakin's store. He took some things, but not so much as I expected. In settling up he said (Ambler was not there): "Ambler borrowed forty pounds off you when in town I understand." "Yes," I said, "Well ," he resumed, "Mundy, if I pay you for these things I have got today I shall have to owe you twenty pounds of the forty Ambler borrowed off you, but you shall have it next time you come. I'll give you a pro-note payable on demand for twenty pounds. Will that do?" "Yes," I answered, "but I shall expect it when I come again." "You shall have it," he said, "without fail." Five or six men were in the store when I was paid, who were looking for a drink, as they knew who I was, so I asked them all to have a drink. All of a sudden the cry of "Joe, Joe," ran like a lightning flash along the lead "Oh," all exclaimed, "a digger hunt, we'll see some fun now."

At the distance were seen about twenty men, marching on the side of the lead, with two constables one on each side of them. With musket and bayonet in hand, guarding the captives, the paperless men were ready to fire on anyone who attempted to escape. Two troopers, swords drawn in readiness, pistol in holster, galloping up one on each side of the lead ready to intercept any runaways who were making for the bush. Ten or twelve police also armed with bayoneted muskets, marching among the diggers, accosting all they met with "Show yer licence." Those who happened to be licenceless at the cry of "Joe" would whip down the holes and out of sight if any drives had been commenced.

If any claim had only just bottomed or was being sunk the policeman would look down and seeing the man below, would call out pre-emptorily, dropping the butt of his musket on the ground: "Come up you and show your licence." As a rule they obeyed the order meekly enough, but in instances, the man waited, defied the policeman, telling him to come down and fetch him, in which cases the police were nonplussed and near always left him.

An old heavy duty dray of the type Henry owned and used so effectively.

Edwin and I got into the dray and looked on as they passed the store. The diggers were shouting out at the police: "Ice, ice, I'am his tail. Boy wouldn't your mother be proud of her son now, the dandy policeman with his muckstick in his delicate paw, bow, wow, wow how's your friend ice La trobe, is he well? Haw, haw, ah, ah, haw!" accompanied with such demoniac yells, it is impossible with pen and ink to describe. They passed on steadily, not heeding the clamour, taking a prisoner now and again.

Most of the diggers on the main lead on gold were provided with licences; the principal victims were the outsiders, prospecting for spurs or off-shoots from the main lead, some were sinking, others only shepherding. There was no get away for them. These helped to swell the prison gang very considerably. Poor wretches, perhaps some of them had not the price of a meal. One fellow for a bit of fun bobbed up suddenly out of a hole and seeing the traps, pretended to be scared, commenced to run as if to escape - he ran over the most difficult and dangerous places he could see. Three police were after him, pell-mell coming to an abandoned shaft where the windlass and logs had been removed, the runaway doubled adroitly, nearly within reach of the policeman nearest him, who made a grab at the fugitive; missed him and fell sliding down to the gaping chasm. The chased man, on looking round seeing the danger of his foe, hesitated for a second or two, when he was securely pinned by the two other chasers.

The man who had fallen looking very scared just picked himself up at the pits edge but his musket had gone down. "Show your licence," was the angry demand of the two men. "Licence," the man said, "is that all?" He pulled it out of his pocket and showed it, amid the prolonged uproarious laugh from the crowd of diggers round. Alluding to the man who had lost his gun, "He looks sick doesn't he?" one would remark. Another: "Oh take him home to his mamma, poor dear, she'll put him to bed and give him some gruel." "Where's his muckstick?" "Oh, he's been playing and lost it." Etc. etc.

As the hunt had passed on, Edwin and I left for Bakery Hill, calling at Bradshaw's as I had some goods not sold, but he was not in want of anything I had. He told me he intended to give up grog selling. The hotel being built, he said, will alter the state of things. The licencee will have his own spies out, with that and the police together, the game will be too risky.

As I had not disposed of all my goods, I had to stay Sunday in Ballarat. The principal right on Sunday morning was the diggers washing their clothes, playing quoits or shooting at a target; though the greatest were in the shanties worshipping Bacchus.

There was little difference in their clothes which they wore on working days, only perhaps cleaner, having been through the cold water cleansing. Very few shaved, except those of dubious character, rogues and thieves, but wore a full beard and long hair. An unkempt looking lot. Here and there a person could be seen elevated on a fallen tree, a stump or a dray, holding forth to a small crowd, who were continually coming and going. Some half drunken fellow perhaps would come up and after listening seriously for a while, would commence to ask the parson questions or contradict him; when some of the more seriously inclined would tell him to shut up, or clear out. Some of the shanties possessed a bagatelle board; all kept cards. Gambling for money or gold was another Sunday's amusement. Concertinas and fiddles were evident everywhere.

After dinner, Gribble, Mrs Gribble and I had a long talk about things in general, principally about our life on the station and the sheep and bushfires that we had to put up with. The early days on the goldfields, of our luck in finding gold, but we did not like the chances a newcomer had. Where fifty were on good gold, there were five hundred looking for it. It was a moot question whether all the gold that was raised would pay small wages for everyone on the goldfields, whether, considering all things, the gold obtained paid for the getting.

Look at the many poor devils who arrive on the diggings with only a few shillings or perhaps no money at all, nothing but what they stand in and their little calico tent 8' X 6', thinking to pick up gold, as soon as they land. What privations the most of them had to go through. Hard living, hard lodging, bad drinking water, that often brings on Colonial fever or dysentery. They take to their miserable couch. Their next neighbour may miss him and lift the flap of his tent, and look in to see a poor suffering fellow mortal, maybe on the point of death, perhaps dead. If living, he tells the neighbours round who readily do what they can for him, bring him a pannikin of tea or some hot gruel, telling him to take that and cheer up, he will be better soon.

In case of death the diggers would knock up a coffin of rough boards if he had no friends to claim him, and bury the body in some secluded spot in the ranges; there to lie till the resurrection day. Perhaps six months since his friends in the old country with hearty demonstrations of good wishes for his success had bidden him adieu.

This latter picture of things seemed to depress Gribble's spirits; so I went to our tent and brought back a bottle of rum and John with me. After the second tot he cheered up wonderfully, and he said: "Look here Mundy, I'll tell you what I'll do. I was lucky once the first time I went to the diggings, so this is the third time I have tried my luck and if I don't get on gold soon I'll tell you what I'll do, I'll sell the houses in Geelong and you and I, if you like, will buy a farm together and work it between us." "What do you say old woman?" "A very good plan," she said, "if you would only keep steady, but you are not to be trusted." "That is just the thing that would keep me steady," Gribble replied. "Ah well," she said, "we'll see."

On Monday morning, I yoked up early and went round among the stores and shanties in order to dispose of what few things I had left. It did not take me long. We started then right away for Geelong and reached there Wednesday forenoon. On our way down, we met the bullocky of the leaking

A Cobb & Co changing station typical of those it had at regular intervals throughout huge stretches of Australia. Old coach drivers formed an association which had meetings as late as 1935.

GOLD FOUND OUTSIDE BALLARAT

At the end of 1851 gold was found at Mt Alexander which became the town of Castlemaine, and in six months £3,000,000 of the precious metal had been collected by the fortunate few as people walked out of Melbourne and other towns to follow their luck in the bush.

porter barrel. He had found his bullocks at last, and was making headway for his destination.

Mother's health was considerably improved but she still kept the servant. I went to see my girl and Fanny in the afternoon. Both were hard at it making flannel shirts. I told them about Gribble's being duffered out, and how disappointed he was and if he did not succeed soon he would very probably be coming home. "Oh bother," said Ann, "he thinks he's going to pick gold again the way he did on Bendigo, he's got no patience. I wish I was a man I'd bet I'd find gold before very long. There's Blackney here next door, he and his boys have dropped on gold again, pretty good they say, and they did pretty well before." "Why doant'e put on a pair of breeches maid and dress up like a man and try thee luck?," Fanny joined in, "So I will Aunt, if you'll do the same, and we'll take Old John with us." "Oh drat auld John, thee beest allus telling about 'e." "What is old John still persisting of paying his devoirs (duties) to his lady love?" "His what," Fanny enquired. I said: Does he still come accourting after all the rebuffs you have given him?" "Be's that he do," she replied, "after me telling him jump blunt, I'd hae nay more to do we'un, yet he still do keep on coming, I hate to zee un, that I do."

Three more trips to Ballarat finished my carting career for the time. The next trip I made, Eakin and Amber took but a few goods off me, which they paid for, but could not pay me any of the £20 they owed. Things seemed, in my line of business to be going worse. The roads about Buninyong were made more passable; Scott's Swamp and other bad places had been planked over, carriage came down, more bullock teams were competing for loading so that most of the storekeepers went to town and purchased their own goods. The second trip Eakin and Ambler bought off me pretty liberally, on condition that I would let £10 stand over till next trip.

Lanky and Squat had got what they required off some other dealer. The next and last trip I brought no spirits, but only oats, bran and fruit, which took me two whole days to sell, at what I considered low prices. John had yet some drink in the tent, which took a few days at lowered prices.

Gribble and Grace were still out of luck, without any prospects of better things. I told Gribble of my intention to give up the roads for the present, and was not coming back again. "Well," he said, "Mundy, if you are not coming back again we'll go too." "What do you say?" turning to Mrs Gribble. "Yes, yes," she said, "we might as well, I want to see the maid and you don't seem likely to do any good here."

So leaving Grace still there, on the morrow we sold our tents, packed up and went off for Geelong. The evening I had interviewed Eakin and Ambler, they promised to send me the £30 they owed me in a month's time. I had to be content with that. Mother and daughter, or correctly speaking Aunt and niece had a joyful meeting, much to tell of what they had heard and seen. They were very fond of each other. Gribble kept wonderfully steady for weeks. "We can live on our rents Mundy, you know if we are careful," he told me.

I had given up the roads for the time, I could have made a pretty good living carrying for hire as horse teams were preferred to bullock teams for despatch and got a trifle more, but it was a hard, worrying, unsettled life, so that I got totally sick of it. I resolved to sell my horses, and dray, and have a spell for a while.

Edwin went to work for his Uncle Jim Gillingham who owned a farm at Mount Mistake on the other side of Fiery Creek. I kept the horses in the stable for a week or two to get them into good condition, thinking to sell them privately, but getting no satisfactory offer I took them to the sale yard where they realised about what I gave for them. The dray, through being built under stress of great demand had been made of not too well seasoned timber and the spokes and joints were beginning to work, but keeping it well covered with wet bags for a few days made it as sound as a bell. I did not lose much on it.

Father kept one horse and did light jobs about town but occasionally took a trip to Ballarat with light loading. On one occasion about a fortnight after I had given up the carting, he engaged to take a woman to her husband in Ballarat. Father was always one for an early start so that the woman was invited to stay at our place the previous night so that there would be no delay in the morning. My brother had a gold watch lying on the mantle piece, which sometime during the night had disappeared. John knew where he had left it, and others had seen it there. No other

Tens of thousands travel to Sovereign Hill for a taste of life in the goldfields.

In the margin beside these lines in Henry's original manuscript was written: *"My eightieth birthday, June 25, 1911, 129 Argyle Street, St Kilda. H.M."* The address was that of his daughter.

The house has since been demolished, but adjoining properties, which are all identical, show it was a very fine two storey attached brick terrace.

JAMES GILLINGHAM
Uncle to Ann and a farmer. Married Susan Stukeley Templeman at Raglan (near Fiery Creek). Had three children Isaac John (1867 at Raglan), Charlotte Marcelia (1871 Raglan) and Elizabeth Susan (1885 and died the next year). Susan also died at Raglan, probably in childbirth.

FIERY CREEK
Fiery Creek is today the town of Beaufort.

Walter Craig had this painting of Nimblefoot and jockey in his colours with black arm band painted before his unexpected death! It remains in his hotel.

BATH'S HOTEL AND CRAIG'S DEATH PREMONITION

Thomas Craig was born in Cornwall in 1820. He became a butcher before going to sea and settling in Geelong in 1849 where he took up his trade again and married. Between 1851 and 1853 he also tried prospecting, and was successful enough to own large amounts of land around Ballarat and launch himself as its first legal publican.

He and his very respectable hotel earned a fine reputation, and he became a very successful and enterprising businessman and later benefactor.

In August 1857 he sold his hotel to Walter Craig. Both young men were keen on horse flesh, and became such good friends that Bath was a benefactor of Craig's will when he died.

The hotel grew rapidly, and buildings nearby were acquired and demolished for the expansion of the hotel with no expense spared. It was *the place* to be seen when drinking and dining in the best company in Ballarat. Esteemed guests included Mark Twain, Prince George, Prince Albert Victor and Prince Alfred (the Duke of Edinburgh and Queen Victoria's second son).

In 1867 famed poet and horseman Adam Lindsay Gordon rented stables and ran a livery business

conclusion could be arrived at but that the strange woman had stolen it, of which she was accused straight away. She strongly protested her innocence and appeared greatly indignant at the charge. However, there was nothing for it but she must be searched. Mother called in a neighbour and the two searched the woman over and over again, but no watch could be found, nor ever was seen again.

Father started on his journey with his female cargo, the woman was pregnant and near her confinement and passing Buninyong, the pains of labour came upon her. She told father, who proposed to leave her at Mother Jamieson's Hotel, but the woman objected to that, she insisted on being taken to her husband, eight miles farther on. He did manage to land her safely just in the nick of time. I never heard father swear, but he came very near it, when he told of his troubles with that bothering woman.

Nearing the end of 1852 Geelong had become quite a prosperous place, a large amount of money was being expended on the roads, a new iron bridge replaced the old wooden one over the Barwon; the building trade was brisk, buildings in Chilwell Flat were springing up like magic. More ships crossed the bar to Geelong than anchored at Hobson's Bay. New wharves were built, on which the traffic was immense. It was the nearest route from Melbourne to Ballarat and the surrounding gold fields. Goods came from Melbourne for Ballarat in lighters and steamboats and reloaded for Ballarat as it was £10 a ton cheaper than going direct to the diggings from Melbourne. There were three cattle sale yards and five auction sale rooms doing an immense business.

To pass my time for the first two or three weeks, I visited the sales. The old clique had seemingly got broken up, as I saw some of them, but everyone seemed to be buying on his own. A great game was selling unopened parcels or bags or boxes with something in them left at hotels, found on the road or sent for sale by some one unknown.

The auctioneer would introduce a bundle tied up in a handkerchief with the toe of a boot sticking out of one corner. "Now gentlemen," he would say, "here's a parcel, what its contents are I don't know, might be bank notes for all I know, speculate for luck, now's your chance, nothing ventured, nothing won. How much for the parcel?" It was surprising to see what spirited bidding would ensue for that bundle of mysteries. A man I knew well during my stay in Geelong before the diggings started, a bricklayer by trade, glad to get a chimney to build or any other little job, had been attending the auction rooms for a considerable time, did nothing else, he told me. He had made as much as five pounds some days by buying at one room and selling at another. I thought to try my luck at it too. I tried it for a while but did not succeed very well. Sometimes I gained a little, but very seldom lost anything. One venture I went into was buying a dozen fine looking watches, gold to all appearance, for £2 each, I resold ten of them, put up singly £2/10/- each, the other two sold for £2 each. If I had stuck to the business and got further experience in the mysteries of the swindles carried on, I might have made money at it, but it did not suit my taste, so I gave it up.

Eakin and Ambler had promised to forward me the £30 they owed me in a month, but two months had passed and receiving no word from them, I resolved to pay them a visit. So, booking in Cobb's Coach one morning which was £5 to Ballarat, opposite Golden Point, I left the coach for Eureka on foot. Passing along the gravel pits, I ascertained that a digger hunt was going on, by hearing the frequent yells of "Joe, Joe." The hunt was making towards Eureka. I walked leisurely up and was going past, when an officious policeman turning to me said: "Show your licence." I said, "I'm not a digger, I have just arrived from Geelong by Cobb's Coach, I'm here only on business." "Oh, that'll do," he retorted: "you have no right on the diggings without a licence. Haven't you got a licence?" "No," I said, "look at my dress, you can see for yourself, I am not a digger." "It does not matter about your clothes, you can't show your licence so fall in with the rest." I asked him if the hunt would pass along Eureka Lead. "Yes," he said, "Well," I said, "there is a storekeeper named Eakin, he can tell you I am only a carrier" "Very well," he answered, "if Eakin can satisfy us you are a carrier, it will be alright." So I joined a crowd of about twenty more and we were driven slowly along like a flock of sheep. When we got to Eakin's store both he and Ambler came out to have a look. I quickly made myself seen by Eakin, who sang out: "Hullo Mundy, have they grabbed you too?" The man who had arrested me came up, Eakin calling the man by name: "You have made a mistake, Mr Mundy is not a digger, he is a carrier." "How do you know Eakin?" he enquired. "Know," Eakin replied, "he's been carrying for me for months back." "Oh well," the policeman said, "if you know he's only a carrier Eakin, its all right, he can go." Two more policemen came up then, I whispered to Eakin: "Is it safe to ask them to have a drink?" "Yes," he said, "it's quite safe." I shouted for the three policemen, Eakin, Ambler

CRAIG'S ROYAL HOTEL

"The Pride of Ballaarat"
- Mark Twain

DIEU ET MON DROIT

Craig's Royal Hotel is an institution in Ballarat and this is its beginning.

and myself and all had a good laugh over my recent arrest.

Eakin and Ambler paid me all but £9 which they promised to send in a fortnight. I was obliged to be content with what I got, and that evening visited Bath's Hotel, the building of which was so far advanced as to enable Bath to procure his licence.

The most remarkable thing that struck me on entering Bath's Hotel, was the length of the counter. I guessed it must be forty feet long at least, thronged with diggers on one side and a plentiful supply of barmen on the other. It was a shilling a drink. The crowd though talking and shouting loudly was orderly enough. I had a drink myself and stood and looked for a while, then thinking, advised by my stomach that as I had not had a square meal since breakfast, I would try to find something to eat. I went into the dining room, sat down and was supplied with a rough meal, with tea. I think the meal was half a crown. I asked for a bed. No, none to spare, all taken up. All things seemed to be in the initial stage, and unsettled. I did not know of any accommodation in shape of a lodging house nearer than Mother Jamieson's in Buninyong, that was eight miles away. Well, what of that, that was nothing of a walk. So I started straight away.

There was no moon but the night was clear and bright. I knew well every inch of the road. Arriving at Jamieson's, hilarity seemed to be the order of the night. Three troopers and several others, all sorts were congregated in the large sitting room. When I entered one of the troopers was singing "Down the Swannee River." I ordered a brandy spider and enquired if I could be accommodated with bed. After enquires I was told: "Yes," could have a bed. Satisfied as to the bed, I joined the company. It was a jolly crowd, many good old songs were sung. The company did not break up till one o'clock.

During the evening one asked me if I was going to Ballarat. I told him I had just come from there, and was bound for Geelong. "Going by the coach." he asked. "Not if I can get any other conveyance," I replied. "Cobb's coach would cost £4/10/- from here at least." "I think I'll walk it." "Why, hold on a bit," he said, "there's Bill Jeffries stopping here tonight, he drives a spring wagon, he's going back empty. I'll bet you can get down with him for a couple of notes." With that he went to bring Jeffries to me. I knew the man by sight and he recognised me, we had often met or passed on the road. "Oh, it's you is it?" Jeffries said, "that wants a lift to Geelong, where's your dray?" I told him I had given up carrying for the present, and had been to Ballarat only on business. "Will you be in Geelong tomorrow night?" I asked him. "Yes, if all's well." "How much will you take me for?" "Oh, we'll say thirty shillings." "All right," I said, "I'll go with you, let us have a wet." We three had sundry drinks together. The man who introduced me to jeffries sung a song. "The minute gun at sea." I was called upon but begged to be excused on account of a sore throat. I enjoyed myself very much that night.

A little after sunrise, Jeffries was ready harnessed up for the road. It was as comfortable as Cobb's Coach, he had two good horses in the pole; the wagon had a good tilt on it and a bag of chaff to sit on. My companion was not very talkative for a while but coming to a spot near the Stoney Rises, he said suddenly: "Do you see that thick clump of honeysuckles over there?" "Yes," I answered, "Well," he said, "about six months ago I was stuck up there by two masked bushrangers going back to town as I am now. The wind was behind me and not too warm, either, so I had the two hind flaps fastened together. All of a sudden, two men on horseback with masks on, rushed from behind, one on each side, each presenting a revolver at me, crying out "Bail up." So I called "whoa" to the horses and they stopped. "What's the meaning of

there.

Craig became very heavily involved in horse racing, and the still prime VATC (Victoria Amateur Turf Club) had its origins in 1876 at Craig's Hotel.

One night in May 1870 Walter Craig dreamed that he was watching the running of the Melbourne Cup in November. He was amazed to see it was won by his own horse, 'Nimblefoot'.

He had walked over to the jockey, and while congratulating him noticed that he had a mourning band of black crepe paper on his arm.

The jockey explained that he was wearing the band for the owner who had died three months ago.

Craig was struck by the dream, and told all of his friends to put large bets on Nimblefoot to win the Cup despite the horse having little chance of success.

A Mr. Slack placed a bet of four beers to 1000 pounds with a local stock and station agent!

On Melbourne Cup day all of the interest in Ballarat was centred on Craig's Hotel, and about four o'clock a telegram was received by Mrs Craig who immediately burst into tears - Nimblefoot had won the Melbourne Cup. His his rider wore a black arm band - because Walter Craig had died three months before!

Mrs Craig stood good the 1000 pounds owed by Mr Slack, and also other bets which had been placed on Nimbleoot at her late-husband's urging.

Craig had died of pneumonia after years of rheumatic gout. The hotel was offered for sale, but his widow died thirteen months after her husband and before it was disposed of - he was only 45 - she was only 43.

The hotel has been through many hands since, but remains truly one of the finest classical hotels in Australia.

this?" I said startled. "Oh, you know what it means well enough," one retorted, "hand over that roll of notes you have on you and that quick or you will have a bullet through your hide." "Oh, bushrangers is it?" I said. "Yes, gentlemen of the road or bushrangers if you like that better, come be smart and fork out quick, your life's in danger," the first speaker snapped. "If you give it up quick and quietly we don't intend to harm you, quick." "Well, gentlemen of the road," I replied, "it's lucky for me and unlucky for you, I must tell you that I took a fair sum of money in Ballarat this trip, but I paid it into the post office and got a post office order for it, payable to myself in Geelong. All that I have on me is a couple of ones, I suppose you'll have to have that."

"Tell that tale to the Greeks," the fellow snarled out: "All bunkum, get out of the wagon," signalling to his mate to search me which he did, turning all my pockets inside out but found only two one pound notes and a half crown. He felt my clothes all over, took off my hat and found nothing more. "You have no fire arms?" "No," I said, "I carry no arms and very little money." The fellow who had been covering me with his revolver, lowered it and growled: "Take off your boots." I took off my boots, which were minutely searched, my socks examined - nothing. "Search the wagon now," he said. The fellow sprang into the wagon, he searched my overcoat, bedding and tucker box. I had a butt of oats in a bag and half bag of chaff which the man emptied on to the floor of the wagon and clawed carefully over, but got nothing for his pains. "Nothing here," he sang out, as he jumped down and mounted his horse. The one who had remained mounted said: "Look here, if you tell of this to anyone within twenty-four hours, we'll wait for you when you pass again and shoot you dead." "Thank you," I said. Then they scuttled off into the bush."

"They gave you a thorough overhaul," I said: "It is a good plan to take out a post office order. I have done that too sometimes, but at other times have hidden my money in the best place I could think of. I have hidden it too in the chaff bag, in which case, if those fellows who stuck you up had visited me I should have lost it."

We passed through Meredith then in its initial stage. At the Separation we stopped a few minutes to have a drink. We had another at Bates Ford and reached Geelong in good daylight. I went to Gribble's after supper to see my little sweetheart; she was looking more charming, I thought, every time I saw her. Fanny had rented a house in Autumn Street and lived there with her son Nathan. Gribble was still keeping steady. He broached the subject again about him and me jointly taking a farm. I was quite willing but land was so awfully dear. There were some blocks of Government land advertised in the Geelong Advertiser: He said: "Shall we go and look at that?" It was on the North shore on the other side of Cowie's Creek, to be put up in a few days. "All right," I said, "I do not intend bidding for land again before I have seen it."

So the following day, we walked out to inspect the blocks. We easily found it, by keeping along the sea shore. It was a large level swamp elevated about four feet above high tide, covered thickly with tussocks of wire grass three or four feet high. The north, east and west were all a rocky plain, not a tree within miles. We unanimously came to the conclusion, that a farm there would not suit us. Gribble said: "No doubt it is good land right enough, but it has to be drained into the sea and all those tussocks cleared off and that would take a fortune."

We tried to find one hundred acres of suitable land for private sale in the Moorabool and Barwon Flats, at the Heads, Mount Moriac and other places, but nothing could we find to suit us under £25 or £20 an acre, which was beyond our means.

I bought half an acre of land running from Hope Street to Autumn Street near the Government Road off a bullock driver named Bedwell for £120, resolved to start a market garden. It was well fenced but had only a bush hut on it, thatched with long grass. I started digging and delving, with a will. After working for a fortnight I had a fairly good piece turned up. I then procurred a few hundred cabbage plants and set them out. I sowed some onion, carrot, parsnip and other seeds, nicely finished up in beds. I had done a little gardening in England; my father was an excellent gardener and I took a great delight in it. I surveyed what I had done with great satisfaction and felt proud of my new venture.

This anonymous piece of land on the corners of Hope Street, Autumn Street and Shannon Avenue is the site once owned by Henry Mundy and intended to be his market garden.

I imagined what it would be when I had had all my projected plans carried out. But alack, the best laid schemes of mice and men, "Gang aft a glee," as the Scots have it. Bedwell returned from a trip to the country late one night, thought no harm of turning in his team of bullocks for the night; as he gave them no feed they wandered up and down all over the place, ate all my plants, tramped over my beds, pulled the thatch off the hut and did all the mischief they possibly could. The next time I went and saw the mess, Bedwell and his bullocks were gone. I felt so disgusted and disheartened I gave market gardening away. I saw him sometime afterwards and expostulated with him for his conduct. He said he was not aware anything had been done on the ground. When I asked him to indemnify me for the damage he flatly refused.

Gribble, with so much idle time on his hands and nothing to do, broke out drinking again, and there was 'war to the knife' between him and his wife. He had had an offer for the shop and one house and swore he would sell in spite of the old woman, which he finally did. What he got for the houses he would not tell, it must have been four or five hundred pounds, the bulk of it he put in the bank but always had his pocket well filled with notes. He used to go out and get as drunk as he could, just manage to walk home, then lay down in the stable to sleep it off.

One day when I was there, for I was there very often, I saw him come and go to the stable and lie down. I went to him and asked him why he did not come inside and lie on the sofa. "Look here Mundy," he said, "I come here for peace sake. To go into that house is like going to hell, no saint could stand that woman's tongue, she's the very devil." I knew he would listen to me before anyone, but it was no good advising him then. While talking to him I noticed the end of a roll of notes in his trousers pocket. I went inside and said to Mrs Gribble: "He has a handful of notes in his pocket, when he is asleep you take them out and every shilling he has. When he wakes and finds his money gone he will no doubt blame you, but deny knowing anything about it, but don't bully and call him the names you do. I believe if you would let him take what drink he likes, let him alone and don't abuse him so, he would not be half so bad." "Ah I zee," she said, "thee ut taking his part, you don't know what I've got to put up we." Ann came forward as my champion and said: "Yes, mother I believe Mundy is right. Try it Mother, let him drink as much as he likes and let us have peace at any cost. I am so tired, mother, of this miserable life," and began to sob and cry. My poor dear little girl. How I wished to have her and hold her as my own, but the plea was she was too young to marry. The objection I knew was good, therefore I was willing to wait and watch over her.

Gribble did not rouse up during my stay. When I called next day he was sitting on the sofa looking terribly bad. A robust plump looking man when in health, his eyes now seemed starting out of his head, his face was hung with great flabby wrinkles, the colour of white soap. Mrs Gribble was making him some gruel, which he protested he did not want. He wanted some brandy, which if he did not get he would die, while his wife said: "Die then, for not a drop thee'l get from I." "Lend me a shilling Mundy," he said, "I lost all the money I had." "Lost it. It might be in the stable but looked everywhere there, but could not find it, perhaps that old cow has picked my pocket, I haven't got a shilling so help me God." I said: "If I get you a drink, will you swallow the gruel?" He looked at the gruel then said: "No, you won't lend me the shilling." "Very well, I can get as much tick at Dick Ruffin's as I want, but it looks so mean." I said no more, but went to Ruffin's and got a bottle of Martell's brandy, and cautioned Dick not to give Gribble any drink, as he was on the eve of the horrors.

"All right," Dick said, "you can taper him off with that bottle." "That's my intention," I said. When I returned with the brandy, I went into an adjoining room, drew the cork and poured out a stiff nobbler and gave it to him. "Now," I said, "You'll have to take something nourishing, take the nice gruel made for you," which he did and in half an hour was quite cheerful." I feel better now old woman," he said, "after this is over, I'll take the pledge and give up drinking, you have no idea how I felt this morning. I'll have to taper off now and when I get right again, I'll have no more for twelve months." After three hours I gave him another dose. He so far recovered, as to take some tea.

Next day I called in to see how things were going. Gribble was quite sober and as meek and humble as a lamb. He had had a shave and cut himself in two or three places, his face was shrivelled up and ghastly; his hands trembled, so that he could hardly hold a cup of tea without spilling. "That bottle is finished Mundy," he said to me, in a piteous tone, "don't you think I'd better have another?" "Perhaps you had," I answered, "but remember and do not forget you are tapering off. Let the wife dole it out to you, always less and less."

Gribble got over his spree all right and kept from drink for a week or two when, he began to take it in wonderful moderation and kept himself respectable a long time. He was very much relieved in his mind and thankful when his wife told him she had picked his pocket in the stable.

My brother John had made an acquaintance of a young man, a carpenter and induced Mother to take him as a boarder. John and I were doing nothing. I said to John one day: "There is plenty of room on our allotment to build another house. Tom your friend will show us how to do it properly." "All right Henry," he answered, "a good idea, I'm sick of walking about doing nothing. Let us see what father says." Father was consulted about the building of the new house and was quite pleased at the fit and the new idea that had seized us. So it was decided to build a four-roomed weatherboard house, 24 X 24 feet.

This house is an original and a splendid example of the period when Henry built in Geelong.

Father said: "You do the building, lining and paperhanging and painting outside and I'll do the painting inside." So we started our building right away. Tom was willing to superintend the job, give us instructions mornings and evenings and when he came home to dinner, so we got on very well for amateurs.

While we were busy building the house, a man named Budge came to Gribble's. He was a professional bullock driver. He was an old acquaintance of Gribble, having known each other on some station where they had been working together. Budge had recently lost his wife and had one child, a girl about five years old. After the death of his wife, he sold his team of bullocks and dray and came to Geelong for the purpose of placing his child with some respectable family where she would be taken care of. Having met with Gribble in the street and after having a drink together, Gribble invited him to his house, and requested him to make it his home for a while, which he did, after placing his child in safe keeping.

Budge was about thirty-two, he was not a heavy drinking man, but could take his share with the rest without showing any ill effects, in fact what was called a moderate drinker. There were three classes of drinkers in those days, one was like Budge, another would drink moderately for a time, then would break out and have what he would call a bust, perhaps for two or three weeks. The other class were always drunk, except from an occasional attack of delirium tremens, when they had to taper off and suffer a recovery or die. Of total abstainers there were none; at least none ever came under my notice.

Budge after a few weeks conceived a notion of trying his luck on the diggings and wanted Gribble to go with him. Gribble who was tired of loafing about was willing if the old woman, Ann and I went too. I was afraid that if I did not consent they would be taking Ann away, so I agreed to join them as soon as I had finished, with John, building the house which would not take long. For some cause or other, very soon after, Gribble broke out on the bust again and upset all peaceable arrangements and did not care whether he went or not. But Mrs Gribble was bent on going in order to get her husband away from Geelong and his boon companions. So we hired a dray to take us to Ballarat, as fresh rushes were continually happening there.

The main road leading up to Bell Post Hill, and out of Geelong to Batesford, Hamilton or Ballarat.

Being all ready to start one morning excepting Gribble, we hunted for him for over an hour without success. The drayman became impatient and declared he would wait no longer, that he would be sure to catch up to us at the first camping place, the Muddy Water Holes. So we started. Budge had a saddle horse, Mrs Gribble, Ann and I rode with the driver. The first incident that occurred on the journey was at Bell Post Hill, the steepest ascent between Geelong and Ballarat. The driver got down and suggested as the load was heavy we might get down and walk to the top of the hill, which we did. Budge had a saddle horse and was riding, seeing us on foot he dismounted and joined us, saying jokingly to Mrs Gribble: "Get up and have a ride on horseback." "So I will," she answered, "if you'll fix the stirrups and lift me up. That was soon done. She sat the horse all right to the top of the hill at a walking pace, when somebody said: "Now make him trot"; with that she gave the horse a touch with the whip. As likely as not she had never been on a horse's back before, when the horse started on a gentle trot, the rider went bump, bumping up and down in a most unhorsewoman like fashion for about fifty yards, when over she tumbled with her foot through the lower stirrup. The horse, after going a few more steps dragging her with him, for a wonder, stopped, till we were able to extricate the amateur rider, not hurt but "plenty frightened," as the blacks used to say.

We camped for the night at the Muddy Water Holes, but no Gribble appeared. Continuing our journey the next day, we camped at the Stoney Rises. Just before sundown Budge and I were fixing the tent for Mrs Gribble and Ann, when up rode William Gribble on horseback. "Ah," he said, "I've caught up to you, I thought I'd come up with you here. I started from Geelong this morning," and then began to apologise for not being ready to start with us, with a jumbled up lot of lies about business, which no one believed. I saw he was very nervous and wild looking; his tremulous hands could scarcely hold the bridle.

He knew we had liquor on the dray and said: "Mundy give me a drop of brandy, I have not had a drop since I left Geelong. I feel used up." I knew that was a lie. I poured him out a good stiff dose in a tea cup which he swallowed straight. His opinion was that it spoilt grog to water it. Mrs Gribble and Ann were preparing supper. Gribble would not have any. His excuse was that he had had such a big feed at the Separation, another lie. We sat, some on the grass, some on a big log before the fire and talked for about two hours and had a drink or two each, when Gribble said: "Old woman, have you made up the bed?" "Oh yes," she replied, "e' can go when e' likes." "Ah well," he said, "I'll turn in I had very little sleep last night," which he did straight away.

After I suppose an hour, his wife went to bed too. It must have been I think about eleven o'clock when the end of the tent was suddenly burst open by Gribble rushing through it, roaring out: "Murder, murder, stop 'em, they're going to kill me, murder, murder," with nothing on but his shirt; running like a hunted hare straight into the bush. Budge said: "He's in the horrors." "Come," I said, "let's fetch him back." "Not I," Budge replied. "I'm not going to risk getting shot. You know he carries pistols about him." "How can he carry pistols," I said, "he's nowhere to put them." "Oh," he said, "he may have one in his hand."

The yelling still continued till it gradually died away in the distance. I said to Budge: "If you will not go with me, I'll go by myself." "More fool you," he said, "I would not go a step after him, besides undressed as he is, he'll feel the cold and will soon be back." I got up to make a start, when Ann said: "No, don't you go Mundy," catching hold of my arm, "I won't let you, he'll come back when he misses his clothes and feels the cold." It was not a cold night but the air was keen and still, a night on which I should decidedly object to leave home without my pants.

After a while Budge said: "I'm going to turn in under the tarpaulin." I said: "I'm not coming till Gribble comes back."

Ann said: "I'll stop with you Mundy." I made up the fire afresh. Ann and I sat side by side on the log in front of the fire, my arm was round her waist, very little was said, alternately looking into the fire and towards the direction Gribble had fled, hoping to see his ghostly re-appearance through the darkness. But he came not, nor was there any sound. The wonder was, did he keep straight on in his mad career, or did anything induce him to stop?

Time passed on, hour after hour. At last Ann said: "I feel so sleepy." I replied: "Go into the tent, then to your mother and lie down." She answered me abruptly: "No, I won't." I then gently drew her head on to my shoulder in which position she was soon peacefully sleeping. She slept that way for two long hours, when she woke up saying: "Mundy, I'm cold." "So am I," I said, and went about getting more wood to freshen up the fire, which had gone low. Another hour passed, and the welcome streaks of day were visible in the east. As soon as I could well see, I said to Ann: "I'm off now to look for the madman." "Alright,"

she said, "I'll stay here and put the kettle on. He'll want something hot, if you find him, but do not be long away, if you can't find him soon come back and we'll tell the police about him when we reach Buninyong."

So I started in the direction I had heard the last sound of his voice. In half a mile I came upon a nondescript object, something out of the common. It was Gribble. Darwin's theory is that man is developed from the monkey. If his theory is correct, Gribble would have seemed to have retrograded unknown centuries back to his ancestors; he looked so much like a monkey. His back was bent, his legs half doubled, his two hands hanging down between his legs. Coming up to him I sang out: "Gribble," he started, turned half round and muttered something. "Gribble," I shouted, "what the devil are you doing in this plight?" At that he turned enough to face me. "Oh Mundy," he cried, "I'm so glad to see you." "Come away to the tent," I said, "and get into your clothes." He was trembling from head to foot, his teeth clacking in his head. "I can't," he replied, "that fellow won't let me." "What fellow?" I asked. "Why," he said, "that fellow standing there." Pointing to a denuded stump about three times the height of a man, he tells me: "I shan't go till I eat all that pudding," pointing to a prostrate log a foot thick, and two yards long. "Oh come on, you are mad," I said, catching him by the arm and giving him a fierce drag.

He stumbled on a few yards and looking behind with abject terror in his eyes: "Is he coming" he asked? "Come on, come on" I said "if he interferes I'll soon settle him." "Ah," he exclaimed with great confidence. Yet he could not help looking back now and again, for the first two hundred yards. In his proper strength he was a stronger man than I was but now I could handle him like a baby. I hurried him on and at last got him into a trot. Ann saw us coming and ran to the tent to tell her mother, who all dressed, came out with Gribble's pants in her hand. When drawing near she cried out " "You mad wretch, to serve I like this," bewailing her fate, and wringing her hands in frantic frenzy, added "I wish I'd never seen un, I do."

I snatched the pants out of her hand, saying to Gribble: "Here go to the tent and dress yourself and I'll bring you a hot drink of brandy." After he had dressed and gulped down the hot grog, he became all at once quite himself again. Budge then made his appearance to whom I made the remark: "What a constitution he must have, what he went through last night, was enough to kill any ordinary man." "Oh," he replied, "nothing will ever kill him till he is shot."

Ann had soon the breakfast ready, laid out on a rug on the grass near the fire. All partook of it heartily except Gribble, who ate only a few mouthfuls but drank plentifully of hot tea. An hour after I gave him another dose of brandy, which he took with genuine thankfulness, saying: "Oh Mundy, you saved my life." A short time afterwards one could scarcely credit that he had undergone the ordeal of last night, unless he had witnessed it.

Packed up and ready for the road again, Gribble and Budge on horseback, and about to make a start Gribble said: "I'll ride on and pick out the best place to camp and meet you in Buninyong," and off he went. We stopped for dinner a mile before reaching Buninyong. During dinner Gribble came up. He said he had not found a place that suited him yet, he would have another look round. "No, I had dinner," he replied to our invitation to join us, he had eaten a good dinner at Jamieson's. I could see he had been drinking as he swayed about in the saddle. "Look here," I said, "if you go drinking again, you may go to the devil for me I'll wash my hands of you." "By God, Mundy," he said, "there's no fear of that, last night was lesson enough for me." I said: "You have taken too much already." "Well," he said, "a man must taper off you know." "Take care you don't taper on," I replied. "Oh, no fear of that," when off he rode.

The road from Geelong to Ballarat became the Midland Highway. Many of its farm fences, built from the stones which littered the paddocks, remain and the place is generally untouched from Henry's time.

At the back of Mother Jamieson's, we came to a gully having two or three feet of water in it. We watched a team pass over the usual crossing place. Our driver hesitated, saying: "I'm afraid I shall not be able to cross there with this load, let us see if there is not a better place." So we looked up and down the gully and found no place satisfactory as several boggings were evident. There was nothing for it but to risk the common crossing. He suggested taking off half the load and to return for the other half. I said: "Do you think you could cross if you, I and the women were not on?" "Well," he said, "I would chance it then, but how are the women to get over?" "As for that," I said, "I'll carry them over." "Right you are," he replied, and started walking through himself. With a little struggle he got over safe. Budge then said: "I'll take the women over in front of me on the saddle if they like." "Oh," Ann said, "Mundy will carry me over, I'm not very heavy." So I took her in my arms, saying: "Hug me tight round the neck, as tight as you love me." We crossed all right for she was very light. I then returned for mother, who preferred being carried too. When I lifted her I felt an amazing difference in the weight, and she hung frontward in such a lolloping way, I could with difficulty keep my balance. I told her to keep close and hold me round the neck. When about the middle of the current, I stepped into a shallow hole and nearly lost my equilibrium; if I had we should have gone, side on into the wet together, but as luck would have it, I recovered myself, and Jordan was safely crossed.

We made over the ranges to the back road to Ballarat. I knew of a nice camping place about three miles from Ballarat, somewhere near where the Magpie lead broke out later on. Budge and I both thought the spot would suit very well, as the new rushes were continually approaching Buninyong. So we pulled up and got fixed for the night, but there was no sign of Gribble. Where he had gone to, nobody knew, and I believe, very little cared.

Next morning, we went to work fixing our tents for a permanent stay. We fixed the women's tent first and made it as comfortable as we knew how. We made a little galley too, with bark roof for the women to cook and wash in. This work took us all day, although we worked with a will. No Gribble made his appearance. The next day we finished our own tent to our satisfaction. In the evening, Gribble turned up. On being questioned where he had been, he replied: "Looking for you, I found a splendid camping place near The Prince Regent, but then the trouble was to find you." "Served you right," I said, "why did you leave us? What have you done with the horse?" "I sent him back to Geelong," he answered, "with a man I knew, tied behind a dray." But I knew it was no good asking him questions when in drink; all that one could get out of him would be only lies. He was nearly drunk then. "Have you got any grog left?" he enquired. "No," I said, "Budge and I drained the last bottle this afternoon." The place where we pitched was not thronged with tents only one here and there - there was a store a quarter mile away. Gribble saw the store and made for it. In a short time he returned saying: "I tried that store for a bottle, but they told me they didn't keep a shanty."

We all turned in pretty early that night, expecting a repetition of the affair of the Stoney Rises, but the night passed off quietly. Gribble could not eat any breakfast unless, he told us, he had a nobbler first and started forthwith in search of an appetiser. Budge and I had half a dozen bottles in our tent, but neither of us spoke up. That was the last we saw of him for six or seven weeks. Mrs Gribble told us he had a roll of notes in his trousers pocket which she tried to get hold of, but he gave her never a chance. She told him she had no money and asked him to give her some. After a deal of badgering he drew a note from his pocket and said, here's a one for you and make much of it, but the one happened to be a five.

Budge and I had a look round for a day or two then resolved to try our luck at the head of (I think) New Chum Gully. We bottomed too shallow, on the reef at fifty feet while the gutter was sixty or seventy feet where the lead ran. That was our first duffer. We then sunk for a leader running from the range to the main lead. That was duffer number two. We made up our minds then to go a prospecting in and on the many hills and gullies round, but fortune did not favour us.

What a mockery there is in fate. A man is anxiously desiring a certain thing, he hunts the wide world over to find it, but still it eludes his reach and still it is close beside him if he only knew it. We had been sinking, prospecting and sinking holes, one, two, three miles from our tent for gold and got not a pennyweight, and at the same time we were living near to, if not actually on the famous Magpie Lead discovered three years later. It is said, by some, there is no such thing as luck, that every man is the architect of his own fortune. Such people had never been gold digging.

We were both down on our luck, but I had Ann with me and was happy enough. Budge was sick of it and Mrs Gribble was afraid her husband would sell the other house. We might have stayed longer but Mrs Gribble's brother Jim, who was carrying with his bullocks between Geelong and Ballarat, happened to run against us. Jim received a full account of Gribble's conduct from his sister. "I wonder what's become o' un," Jim said at last, "he may have fallen down a hole." "I hope to goodness he has," she rejoined, "and broke his neck, that would be the end of his misery and mine too." "Now Ann," Jim said, "as Mundy and Budge

NEW CHUM GULLY
There were five New Chum Gullies in the goldfields.

ain't got no luck, please yerselves, I'm going back empty, you all and your trap can go with I. I won't charge you nothing. I don't see what good it is for el waiting for Gribble to turn up, he won't come now." So it was agreed to go back to Geelong again. Budge having a horse could have gone on, but he chose to travel all the way with us.

When we arrived in Geelong, Ann and her mother went to Fanny's to stay till the tenants who occupied their house could find other quarters. Gribble was in Geelong and had been there for weeks still drinking. There had been a rupture between John Crosby and Fanny. He had made her a present of a nice clock thinking that that would soften her hard heart and bring her to, but she told him to "clear out and take his auld clock we 'un, as she wanted neither he nor his clock." As John had expected a far different reception than this base ingratitude, for a wonder, got angry, and they had hard words; the end of it was John took up the clock and limped off. Fanny made us laugh the way she mimicked him going away with the clock.

After they had been at Fanny's two days, Gribble heard of it and paid them a visit. He was a deplorable looking wreck, his dissipated wrinkled face was shocking to look at, his clothes dirty and hanging about him in folds, his black bushy whiskers were one mat. He begged of Fanny to let him stay there, till his house was ready and persuade the old woman to go home with him. Mrs Gribble who had seen him coming had hidden herself in the next room, where she could hear and see and not be seen, could contain herself no longer and flung open the door. "William Gribble," she burst out, "never while I have breath in my body, will I live with e' again, after the way you've treated and deserted me this last six weeks, left me and Ann in the bush with only one miserable pound, if it had not been for Mundy we should have had nothing to eat." Fanny told me she abused him so, that she felt pity for 'un, while Gribble "looked as meek and as penitent as a chiel."

After she had vented the last word of anger upon him, she went into the room again and slammed the door. After this tirade he sat on the sofa in a total collapse. At last he said: "Have you seen Mundy?" "Yes," Fanny said, "he was here an hour agone and took Ann away with 'un for a walk." At that he left, saying: "I might drop across them." I did not see him till next day. I met him in Moorabool Street quite sober. To all appearances, he had recently awakened out of a sleep in some shed or stable as was shown by the loose straws sticking about him. "Hullo Mundy," he said, in a shaky voice, "I've been looking for you. Where's the old woman?" "You know where she is," I said, "she's at Fanny's." "Yes," he said, "I know, I saw her there yesterday, she swore by all that was good, she'd never live with me again." "No wonder," I replied, "the way you have treated her, no woman on earth, a woman at all, could put up with your carryings on." "Yes," he answered. "I know I am a beast, but so help me God I can't help myself , when the drink is in, I have a sleep and wake up sober and realise what a fool I am making of myself. If I didn't have a drink to revive my spirits I should commit suicide."

"I believe Mundy, you are the only true friend I've got, tell me what to do." "It is very easy to tell you what to do but will you do it? You know very well yourself, all the advice in the world is useless, no one can help you if you don't help, or try to help yourself. As for friends," I said, "Ann is your friend, only she feels degraded with such a stepfather, your wife too would feel proud of you if you would only keep yourself respectable."

His face began to twitch and big tears trickled down his prematurely wrinkled cheeks. "God help me," he moaned. "Look here," I said, "go to the barber's, get a shave, your hair and whiskers trimmed, tidy yourself up to look decent, and keep sober; in three days time they will be home; come then and see them. In the meantime I shall see them and endeavour to make things straight." "Oh Mundy," he blubbered, "You are too good to me, but I must have a drink, just a few, one now and again." "Yes," I said, "it would be best if you could manage that, but if you take one you take two and half a dozen." He took a bullock driver's solemn oath he would do as I advised him.

I went to Fanny's house in the afternoon. I told Mrs Gribble and Ann I had met Gribble and what a deplorable and penitent state he was in, not forgetting to mention the tears and how he had promised to mend his ways, adding that I thought he would be a different man for the future; he sees that he is going to his death at railway speed the way he is going. Ann said nothing. Mrs Gribble took up the cudgels, bursting out: "I wonder at thee Mundy pleading for he when you know so well how he has treated I." "I plead for the man," I said, "because I like him, a truer, kinder-hearted man than William Gribble never trod shoe-leather. It was his misfortune to get money easy, like thousands of others, it has driven him mad. Why do you not be kinder to him and nag at him less, try to wheedle the money from him and put it in the bank in your own name? If he had no money to handle he would be the good old Gribble again." "No Mundy," she said, "he'll not give his money up to I. I've taken a solemn oath not to live with 'un again and that I never will."

After a while Ann and I went for a stroll and talked over the miserable state of affairs. I said: "If your mother breaks off with Gribble, how is she going to live, he won't keep her and what's to become of you?" "Me," she said, "I can do as Fanny does, work for the shops and mother can do the same." "I know of a better plan than that," I said, "let us get married then mother can come and live with us." "No," she answered, "that won't do, I don't intend to marry for a year yet. They will make it up again you'll see if William only keeps sober. Mother does not mean what she says, only for the time."

I told her then what I advised Gribble to do about tidying himself decently and to come and see you as soon as you went home, and when he does come you try to persuade mother after the first meeting is over (it will not do to be too kind at first) to treat him kinder by degrees and keep her biting, nagging tongue still, till she gets into his confidence and you will see she can do anything with him, the mood he is in now.

Hope Street, Ashby looking towards Pakington Street. The Gribble houses and shops were on the opposite side of the intersection.

Let her coax him over to hand what money he has left, to hand it over to her so that she can place it in the bank in her own name. That would be the means of saving his life, which he must know himself if he is not a bigger fool than I think he is. After a while I took her home promising to call at seven to take her to the theatre as there was a good piece on that night, 'The Lady of Lyons.' We went to the play that night, Coppin was at his best on the occasion and we enjoyed ourselves to our hearts content.

In due course Ann and her mother moved into their own house, and Gribble very soon paid them a visit. His reception from his wife was not a very welcome one at first, but by degrees she became more sociable and attentive, till one would think nothing disagreeable had ever happened between them.

Gribble evidently suffered his recovery with pleasure. Under the influence of broths, niceties, strengthening food and kind attention from both his wife and Ann, he recovered himself considerably. His wife said to him one day: "What a fool I be to take all this trouble nursing t'ee up and getting tlee strong again for another bust." Gribble cut her short. "No, old woman," he said, "by Heavens I'll never drink again as I have done, because I know full well if I do the next bout would be the end of me." "But thee sayest," she replied, "when thee gets over a certain stage thee can't help theeself, to make sure why not give the money to I to hold. I could give thee enough to spend to be decent with and stop thee when going too far." "A very good idea old woman," Gribble said: "I'll think over that tonight and tell you what'll do tomorrow."

On the morrow after breakfast Gribble said: "I am going, old woman, to make you and Ann safe, if anything happens me. I'll will this house over to you in this way, to be your's while you live. At your death it goes to Ann, and after to Ann's oldest child. I think that's fair enough. We'll see the lawyer today and get the Will made out. What do you say?" That seemed a concession in the right direction, so for the time she was bound to be content, and promised to go together to the lawyer with him, which they did and the Will was to be ready for signature next day.

I saw Mrs Gribble in the evening, Gribble happening to be out. She was in good spirits and told me about the Will Gribble was going to sign. I was not much of a lawyer myself but said; "I do not think this Will can hinder him from selling or making a fresh Will whenever he likes." "Don't e," she replied, "if that be so, a Will be no real protection to us at all." "I'll ask Mr Gregory, the lawyer tomorrow about that." Accordingly she asked the lawyer what guarantee the will would be against Gribble selling the house afterwards. "None at all," he said, "a Will has no force till after the testator's death. While he is alive he can do with the property what he thinks fit. To preserve confidence between you, I advise you to lease the house to some trustworthy friend for a term of say seven to fourteen or twenty-one years, then it cannot be sold without the lessee's consent. Lease it for fourteen years at something near its value, say £2 a week." Gribble objected to this arrangement. "Who," he asked, "could they find fool enough to risk the liability of being compelled to pay £2 a week for fourteen years?" "Mundy would," she replied. "Oh, well," Gribble said, "if Mundy will do it I am agreeable." So I was afterwards consulted on the matter. "There's no knowing what may happen in fourteen years, it looks a bit risky," I observed, "but no matter, I'll sign the lease." I never paid any rent nor was I expected to.

After the Will and lease business was completed, affairs went on smoothly for a while but Gribble did not cease drinking more than was good for him, and his wife was ever urging him to let her hold the money until at last he promised to hand it over to her. It was agreed they should go to the bank for the purpose, and I was requested to go with them as witness and see that the transfer was done properly, as Gribble could neither read nor write. So we three started for the bank one morning to complete this important business. The bank, I think, was the Victoria, situated at the corner of Corio and Moorabool streets on the bay side; on the opposite corner the watch house or 'Stone Jug' as it was called, a small building built of blue stone. It has long disappeared and on its site now stands the Savings Bank. Gribble to me seemed pretty sober and in earnest. As we were passing the watchhouse gate before crossing Corio Street, Gribble suddenly grabbed his wife round the waist and dragging her violently toward the watchhouse crying out: "This is the bank I'm taking you to, you old ..."

I stood thunderstruck for a second or two at his treachery and to think I should have been brought

The corner of Corio and Moorabool Streets in 2003. It is the spot where Henry was assaulted by his future father-in-law and where both were arrested.

there on such a fool's errand. I made for him straight; he loosed the woman then to face me. The upshot of it was he went over into the gutter with his heels sticking up on the curbstone. As I stood looking at him with my back toward the watchhouse a policeman sprang up behind me, and catching me by the arm said: "I arrest both of you for fighting in the street." There was nothing for it but to submit, for either of us.

After digging his hand into our pockets and possessing himself of all the money we had (I had two pounds and some silver) pushed us into different cells and locked the doors. The cell was lighted only by a row of vertical iron bars near the ceiling, so that at first I could not see very well, but kicking against a box I sat down on it, and wondered what there might be going to happen next. I sat ruminating for a few minutes, thinking I was alone when a fretful voice from out of a dark corner said: "What's the charge mate?" "What, what's the charge." "What was you run in for?" "Oh," I said, "fighting in the street the policeman calls it." "Have you got any friends?" he further enquired. "Yes, a few," I told him. "You've no occasion to worry then, they'll soon bail you out. I've got no friends nor any money, so I got to stop and do my time."

"What brought you here?" I enquired. "Getting drunk and resisting the police," he answered. "How long are you in for?" "A week," he said. "I done four days." "How do you pass the time?" "Pass the time," he replied, "principally in thinking what a fool I've been. I tell you mate, I'm as miserable as a shag on a rock." And he looked it. "This is not the first time you've been in quod?" I said. "Oh no," he replied, "worse luck." I knew the man was an old convict. We said no more for a while. He was just going to tell me something, I thought of importance, when a key turned in the lock of the cell door and there stood the policeman and my brother John behind him. "Bailed out," the policeman said briefly: "to appear before his worship the Mayor at ten o'clock tomorrow. Here's your money."

I told John how I happened to get into the lockup, and we had a good laugh over the adventure, and went into the Victoria to have a drink, where John told me how Mrs Gribble came, in a very excited state to our house, to tell them that Gribble and I were in the lockup, with a long rigmarole how I had knocked Gribble over as he was going to put her into the watchhouse, a story of which no

Autumn Street looking from the quarry end towards the city and Corio Bay.

one could make head or tail. Only one fact was plain, I had got myself locked up. Whereupon mother got exceedingly wrath, and said: "go John and bail him out. I expected something would happen in the long run with Henry mixing himself up so much with them Gribbles, he's hardly ever at his own home." Mrs Gribble then ran home to tell Ann the news. And there was trouble in the house of Gribble till John and I made our appearance. Ann laughed over the affair but I could see her eyes were red. Where was Gribble, was the question. Out no doubt as he had money enough on him to bail himself out.

When I arrived home, I found father very much put out to think that I should have been locked up. And mother gave me a severe lecture saying Mrs Gribble and Gribble were looked upon as people of little account, and as for the girl there were many better girls than she was. "There's Margaret," she said, "is overhead and ears in love with you, as good or better girl than Ann Gribble." "Mother," I said, "Margaret is a nice girl, I have nothing to say against her, but Ann is my choice and if possible, marry her I will. She is young I know, and if she had a happier home, I would willingly wait two or three years for her, as things are, I am quite willing to marry her tomorrow." There was terrible upset at Fanny's that night. Mrs Gribble had gone to Fanny for condolence in expressing her outraged feelings. Gribble hearing where she was, went after her as drunk as he could be. Then commenced a scene of mutual upbraidings.

After going to their house and finding no one in, I guessed where they might be, so I went directly to Fanny's and dropped in, in the thick of the turmoil. Mrs Gribble had gone into hysterics, while Gribble was calling her all the beastly names his bullock driver's tongue could utter. There were unlacing of stays, applications of smelling salts, sprinklings of cold water on the face and hands, accompanied with screams and kicking and plunging of the patient. All at once she made a spring, ran out of the door, her dress all in disarray, hair all hanging down, and ran like mad down Autumn Street and Ann after her. She ran about a hundred yards when Ann caught up to her in a state of collapse. We got her inside again and placed her on the sofa where after a time she went to sleep and Gribble staggered home.

Fanny was greatly annoyed that such a scene should have been enacted in her house, and said to Ann and me: "They be always rowing, why don't 'em quarrel at their own wh'um and not come upsetting I, bringing the whul street gaping to my door. I shall be put down as bad as they for harbouring 'em. They are always rowing they be; they be miserable therselves, and make everyone else the same. Ann poor maid must have a wretched time among em, why don't e' get married and have a home of yer own; yes chiel, get married to once, thee'lt never have any peace living with they."

In walking home with Ann that night she said: "You'll have to go to court tomorrow, I wonder how you'll get on?" "Oh," I answered, "either be fined or go to jail." "Go to jail," she gasped, "what, for taking mother's part?" "It is all according how they bring it in," I said, "but I think there will be option of a fine." We tarried a little while at the gate, when Mrs Gribble came up asking where Gribble was. We did not know, but I said: "I'll look in the stable," where I found him snoring off the effects of his drink. I bade them good night then and went home.

On the morrow at ten o'clock, Gribble and I appeared at the Court House. A short time after Dr Bailey, the Mayor, with great dignity, took his seat on the bench. After a few drunks had been disposed of, a policeman called out, "Henry Mundy" three times, when I walked up and announced myself. "What's the charge?" "Fighting in the street your worship." "Guilty or not guilty?" I said, "Your Worship, I had no

219

intention of fighting, I was only defending a woman." "You hear the charge, guilty or not." So to cut matters short I pleaded guilty. His Worship answered: "I fine you five pounds. Next case." When Gribble was called and dealt with the same.

After our cases were heard neither of us had any curiosity to watch other cases, so we both left the Court House together. "Look here Mundy," Gribble said, "I'll pay that fine for you, I was a jolly ass to act as I did. I had not the least notion of putting her in the watchhouse till I came to the gate, when the devil seemed to have got hold of me. It was a foolhardy business anyhow. I hope you don't bear any malice with me for it Mundy, that is the only thing that troubles me." I said, "I cannot, with common sense, bear malice against a madman, but I feel ashamed to be seen in his company."

There was silence for a while, when passing the Black Bull, he said: "Come and have a drink Mundy." "No," I said, "I want to get back and tell the women how our trouble has been settled." "Oh I see," he answered, "you bear me a grudge and are going to be unfriendly, look here Mundy, I'll swear." "Don't waste your breath man," I said, "what's the good." "Well then, come in and I'll give you the £5 you were fined through my foolery."

Under the circumstances I thought it advisable to take his drink. At the bar he drew from his trousers pocket a roll of notes and counted and gave £5 to me, holding out his hand, saying now let us be friends again. "That all depends," I said, "on the way you carry on for the future, I shall certainly not put up with you, if you do not alter from this out." "Ah well," he said, "you'll see." With that I left him.

When I arrived at the house and told Ann and mother how things had been settled they were both highly pleased, especially at Gribble's paying the fine. In the evening Ann and I took a walk out and called to see a friend of our's, Mrs Charlton. She was a shipmate of Ann and her mother from the Old Country. A jolly, good soul was Mrs Charlton, she had a joke and a pleasant word for everyone. A woman about forty-five years old, the most famous midwife round her quarter. She and her husband hailed from Nottinghamshire. According to her native country her talk now-a-days in this squeamish generation would be looked upon as coarse, but no one could be offended at the way she told her stories.

As soon as she saw us coming she held up her hands crying out: "Eh lad, I'm so glad to see ye. I heard both you and Gribble were in quod, how did'st tha manage to get cot of it." Then I had to tell her the whole story. "Well now," she said, "What an ass he must halbin to think he could have put her into t'watchhouse and thee must have been too to think he could." "But" I said, "what a fool he made of me." "Yes, yes lad," she replied, patting me on the shoulder, "thee didn't stop to think did'st thee?" She continued, "I'll tell thee two what's best to do, go and get married and have a house to your own selves. Ann poor lass, will know no peace nor you either, until you do. Na, lad, I just will tell you what I know there's faults on both sides, though Gribble is the worst of the two. If he had no money or very little to spend he would keep sober and a quieter more civil man I never met, when out of drink. "

When we left Charlton's, I was anxious to go home and tell my people how matters had been settled and wanted Ann to go too; but I could not persuade her to go. Unhappily there existed between mother and Mrs Gribble a coolness which the latter endeavoured to instil into Ann. My mother was a very straight talker, perhaps too much so, but she never bore malice, but Mrs Gribble, as I found to my sorrow in after years, was very vindictive.

We went back to Gribble's. He had not come home. "I expect," she said, "when he does come, it will be as usual, drunk." I told her what Mrs Charlton had said about us getting married, when she began to lament saying: "What'll become of I, alone in this house with that man, it's bad enough as it is, but what'll it be when thee art gone and I have no maid to talk to and take my part?" "As for that," I said, "you will be welcome to visit us whenever you like, and Ann can come to see you as often as she likes, and if Gribble becomes unbearable you can come and stay with us till he mends his ways. If he comes to my house drunk and quarrelsome I'll see that he does not come in, if I am there." "Oh, I know," she replied, "the poor chiel is miserable in living the life she do, and I think it would be selfish of I to stand in the way of her happiness for I know you are fond of each other, but I do wish she was a year older; she is so young."

During this talk, between the mother and me, Ann said nothing. Mother sat silent for a few minutes, then said: I'll give my consent that you and Ann get married as soon as everything is ready." Ann then said: "You two seem to be settling this business between your selves, haven't I anything to say in it?" "Yes, my dear girl," I said, "you have, you have everything to say in it now." "Oh well," she replied, "I suppose I must not be disagreeable. I will say I'm willing."

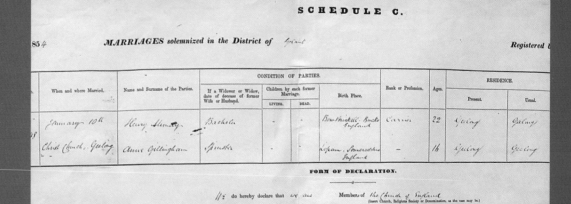

Henry and Ann's marriage certificate.

Christ's Church, Geelong.

ANN MUNDY AND A FAMILY

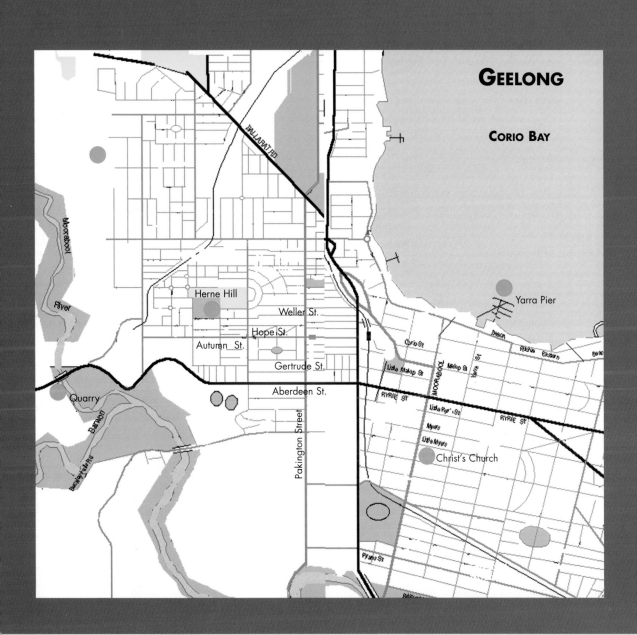

GEELONG

CORIO BAY

Yarra Pier

Herne Hill

Weller St.

Hope St.

Autumn St.

Gertrude St.

Aberdeen St.

Quarry

Pakington Street

Corio St

Little Malop St

Ryrie St

Little Ryrie St

Myers

Little Myers

Christ's Church

Ryrie St

Moorabool

River

Barwon

Berkeley Rd

Ballarat Rd

Malop St

Yarra St

Ryan St

Barwon

MARRIAGE, EXCITEMENT THEN TRAGEDIES
HENRY AND ANN MARRY, START A BUSINESS AND SOON A FAMILY, BUT ...

When I went home that night I told my father and mother and John all the news of the day, that Ann and I were going to be married soon. Father said: "I'm glad to hear it my boy, you'll be more settled in your mind now and make a start to do something, these last three months you've only been idling about doing nothing. You will have a home of your own and away from that Gribble."

This was near the end of the year 1853. Ann would be sixteen the coming May, and I would be twenty-three in June. I sold the block of land of my prospective market garden business and made about £10 on my bargain after holding it eighteen months. I bought a horse and dray for £120 intending to go carting again, but our chief concern for the present was the household furniture. Nothing common would suit us, we must have the best, and furniture was very dear then. I recollect some of the items - wooden bedstead £6, pier glass £3, two cut glass decanters 18/- each. A set of china £2 etc. We rented a four roomed house in Kildare, I forget the rent. The wedding dresses to be bought and made a get-up for the bride, also for the bridesmaid. Mrs Gribble was to be bridesmaid, and the dresses were of Chinese silk, blue plaid on white ground. My dress was stylish for the occasion. One article made an indelible mark on my memory, that was the waistcoat; it was of white satin worked over with satin flowers and cost 25/-. All things being in readiness and in order, a few of our most intimate friends were invited, including father and mother, sister, John and his sweetheart, Gribble was expected to come but he did not turn up. Wedding guests in those days were not looked to bring presents.

The bridegroom had to fork out for everything expecting no favour from any one except, perhaps, from his nearest relatives.

The day fixed for our wedding was the 10th January, 1854. I engaged a livery stablekeeper to bring a fine pair of roans in a double-seated, tip-top carriage to drive us to church and back, about a mile and half for £4. We all had to wear white gloves. in presenting a pair to the driver "God bless the woman," he said (old Roach being a bit of a wag in his way). "Do you think I could put them on, my hand is like a frying pan?" Stretching out an immense paw proved what he said as far as size went.

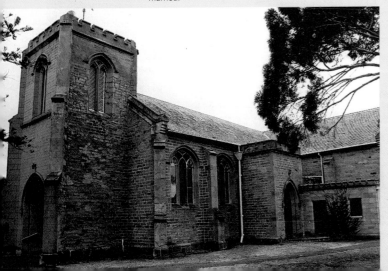

We arrived at Christ's Church about eleven o'clock where Archdeacon Stretch was waiting for us, who joined two loving hearts together in the bonds of holy matrimony. I had attained the consummation of my hopes and wishes and was supremely content.

When we returned home the wedding dinner was soon ready as there were plenty of cooks and waiters. After a satisfactory meal and two hours chat, some one suggested a drive round the town. I asked Roach, who had stayed to dinner, what he would charge for a run round. "A couple of pounds," he said. "All right," I said, "agreed on." The carriage was filled with as many as it could contain, including John and his girl and my sister. After a good run round for two or three hours, we returned home, having enjoyed ourselves to our hearts content, quite ready for another meal. We passed a very pleasant evening, or rather night, for we did not break up till four o'clock. There was plenty of all sorts of drink, and everybody sung except father and me. Some got a bit boozey toward the end, that is the men, but the ladies were all abstemious enough excepting one. She enjoyed herself rather over much and was anxiously intent, to my wife's annoyance on kissing me, but she was disposed of by the other women putting her to bed.

Being now a married man, I felt keenly my responsive altered situation. I was anxious to be doing something to make up for the idle time, and the money I had spent. We had no desire for a honeymoon, we two. The third day after the wedding I saw in the Geelong Advertiser, an advertisement from a road contractor, for a man with horse and tip dray. As mine was a tip dray, I applied for the job at once and saw the contractor, whose name was Trotter. He had a contract for widening the road at the end of Yarra Street, which was a cutting seven or eight feet deep sloping to the pier, and filling up nearer the bay.

The Yarra Pier in Geelong was a busy place in the 1800s, and the same port over 120 years later is on the left.

Yarra Street leading to Corio Bay.

Trotter engaged me with horse and dray for 30/- a day. I worked for him a week. Ann brought my dinner every day, but before the week was over father had got a job to cart two loads of furniture to Ballarat, for a new hotel called the George for £15 a load and wanted me to take one of the loads, which I agreed to do. At the end of the week I told Trotter I would not be able to come again as I had engaged to go to Ballarat. He did not seem very well pleased at my leaving him so abruptly, he liked the action of my horse, he was very quick and took such little time in delivering his load and back.

Monday morning found father and me on the road to Ballarat. Our loads were bulky but not heavy. We arrived there without mishap and unloaded in three days and staying for the night there. I visited Bath's Hotel. It was vastly improved since I saw it last, the bar and rooms were densely crowded. Grog shops were little patronised within a mile of Bath's. How the proprietor, I thought, must be scraping money in. The Royal or St. George (in after years it always went by the name of The George) was the second hotel built in Ballarat. Wholesale wine and spirit stores followed soon after.

The entrance to the George Hotel in Ballarat - the second hotel in the city and a serious rival to Bath's hotel.
It is seen on the left and remains an imposing structure.

On Wednesday, early, we were on our return journey. Father when on the road, especially when returning empty, was one of the most fidgety mortals I ever knew; he wanted to be always going. We camped that night near Meredith. After we had fed and hobbled the horses putting a bell on one, we turned them out, and we turned in. We both slept at least I thought so, for I could not tell what time it was. I know it was very dark, I heard some one cooee. I said: "Father, there is someone cooeeing, I suppose it's somebody got lost." As I received no reply, I spoke again, receiving no answer. I put out my hand and found his place was empty. I slipped on my pants saying to myself: "I'm blowed if that fidgety old fool hasn't gone out in the dark to look for the horses." Slipping out of the tail of the dray, I cooeed as loud as I could which was answered. I looked for my boots to go to meet him.

My boots were not to be found, but I found his. "Blow me," I said, "if he has not gone in my boots, which were two sizes too large for him." I would have gone to meet him but had no boots and the ground was too rocky to go barefoot. I had to wait till he came flop, flop, flopping leading the two horses.

"Why didn't you answer my cooee?" he said, quite out of temper. "I've been shouting this last half hour." "So I did," I said, "as soon as I heard you, why in the name of common sense did you go at all, I want to know?" "Well," he said, "I couldn't sleep, I listened to the bell a long time when all at once it stopped. I lay a while till I got uneasy, I did not wake you because I know if I did, you'd only laugh at me. A pretty pickle we shall be in, in the morning to get up and our horses gone. I could not rest any longer but got up to look for them to make sure. I could not find my own boots, so I put on your's. I went straight to where I heard the bell last, and there I found them as swell as mice." "Of course," I said, "their bellies were full." "And when," he continued, "I had put the ropes round their necks, and taken off the hobbles, for the life of me I couldn't tell which way the drays were. Our fire had got so low I couldn't see a sign of it. I knew it was no good going anywhere in the dark when you're lost so I stood still and cooeed for ever so long till

I heard you." "Ah well," I said, "it cannot be far from daylight (neither of us carried a watch). We will feed them now, get our breakfast and be ready to start by break of day." Father agreed to this willingly.

We reached father's place early in the evening. I kept my horse in father's stable. Arriving home I found my little wife as happy as a queen in company of an intimate friend of her's, Charlotte Kircaldy, both busy making and stuffing sofa pillows. After a little talk about our trip, she told me she saw mother every day, mother either came to see her or she went to see mother. Gribble, whom I had not seen since before the wedding, was keeping very steady, and they were living more agreeably together. He was talking, too, about buying a horse and dray as I had done and going to work. "The very thing," I said, "that will keep him out of mischief."

I saw no chances just then of another trip to Ballarat to suit me. There were drays wanted to cart bluestone from the quarries near Levien's Punt to the Geelong Jail for the prisoners to break. I got a job at that at ten shillings a yard. I could do four trips a day, carrying about a yard each load, but it took two half days a week to stack the stone for measurement. There was great art displayed in the stacking, so as to make the inside of the heap as hollow as possible. This swindle was carried on by some of the carters to such a degree that the inspector could not help to notice it, he caused one heap to be restacked by the prisoners, which brought it down to three quarters its original size. The prisoners were all short-sentenced men, petty thieves, runaway sailors and condemned to hard labour, hard labour forsooth they made it easy enough. They were a pest to the carters when opportunity occurred, asking for something, principally tobacco. I did not smoke so I had no tobacco; it was too risky to supply them with anything.

At the top is the quarry which Henry worked, and below as it was in the late 1880s when horses hauled heavy loads up the massive Hyland Street hill into Geelong.

When the stone carting was done I had a spell for a few days and finding nothing better, I applied for light loading to Ballarat and travelled by myself. I went three trips, the first two paid me fairly well but the third was disastrous. I had arrived in Ballarat safe enough. At the end of the Gravel Pitts near Bakery Hill I came to a difficult piece of road between the holes and heaps of dirt to get to where I wanted to deliver my load. In passing one heap of mullock the off wheel rose so high that the load, which was rather high, lost its perpendicular and fell over on to its side, throwing the horse over on to his side with it.

The old Geelong gaol.

Several diggers came to my assistance and soon extricated the horse and got him on to his feet, but he was hurt on the near shoulder and when he attempted to walk, dragged the toe of his near leg on the ground, quite useless. One man who appeared to understand the nature of the injury said he had received a serious hurt in a certain part of the shoulder joint; it would be a long time before he recovered the use of the limb again the same as before, if ever he did. He called it the shoulder lameness.

The dray was partly unloaded when they dragged the dray and what was in it past the mullock heap, and I put the horse in. I had but three hundred yards to go to my destination and the road there was fairly good. The load was soon fixed up again and the poor brute hauled it to the journey's end on three legs.

I told the storekeeper what had happened. "What a pity," he said, "but stop here tonight, the horse may be all right in the morning." I sought out a veterinary surgeon. After examination of the injury he gave a similar account of the damage the other man had done. He clipped off the hair and told me to bathe the part for an hour with warm water, while he prepared blister. "The best thing you can do," he said, "is to turn him out on the grass for a time, give him his free liberty, he will recover sooner that way than keeping him in a stable. It may be months or it may be six before he is himself again, but I doubt that he will ever be the horse he has been.

In the morning he seemed very little better, so leaving the dray and harness at the store, with a rope round his neck, started homewards. It was slow toilsome work. I succeeded in getting him beyond all the diggings towards Buninyong, where I made up my mind to let him loose among the ranges, my £80 horse to go where he liked and perhaps I might never see him again. I could not see any better plan

LEVIEN'S PUNTS
The punt which the bullock teams used to cross the Fresh Water River into Footscray was owned by Benjamin G. Levien (above). He would later own the punt over the Barwon River which Henry used often in his business. In 1840 Levien was the licencee of the Victoria Hotel on the banks of the Fresh Water River on the Footscray side. Soon after he established his punt which was large enough to cater for a 10 bullock team, and had lights for night crossings.
Thomas Watt had run the first hotel there in 1939 but was bought out by John Stewart Spottiswood who ran what was described as a rough and foul business. By 1850 it was respectable and its name was changed.
Levien ran a number of punts including one in Melbourne and another in Geelong.

226

under the circumstances. I had been troubled with an attack of dysentery for the last few days, and my late worry seemed to make it worse. I walked two miles to Mother Jamieson's to stay there and have rest the remainder of the day and sleep there the night and catch Cobb's Coach on the morrow.

There was no other chance next day but to take Cobb's Coach. I had to pay £4/10/- to Geelong. I felt very unwell and I was not a very pleasant mode of transit for one to ride fifty miles in Cobb's heavy lumbering coaches when one is sick. Thought pretty nigh exhausted I arrived home safely. When I went in Ann assailed me with half a dozen questions at once. "What's the matter with you? Where's the horse and dray?" etc. etc. I told her then of my mishap and I was not well. "No wonder," she sympathetically replied, "you are not well. Go to bed directly and I'll give you some nice hot tea and something to eat. suppose you've had nothing to eat since you left Buninyong." "Yes," I said, "I had a bit of dinner at Meredith. But give me some hot brandy instead of the tea. I do not want anything to eat just now, but I want some medicine for dysentery. You know where it is, which I always take for this complaint." "Oh yes" she answered, "I know, castor and fifteen drops of laudanum." After taking the brandy and physic I went to sleep, but was disturbed several times in the night. It was a fortnight before I got to be nearly well again, but very weak.

I attended the auction rooms for a time and the sale yards, where I often met Budge. He was making a little at horse dealing he told me. One day there was a likely looking filly put up. "What do you say," he said, "if we bid for that, we can break it in ourselves." "All right," I said, "you bid for it but don't go over £30." So he bid for the unbroken filly which was knocked down to him for £27. We broke it in between us. She did not take much trouble, a very tractable, quiet beast. I had an idea of buying his share and keeping her. I kept her in father's stable by night and let her out hobbled on the common by day. But one morning I turned her out and looked for her to take her home a usual, when she was not to be found. Both of us searched all next day but could not find her, she had disappeared utterly. He had no idea he said what could have become of her. I had an idea and told him so.

A restored Cobb & Co. coach.

A horsethief had taken her and had ridden during the night to Melbourne and sold her that day at one of the horse sales which had been a common occurrence lately, as there was then no telegraph at that time to stop those tricks. But before the end of that same year a line of posts with one wire was erected from Melbourne to Geelong. I could not help but think Budge had something to do with the disappearance of the filly, he seemed to take it so lightly and unconcerned; although a man very plausible, and straightforward to all appearance. I could never make a confidential friend of him. However, I never heard anything more of the filly.

The railway from Melbourne to Geelong had been started. I thought of buying another horse and work on the line, not that I cared much for navvying. I had heard much about navvies and gangers, I thought it a low game and being pretty full up with horses at the time, this new venture came to naught.

Having nothing better to do the idea struck me to build a house for myself and not be always paying rent. So I bought an allotment of land in Thomas Street, Newtown, not far from father's. I got John to help me as he was doing nothing, a two roomed weatherboard, 24 X 12.

After finishing the house and settling in it, I resolved, by borrowing a horse from my father, to go to Ballarat and fetch my dray and harness home, and try for any possible tidings of my horse. I immediately started on horseback for that purpose, taking nothing with me beyond what I stood in but an overcoat.

Thomas Street Geelong, running between Autumn and Hope Streets.

When I passed Meredith it was too early to stay for the night. I went on intending to travel as long as I could see, which brought me nearly to Burnt Bridge, when I pulled up, unsaddled the horse, hobbled him and turned him loose. There was an abundance of wood about. The next thing I did was to make a blazing big fire. Ann had insisted on my taking something to eat in case I might feel hungry. Overhauling the overcoat I found a pretty generous supply. I had provided

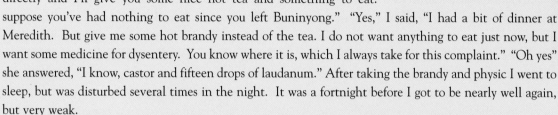

BURNT BRIDGE
It is believed Burnt Bridge was just north of Meredith. It does not exist today.

227

In the late 1990s the old Cooper's Hotel (Crown) in Buninyong was offered for sale through a public raffle.

Buninyong faded and was captured in that state by artist John Darbyshire in the late 1960s. Forty years later it would revive.

myself with a pint bottle of Martell's brandy, so I felt pretty comfortable alongside the fire. I could hear the horse's hobbles clinking now and then.

After a time, feeling sleepy, I wrapped the overcoat round me and dozed off to sleep. I must have slept three or four hours when I awoke with the cold. The fire had gone low, my first care was to heap more wood on it, and take a mouthful of brandy. I could not hear any sounds of the horse, he might be standing still, or lying down or out of hearing distance. That troubled me little. My trouble was to keep warm. I found out before long there was a very severe frost. With the brandy I had swallowed, together with the heat of the fire I felt very sleepy. I lay down again in front of the fire, but could sleep only at short intervals, turning like a roasting leg of mutton on a roasting jack, as one side got hot the other got cold. I was thankful enough when I saw the day breaking.

As soon as I could see I went in the direction I had heard the hobbles last, but failed to either hear or see anything of the horse, but as daylight was increasing I took a short circle round the fire and then a wider one. By the time I had done this it was broad day, but no horse could I find. I then resolved to make a wide tour to try and pick up his tracks. When I had gone a little more than half round I picked up the track of a hobbled horse sure enough. The tracks were making for Meredith. The tracks were easily seen in the white frost on the grass. He was making back for home. I followed for three miles or more when I came to a bullock dray camped. I asked a man if he had seen a heavy bay horse pass along. "Yes," he said, "he was hobbled, he went past here a quarter of an hour ago." Hastening on I very soon came in sight of him and very soon interrupted his journey.

I reached Buninyong early in the morning, went to Cooper's Hotel, gave my horse a feed and had dinner there. After a couple of hours rest I proceeded to Ballarat to the store where I had left the dray and harness, which I found all right. I harnessed up and returned to Cooper's, where putting the horse in the stable and put up there for the night. I gave the groom half a crown with strict instructions to feed the horse well, as I intended, with an early start, to get as far as the Separation next day.

While I was having my breakfast I asked the groom to put my horse into the dray as soon as he had done feeding. After settling my bill and securing a square bottle of Hollands with some biscuits and cheese I went to the stable. The horse was in the shafts and ready for starting. I remarked to the groom: "He looks thin and pinched up, I hope you have not neglected to feed him well." "Feed him well is it," he retorted, "sure thin, he's after scoffing the full of that box there, "fonent" ye, devil a word of a lie in it, of good chaff and oats this very morning." "Oh well," I said, "if he has gorged all that he has not done so badly. Perhaps he wants a drink, but I can give him one as I go along." There was plenty of water in the crab holes.

At a considerable distance from Meredith I turned off the main track well to the right, to avoid some bad road I knew of. In so doing I struck the head of a blind creek which I supposed to be a tributary of the Leigh. I knew I was on the wrong side but it led at first in the direction I wanted to go and was easy to cross if I wanted to. As I proceeded the creek became deeper and narrower and what was worse, its course turned too much to the right, and taking me with it. So I thought it best to cross to the opposite bank. It was a short distance from the bed of the creek so I jumped from the dray and went to see for the best place to cross. I found on examination that there was a narrow water cut gulch two feet deep right in the bed of the creek. "Oh," I concluded, "I'll go a little farther on, there is sure to be a good crossing if I go a little farther." After a while I saw what I thought a good place. The gulch had disappeared and instead were small shallow water holes, not far apart but with plenty of space for a dray to cross between. The bank down was pretty steep and the horse seemed to like it and was inclined to go too fast. When I stopped him, got down and saw the bank was steeper farther on, I thought to go back, and tried to turn him round. I got him half round but no farther.

I tried then to take up the bank by degrees slantingly, but no, he would not do that. Whenever he moved his tendency was down hill. At last he was so determined to go down I had him by the head, did my utmost to stop him, I saw he was running straight into a water hole. I dragged his head back till it nearly touched the shaft to alter his course, but it was no use. I held on to him till near the water hole, and not feeling inclined to go into the hole with him I let him rip. Before he could see where he was, he found himself over the bank of the hole about three feet high with his head ploughing through eighteen inches of water and mud while my overcoat, half a bag of feed, my dinner of biscuits and cheese, and the Holland gin followed suit on top of him.

I rescued them all but the tucker which rolled into the muddy water. The horse's head was above water and the wheels were in the hole, the body of the dray would have been too only for the point of the shafts pitching into the mud; it was just hanging by the pummels, but from the horse's struggles that came down to the level. Here was a fix to be in. I was more than two miles off the main traffic, not a hut or soul in sight, not even the sound of humanity anywhere to be heard. I had neither axe nor spade. I have been in many tight fixes during my life, but must say this was the tightest, for the time it lasted. From the position of the dray the tug chains happened to be loose which I unhooked, the back chain had slipped over the front of the saddles. That with great difficulty I unhooked, but it was impossible to free the breech in from the hooks. I tried for a long time to reach the buckle of belly band of the saddle, but not succeeding, I cut it. All the time I was operating, the animal was struggling to get up which he succeeded in doing at last, leaving the saddle and breeching behind. The horse was saved, so far, so good.

I had still two hours of daylight and no intention of leaving the dray there. Oh, if I had only a spade and an axe, but I had not. Lucky it was for me the other side of the creek was fairly level. After several contrivances I got the points of the shafts out of the mud and pulled the dray till the wheels reached the middle of the hole. Beyond this I could move it no farther straight forward; by twisting to one side I could move one wheel a few inches.

A new idea then possessed me. I found two short junks of wood and twisted the dray to one side as far as I could and blocked the wheel on that side, then the other wheel the same. I wriggled on that fashion till I had the dray out of the hole and on level ground. The sun had set leaving me light enough to reconnoitre the situation. A few yards farther on the way out, the ground began to rise pretty stiffly. I knew the horse would not face it. I had heard my father tell of his jibbing qualities. "That horse," he told me, "if you don't stuff him with all he can take in, will jib in any place at any time." He had been feeding out of the bag all the time I had been at work. I was wet through, nearly from head to foot and the thought of passing another night like the one I passed, going up, in my wet clothes, made me conclude to drag the dray up to level ground myself.

I found I had, for safety against the jibbing horse, to take it quite a hundred yards. I had no dinner in fact I had not thought of eating and what food I had was in the muddy water hole, but I blessed my stars I had plenty of gin. My first performance was to tip the shafts up as far as they would go till the hind part of the dray rested on the pummels, then a deal of hunting round in the twilight for a prop to put under the front part of the dray, so as to lift the shafts high enough to lift the wheels off the ground. This was a tough job, however I managed to do it. Taking off a wheel I wheeled it up to a level spot I had chosen for a good start, went back for the other and did the same. I lowered the dray body down then and endeavoured to twist it along as I had done with the dray in the hole, but advanced with such slow progress and with such hard labour that I feared I should never be able to accomplish it, and sat down for a rest and to devise some better plan. I wonder, I thought, could I turn it over. It would travel easier on the guard irons. I tried to turn it, could lift it till the opposite axle arm touched the ground and no farther. Being a tip dray I easily took off the shafts which lightened the weight considerably. With one corner of the front of the dray and the point of the opposite axle arm on the ground I managed to get it to the balance and over it went. I did not smoke in those days, if I had I should have sat down and taken a good long draw; but I had some gin and that had to do. After a short rest I fixed on the shafts again and found I could wriggle along on the guard irons much easier and make greater progress than I had done before.

It was a terrible night's work, but to cut the story short it will be sufficient to say the sun was well over the tree tops when I had the horse in and ready to start. I was quite dry but what a beastly mess I was in. When I had left home I was fairly well dressed in tweed trousers, and vest, a white shirt,

This stretch of the road to Ballarat from Geelong was the early track through Meredith.

PUNTS AND FERRIES
Without bridges in the new settlement the only means of crossing the rivers was by punts which operated on the Yarra and Maribynong Rivers (Salt Water River and Fresh Water River). A ferry also ran between Williamstown and Port Melbourne.

The first punts to cross the Yarra began in 1838 and were owned by the government and private business. John Welsh's punt ran across from Swanston Street, and John Scott ran another from Coles Wharf below the falls from 1844. Dr James Palmer, for whom Henry later worked at Mustons Creek, opened a punt on the Yarra at Hawthorn which saved woodcutters three miles between Stringybark Forest and Melbourne. In 1843 he opened another punt at the Bridge Road end of Richmond, and without opposition charged such high prices that many protests were lodged.

John Hodgson built a punt to operate from Studley Park, but when the business became too busy and new large punts were needed, Palmer sold his in 1849 to concentrate on his other businesses and politics.

Wellington boots and monkey jacket, which as I had taken off was intact. All my other clothes were thickly covered with mud and grease from the axle arms. I did not remember ever having felt so used up. My intention was to make for Meredith and get some breakfast for I felt as empty as a bladder, having had nothing to eat since the morning before.

As near as I can guess I had gone about a mile when I saw a shepherd's hut not out of my way much, which I made for. The sound of my wheels brought out a middle aged masculine-looking woman with a large sunbonnet flopping over her face. On seeing me she stood and stared. "Good morning," I said, "how far is it to Meredith? I had an accident last night," I continued: "my horse jibbed and ran me into a water hole." I gave her a brief explanation of affairs, which she did not seem at all to understand. "My good man," she said, "you look as if you had been rolled in mud hole." "I should not wonder if I did," I answered. Then she asked me if I had breakfast. "Yes," I said, "I had yesterday morning not a bite since." "What! Almighty, get down off that dray and come in and wash your face and let's see what kind of man you are, whether you are black or white, while I cook you some breakfast." She brought me some water and soap in a wooden tub and I gave my face, hands and arms a thorough good cleaning and wiping myself on a very coarse towel. I showed myself to her by the fire. "My word," she said, "what a difference! You're not a bad looking man after all." Under the effect of this flattery I went to the dray and took the remaining half bottle of Holland's I had left and invited her to have some. "By the powers yes," she said, "that I will." I poured her out nearly half-a-teacup full, which she swallowed with evident satisfaction. Her tongue went without ceasing after that. She soon set before me a pile of mutton chops and eggs enough for two men which I did ample justice to, much to her satisfaction. "Why didn't you cooee last night?" she asked. "Me and my man would have come to help you heart and soul." I told her I was not aware of there being anyone so near or I certainly should have come, if I had known which way to go. Then she began to tell me a little of her history, how she and her man had come to Victoria from the other side with the intention of going to the diggings; how the squatter they were working for, fell across them and offered them £70 a year and their rations, she as hut-keeper and he as shepherd.

"I have to shift the hurdles, but Jim helps me a bit in the morning while the sheep are in sight. Its only a bit of pastime for me for I do feel so lonesome sometimes. I think when our year is up, we shall try the diggings, we may make our fortunes as so many have done. "Better stay where you are," I told her, "and make sure money, for the hundreds who make fortunes, there are thousands who are making nothing, and are living on the means they brought with them. I assure you there are plenty who do not know where the next meal is to come from unless some storekeeper gives them tick." "You've tried the diggings yourself?," she asked. "Yes," I answered, "I tried it twice. I got a little gold but nothing to boast of and met with a great many more blanks than prizes."

After a little more talk I told her I had to be moving on as I wanted to be in Geelong that night, and as I had a horse I could not depend on I wished to take advantage of all the daylight I could. I poured her out another drop of gin and had one myself. She pledged my safety home and I to her and her husband's good luck, and thanked for her kindness, observing at the same time there's a drop left in the bottle you can keep that and give your husband a drop when he comes home. So I bade her goodbye and seated myself on the dray, when a thought struck me. "Oh, bye the bye," I said, "have you ever seen a lame grey draught horse about here at any time lately? I turned one out to take his chance a while back and if he would be making back home he would probably pass here somewhere."

"No," she said, "I have seen nothing of the horse you describe, but Jim my man may, as he is out every day on the run. I'll ask him to-night; leave your address and if we find out anything about your horse we'll write." After giving her my address we parted.

When I had gone a few hundred yards I happened to look back, she was still standing where I had left her, she waved her sunbonnet and I waved my cap. A few yards more and the trees hid her out of sight. She was one of the motherly old convicts who had suffered for years, of grief and trouble, perhaps for a mere trifle. There were many such both of men and women; banished from husbands, children, wives, or sweethearts forever, with not the slightest hope of ever returning. The English Laws were terrible cruel in the bygone years.

At Bate's Ford I stopped for an hour to give the horse the remainder of the feed I had. I was afraid to venture to put him to face the Moorabool hill on an

TELEGRAPHIC 'MODERNISATION'
The first telegraph line in Australia ran between Melbourne and Williamstown. It began operations in 1854.

The current hotel at Batesford replaced the original which is behind the trees and now a private home. The old bridge has been replaced too.

230

empty stomach, but he met it bravely, one inducement he had he was nearing home.

I reached home an hour before sundown, my wife was out, gone to her mother's. I knew where to find the key so I went in and changed my clothes before taking the horse to father's. He was home when I went in. I told them about my unlucky journey. "You may depend upon it," father said, "that hostler never gave the horse any feed that morning or he would not have jibbed like that with an empty dray. I've always told you when you are travelling to see your horse fed yourself, there's no trusting these hostlers."

When I went home Ann was there. She had been to her mother's. Poor girl she had caught a bad cold and looked ill and miserable with a band of red flannel round her throat and so hoarse she could scarcely speak. She had been in the bedroom and seen my dirty clothes. "Where-ever have you been" she asked 'to make your clothes in such a mess as that. They are quite spoilt, I shall never be able to wash that black tar out." I then told her. "You are ever getting into trouble lately, first losing your horse then losing the filly and now this trouble you got into, the horse might have knocked you into the hole too, and the dray on top of you; the next thing will happen, you will be getting killed and will be brought home dead. What shall I do then?" At that she began to cry. It was my turn now to turn comforter. I took her on my lap and said: "My little pet, you are ill and low-spirited, we cannot but expect but to have troubles sometimes." "But," she said, "you had no trouble before you had me," with a fresh burst. "Oh do stop it dear," I said, "I can't bear to see you cry. I'll tell you honestly, and truly, the best fortune I ever had was to win you." I then told her of the woman of the shepherd's hut who acted the good Samaritan who took me in and fed me when I was hungry, and her kindness and what she said. Thinking to make her laugh, I told of her waving her sun bonnet at parting, but she didn't, but only asked: "Was she good looking?" "Good looking?" I laughed and said: "I'll tell you who she was like, mother Broughton who lives next door to mother, both of them are othersiders." Then she laughed.

My wife in course of a week recovered from her cold and I took a weatherboard kitchen to build for an acquaintance, which led to another small job or two; after that I did a bit of business at the auction rooms, during which time a month had passed. I advertised for my horse, offering one pound reward to anyone for information where he could be found or two pounds for delivery to me.

In a week's time I received a letter from a shepherd employed on Sutherland's outstation, not far from the Muddy Water Holes informing me that a few weeks ago a horse answering to my description was on his run, but had suddenly disappeared. He probably was not far away. I resolved at once to see this shepherd; accordingly with a light rope over my shoulder I started to walk next morning. It was only about twenty-four miles. I found the hut early in the afternoon. The man, of course was out with his flock, but his wife was there, who asked me to wait till her husband came home, which I agreed to. She gave me a pannikin of tea and some bread and butter, saying: "If you like to stay tonight I'll make you as comfortable as I can." She had seen the horse herself, she told me, and was pretty sure it was the same.

When the shepherd came home in the evening, he gave me a full description of the horse. I knew it was mine. He has passed on no doubt I said, farther towards home, and I may have passed him on my way from Geelong. "The last time I saw him," he said, "was not far from our home station; have a look round there before you go back," which I agreed to do. They were a very decent couple and like myself came out as emigrants but a year previous to our arrival, and hailed from Kent.

He said they had been working with the squatters ever since they came out. "You have no inclination to try the diggings?" I asked. "No," he replied, "my girl and I have saved a little money, and the wages are higher now than before the diggings, and I hear that gold-digging is very uncertain and risky work, so that we might lose our little all, and that would be heartbreaking. No, I and my old girl are quite content to stay as we are a few years more; our ambition is to buy a piece of land, make a farm and establish a home for ourselves." "You have no children?" I remarked. "Yes," he said, "but only one, a son whom we left with his grandmother in Kent. My mother has a little property which, when she dies, our son is to have. She fretted a good deal when we left and begged us to leave the boy with her, I believe the poor old soul would have broken her heart if we hadn't. She is over eighty now and cannot live much longer, and when she dies, if we are spared, will send for the boy."

The following morning I walked to the home station about four or five miles. As I approached I saw a man ploughing in a paddock with two horses, one was a grey. I did not go to him but went straight to the house. As I neared the door a man came out. I enquired of him if he knew anything of a strange grey horse on the run; he had been lamed in the shoulder but as it was three or four months since I turned him loose he might probably have recovered from that. "What were his brands?" he asked. "W near shoulder," I told him. "Yes," he answered, "there has been a horse about here of that description these several weeks past.

Wait a minute," he said, "I'll enquire." With that he went into the house again. Returning he said: "I think I know where he is, I'll go with you." He took me away about a mile into a gully. "He has been seen principally about here lately, but I don't see him now." We walked round for about half an hour. "No, he's not here now, we'll go back to the station and enquire if any of the hands have seen him." At that we turned back.

I saw a grey horse outside the paddock where I had seen the man ploughing but the ploughman had disappeared. "There is a grey horse," I said, "by the paddock fence." On getting closer, I said: "That's my horse." I understood then the ruse he had practised on me. The horse was in the plough, he had returned to the house to give orders to have the horse turned out, while he took me on the bogus pretense of looking for him, but I said nothing. After a little talk he said; "Will you sell him?" He had a slight limp yet and there was a slight protuberance where the hurt had occurred. I had a misgiving that on journeys to any distance he might break down. "Yes," I said, "I want £50 for him." "£50 is too much," he replied, "I'll give you £40 him." "No," I said, "I can't take that. I could get more than that in the saleyard for him." After some haggling I agreed to take £45. "All right," he said, "come into the house and write me out a receipt and I'll give you the money."

I made back to the outstation again which was not far out of my way home, saw the shepherd's wife, gave her a pound with which she was very pleased, got me some dinner, after which I started for home and arrived there a little after dark. "So we have got no horse," Ann said. "What are you going to do now?" "I don't know," I replied, "to tell you the truth I'm rather full up of horses just now. Perhaps I might go to and try the diggings again." "If you go to the diggings," she replied, "I'll go with you, you're not going without me. I'm not going to live in this house by myself." "Do not fret yourself my dear girl," I said, "when I go to the diggings again it will be to stay there for some time, and I'm not going without you, don't you believe it, but then I have not made up my mind about it yet. We shall see how things turn up."

"Oh Henry," she said, "what do you think? Old John and Fanny are friendly again." "Has he brought the clock back?" I enquired. "I don't know, but he has bought a four-roomed house, just above us in Autumn Street. I expressed my belief that John would marry Fanny yet. What a lucky old dog he is, which to cut it short, he did.

Gribble had behaved himself wonderfully well lately, he was not doing any work but talked continually of buying a horse and dray and starting at something. Ann and I, we mostly had our dinner and tea there on Sunday, and everything seemed to pass off quite comfortably.

In Ballarat there had been an undercurrent of discontent among the diggers, brewing for a long time on account of various abuses and maladministration of the law. The chief of these grievances was the exorbitant licence fee and the imperious and arbitrary manner it was collected. It was nearly the same on Bendigo and Forest Creek. The genuine digger was a peaceful and law-abiding citizen but the gold discovery had brought thousands of ex-convicts, among them some of the greatest ruffians alive who came ostensibly to dig for gold, but only to plunder those who had already got it. The consequence was robberies, murders and men missing who were never heard of (the enormous amount of unclaimed gold in the Treasury substantiates this), so that the diggers were looked upon as a turbulent and ungovernable lot. La Trobe advised more police, more assistant commissioners and if possible, to stamp out the drink traffic, which he looked upon as the main cause of all the evil.

Accordingly, more police were added to the force, many of them ex-convicts. The assistant commissioners were mostly scions of the noble aristocracy of the old country, no good at home, and worse here; haughty, imperious and overbearing, when vested with a little authority, a corrupt lot. "La trobe's pets," they were called. The government recommended a more stringent and more drastic supervision over the gold fields; in fact the commissioners were allowed almost unlimited power.

Another grievance, though of minor importance than the licence fee and its collection; the prohibitive liquor law. Almost every man before arriving on the gold fields had been accustomed to his usual glass, now here he was bound to become teetotaller willy-nilly. Imagine a man with a bag of gold, or a roll of notes in his pocket wanting his usual glass, or perhaps he wanted to invite his friends to a sociable evening to celebrate his good luck, or it might be the anniversary of his birthday. He would willingly give a pound or twenty five shillings for a bottle of brandy. The storekeeper knows this, and finds means to smuggle in the much-desired article with great caution. It pays him to run the risk, but with proper management, there was little risk in it.

The government officials all had their price, either a douceur or drink ad libitum, whenever they called. Then there was the poor shanty keeper with his usual hanging shutter and little counter stocked with hop beer, cider, lemonade, ginger beer etc. who could not resist keeping a drop of stuff for his friends; it was the unfortunate shanty keepers who were made the scapegoats who paid the penalty of the pretended vigilance of the police to suppress sly grog selling.

These vendors of soft drinks at sixpence a pint were mostly poor people who could not afford to bribe the police and now and again the commissioner would come with half a dozen jingling troopers, with all the majesty of the law "from information received" set fire to the frail tenement over the owner's head and burn it to the ground and everything combustible in it. Or if they saw a team newly arrived, would accost the driver. "What loading have you on the dray?" Goods for such and such a store would be the reply. "Have you no spirituous liquors in your they would say, loading?" "No." If the police had any suspicion, "We must search," consequently the tarpaulin would be torn off, the goods tumbled over in a reckless manner and if no forbidden stuff was found they would leave it to the driver to rectify the load himself. If any alcoholic drink was found over two gallons, the driver was ordered to drive to the camp where all the liquor was spilled; bottles smashed, heads of casks stoved in and contents let run on the ground, team confiscated, the owner fined £50 and sent adrift.

Since the outbreak of the gold fields, the population had increased by many thousands, coming from all parts of the earth, principally from Europe and America, as fine a class of men as any one could wish to see; many of them well educated, doctors, lawyers, merchants' sons; in fact of all trades and professions. Men of pluck and spirit and intolerant of injustice, indignant at the imperious and corrupt administration of the law, were continually taunting the diggers with their mule-like subjection. So the discontent grew and grew, till signs and mutterings were heard of an impending change. Like rumblings of a coming thunderstorm. It only wanted a spark to ignite the conflagration; which culminated in the murder of a man named Scobie at Bentley's Eureka Hotel on the 9th November, 1854.

Scobie, who was a Scotsman, during the day had come across an old friend, whom he had known in the old country. To celebrate the occasion they had various drinks together until it was getting late at night, when they started home to Scobie's tent on the Eureka Lead. In so doing they passed Bentley's Hotel but like most men who have had more than enough, thought they could for the cold do with another "wee drappee." The house

Eureka Street.

was tight. They knocked for admittance but were told the house was closed and they would not be let in; so they started on the road again. After going a short distance Scobie looked back and saw a light in a window, and said to his mate: "You stay here, I'll go and try again," which he did, but did not return. Scobie's dead body was found at Bentley's door in the morning. An inquest was held on the body, and the verdict was he died from injuries inflicted by a person or persons unknown. But Bentley was a noted ruffian; it was well known he had served ten years in Norfolk Island and his wife was little better, and the hotel had a low reputation. The miners were convinced that Bentley and his wife were the murderers. This feeling grew so strong that in deference to it, Bentley, his wife and a lodger were apprehended, and tried at the police court, the presiding Chief Magistrate was a Mr Dewes. Along with him sat Commissioner Rede and Assistant Commissioner Johnstone. Dewes hurried over the proceedings; gave every advantage to the prisoners and finally acquitted them.

It was well known that Dewes was pecuniarily indebted to Bentley for a large sum. Dewes did not deny it. Though he had £500 a year and £150 for allowances, he could not live on that sum, and burned it to the ground and everything in it.

The diggers were indignant at the miscarriage of justice. They held a meeting on the spot where Scobie was killed. A bosom friend of the murdered man named Kennedy harangued the crowd on the merits of his friend and with a rough but genuine eloquence moved them to indignation. The ghost of Scobie, he told them was hovering round the spot in quest for vengeance. An orderly meeting carried a resolution that, not being satisfied with the way the proceedings had been conducted, either at the inquest, or at the trial, pledged itself to use every lawful means to have the case brought before more impartial authorities.

For this purpose a committee was appointed, containing among others, Peter Lalor, T.D. Wanliss and Wilson Gray. £200 was subscribed for that purpose in Ballarat and all things seemed to proceed with order.

233

But unluckily a crowd had gathered in the afternoon round the Eureka Hotel, merely idlers out of curiosity, hooting whenever they saw a sign of Bentley or his wife. About four o'clock a body of troopers arrived to disperse them. They claimed their right to be there as they were doing no harm. The troopers rode into the crowd to scatter them. Just then a boy, out of mischief, threw a stone at the lamp before the hotel door the sound of crashing glass sent the crowd furious, they rushed the house and smashed the windows till there was not a pane left.

The crowd rushed into the house clamorous for Bentley, whom they talked of hanging. The police could no longer keep them in check. The crowd swarmed into the hotel. In a short time the furniture, bedding, cooking utensils, crockery etc. were thrown out. Commissioner Rede arrived and spoke to the crowd but he was not liked and no one listened to him. The report went he was pelted with stones. Just then the cry arose "the hotel is on fire." Some diggers had gone to the bowling alley and set it on fire, and the hotel in a very short time was but a blazing mass. Bentley and his wife though, narrowly escaped to the Government Camp.

Then came a company of the 40th Regiment. The soldiers advanced as if to attack, but the officer afraid to take the responsibility of bloodshed marched them back to the camp. The Governor Sir Charles Hotham looked on this as no ordinary trouble, but a deliberate attempt to introduce from California, Lynch's law into the gold fields. Troops and more police were forthwith, hurried to Ballarat, altogether four hundred and fifty men. Hotham might have sympathised with the diggers for he was certain Dewes had been acting a scoundrelly part, and had acquitted Bentley, knowing him to be guilty. He had appointed a board consisting of E.P.S. Sturt, F.A. Powlet and Dr McCrae to inquire into the conduct of Dewes. The board's report was, Dewes had taken bribes and so had the Sergeant Major of the police. Hotham dismissed Dewes and Sergeant Major Milne, reprimanded the Coroner and ordered the re-arrest of Bentley, his wife and the lodger Farrell.

All this was satisfactory to the diggers; but they had another grievance. Three men McIntyre, Fletcher and Westerby had been arrested for burning the Eureka Hotel. The selection was arbitrarily done. These men were tried in Melbourne and found guilty, the jury adding a rider that these painful circumstances would not have happened if those in authority at Ballarat had done their duty. The judge sentenced McIntyre to be imprisoned for three months, Fletcher for four and Westerby for six. At the same Criminal Sessions, Bentley, his wife, Farrell and another man named Hanse were tried for the murder of Scobie. Mrs Bentley was acquitted; the other three were condemned to three years hard labour on the roads.

There was no doubt, but that the authorities and the people in Melbourne sympathised with the diggers and wiser administration would have prevailed in the course of time; but the people of Ballarat looked upon it as dishonourable to let three of their number suffer for what they all had a share in, while they themselves were equally to blame. They held a meeting and appointed three delegates, George Black, the editor of the Diggers Advocate, Thomas Kennedy, who had seen Scobie's ghost, and John R. Humphrey a well educated Welshman and secretary of what was now called the Ballarat Reform League.

The delegates met the Governor W.T. Stawell, the Attorney General and John Foster, the Colonial Secretary. After a long conference they submitted a resolution of the meeting of which they were delegates demanding the liberation of McIntyre, Fletcher and Westerby. Hotham objected to the word "demand." He intimated that if a proper memorial had been addressed to him, he might have complied with it, but the men had been tried, and found guilty by a British jury, they had been sentenced by a judge who had heard the evidence, to the lightest punishment the law provided for; he could not listen to any "demand" for their release. The deputation withdrew regretting that their message had not been more carefully worded.

A great deal of political agitation had been mixed up with this, which was after all, only a personal matter. The first great meeting of the Ballarat Reform League had been held on the 11th November. 10,000 men gathered on Bakery Hill. They carried resolutions that it is the inalienable right of every citizen to have a voice in the making of the laws he is called upon to obey, that there should be no taxation without representation, and that therefore the following political changes should be demanded:

(1)   *A full and fair representation*
(2)   *Manhood suffrage*
(3)   *Abolition of property qualifications for members of the Legislature*

(4)   *Payment of members*

(5)   *Short duration of Parliament*

In addition to these, the Ballarat Reform League demanded an immediate alteration in the government of the gold fields, and a total abolition of the licence tax.

Hotham dispatched more military to Ballarat. There were already 450 men there, but he hurriedly sent off a detachment of the 12th Regiment in vans for greater expedition. The miners looked upon this concentration of troops on the goldfield as a threat intended to suppress free discussion, and the news burst from mouth to mouth, that more force was coming to add to that already in the Camp; their indignation burst forth. As the carts filled with soldiers reached Warrenheip Gully, the cry of "Joe" began to echo through the gully, and a great crowd of miners lined the road to see them defile past on their way to the camp. Unfortunately a few of the most forward threw clay, mud and stones and broken bottles followed. Further on a number of the Gravel Pitt men hearing the tumult gathered in a crowd and intercepted the first cart and upset it. They took the weapons, and ammunition from the soldiers, who ran away and hid themselves, as the other carts were detained some distance behind.

The officer-in-charge got his men out and formed them in line but they were badly ordered, seemed confused and disconcerted. The scene degenerated into a mere riot, for which the rougher and less respectable diggers were responsible, the leaders of the League being conspicuous in their efforts to prevent disorder. In the scuffle six of the soldiers were wounded with pistol shots, one of whom afterwards died. It was only with slow progress and great labour, the soldiers reached the camp. Then the mounted troopers made a sortie charging in among the crowd and wounded a number of men. The detachment were all safely received into the camp at eleven o'clock at night, and anxious watch was kept throughout the darkness, while the more foolish diggers celebrated the affair all night long as a triumph for the populace.

The exact site of the Eureka Stockade is unknown because the scene was merely a spot on the busy goldfields and no permanent buildings were constructed. Today a very worthwhile museum and commemorative building is a popular tourist attraction in the approximate area.

Unluckily, next morning 29th November, was the time appointed by the meeting to receive the delegates sent to Melbourne. About midday they gathered at least ten thousand round a platform from which floated only the Australian flag; its blue folds and snow white stars meaning mischief. They waited quietly for the delegates, who had come from Geelong by coach, and gave them time to join the meeting. Timothy Hayes was voted to the chair. The report of the delegates was heard attentively. They did the Governor full justice, but said that he was powerless to grant their demands. indignant speeches followed from Lalor, Vern, Brady, Kennedy, Humphrey, Ross and others. A resolution was carried that the members of the League should all forthwith burn their licence and pledge themselves to take out no more.

The greatest enthusiasm prevailed. Fires were lit there and then, and licences were thrown onto the fire by the score. It was agreed that if military or police should arrest any man for having no licence the entire League would unite in his defence. When these and other resolutions were carried volleys of fire arms were fired into the air, indicating their delight. But on the whole the meeting passed off quietly. Detachments of troops and police were placed all round the place lest disturbances should occur, but they were not needed.

During the night there was strict watch kept at the camp, and screens of sand bags and bags of flour were thrown up around the tents and wooden buildings. But the morning dawned without any mishap.

All attentions were now directed towards the next 'digger hunt'. If the diggers kept their promise, there must be a decided conflict. The authorities resolved that the crisis should at once be brought to a head, and ordered a digger hunt for the Gravel Pits next day, the 30th November - the last that ever took place. The miners were all quietly at work when the cry of "Joe" echoed from claim to claim. It was Assistant Commissioner Johnstone with a body of police. He was pelted with stones and compelled to withdraw. Commissioner Rede then took a much larger body of police and marching down met a large crowd of diggers on the road. He told them he must carry out the law. He appealed to the well disposed to retire, and many did so; but others kept their places. He read the Riot Act and sent for the military to come up. The crowd dispersed. Captain Thomas brought a large force of redcoats on the field; the infantry extended in skirmishing order across all the flat with cavalry at the wings, and in centre. No resistance was made. The troops swept the field and Johnstone made the diggers show their licences, those that had any, those who had none escaping as best they could. Eight prisoners were taken, and with these in charge the police returned to the camp.

The diggers had now to make good their promise. Eight of their comrades were in gaol. At three o'clock in the afternoon another meeting was held on Bakery Hill round the platform whereon the Australian flag once more floated. Peter Lalor, an Irishman son of a former member of the House of Commons, became the leading spirit. He mounted the platform and called on the diggers to fall into companies, and prepare for drill. About five hundred at once complied. Lalor, standing with the butt of his gun resting on his foot and the muzzle in his hand, addressed them. He warned them that a collision was inevitable, but entreated them to let no destruction of property or pillage or plunder sully the cause they had to fight for.

At a meeting held in Diamond's store, Lalor had been appointed commander. He now directed that all those prepared to fight should swear to be faithful to their standard - the Southern Cross, that all others should retire. The companies then formed in order round the flagstaff; each advanced in turn its leader repeated an oath to defend their rights and liberties and the others kneeling with heads uncovered answered with a deep Amen. They were very much in earnest. The five hundred hands that pointed up to the streaming standard were ready for grim work. All of them knew that by the law of the land their lives were forfeited if they miscarried in their venture. Foolish as the effort may seem to us they were actuated by ardent motives. It was a pity that warmth of feeling should have urged them into a course that was, to say the least of it, precipitate.

For the reform they wished for would have come about, no doubt, in the course of perhaps a long time, but the sudden determined attitude of the miners against the governing authorities, the corrupt and maladministration of the law on the diggings startled the public into thought. The governor too who, no doubt meant well, was anxious to put matters right if he only knew how to proceed; for there must be something radically wrong to cause such hostile demonstrations. Hotham appointed a commission of inquiry to make a careful examination into the grievances of the miners. William Westgarth became chairman. The other members were John Fawkner, James McCullock, William H. Wright, John Hodgson, John O'Shannassy, and Charles W. Carr was added to the commission as Secretary. Thus Hotham showed a sincere desire to do substantial justice.

He directed the commission to determine the most suitable method for levying that tax the miner was in honour bound to pay, as the price of order and protection; to inquire into the feasibility of granting mining leases in order to encourage the investment of capital on the goldfields, and to inquire into the conduct of the officials complained of. It was fortunate for the Colony that the Governor was a man of these views, and sympathies. For the issue of this commission a fortnight before the collisions at Ballarat disarmed the great bulk of miners and converted what might have been a formidable explosion into a small conflict, lamentable but hopeless.

A different tone on the part of the Governor would assuredly have gathered from five to twenty thousand miners according to the degree of exasperation they received; and a month or two of disorder, and a miserable amount of bloodshed would assuredly have ensued. As it was the more thoughtful, the more sensible of the miners withdrew from the hot headed five hundred, who had reached the ridiculous conclusion that only the sword could secure the redress of their grievances.

The great bulk of the Ballarat Reform League declined to imitate their fiery zeal; even the secretary, J.B.Humphrey, disapproved of the violence which his friends were aiming at. All reasonable people were willing to wait till the commission had finished its labours and its report. And, therefore, although there were fifty thousand discontented miners (though there were twenty thousand not disinclined to resist what they regarded as oppression) yet only five hundred responded to the call to arms. Probably even these would not have gathered had it not been there was so much distrust of some of the members of the new commission of inquiry. However, the afternoon of that Thursday was spent by the ardent spirits in drilling on the slopes of Bakery Hill.

In the evening bundles of slabs, intended for stabbing the shafts were carried to the Eureka Plateau, to be used in raising a palisade for defence when the military should attack. All night long the men coming from a distance continued to drop in, some with fire arms, some with rudely manufactured pikes. As the darkness deepened the numbers steadily increased, till there were eight hundred men present within the space marked out for a stockade. Vigorous moves went on by lamplight and the gleam of fires. A meeting of the council was held. It was resolved to send a deputation to the camp to demand the release of the eight prisoners, and an assurance that in the meantime there should be no more licence hunting until the decision of the Legislature could be made known.

George Black and Carboni Raffaello were chosen for the purpose. On a moonlight night they made their way to the camp, which had been heavily barricaded during the afternoon. They reached the presence of Commissioner Rede and Black, remonstrated with him on the imprudence of sending soldiers with bayonets to inspect licences of a body of exasperated diggers. He concluded by demanding the release of all the miners who had been apprehended that morning. Rede was indignant at such a message. The men had been legally apprehended and must be legally acquitted before they could be discharged. Black then asked for an assurance that there should, in the meantime, be no more digger hunting. Rede replied that it was all nonsense to pretend that the digger's agitation was intended solely to secure the abolition of the licence fee.

He knew that it was a strong democratic agitation by an armed mob. Raffaello allowed that there were indeed other subjects of contention. The miners wished to be enfranchised, and they all re-echoed the cry "unlock the lands." But these questions were not immediately pressing. The diggers were in arms solely to secure, in the present, the abolition of digger hunting. Rede was courteous and even considerate to them, but was firmly of opinion that his duty forbade him to give any pledge of the kind required. Far on, in the evening, a meeting was held to receive the delegates. The answer was heard in silence, and the meeting was adjourned till next morning at five o'clock.

At that hour a crowd again gathered, and commenced their drill. The slabs there were lying in disorder, and began to be set up in a close palisade. At ten o'clock the rumour spread that the soldiers were setting out from the camp on another digger hunt. All work was stopped on the goldfields and a time of painful suspense occurred, but the rumour was false, the day passed quietly. But at the camp there were breast works raised with firewood and trusses of hay and bags of corn to make all ready, for it was unknown how many thousands there might be of the insurgents, and an attack was expected for the release of the prisoners. The diggers, however, had no such design; they were busy throwing up their stockade, within which a German blacksmith worked incessantly making pikes for those who had no fire arms.

On receipt of news from Ballarat Sir Charles Hotham at once despatched all the remaining troops in Melbourne. With two field pieces and two howitzers, they set out together with a company of marines. Major-General Sir Robert Nickle went with them to assume the chief command.

Meantime the diggers had also been reinforced, but not to the same useful purpose. Four hundred men from Creswick had arrived, but they had with them no provisions, and little in the way of fire arms. They had expected everything to be provided in plenty at Ballarat, but the diggers were then themselves inadequately supplied. They shared their quarters as well as they could, however, with their Creswick comrades and for those who could not find a tent to sleep in, a large bonfire was lit, round which they slept in tolerable comfort in spite of a three hours thunderstorm. But these new comers, not liking the general prospect of discomfort and failure mostly returned on the following day.

During the night the soldiers saw signals flashed across the goldfields, from tent to tent, and feared arrangements were being made for a night attack, and the troopers each beside his horse were stationed as outposts in dreary inactivity throughout a dark and rainy night. During the whole of Saturday drilling went on in the stockade, but all anxiety was at an end in the camp when it gradually became known that only a small fraction of the diggers were in arms - that not more than seven or eight hundred at the utmost were concerned in the rebellion while there were nearly eight hundred soldiers and constables in the camp, much better armed and disciplined. Others were on their way to Ballarat.

The diggers resolved to intercept these

qualified, that not one per cent of the diggers were practical miners. The yields of gold were difficult to conceive. He remembered one occasion when a man brought to the Bank of Australasia a 68 lb nugget from the Kohinoor. James Oddie elaborated on how gold was responsible for the booming conditions, and how the establishment of the School of Mines was the outcome of mining. He concluded his interesting address by assuring his audience: "It was no wonder the Ballarat people were noted for their health and physique when their fathers and grandfathers represented the finest types of manhood the 'Old Country' could produce."

The graves of those victims of the Eureka Stockade rebellion are located in the old Ballarat cemetery in the north of the town. Near the site of the uprising a large park has precluded any development of the area which is so significant to the maturity of Australia and its characteristics.

EUREKA STOCKADE MEMORIAL PARK

reinforcements, which must pass with their cannon along the road from Melbourne. The stockade was enlarged so as to stretch across the road, and Frederick Vern, a Hanovarian of turgidly revolutionary instincts, took command of a detachment to guard the road. But so little of true military management was there in the place, that at midday, almost all went off to their dinners to various places in Ballarat, and left the place deserted. They came back by twos and threes and at 4 o'clock there appeared a corps of Californians, two hundred of them in something-like uniform, and all armed with revolvers. The stockade grew noisy, marching and counter-marching, stentorian orders and clumsy evolution's. A company of people all managing and yet nothing being managed properly.

The diggers now felt themselves, that the struggle would be unequal. They wanted more arms and more ammunition. They sent out men to press for these requirements, and an armed body proceeded to the camp of Commissioner Amos, which was detached, and not far from the stockade. They took him prisoner and brought him to the camp; but let him go, keeping his horse and arms however. Father Smythe visited the stockade in the afternoon and warned the diggers of the madness of their attempt. He advised all of his denomination to be at mass the following morning, and to abandon their desperate plan.

Till midnight the diggers kept watch upon the Melbourne road, but, as the night was wet and dreary, and there was little sleeping accommodation in the stockade, the great bulk of them withdrew to their various homes, leaving only about one hundred and fifty to guard their fortress which was badly constituted and on a badly chosen situation.

Captain Thomas who was in command at the camp, resolved to strike the blow at daybreak. He gathered an attacking party of two hundred and seventy-six men - eighty-seven of the 40th Regiment under Captain Wise, sixty-five of the 12th under Captain Queade, thirty cavalry, twenty-four foot police, and seventy mounted troopers. The sun was not yet risen but it was fully light; it was chilly, and the soil was wet underfoot, when they set out on their march at three o'clock in the morning.

Half an hour brought them within three hundred yards of the stockade still unnoticed. They halted while detachments extended in skirmishing order. The mounted men were sent to move round by the left as if to attack the stockade on that side, while the real attack was to be made by the foot-soldiers, right in front. These dispositions made, the tramp of the soldiers was heard as a muffled sound, when a single shot fired into the air by an insurgent sentry warned the defenders that the crisis had come. They rushed from their resting-places to man the stockade. They saw a line of redcoats approaching, and when these were one hundred and fifty yards distant a little fellow formerly a barber, coolly fired at the nearest officer, who fell. At that signal a volley rattled irregularly through the palisades, and several soldiers dropped.

The bugle sounded the order to commence firing, and a sharp volley rang out from the long red line of troops, who then continued to advance firing incessantly for about ten minutes. Lalor was by this time at his post within the stockade. He climbed on a heap of palisades that lay beside an empty claim. As he stood looking over the fence in order to see what dispositions were necessary, a soldier picked

A stylised interpretation of the fighting which took place at Eureka. The truth of the slaughter was not half as glamorous as this romanticised version.

him off with a bullet, and he fell apparently dead. The diggers behind their palisade had a favourable situation, and so long as the conflict was with firearms they could hold their own. But when came the ominous sounds of fixing bayonets, "Charge" was the word that rang out, and with a loud cheer the soldiers rushed for the fence. It offered no difficulty they easily leaped over, and found that those diggers who had guns were without bayonets, while the number who had pikes were inconsiderable.

When the troops were over, therefore there was no defence, a few diggers made a light resistance behind a cart, but most retreated to the empty claims or behind heaps of clay that dotted the enclosure. The soldiers ferreted them out, and hand to hand encounters took place, the diggers in the end being generally bayoneted by the soldiers. A policeman climbed the flagstaff and brought down the Southern Cross amid a wild hurrah from his comrades. Meanwhile the great body of the insurgents had withdrawn to a cluster of tents behind the blacksmith's shop. The troops set fire to the canvas, and as the diggers rushed out pistol conflicts and duels with pike against bayonet took place; but in ten minutes after the charge the fighting was over. Many of the insurgents escaped, but one hundred and fifty were captured. About forty men were lying in pools of blood here and there in the enclosure, eleven of them lay dead close by the stockade. The troops first marched their prisoners off to the camp, and then a detachment returned with stretchers for the wounded.

Peter Lalor, during the confusion. had been dragged by some of his friends out of the way, and covered over with some loose slabs. While the troops were gone he managed to crawl out, and before they came back he was out on the flat, and among crowds of peaceful diggers. Ere nightfall he escaped into the ranges, where a doctor amputated for him his left arm.

This spectacular monument to the uprising lies quietly in Eureka Stockade Memorial Park in Eureka Street.

In the afternoon there was the melancholy task of burying the dead whose livid features lay upturned on the scene of conflict. Only one soldier had been killed outright; a great crowd of diggers looked on in respectful silence as his body was buried in the cemetery. Then came the bodies of fourteen diggers all found dead within the stockade.

But that represented only part of the loss of life; for of the sixteen soldiers severely wounded, four subsequently died, and Captain Wise lingered but a few days, when he too succumbed to the effects of two wounds he had received. He was buried with military honours, also in the rustic cemetery. Of thirty diggers severely wounded, eight subsequently died, including Lieutenant Ross who had been the standard bearer of the insurgents. The total number killed on both sides was twenty-eight.

While the rough work and tumult was proceeding in Ballarat I was peacefully haymaking on Herne Hill. Gribble and another man had contracted to mow two paddocks for hay, and I was getting 10/- a day, and beer for helping make the hay and stacking it. We heard daily exaggerated reports of what was going on there. Both Melbourne and Geelong were in dread of an invasion by armed diggers.

It was reported that twenty thousand men were ready for mischief. In addition to what force was left in the city 1,500 special constables were sworn in, in case of emergency to protect Melbourne. A proportionate number was also enlisted in Geelong for the same purpose. There was a universal dread that evil was impending. So there might have been, but though the malcontents were numerous enough there were but few who were ready to take up arms to enforce their rights. If the diggers had come off victorious in the contest, they would have most likely got what they asked for, but there were plenty on the diggings and in the towns who had no grievances, who lived only on the industry of others, and who were ready in case of the weakness of the Government and disorder, who would make use of the adventure to rob and plunder.

It is to be regretted that a few lost their lives over the disturbance, but it did good to the people in the end. It showed they were in real earnest and hastened the settlement of the dispute to an early and prosperous issue.

After I had finished hay making I had a few small jobs carpentering. When I had nothing else to do I attended the auction rooms but to little purpose in the way of gain. Gribble did at last buy a horse and dray and the first thing he did with it was to invite his friends to a picnic at the Heads. There were Ann (my wife) and I, Mr and Mrs Charlton with their friend, Fred Green, another married couple and Mrs

Gribble and Gribble himself. We arrived at Bream Creek about 3 o'clock, and Fred Green, who was an expert in the piscatory handicraft threw out his baited lines at once, and in a very short time Mrs Charlton was busily frying delicious bream, while Mrs Gribble, my wife and the other woman were attending to other arrangements, preparatory to a meal for nine hungry souls. The locality was swarming with wild fowl. So we men marched off to have a shot or two before dinner.

Among us we brought back six fine fat ducks, which we told the women, while we were eating our dinner, they would have to cook for supper, but the women folk overruled this, and promised to have them ready for breakfast. It was a splendidly calm night, and the moon was at its full. Some one proposed to go opossum shooting. No sooner mentioned than all agreed. Mrs Charlton went with us to carry home the game. The animals were plentiful enough, scuttling up the trees at our approach, looking down at us now and again, then going a little higher till the topmost branch was attained. They stopped and looked down on us. Then bang went his death warrant, two or three twists in his death agony, then down he would drop on the ground with a thud. Mrs Charlton gathered up the dead until her apron was full and the burden grew too heavy. When she cried out: "for goodness sake stop shooting the poor things for I can't carry any more, I only wanted a few skins to finish a rug, and I'm sure these are enough." So we stopped firing and set our faces towards camp, sharing the old lady's load among us.

Barwon Heads - the bridge to Ocean Grove.

The sea beach was about three hundred yards distant; the roar of the waves beating on the shore was incessant. Ann and I took a stroll to the edge of the turbulent ocean, where at times we could feel the spray of the waves as they madly dashed against the overhanging cliffs shooting up, twenty or thirty feet into the air; the frothy billows with wild violence, as if angry of being so suddenly intercepted by anything earthly. The moon well-up in an unclouded sky shone down upon us, with a soft silvery light as if to bless us, and all the created world. We selected an elevated rock overlooking the sea and sat down to contemplate the magnificent scene. The shifting waves out at sea looked like so many brilliant stars coming and going by the reflection of the moonlight. At times our vision was obstructed by an incandescent foaming wave, and spray shooting up and falling like a shower of diamonds from fairy land. The scene was impressive, majestic, awe-inspiring and made one's thoughts revert to the great Creator, who had planned it all. In after years, even to the present day I have often recalled to remembrance the solitary hour we sat on that rock, side by side, hands clasped in the morning of our lives; with hearts full of grand expectations and hope in the years to come. Alas.

The rugged coast line near Barwon Heads.

When we returned to the camp a tent had been erected not far from the dray. Fred Green had skinned the opossums for "ahr dame," Green and the Charltons were shipmates from the old country from Nottinghamshire and both her husband and Green spoke of Mrs Charlton as "ahr dame." Green was a shoemaker by trade, but did a little fishing and bird and animal stuffing at odd times.

All hands were congregated inside the tent, and the bottle was passing round freely, all seemed in the height of good humour and enjoying themselves. Mrs Charlton told some of her racy jokes, which were none of the choicest as far as language was concerned; redolent of old obsolete Saxon words in daily use in her native County, which among the squeamish of today would be considered vulgar. She could see no harm in her talk nor cared if others did. She was a kind, goodhearted and well meaning woman, was "ahr dame." When it got late, or rather early in the morning the beds were made amid much joking and fun. Fred being an old bachelor was relegated to the dray with a sheet over his head. The jokes continued in bed for a short time, but eventually everyone had dropped off to the land of nod.

We had not been long asleep when Fred in the dray got up such a terrific snore that would have awakened the 'Seven Sleepers'. Ann gave me a poke in the ribs with her elbow saying: "Henry, Henry do you hear Fred Green?" "Lord yes," I said, "I should think I do, I wonder how long he's going to keep that up?" Charlton was awakened too, when he sang out: "Fred, Fred, turn over on the other side man, you are keeping us all awake with thee snorting." Fred must have heard, for he gave a great gasp as if recovering from a choke, when all was silent.

I awoke in the morning on hearing Gribble feeding and talking to his horse. It was broad daylight, though the sun had not risen. I sprang out of bed, and looked round, it was a beautiful calm fresh morning; the dew was on the grass, and the soft balmy breeze from the sea was so fresh and exhilarating that it made man glad to be alive. "Get up Ann," I called, "and let us have a walk on the beach before breakfast." She sat up rubbing her eyes. "Why", she complained, "I haven't had half a sleep yet. Oh Henry," she begged, "do let me sleep a little longer." "No," I said, "out, out you come, you'll soon be wide awake enough when you see this beautiful morning." Without more ado she dressed and came out. "Oh," she exclaimed, "isn't it nice." "Come on," I replied, "down to the shore, and see what we can pick up, it is low tide now and the waves are just mere ripples." The water had retreated fifty yards from the foot of the cliff, leaving a smooth sandy descent to the water's edge among rocks, that had been torn from the high, overhanging shore. We experienced a little difficulty in finding a way down, but at last discovered a narrow gulch which former travellers had evidently made use of for descending. We were requited for our morning's walk by finding curiosities we had not seen before, fragments of sponges of various colours, innumerable varieties of sea shells of all colours which had been excavated from the high shore by the ever-recurring tides of the numberless past centuries, perhaps deposited millions of years before.

We collected a number of shells, and sponges in our handkerchiefs, and feeling in good trim for breakfast, we returned to the gulch and made for the camp. Mrs Charlton, conspicuous among the women folk, saw us coming, sounded the gong (the frying pan) indicating that the meal was ready. A white table cloth was spread on the scarcely yet dry grass, the spread consisted of cold wild duck, bread, butter, jam and delicious coffee; sauce we had none, except our appetites which to all appearance, answered well enough.

After breakfast when Gribble and Green had had their smoke, we made it up that Fred Green should catch more fish while Gribble, I and Charlton with the other George Trembling should make a raid on the wild fowl, so as to have some fish and fowl to take home with us. Trembling owned that he was not much of a shot, but for the sport of the thing he would go. Before he started Trembling had borrowed a gun off a neighbour, and laid in a stock of ammunition, so as to be equipped like the rest of us. Little Mrs Trembling strongly protested against her husband going with us, she said: "I don't believe he ever let a gun off in his life and if he goes along w'you shooting, ten to one he'll either shoot himself or somebody else." Mr and Mrs Trembling were both small people and George took umbrage at his wife so belittling him, thus making him still smaller before his friends. He said: "Hold your nonsensical tongue Sarah, I tell you I am going with them, I might not kill anything I can only try; as for never having let a gun off in my life, how do you know?" "Ah well," Mrs Trembling remarked, "it's no good me saying anything more; when once he's put his foot down."

When on the war-path Gribble was a terror for shooting. He burnt a lot of powder, but seldom shot anything; he seemed to have little idea of the proper range. After we had gone a quarter of a mile we sighted a lagoon with a couple hundred ducks on it, busily feeding close to some scrub. Charlton said: "Look thee here lads, there's a fine chance if we only act right. Let us go well back and come upon the mob behind the scrub, which is low near the water's edge; we must crawl on our bellies through that and when we get well within range, I'll give the signal by a low whistle and let us all fire together." We intended to follow his advice but Gribble not waiting for the signal when we were pretty close, saw half a dozen pretty close together, and let fly. The flock rose immediately and circling round twice we all had a bang at them flying; all but Gribble whose piece had been emptied to no purpose. Charlton secured four, I got two and by the powers above Trembling got one to his great delight. Gribble said he saw George shut his eyes when he fired, but we took that as a piece of envy, and spite, because he himself had been unsuccessful. Charlton annoyed at Gribble's precipitancy, said he would go alone. So we all, after that, went different ways, George back to the camp, triumphantly carrying his duck to show to his wife. "I shot it flying," he told her.

At midday we all mustered at the camp. Charlton brought home about a dozen birds, I had five ducks and a swan, Gribble had managed to shoot four ducks, and Green had caught a lot of fine bream some of which we had for dinner. It was resolved to make for home that night; so as soon as might be we packed up, and were on the return. We arrived home about dark; all well pleased over our night's outing.

A few days after our picnic Gribble was offered some loading by a contractor who was erecting a bridge over the Wardiyallock Creek, forty-five miles distant. There were two one horse loads to go. I had a dray but no horse. I offered father half the proceeds of the trip if he would lend me his horse Damper, the one that played me such a dastardly trick coming from Ballarat. "All right, and I'll find the feed; you must take care to feed him well, and you will get on right enough." So it was arranged that we should take the two loads at £20 each. Ann and Mrs Gribble went as far as Fyan's Ford hill with us, and then returned home. The Moorabool River in those days had long steep banks. The descent from the Geelong side was

the worst, but we made the descent all right. The crossing of the ford was the next venture as the stream was flowing three feet deep.

It was arranged for Gribble to go first as I was doubtful of my horse facing the water. We both walked through, taking the horse by the head, and crossed over safely, and likewise to the top of the other bank

Looking to the Barrabool Hills from near the Moorabool River at the north east of the city.

without trouble, where we stopped to congratulate ourselves and have a nip out of Gribble's bottle. We went as far as Murghebolac that day and camped at a farm occupied by an old couple, who made us very welcome to what they had. Gribble got a bit boosey that evening. Before going to bed we fed our horses plentifully, and my mate, instead of fixing the feed bag between the shafts, seeing an empty wheelbarrow handy threw the feed into that, and tied his horse to it. After we had turned in and got properly settled a great commotion arose outside, Gribble's horse had run away with the wheelbarrow. We both sprang out, and gave chase but the clatter had ceased; we found the barrow stuck on a sapling

Celebrations in Melbourne broke out upon the release of prisoners arrested for their involvement in the Eureka Stockade.

minus a leg but the horse was not to be seen, and it was pretty dark too. After a quarter of an hour's hunt we found him quietly feeding on something in the old man's garden.

In the morning Gribble told the man what had happened, and offered to pay for the damage but he refused to take anything only observing: "What a fool you must have been man to fasten a horse to a wheelbarrow." Our next day's journey was over bare plains; a good road only rocky in places. We reached our destination in the evening twilight, but did not unload till the morning. We unloaded early and everything being satisfactory we got paid, and were soon on our return journey. The locality, well known to me before, was perfectly treeless with the exception of a few stunted gums along the creek.

The journey home was monotonous and dreary. Gribble stretched himself in the dray bottom intending to sleep but it was no use; the unguided horse choosing his own road took the wheels over rocks from six inches to a foot high would wake the dead. We camped that night about two miles before we came to the old couple's farm, and got home early the next day, just four days away. I gave father ten pounds with which he was highly pleased, and well he might be, after paying for the horse's feed he would have over nine pounds; not so bad even then for the hire of a horse for four days, but he was my father, I did not grudge it him.

I make no pretensions to write the history of Victoria, but only to describe what affected me personally and the times I have lived through. I will here give a brief and concise relation of what followed the failure of the Ballarat insurrection. Well when I say failure, it was anything but that; those few poor fellows who gave their life's blood (mostly educated men, hating tyranny and oppression) for the liberty of their fellow men, excited and assured the sympathy of not only all classes in Australia, but the Government of the old country. The English Government granted to the colonies permission to make their own laws, and to frame their own constitution to suit themselves, reserving to itself the right to appoint a governor as a vice-regal representative of the English throne. That insignificant skirmish of the Eureka Stockade was the commencement of the eve of democracy in Victoria which has grown and grown till it is today the most democratic country in the world. The working man is not only assured of good wages but plenty of leisure for recreation.

Four days after the fatal Sunday morning at the stockade, the Royal Commission arrived at Ballarat to inquire into the grievances of the diggers. They took abundance of evidence, sifting all the troubles the miners complained of. This report was not handed in till March 1855.

It stated that the unseemly violence with which the licence was often collected had naturally exasperated the miners, that the high price of living from scarcity of farm produce owing to high price of land had caused a great deal of distress among those who had been unfortunate and lastly the want of all political rights was naturally felt as a grievance by a body of men who were intelligent and active.

It was proposed that the licence should be abolished, but the public right to gold found on waste lands should still be vindicated by paying a fee of one pound a year by every miner; that no active means should be employed to compel this fee which was no longer to be called a licence, but a miner's right, which should protect the holder from aggression from anyone infringing on his rights as a miner. And again the possession of a miner's right should enable him to vote at an election. Also the Commission recommended, that land wherever it could be found possible, to be sold, at not less than one pound per acre. It was also proposed that a miner by a mere possession of a miner's right should be entitled to vote at political elections.

Finally the Commission suggested the propriety to the Government of granting a general amnesty to the prisoners taken at the Eureka Stockade. The report was conceived in a very democratic spirit, and was so hostile to the officialism which had been rampant on the diggings, that Mr Wright the Chief Commissioner of all the gold fields refused to sign it. Of course, he naturally felt annoyed at the reflections cast upon himself and his subordinates.

There is no doubt, but that Fawkner was the most active member in making out this report. Its recommendations were by no means relished by the Government. There was scarcely a passing reflection against the diggers, not even those who had taken up arms against the authorities. By implication the Government was condemned at every turn not only on the goldfields but in the cities also.

When the news had reached Melbourne that the diggers were in arms, the mayor called a meeting for the protection of the city if it should be attacked. Many members of the Legislative Council were present, and the proceedings started with resolutions intended to strengthen the Government, but when two had passed and a third being discussed, the real temper of the meeting broke out. In great confusion, the mayor left the chair, which was taken by Dr Embling, and several resolutions were passed, expressing sympathy with the diggers, and calling on the Government to take measures to redress their grievances. On the following day the people convened a monster meeting to be held where St. Pauls Cathedral now stands. Five thousand persons gathered there on a Wednesday afternoon. Then overnight there had come the news of the conflict at the Stockade, rumours reporting that from fifty to a hundred miners had been killed, and that the whole of the Buninyong district was under martial law. The feeling of the meeting was extremely hostile to the Government. A resolution was passed condemning the miners for their appeal to arms, but others expressed their disapproval of the coercive measures of the government. The speakers were John Fawkner, David Blair, Thomas Fulton, Dr Embling and others, whose speeches were anything but complimentary to the authorities.

All round the place of meeting Hotham had placed bodies of men fully armed; consisting of three hundred police and a hundred warders from the jails. One hundred gentlemen volunteers were stationed at a short distance, while the seamen and marines of Her Majesty's ships Electra and Phantom guarded the treasury and powder magazine. But these precautions were all unnecessary.

One hundred and thirteen prisoners were taken at the Eureka Stockade. A hundred were released, but thirteen, who had all been moving spirits in the rising were remanded for trial, but the actual leaders were at large; five hundred pounds had been offered for the capture of Vern who had made it be believed he was the actual commander-in-chief of the insurgents, but no one betrayed him; he lurked for months among the tents in Ballarat among his friends.

Two hundred pounds each had been offered for the capture of Peter Lalor and George Black, but they too had staunch friends among the miners in the ranges who concealed them till all trouble was blown over. The thirteen destined for trial were placed in Melbourne Gaol to wait there during the Christmas recess to wait for the next criminal session. An address was presented to the Governor signed by 4,500 inhabitants of Ballarat desiring him to grant a general amnesty. The Royal Commissioner of the gold fields made the same request, but Hotham declined to interfere with the law. The prisoners in gaol were not treated as felons, and their conditions were made as comfortable as possible. Joseph MacPherson Grant undertook to prepare for them their defence gratuitously and the popular Aspinall gave his services for the defence as their counsel Archibald Michie and R.D. Ireland also offered their services.

The first case that came on was John Joseph, a negro from Boston; well known on the Ballarat goldfields. It was well known and proved that he had been firing out of the stockade upon the soldiers. No defence was offered, only that if he did drill and helped to build a stockade, he did fire on the attacking

force, and resist when being captured. He had no treasonable intentions; the jury accepted that view and after an hour's consultation returned a verdict of "not guilty." A loud peal of applause followed the verdict. Judge a'Beckett not pleased at the result of the trial showed his displeasure by committing to gaol for a week the two most uproarious who had dared to desecrate the court with applause, and though they humbly apologised, it was of no avail. They had to pass their seven days in gaol.

The trial of John Manning came next. He had for his counsel that able Barrister Archibald Michie. He followed the same line of defence. John Manning was a reporter of the Ballarat Times, he admitted being drilled in the pike company and having fought within the stockade, but he was in arms, only in self defence against licence hunting policemen, and he had attacked nobody. He was acquitted; much to the wonder of Gurner, the Solicitor General and Stawell the Attorney General, who were in court conducting the trials. They postponed the other cases, hoping that a new panel would give them juries more disposed to support the Government.

A month passed, and the trials were resumed before Judge Barry, who won the popular favour by his kindly and courteous manner, yet he was strictly impartial. On the twentieth of March, the trial of Timothy Hayes came on, who had been chairman at the meeting, when the licences had been burnt; a decent fellow with a wife, and six children. His case was a difficult one on which to secure a verdict. Stawell nevertheless used all his skill in the prosecution, yet he was strictly fair. The evidence he produced was conclusive. Barry summed up in such a manner that showed his sympathies were with the diggers. He informed the jury that the mere firing did not constitute treason, even on Her Majesty's troops. Circumstances might justify, and often had justified, resistance yet he thought in strict law the prisoners had been guilty of treason. He as well as others was anxious to hear from the jury whether the Government might be opposed by armed men or whether it should be carried on however obnoxious a minister or his measures might be, till that minister was removed or that measure altered by constitutional means.

The jury would not take the judge's view. After twenty-five minutes consultation they returned with a verdict of "not guilty." A murmur of satisfaction filled the court, but the people were cautious. The word however passed out to the great crowd in the street, and the cheers were loud and prolonged. When Hayes came out a free man he was conducted down Stephen Street, as the hero of the day.

Two days later Carboni Raffaello was placed at the bar to answer to the charge of treason. In his case there was contradictory evidence, but it was clear he had been prominent in the disturbance. Both Aspinal and Ireland maintained that he had been justified in resisting the unconstitutional violence of Commissioners and police by the use of force. Barry summed up, taking notice of the fact that Raffaello had come sixteen thousand miles to escape Austrian tyranny, and that he complained of having met oppression quite as bad on the goldfields. The judge, however, said in a British community there were provided abundant means of agitating in a constitutional manner. But the jury again returned a verdict of "not guilty." The Government found itself completely defeated. The legal advisers of the Crown wished to abandon all the other cases, but Hotham objected, and said if the juries would not do their duties he did not see any reason why he should not do his. The trials proceeded in a purely formal manner; each prisoner was acquitted in turn, and the particular cause had won a complete triumph. Hotham confessed as much, when a short time after he granted an amnesty to all concerned.

From that time forward the era of democracy was fully commenced in Victoria; the people were completely masters of their own course and able to shape their own destiny.

After having related what followed and the results of the Ballarat disturbance I will continue my own personal history.

With the exception of a trip to Ballarat with a load with my father's horse in company with Gribble, I had done very little for two months. I had a price offered for my house, a rather tempting price, so I sold it with the intention of building another. In the meantime we went to live with the Gribbles. Close by there was a newly-built shop to let in Weller Street intended for a grocery business. My wife urged me to take it as she was anxious to make herself useful in doing something to make money. So we decided to start the grocery business. There were only two weatherboard rooms beside the shop. The rent was two pounds a week. We had in a pretty fair stock of goods, and did fairly well at first, but both of us were novices in making up parcels, yet we soon improved. I bought a good portion of the goods at the auction sale rooms. I also bought about four hundred books and started a circulating library, charging 2/6 deposit, and threepence for exchanging each book.

There was another grocery shop in the same street not far distant, which was doing a profitable business, and he, the grocer, carrying on the trade for some years became to know his customers, gave credit to some whom he could trust for short terms. We considered it necessary, if we would keep up our custom, to do the same. First one then another began to ask for accommodation, under various pretences. Some paid up according to promise, others again would beg off till next week. Husbands on the diggings or carting on the road had failed to send her money, a very strange thing; she wondered whatever could be the reason such a thing never happened before. The end of it would be she would secure another stock of a week's groceries promising to write to her husband forthwith; most likely we would not see her again till I hunted her up, probably in vain. Some got at us for three weeks and one for a month. I asked a friend of mine who lived near her if he knew anything of her. "Why?" he asked, then I told him how she had served me. "Oh," he said, "is that it; look here Mundy that woman is a bad egg and there are a good deal like her about here. It is not safe to give credit to women unless you know them well."

Stephen and Amelia Hubbard
They had a son Matthew born in Ashby in 1861.

There are a good many grass widows and I'm sure I do not know how some of them get along, and some of them have large families." "I hear," I said, "that Hubbard (the other grocer) gives tick to a good few, and he seems to get on all right." "I believe he does, but believe me," "Yes," my friend answered, "Mundy he knows his marks, he's the wrong man to run much risk and he's been in the business here a long time, and knows everybody. You and your little woman are new in the business, and do not know the people well enough to get on with them safely. I would advise you to give up shopkeeping, and do something else for a living." "Well," I said, "I believe you are not far wrong. At any rate I'll give no more credit." I told Ann, my wife when I returned home, I was determined to give no more credit to anyone, unless we knew they were sure and trustworthy people we knew. "How about them who are in our debt?" she asked? "Oh," I'll frighten it out of them, but do not let them have anything more, unless they pay down on nail for it; tell them we are only new beginners and cannot carry on unless we get our money in." "Ah well," she said, "it's awfully aggravating when you try to oblige people in distress by letting them have your goods, and perhaps have no prospect of means, or may be no intention to pay for them. You may depend upon it if we refuse them any further credit they'll do all they can not to pay at all." "So be it," I said, "but the first loss is the best. We'll see how we get on." When Saturday came the most of the moneyless are in evidence again with all manner of plausible tales, but I told them right away we would give no more credit to anyone, simply because we could not afford to do so.

The wholesale dealers had to be paid cash down when they let us have the goods, and it was impossible to keep a good stock in our shop if our customers did not pay us. I appealed to their own common sense if that was not reasonable. Accordingly, to all defaulters who asked for more things on the same lay I told the same story. Some bought a few things as far as their money went, promising to pay up as soon as they were able. The woman who owed for a month came with a long rigmarole of how she had been disappointed, and how thoughtless husbands were when away from home, and how she knew very well he had bottomed on gold for in her last letter he had told her he was dead on it. I told her I could give her no more credit in fact I would give no more to anyone from that out.

At that she bristled up and put on indignant airs. "What," she said, "What a fool I have been. I dealt with Hubbard before you opened thinking to do you a good turn as a new beginner. I left him to deal with

This old shop in Weller Street is believed to be where Henry and Ann operated their grocery.

you, as a new starter in the business just to encourage you, and now after spending all my ready money with you and because I'm a paltry 30/- in your debt you refuse to help me any farther, and my husband on gold too. Oh, I do wish I had stuck to Hubbard, I have paid him a lot of money, and I know he would not have served me like this". "Perhaps," I suggested, "as you have been such a good customer to him in the past he will be ready to help you in a fix." "After spending all my ready money with you?" she snorted. "Well," I said, "Mrs — I cannot afford to let you have any more of my goods on credit and if the outstanding account is not settled in fourteen days you will hear from my solicitor, that's all I have got to say at present." With that she snapped her fingers, saying: "Do your best," cocked her nose high in the air and majestically sailed away.

After the "bad egg" had departed none but ready-money customers came in till about nine o'clock when a delicate-care woman came in looking ill at ease. She owed only a small account for last week's groceries. "I hear," she began, "you have refused to allow any more credit to any one." "That's so ma'm," I answered, "we have been acting very foolishly to ourselves in giving too much already and we are obliged to be cautious; one week's credit is nothing if customers would only pay the next, but when once they get into one's books the only pay I can get is excuses and promises. Really we cannot afford to give credit unlimited as our capital is small and we have to pay for our goods as we get them." The little woman looking very disconsolate dropped herself onto a box as if not able to stand, a picture of misery. She said nothing for a while; then suddenly said: "Oh dear, oh dear, when I-I go-go home and tell-tell the children they'll have nothing to-to eat tomorrow oh-oh," and suddenly burst into tears. "Whatever shall I do?" My wife, I thought, was going to break down too, out of sheer sympathy. I felt a bit queer myself, I hate to see women cry when in distress, especially. I have often been bought, aye, and sold too, from being over-soft.

I went out into the back room leaving the two women to settle matters by themselves. I knew well how it would end. The woman would get what she wanted. After a while when I knew the woman had gone I went into the shop. Ann said: "Henry don't be vexed I had to let her have a few things, some flour, tea and sugar and codfish." "Yes," I said, "you'll be the ruin of us with your liberality." "I could not help it, there now. And thoughts of those little children. I am sure the woman is honest." "Why you little goose," I said, "you've been crying yourself," for her eyes were red. "Well who could help it." She replied, "to hear how thankful she was." "All right, my pet," I assured her, she had done what I expected she would for I'm sure I should do the same myself under the circumstances. Some of those who owed us money paid but never dealt with us after, and some never attempted to pay.

I sent various letters bristling with threats and evil consequences if accounts were not squared at certain dates, but of no avail. Our custom too fell off by degrees, so that it evidently failed to pay to keep it on.

The library as an accessory was a good help but no good by itself. Finally I said to my wife: "We are giving £2 a week for this shop, and we are keeping the shop instead of the shop keeping us, do you not think we had better give it best?" "Well she said, "it is certainly no use keeping on when we are not making our living out of it, but what are you thinking of trying next?" "Go to the diggings," I said, "and try our luck there." "Yes," she answered, "I'm quite agreeable; you will be sure to be lucky if I go with you, was not Gribble lucky the first time he tried when I was there." So we gave up the grocery business, took our stock of goods and books to the auction rooms and in a short time they were disposed of, some at cost price and some for less.

When Gribble knew we intended to try the diggings again, he was all for going too and Mrs Gribble was anxious for it also for she said: "I can't think of letting the chiel go without me, she will want some one to look after her soon." So in about a fortnight's time we were ready for a start. My brother John was anxious to join me as mates. Gribble, as John was going with me, joined with another man named Lamb. Two in those days was considered enough to start a party.

It was planned to go first to Happy Valley, a diggings recently broken out. Gribble had a horse and dray of his own. We got father to take us. We had a plentiful supply of provisions and mining requisites. Happy Valley, as near as I can guess, was about forty-five miles from Geelong, a narrow gully running east and west. The sinking six or seven feet there was very little alluvial washdirt; the gold was found

principally between the blue clay slate on the bottom. It ran only about one claim wide; and was at that time the only gully where gold could be found. We had been about a fortnight there without any success when a fresh goldfield was discovered on Mrs Linton's station, six miles away towards Ballarat. We struck our tents and shifted there. One gully, called Bloomer's Gully, was being worked with fairly good returns, but when we arrived it was all taken up. Over the range, close by, was another gully similar to Bloomer's which hitherto had not been prospected which in a short time turned out pretty good; afterwards called Nuggety Gully.

It struck me very forcibly there was a great probability of payable gold there; so John and I marked out a prospecting claim eighty feet square and began to sink. Gribble and his mate Lamb started farther up. We both bottomed at about the same depth, twenty-five feet, but we found no wash only raw sand. We did not think of driving but gave up the holes as dead shicers. This would not have happened if I had had then the knowledge I gained in after years of the geological changes on gold deposits. It is a well known fact that when alluvial gold was deposited it was the lowest part of a running stream of water, but through the course of the incalculable ages, by denudation of the banks of the stream, would fill up the original water course and most likely would change its course and often cut a deeper channel. The novice in gold-seeking not aware of this, chooses the lowest part of the gully or creek for his guide, where he considers the gutter is, is nearly always disappointed.

The run of gold in Nuggety Gully was some yards from the deepest part of the gully on the surface; hence we missed it. A few days after we had left it some one struck the run of gold, and we, not being on the spot at the time, missed a chance. When we heard of it and went, the whole length of the gully was swarmed with diggers and left us with not a ghost of a chance. If we had sunk again twenty yards on one side farther on the eastern bank we, with our prospecting claim, we would have been right for a thousand each - but we didn't. "Life is full of mistakes, disappointments and might-have-beens."

John and I tried our luck next on a small hill projecting into the main creek among other straggling workers and bottomed at twelve feet on a pennyweight to the tub; a tub was four common bucketfulls of wash dirt, just what was called a "tucker hole". We worked there three or four weeks till the yield came down to halfpennyweight, when we resolved to try our luck in the bed of the main creek. We got down dry till we struck water and drift sand at twenty feet; it was necessary then to timber our shaft. Not to be beaten we went into the ranges and split a sufficiency of slabs to timber thirty feet. After stabbing to the surface and logging three feet higher we started sinking again.

The water as we sunk lower became stronger and the fine white sand washed in upon us as fast as we could send it up. Plenty were watching us, ready to slip in if we struck gold. One of the onlookers who knew a little more than we did, advised, and showed us how to make a box. That consisted of four wide slabs bevelled sharp at the lower edge, with a cleat nailed on the ends of the long slabs so that the short end slabs would slide down behind; so by digging under the box we could drive it down by degrees and stop the drift from coming in on us and when low enough for a set of slabs on top to fix them in. Having got in its place, we made another start, and succeeded in sinking another foot, but the water increased rapidly. I was below and John was heaving up the mixed water and sand as fast as he could; we had a pretty large galvanised bucket on. I do not know how far it had ascended when the handle broke, when down it came and struck me on the back of my head as I was stooping.

Down I went as if shot, I thought my skull was smashed in. I did not lose consciousness altogether, but seemed paralysed. Resting on my knees, I could not hear or utter a word. The first thing I knew was John alongside of me lashing me on the rope, and then being hauled up. Several people were on the surface round the shaft asking me a lot of questions. After a while I came round and was able to walk home about half a mile. The rim of the bottom of the bucket had cut through my cap, through my hair as if cut by scissors and made a large gash in my scalp, but being a strong part of the skull, it was not injured; a doctor told me if the blow had been fairly on to the top of my head it would have been serious, if not fatal. I only suffered with a stiff neck for a few days, and was all right again.

The water in the shaft rose to four feet. We were advised to increase our party to four men, to put a pump or a whim on it and make the shaft larger as the water was evidently too strong for a windlass and buckets. This would have cost considerable expense; besides after all, it was only prospecting; so after six weeks hard work we gave it up to look elsewhere.

There was another lead of gold struck through black clay sixty feet sinking, called the 'Black Lead' but the results were not very encouraging. In the meantime another digging had been opened six miles farther on, nearer to Ballarat. A good many were leaving Lintons to go to that. John and I went to look at it. It did not seem according to reports to be up to much. Gold was being found on two different hills not far apart. This was called Brown's Diggings. We pegged off a claim. Next morning we packed up some blankets, a few tools and a small tent; with these on our backs we started for Brown's. I would have shifted there right away only my wife was near her lying in and the risk of shifting was too great, she was with her mother where she was. I went home every Saturday night and cut as much wood on Sunday as would do her the week. We bottomed our hole at fourteen feet at Brown's and obtained four dwts off the bottom which was not too bad, with the prospect of an improvement. On the second time of my home coming, my wife took ill on the Sunday night. I aroused her mother who was with her while I went for the doctor,

DURING THE GOLD RUSH
By December 1851 word of the massive Gold Rush had reached England and the scramble to get down to Port Phillip was immediate. By the end of 1852 86,000 Britons had arrived and a similar number hit the shores in 1853 and 1854.
Many more arrived from the Californian Gold Rush and also from Europe and China.

who did not live far away. He was still up. It was about two o'clock, so we soon returned. I went to Gribble's tent and sat down to wait; he was awake. After talking a while he said: "I don't think there is much chance on Linton's; after Ann gets all right and strong again I think we had better shift to Brown's, what do you think?" "Yes," I said, "I intend to anyway. I have no great opinion of it but I think it better than this place." Gribble and his mate had sunk on the head of a gully running parallel with Nuggety and bottomed at twenty-five feet on hard bare slate.

I sat waiting with as much patience as I could, hour after hour. I saw Mrs Gribble passing back and forth to the outside fire, but every thing was quiet in the tent except the suppressed cries of the patient. Half an hour after daylight Mrs Gribble came in and asked me to go for Mrs Bateman and told me the doctor was going to his tent to see his partner to arrange with him to attend on his other patients as he would not be able to leave Ann - adding: "Poor chiel, I believe she is going to have a hard time; though the doctor says everything is going right." Things went on during the day much the same, waiting, waiting for good news but none came. The women looked gloomy and distressed. I walked about till I was leg weary. The situation had got on my nerves. Late in the afternoon the doctor came out to me and said: "Your wife, Mr Mundy, is having a difficult time; things are not going at all as I would like to see them." "How is that doctor," I said, "is there any danger?" "Oh no," he said, "there is a way out of danger by sacrificing the child, which I do not like to do if it can possibly be helped." "For God's sake," I answered, "save my poor little wife's life at all hazards; do not let her life be endangered for the baby's sake." He then said, "I will go and consult my partner, and bring him with me if he is at home."

In half an hour the doctor returned bringing another doctor with him. They were inside a considerable time; the sun had gone down, and it was getting dark. When the doctors came out and told me the trouble was over, the mother with care was all right but the baby was dead. They said they could not possibly save it. "Never mind the baby," I said, "as long as the mother is out of danger. I am satisfied doctors, you have done your best, and no one can do more than that." "You can go in soon now, she has been asking anxiously after you." He added: "Your presence will have a soothing effect upon her, but talk very little. I have given her a sleeping draught, and the sooner it takes effect the better. I will call again tomorrow. Good night."

On going into the tent I was greatly shocked at seeing the poor white exhausted being on the bed. I took her hand and kissed her, she smiled faintly, and closed her eyes. I sat on a box by the bedside and held her hand when she was soon sleeping. I advised Mrs Gribble to go to bed, and get some rest as she must be knocked up with the long watching and worry. "No." she replied, "you had better do that, go and lie on our sofa. I will stop with my chiel for a while yet, she's asleep now and might wake and want something that you can't do for her. Do 'e go now I'll call el after a while and you can come and bide by her while I take a rest." The doctor came next day and was quite pleased at the condition of his patient, said all she wanted now was good nursing and she would be soon strong again.

John came over during the day anticipating the cause of my not returning on Monday; he said he had driven as far as he could, till he was quite mullocked up. He could hardly crawl out, and could not do any more till the pipeclay was hauled up.

The next day John and I buried the baby in a rough box on the side of the range and fenced in the grave with barked saplings where no diggings were likely to occur.

The day following, leaving Ann convalescent and in good spirits, we went back to Brown's to attend to our claim, preparatory for our first washing. We put through four loads which yielded three ounces to the load, £12 worth, which we considered payable. On Saturday when I went home, Ann was still in bed but was getting on splendidly. Gribble had carted a few loads of wash dirt and fire-wood for people. Lamb, his mate, had left him to go to another diggings. So we agreed that the week after the next one coming, for both of us to shift to Brown's.

The Saturday after when I came home, taking half a day's rest, we commenced packing as far as we could for an early start on Monday morning. Our things were taken first

JOHN BATEMAN
Born in London in 1789 and died in 1873. Married Emma and had a son John born in Newtown, Geelong in 1850.

From near Buninyong to Happy Valley where the Mundy's baby is buried.

248

with Ann and her mother on a comfortable seat. We reached Brown's about ten o'clock; when John and Gribble went for his own turn out. By the time they returned I had our tent fixed. It was not much trouble as we had all the sticks with us, and by the time it was dark both tents were in habitable order. Ann was in excellent spirits and so were we all as we sat on a fallen tree trunk and ate our suppers like a jolly set of diggers as we were.

Gribble resolved to stick to his carting as the chances were in his favour. The local water supply for washing the dirt was nearly all either turned into sludge or dried up, and wash dirt had to be carted two miles to the nearest creek where water was obtainable.

The hill John and I worked on was partly occupied by Chinamen, rather unusual to find, John sinking on his own account. Their usual habit was to follow the white man and wash his tailings or sludge over again. John Chinaman was looked upon as a superfluous, useless pest picking up the crumbs that might, if need be, keep a white man from starving. He was considered to have no rights either human or legal, by the diggers.

There was a capitation tax of £10 a head on every Chinaman who landed in Victoria but to evade this tax the greater number of them landed in Adelaide, and walked overland five hundred miles into Victoria in crowds of forty, fifty or sixty together. It was a common thing to see them marching on to a diggings all in Indian file, with their great basket hats, carrying heavy loads in large cane baskets, swung on each end of a pole resting on their shoulders; all in a jog trot.

Generally one among them could speak a little English and acted as interpreter. None of the others could yabber any tongue but Chinese. We worked at this claim several weeks, as we were not jammed by neighbours and had plenty of room till at last the dirt grew too poor and the last few weeks we had to pay for carting to the creek. The drinking water had become used up, so we gave it up and shifted our tent to the main creek and Gribble shifted too, about three miles on. There were several patches where gold was being got, but poor. We then pitched in on a place called Watson's Hill and bottomed at ten feet and got one dwt to the tub. We worked at this a few weeks up till Christmas when father, mother and sister came up to pass Christmas with us, when we had a jolly good time for they did not forget to bring plenty with them.

Our next shift was to a place called the Black Hill, six miles from Smythe's Creek, just a poor and shallow diggings. Half the population there was Chinese, a good few of them had claims. We got in among the crowd and succeeded in getting a little gold, but there was a continual disturbance between the two races. A man I knew well, called Humpy Bob, one day insisted on going down a Chinaman's claim to get a prospect just for satisfaction to know if he was getting anything payable, when the Chinaman opposed him with his long shoulder stick. Bob threw the bucket at his face and the rim of the bottom of the bucket cut him on the cheek severely. The Chinaman put his hand to the hurt and seeing blood smeared it over his face, and dropped on his back, as if he had been knocked down.

The Chinese were very important to life in the goldfields and their legacy is to be found throughout Australia. However, they were the subject of a lot of prejudice from the government and public in the 1850s.

To look at his face one would think he had been murdered, for he never stirred or showed any signs of life. His countrymen gathered round in a furious rabble. A crowd of Chinese collected in a very short time, armed with bamboos yelling, and screeching, when Bob and those who were with him thought it safest to clear out. As soon as they made a start the Chinamen rushed after them, when a general riot began, accompanied with a terrific Chinese clamour.

I happened to be at my tent at the time, doing something nearly a quarter of a mile from where the trouble commenced. My tent was one of a row facing a gully and Humpy Bob lived close by me. As soon as it became apparent that a mob of Chinese was driving white men before them, European blood was up and ran to the rescue with any weapon a man could at the moment lay his hand on. The Chinese had the command of the situation for a little while but as the race lengthened every white man in sight ran to help, till the force got pretty strong, when a dead stand was made.

One man took upon himself the office of commander for the time being, sang out: "Close on 'em boys." Chinamen fight mostly with long weapons to their great disadvantage. They can get only one blow unless the enemy stands back to give them a second chance. In leaving the tent I had snatched up a pickhandle. One ferocious looking fellow made a sweeping cut at me which I easily dodged before he could raise his pole again. I sprang in and gave him a smashing blow on the wrist with my pick handle, which made him drop his stick like a red hot cinder, and bellow like a bull. Some had no weapons at all but used their fists, and punched and kicked away till further orders. Several Chinkees in a few minutes lay sprawling on the ground all yelling like demons. The consequences were the celestial enemy made a hasty retreat, leisurely followed by the conquerors to ascertain what the row was about, for very few of us had the least idea of what the fracas was about, but the spectacle of seeing Chinamen chasing a handful of white men was an ample excuse for intervention. Some got slightly hurt but no one was killed. To say there was no bloodshed would be a lie, for there was plenty of it principally from the noses of the heathen Chinese.

When I returned to my tent my wife and her mother were looking pale and frightened. Ann said: "Why did you run into that fight, you might have got hurt?" I said: "you would not like to see me stand and look idly on, and witness a lot of rascally Chinese hunting white men would you?" "Well no," she said, "but what's it all about." "Humpy Bob was determined to go down a Chinaman's claim to get a prospect to know what he was getting and the Chinaman struck at him with a long stick; when Bob threw the bucket into his face and spoilt his looks, the Chinky turned on him and those who were with him and meant slaughter." Then Mrs Gribble said: "We will not be safe in our beds after this, there's such a lot of Chinamen here. I wish we were somewhere else." "Don't worry," I replied, "they've had enough of it for the present."

Several days after the fight another incident happened between the Europeans and Chinese of quite a different character. Some Chinese in shallow ground were gouging and excavating under a projecting bank, when it suddenly gave way and fell; one was buried completely and another partly buried, caught by the legs, who managed by his own exertions to extricate himself; but the other was under two or three tons of dirt.

Plenty of his countrymen looked on in hopeless horror, but not one attempted to save him, but stood and howled in terrific despair. The white men working near, hearing the noise, ran to see what was the matter and taking in the situation at a glance, set to work with a will to dig the poor wretch out. He was soon uncovered and dragged out, but nearly dead from suffocation. After an hour or so he sat up and began to talk, his countrymen gathered round in excessive joy and surprise as if a dead man had come to life again. They talked to him, and felt him as if they could not believe their eyes. It was useless asking any questions for all they could say was "no savvy." But when he got on his legs and attempted a limping walk their joy was excessive. They ran to the nearest shanty and bought several bottles of Holland gin and ran around the diggings offering a drink to every white man they met. After that there was peace between the races.

Black Hill was a miserable poor diggings; it was called a Chinaman's field. They mostly lived upon rice or "lice" as they pronounced it. Gribble said to me one day: "This place is neither good for carting nor gold, let us try some other place." "You are right," I replied, "but where shall we go?" "Let us try Smythe's Creek," he made answer, "All right," I said, "I'm willing, but I'll see what my brother John says." John was quite willing. So next— day we packed up all our traps in one load, the women perched on top. It was only about six miles so we arrived there early in the day. This was out of the frying pan into the fire. No one was getting anything but a few fossickers. It was declared the place had been good but was now worked out; utterly gutted. We lay on our oars for about a fortnight on the "qui vive" for any sudden news of a new rush; ready at any time to make a dart for it. The only incident that happened there was the meeting of Frank Mason, a cousin of Mrs Dwyer of Victoria Valley, who had left the Valley as he said in the hope of making a pile which he had not succeeded in doing yet, but still had hopes.

One day some travellers from Ballarat gave a marvellous and exciting account of a great rush that had taken place near Buninyong called the White Hills; so with all possible haste we started for that, the distance was about twenty miles. Early in the afternoon we reached the River Leigh, about a mile from the new diggings and fixed our tents that day. Early in the morning we went out to reconnoitre. A few claims had bottomed on good gold, and the vicinity up and down the supposed run of the lead and half a mile wide was swarmed with people. It being so near Ballarat the diggers there got the first news, there was not a ghost of a chance for any one who arrived when we did to get in anywhere where the gold was being got. Gribble was right for plenty of employment for his horse and dray. My brother was offered a job at Telford & Page's store on the Magpie to drive out stores with horse and wagon for three pounds a week and his keep, which he concluded to take as he was without a mate.

I joined John Bateman, a man I was acquainted with in Geelong. We took up an abandoned shaft and after driving a short distance struck fairly good gold which gave us several ounces, but it soon ran out; it was only a patch. We tried two or three more holes near but without success. We did a bit of prospecting in the ranges, we got gold in two places, a few specks but nothing to pay.

In our wanderings round we often noticed an old Dutchman always working if not picking up the red clay on the surface. He was puddling in his tub, his answer was always the same. "Sometimes half pennyweight sometimes quarter pennyweight and sometimes noding at all." I had an idea that farther down in the gully there might be gold; so we sunk a hole and bottomed at twelve feet, getting nothing on the bottom. We drove across ten feet each way but without any success.

Having nothing particular on hand to do I walked out to the Magpie one day to pay my brother John a visit to see how he was getting on. On reaching Telford and Page's store, I was surprised to meet father there. He had come to Ballarat on horseback on some business and had called at the store to see John and at the same time to learn where to find me. We were told at the store that John was gone to Buninyong with the wagon; that we might possibly meet him on our road back. Father looked sad and dejected I thought. I asked him if anything was the matter, he told me he had met with an accident about a month previous. "I had started on my way to Ballarat with a load," he continued, "and I had not got farther than Bell Post Hill when I got stuck. I dug away before the wheel and sang out to the horse heaving all I could on the spokes; the horse pulled like a Briton, the wheel was nearly out when I gave an extra push and out it went, but I felt at the last strain I made something snap in my inside. A lump rose in my groin and it was very painful at times. I took the load to Ballarat but how I got home I can't tell you."

"Have you not seen a doctor?" I asked him. "Yes." he answered, "and he tells me I have badly ruptured myself and advises me to wear a truss." "And don't you?" "No," he replied, "if it is God's will I shall get better, if not - well I trust in him." "But you ought father to follow the doctor's advice," I told him. "God only helps those who tries to help themselves." As we neared Jock Winter's crossing we heard a vehicle coming towards us. I knew it was John by the noisy way he was talking to the horse. In a few minutes we met him, quite surprised to see father and me together. We talked father's trouble over together. "By all means," John said, "you should listen to the doctor's advice and get a truss. What's the use of consulting a medical man if you do not do what he tells you." After a little more talk father said. "Well my boys. I am glad to see you both together once more, I knew where to find John from his letter and he knew where to find you, so I was in hopes of seeing you both, we may not meet all three together again." Prophetic words - we never did.

After leaving John we had about a mile and half to go. He rode his horse, and I walked alongside; very little was said. We came to a shanty near home. I asked him to have a drink of something, thinking to cheer him up, he took a glass of Old Tom but I noticed he only drank the half of it, leaving the remainder in the glass.

It was nearly dark when we reached the tent. Ann had the supper all ready, she was gladly surprised to see father. They were always on the best of terms. I got some feed off Gribble and fed his horse. After supper Ann made him up as comfortable a bed as she could and we soon retired to rest. When he left for home in the morning I went half a mile with him. He seemed very much dejected, I tried to enliven him up all I could. I advised him to follow the doctor's advice and likely he might be as well as ever again. He shook his head and said, "I'm afraid not Henry." Standing for a few moments without speaking at last he said: "Well, I must be getting on I can't ride fast, or I'll be late getting home." Shaking hands he said: "Goodbye, God bless you my boy," and as he turned to go I saw tears running down his wrinkled cheek. He said no more. I stood and watched him going slowly through the trees, his heels always going as was his habit, when on horseback as if he was using spurs, which he never did wear. I

Looking to Mt Buninyong from Magpie - where Henry and John saw their father for the last time.

MAGPIE GULLY

Was the first lead opened up in the area. It started on the surface in a shallow valley in the White Horse Range. It was joined by the Chinaman's Lead, into the Frenchman's Lead, then under the plateau to Sebastopol.

MAGPIE

Starts in the north from the Whitehorse Lead at the Sebastopol-Mt Clear Road, south to the Star and Garter Hotel on the corner of the old stock route, which is the road to Geelong, east of the new bridge at the southern end of Sebastopol, and the old road running away on the left leading to Magpie.

watched him till the trees hid him from my sight. I never saw him again after, living or dead.

About this time a new diggings two miles from the White Hills, and about three from the foot of Mount Buninyong broke out, called the Green Hills. An acquaintance of mine had been to look at it, and had taken up a claim. He invited me and two others to join him to sink right away. I went to look at it next day in company of himself and the other two men. The sinking was about seventy feet. It seemed a very likely show; so we determined to put a shaft down. There was not a great number of people there at the time. Some claims which happened on the gutter were getting fairly good gold, but nothing extraordinary had been discovered as yet. The place was new and very little tested, it was no knowing what it might turn out.

I walked a week to and from my work, which was three miles night and morning. During the week some more holes had bottomed on gold; things were looking up. I wondered the place was not more rushed, but the deep sinking was the objection. The claim alongside of us bottomed on a good prospect. I concluded it was best to shift our tent over at once. Gribble, who had plenty of carting to do, did not care to move from where he was just yet, he would come as soon as things got slack. I got him to take us over. Mrs Gribble was all on for coming too, but he would not leave good work for a mere speculation. There was not much to be done at the Green Hills in the carting line just then. Anyhow, it was only three miles away, the distance could be easily walked.

When we had sunk forty feet we found the remaining portion of the shaft required to be timbered. I and another went into the bush to split slabs while the other two continued to sink. We struck no water but the ground was treacherous. We soon had enough slabs carted in, when the four of us dressed them ready for use and all hands started sinking again.

In six weeks from the start we reached bottom. The wash had every appearance of being the right thing but on trying a dishful we could not raise the ghost of a speck. We then washed a tubful and did raise a few scaly specks. The next thing we concluded to do was to drive towards our neighbour who was getting gold. They told us that their claim was no good towards us. However, for satisfaction we drove to the boundary, but failed to strike anything better. It was evident our claim was a rank duffer. The payable gold lay only in a narrow gutter and our neighbours had bottomed on it. We had sunk on the upper end of the lead which was fully occupied for half a mile. We then went to the other end and pegged out a claim there.

During the day I was talking to two North of Ireland men, whom I knew very well, who had watched us pegging out one of them said: "Going to try your luck there Mundy?" "Yes," I replied, "we have just bottomed a duffer on the upper end; we think now of trying the lower end." "We are in want of another man," he said, "there are only three of us. If we were a party of four we could work two shifts, one man is enough at the windlass in dry sinking; but perhaps you do not care to leave your mates?" "Oh," I said, "they are only mates of mine in sinking the last hole." I saw they were not far from payable claims and already down twenty feet, so I said: "Yes, I will join you willingly." One of the men whose name was George called down the shaft to the man who was working. "Paddy, here's a man we know well who is willing to join us. What do you say?" "All right boys," he called up, "I'm agreeable, just as you like." We all met in the evening and talked over future operations.

We agreed while sinking, unless we struck water to work in two shifts, and spell a couple of hours at dinner time and crib time as one man was enough at the windlass. It would save time, we would get on as fast again. So Paddy and I, it was arranged, were to go on the day-shift till the end of the week, and to Bill and George (I forget their surnames) was allotted the night shift. As it was good sinking, and no rock to contend with, we got on rapidly.

When ninety feet was reached we struck a foot of black clay; under this was a strange kind of earth which none of us had seen the like before consisting of small sticks and very broad leaves intermixed with black sand; caked solidly together like a plug of tobacco. Breaking a cake of it in your hands it cracked like rotten twigs. The veins in the leaves were plainly discernible, quite a different vegetation to any tree then existing, evidently a deposit of bygone ages, perhaps a million or two million years ago, and from the erosion of the higher lands had been covered with ninety feet of earth, and still so perfectly preserved as to be recognisable as unmistakable remains of vegetation.

Six inches of this stuff and then dark clay and sand mixed with waterworn green sandstone boulders. After sinking through six feet of this we struck bottom on soft soapy green sandstone rock. Washing a bucketful of picked wash we obtained a quarter of an ounce of gold. We afterwards found the wash was payable up to a foot. After a few days when the shaft was opened out a bit, we all four worked day shift, three below and one on top.

Gribble had shifted a week before we bottomed and we employed him to cart our dirt to the washing place. The run of payable dirt in our claim was confined to a narrow gutter twelve feet wide. We worked it out in six weeks, and obtained eighty five ounces of clean gold. £340's worth, £85 each. The party broke up, Paddy and I each went on our own; George and Bill being country men had been mates a long time, still continued together. I went to the bottom of the lead and pegged off another claim, intending to do a bit of shepherding as the gully had broadened out considerably, and the sinking was becoming deeper. In such circumstances it was advisable to wait and watch for the turn and course of the lead.

One Sunday morning I said to my wife: "Ann I think I'll go as far as the Magpie today and look John up, to see how he is getting on." It was only about five miles walk so off I started. On reaching Telford and Page's store I inquired for John. The man told me he had left and gone to Geelong, and said: "Are you his brother?" "Yes," I told him. "Oh," he said, "he was looking for you about ten days ago, but he said you had left the place where he saw you last and could get no information where you had gone and was unable to find you. He had received news that his father was dead. The next day he left and we understand he is not coming back."

Father was dead. On hearing this I turned my face homewards to take the sad news to my wife. Dead - a broken down old man at the age of forty-nine. The last ten years he had passed in Victoria which was comparatively a bed of roses to life he had passed in grinding England. He had been put to work almost in his babyhood; his mother had died before he knew her; his father married again to a woman who proved to be a cruel stepmother who grudged him food and half starved him. He told me he often ate his dinner going to his work. He was a small man. I have heard it said it was because he was starved in his youth.

All the Mundy's I remember were of good proportions, not less than five feet ten inches; my grandfather had a brother six feet two inches. My father, before I can recollect, was converted at a Ranter's meeting in the Wesleyan chapel and so great an impression did it make upon him, that he never swerved from it till the day of his death. He entertained a morbid and melancholy view of the pleasures of this world, and used his utmost endeavours to secure a happy resting place in Heaven for which object he worked hard and energetically to obtain.

His work on the farm in England as far as my recollection goes was milkman. He milked ten or twelve cows morning and evening and performed other work during week days. On Sundays after milking he walked a mile to Fenny Stratford to hear a sermon in the morning. After dinner we all went to our own chapel at Bow Brickhill to hear a sermon there. Father would leave half an hour before the service was finished to do his milking. My brother and I had to stay to Sunday school. About seven o'clock in the evening there was another sermon at which we all had to attend. After that a prayer meeting was held for all those who liked to stay. Father and mother always stayed and my brother and I dare not leave. On Wednesday night a prayer meeting was held in the chapel. To fill up the interstices of every other night in the week private prayer meetings were held at member's houses in turn.

When I arrived home and told my wife what I had heard, she was greatly shocked at the news for she had great respect for my father. I told her, I must go to Geelong in the morning to learn farther about it and ascertain how mother and my sister were situated. The coach road was some distance off and by striking across the bush I could save a good few miles by reaching the Geelong road at Meredith. So in the morning I started to walk. It was barely fifty miles and as I had nothing to carry it seemed nothing of a feat, and would at least save four pounds. The first night I reached the Clyde Hotel on the bank of the Moorabool where I put up for the night. I had only walked about thirty-five miles yet my feet were very sore. I had chosen a pair of new boots to travel in, which had proved severe on my feet, leaving a large blister on one of my heels.

The next morning it was with great pain I could walk at all. Cobb's Coach passed the hotel but that would be late in the afternoon; to wait for that the idea was intolerable, so off I limped. The remainder of the tramp was only about fifteen miles, yet it took me till dark to accomplish it. When I arrived at our gate Jane saw me first and cried out "Mother here's Henry." Mother ran to me and putting her arms round my neck, said: "Your father is dead and buried." "Yes," I said, "I have heard." The

HENRY'S FATHER
George Munday (note the original spelling in the official records), was buried at the Geelong Eastern Cemetery in the old Methodist section. There is no headstone.

Pam Jennings (Geelong Cemeteries Trust)

George Mundy died only ten years after leaving Bow Brickhill, but he set up a new life for his present and future families in Australia.

two females then had another good cry while I told them how I came to hear of it. "Where's John?" I inquired. "John," mother said, "has agreed to work the horse and dray, same as father did, he has gone now with a load to Linton's diggings for a storekeeper. He started the day before yesterday. Father, before he died, asked him to do that, and look after Jane and me. Your father wished and prayed he might see you once again before he went, but then we did not know where to find you." "Did father make a will?" I asked. "Oh yes," she answered, "he made a will leaving everything to me for the mutual benefit of Jane and myself." "That was right," I said, "that is just what I thought he would do." Mother had a little money but it could not be much, what it was she did not tell me. She lived in one house and rented the other; that with the profits of the horse and dray with economy ought to be sufficient to keep them.

A fortnight after I had returned from Geelong, Gribble grew anxious to go to Geelong to see how his property was being cared for, and whether it was rising in value, and eventually made up his mind to go, to travel with his horse and dray. Being a good opportunity, I advised my wife to go with him; so she in company of another girl named Ann Bateman gladly embraced the chance to visit their old friends. They were gone a fortnight altogether, and greatly enjoyed themselves. Gribble kept as sober as a judge.

With regard to property, things had taken a downward turn. The Melbourne to Geelong railway had been completed and started working; so that goods intended for Ballarat, its surrounding old fields, and the Western district, were sent from Melbourne by rail instead of coming as heretofore by boat; which caused a great falling of trade in Corio Bay. When Gribble went to Geelong he had a notion of selling his property if he could secure the consent of 'the old woman' and me, but when he ascertained the fact that values had fallen, he contended himself by saying: "I'll wait a while, property will be sure to rise again." A vain prophesy. Two years after, at the end of 1858, the railroad between Geelong and Ballarat was in working order so that freight from Melbourne to Ballarat could pass on without unloading. From that time Geelong began to decline to the veritable 'Sleepy Hollow' as it was called, and remained that way for many years. Geelong rail opened 25 June 1857.

Shepherding came gradually into practice as the sinking got deeper. Few cared to sink far ahead of a lead, except they were far enough away from where gold was being got (half a mile or so) so that they could have the right to an extended area of ground called a prospecting claim. To keep possession of a claim the man was obliged to attend it for at least a few hours every day, and do a little work on it; sink perhaps six inches to testify to his possession, and sit down for awhile, have a yarn with his neighbour or play at quoits or cards to pass time. Failing to attend to his claim every day, Sundays excepted, it was if the show was good, liable to be jumped. In such cases very often angry words would ensue which might provoke a challenge to fight for the contested right of possession to the claim. If the challenge was accepted, there would suddenly be a great commotion among the idlers round. "A fight, A fight". The cry would spread, and no sight was so exhilarating to diggers as a fair stand-up fight, and fair it must be; no foul play.

The two men stripped to the buff, from waist upwards and having chosen their own seconds with

The railway which was opened in 1857 and changed the importance of Geelong forever.

254

plenty of volunteers as bottle-holders, would commence punching at each other for all they were worth. The seconds and bottle-holders would be industriously employed keeping back the pressing crowd. "A ring, a ring" was the cry, "keep back, give 'em fair play." One of the combatants at length would go over, when the seconds took his man on his knee, bathed his face and hands with water from the bottle-holders. After resting a minute or so someone would call out: "Time," when both were on their feet, and at it again. Some of these fights might last half-an-hour or more; some perhaps for only a couple of rounds according to how the men were matched or how much physical punishment they could bear. When one would declare himself satisfied and said: "I give in" it was all over. They shook hands, and the victor could take, if he chose, possession of the claim.

Other disputes again about the right to the possession of a claim had to be settled by bringing the Commissioner to decide the dispute. Next day this official magnate would make his appearance accompanied by four armed troopers. He would ask complainants if they had miner's rights. If satisfactory, he asked what evidence they had to produce. Some neighbouring shepherds would answer to the fact that they had seen them on the claim daily for sometime. The jumpers were then called on to state the reason why they had taken possession. Their answer might be they had passed by there on two different days, and saw it unoccupied. The decision, no doubt, would be by the commissioner: "I decide in favour of complainants."

On one occasion at the Green Hills a party of Tipps (Tipperary men) from Ballarat, arbitrarily jumped a claim in a very decisive manner and flung the tools of the rightful owners away as far as they were able, and swore the claim belonged to them, threatening to slay anyone who dared to interfere, and began sinking, apparently in real earnest. The hole, when they jumped it, was down only three feet. The Goldfields Commissioner was sent for and arrived next day; by then the hole had been sunk to nine feet. The Commissioner examined several witnesses and sifted the matter with great patience, when he gave his decision against the Tipps, and ordered them off the ground. Apparently the matter was settled, and the Commissioner left to attend to another case.

As soon as he was out of sight the jumpers rushed on to the claim again, swearing they did not care for the Commissioner's decision, the claim was their's, and they intended to stick to it in spite of anyone. One of the other party ran after the Commissioner and told him: "Oh they will not agree to my decision and defy my authority." He queried: "Wait a bit, I will be back soon." After a while he was seen coming. The Tipps saw him and all sneaked off. When the Commissioner arrived they were not to be seen "Where are they?" he asked. "When they saw you coming they cleared out pretty smart," was the reply. "Well good for them," he said. "If they interrupt you again let me know," and rode off.

The three of us had now been shepherding over a month; we were considerably nearer claims on the gutter as they kept bottoming. The sinking became gradually deeper and water and a pretty bad drift had been struck. That was all as it was likely to be, but the course of the gutter appeared to be very uncertain and from the trend it was taking lately left us all three in not very favourable positions. However, we intended to hang on for a while longer.

Another, and big rush had broken out again at Brown's. Gribble and I were thinking of going to that when my brother John who was returning from Ballarat called at the Green Hills to look us up. Here was a good opportunity to shift to Brown's Diggings. John could take my things and Gribble his own. So we agreed there and then to be off to Brown's again. We arrived there in a day. The diggings had been rushed about a fortnight before and was thickly occupied. It was very rich as far as it went and was about 80 feet sinking, and in a very unusual situation. Flat, level, country where no one looking at the surface would think of finding a lead of gold, had it not been traced. I had, when there before, walked over it many times, as I remarked to John: "We have walked backwards and forwards to and from our tent for several weeks over this gold to work at Watson's Hill over there for a pennyweight to the tub." "Yes," he said, "is it not aggravating?"

Brown's Diggings when we arrived, was in the height of prosperity; all the pleasures and amusements common in Ballarat were to be found there, a theatre, dancing, saloons, bowling alleys, gymnasiums, concert rooms, Hobart Town Poll with her bevy of girls, Bones, the Bull pup, Cross eyed Luke etc. and grog shanties galore, and all comparatively unmolested and orderly in comparison with two years before.

Things here were much the same as at the Green Hills. The sinking was running into deep ground, and water. All the chance I saw was to go to the lower end of the lead, peg out a claim and shepherd it and await. Gribble, as usual, on a busy diggings got plenty of work with horse and dray carting washdirt, wood slabs etc. He gave me a pound a week to reserve a share for him if I happened to be lucky. So I selected a spot which according to my judgement promised a good chance at the lower end of the lead; which was a considerable distance from where payable gold was being got. This place was more thronged with shepherds than Green Hills. I did not value my chance much. The payable claims were gradually getting deeper and wetter as they neared my position.

My fraternity were jolly enough but were not very enthusiastic over their prospects, yet it was the only thing to be done; to watch and wait. There were two parties of Chinese, next to me, for a wonder, among the crowd. The first Chinese I had seen entering on such a big speculation as shepherding on deep ground. These poor wretches passed a very uncomfortable time among the Europeans whose chief amusement was to tease and annoy the Johns; pulling their pigtails, chaffing them, pelting them with bits of dirt, etc. till the poor fellows were nearly frantic. Some around, myself among them, who disliked to witness the treatment they got, expostulated with the tormentors begging them to leave the poor beggars alone as they were doing no harm. This might have the desired effect for a time, but not for long. I have no love for a Chinaman, but I hate to see unprotected humanity abused. I was on pretty good terms with them. I amused myself by picking up a few words of Chinese which they were always ready and pleased to teach me.

One day the tormentors were going it so strong that one fellow went quite mad. He pulled a knife out of his pocket and stabbed his face viciously in several places till the blood streamed down, then rubbing it about he looked as if he had been butchered; when he fell on his back and roared like a bull. His mates stood and looked on, as there were only a few of them. If their force had been as strong as it was on the day at Black Hill when Humpy Bob struck one on the face with the bottom of a bucket, no doubt there would have been a fight. From that day after the Chinese were not seen and some Europeans jumped their claims.

A stranger, one day, made his appearance among the shepherds; a manipulator of the douching rod, to discover where the deepest water lay underground, which of course would be in the lowest ground and consequently probably the course of the lead. The douching rod is a slim green twig about four feet long.

The once important town of Dunolly was well known by the Mundys for many years and lies in the north of the 'Golden Triangle' and to the west of Bendigo.

The operator with hands at each end of the rod, or nearly so, carries the rod in front of him, and walks through the place to be examined. The end of the rod pointing towards the deepest water was supposed to be felt, sensibly, dipping down, while the opposite side remained unaffected. The douching rod operator was very serious, and silent over his work, only telling the crowd which was following his heels now and again how the rod was affected. A good many there had great faith in what it told them, but the majority, myself among them, believed he was an arrant fraud.

I had been five weeks watching my claim waiting for an encouraging inducement to form a party and commence to sink. The ground for half a mile below me was taken up, but no one had the pluck to start sinking. The claims getting gold had approached considerably nearer, but the area of the lead since striking water was extending in width, and the washdirt was getting poorer owing to the gold being more scattered. When this fact became evident, and each shaft bottoming and obtaining poorer prospects, the outlook became discouraging so that nearly all claims below me were abandoned, and I was still three hundred yards from where gold was being got. Another cause for neglecting Brown's lead was the breaking out of Chinaman's Flat, six miles beyond Maryborough, which was reported to be very rich. Chinaman's had been talked about a week or two before I became discouraged of my present outlook, and I knew it would be pretty certain it would be the old game over again, shepherding. As people were so numerous it would be over-rushed.

However Gribble and I made up our minds to go; to follow the crowd. Gribble took his own belongings and I hired a dray to take my wife and our things. We passed through Maryborough, and came on to the top end of Chinaman's diggings. A dirtier and more begrimed spectacle of humanity I never beheld. The weather was hot and windy. The stores and tents were among the holes; the pipe clay was of a red colour and so extremely pulverised that the air was thick with red dust. The roadway was between the holes, as the sides of the gully were rocky and rough. We stopped at one store, Gribble and I went in to get a drink and get the women some lemonade. The interior of the store and everything in it was covered with a coat of dust including the man and woman. The woman said she washed her face half a dozen times a day, and do all she could, she could not keep the counter decent.

Maryborough is a very prominent ex-goldrush city still.

We started then to go farther on when it became gradually freer of the dust, the gully widened out and the traffic got to the outside of the workings. We pulled up a little below the lower end of the workings to have a look round, and camp for the night. The wash dirt was mostly carted to the Bett Bett Creek another mile farther on. Gribble thought the latter place would suit him best, and resolved to camp there as it would better suit his carting business. My object was to get on as good a show for the lead of gold as I could, so I chose a spot and fixed our tent. A day or two after we had become settled I came across three men with whom I had had a casual acquaintance on another diggings, two of them were brothers named Scarf. I never knew the other one's name, he was known only to us by a nickname Gribble gave him of Fat Jack. He was six feet and as thin as a whipping post.

They were a miserable looking trio each of them, not men I would voluntarily chose for mates. These men held a claim not far from where good gold had been bottomed on the main lead. Their claim, I thought stood a splendid show. To my great surprise they offered me a share. They told me they intended to start sinking and wanted one more man to start with. They held an eightman's claim; if things went well they could sell the other four shares. I thought it the best thing in sight at the time, and gladly accepted their offer. We did not commence work at once but held on for a few days when a claim bottomed on gold almost at right angles to our line of expectations, which caused us to hesitate longer. Another claim bottomed on the same line of divergence which threw a damper over all hope in our direction; it seemed as if the lead had taken a sudden turn.

A good many around us left their claims and pegged out in the new direction. Still there were several going down on our line. The Scarfs and Fat Jack however, gave up in despair to try their luck elsewhere, but I still hung on to await other holes bottoming. After waiting a fortnight longer a hole bottomed on my line on very good gold not many claims away. This seemed to mean that the lead had split into two branches. I made all haste to pick out a party of men to start work at once. This was no difficult matter, I wanted seven besides myself. I could have secured fifty if I wanted them, but eight were all that they required on a claim eighty feet by eighty feet.

Gribble gave up his carting and shifted near to us but did what little we wanted. The party was as fine a lot of men as could be got together. There were Gribble, one Irishman, one American, one Canadian a Yorkshire man, Enoch Holdsworth, a valued acquaintance of mine for many a year after (his wife and mine were great and lasting friends), a county man of mine and another Englishman whom we called the Major from his dominant appearance and the majestic moustache he cultivated and your humble servant. Like others on the two sides and below we started to work at once. Some of us sank a bit, others went to the bush for logs for logging up. Two were told off to split slabs for stabbing the shaft as it went down.

After we had been working a week, the Scarfs and Fat Jack returned from Dunolly, put in their appearance alleging their right to their shares with the tale that though they had been absent three weeks, they had left me in charge of the claim to secure their rights, if anything favourable should turn up; which was an arrant lie, as they advised me to ding (throw away with violence) it too, and laughed at me for still holding on. They were determined they said to have their share of the gold, and to come every day whether we allowed them to work or not.

Accordingly they sank a shallow hole on one corner of the claim and sat by it some hours every working day for weeks; so that they became a real pest. From their extreme persistence some of my mates began to think they must have some legal standing to act as they did. To settle the matter we concluded that it would be best to obtain legal advice. All hands were agreeable to give a lawyer half a share in the claim to see the business through. So I was chosen to consult a lawyer on those terms. The best one I could hear of was MacDermott who lived in Carisbrook. I walked eleven miles into Carisbrook and consulted MacDermott on the case and stating the terms, which he was willing to accept.

All he could do in the matter at present, he told me, was to try and

JAMES SCARF
Married Sophia Searle in 1858.
Son John was born at Chinaman's Creek in 1859 along with Mary Susan. In 1860 Mary Louisa was born in Maryborough and a son died at one day old at Lintons Diggings in 1864.
James Scarf died in 1887 aged 55.

Dunolly was one of many formerly busy towns in that part of Australia which was once the focal point of the world's gold riches.
Now it too lies in tranquility.

Left: Even the large scale old mining operations around Dunolly and the surrounded areas have faded.

257

procure a prohibition. We would, as well as the opposite party, have to attend the Local Court of Mines which sat periodically to adjudicate on mining disputes. MacDermott promised to attend on Court day to conduct our case, and to see to all minor matters.

On the day appointed Gribble yoked up his horse in the dray. Only four of us went as the distance was eighteen miles and the court opened at eleven o'clock so we started early. Soon after we arrived the lawyer came and soon after Scarf and party hove in sight. The second case that was heard was Mundy and Party V. Scarf and party. I stated our case. When Scarf stated his party's case he admitted being absent three weeks but they had left me in charge to hold their claims. "What?" the magistrate exclaimed, "left one man in occupation of eight men's ground? What nonsense is this." "Case concluded in favour of Mundy and party."

That was all. Our party got hilarious over our sudden and decided victory. We went to the nearest hotel and had drinks round. Each of the four shouted in turn and Gribble must needs get a bottle to drink on the road home. All were in a jolly humour joking and singing. When we reached the outskirts of the Alma diggings it was getting dusk, and going merrily along, the horse in a jog trot we all singing "Wait for the wagon," Gribble was sitting in front on the off side driving, when the near wheel dropped plump into an old shallow hole, and the dray dropped suddenly onto the axlebed on that side. Three of us rolled on to the guard iron in a promiscuous heap, sharply yelling to the driver: "Where the devil are you going." We all scrambled over the tail of the dray, and getting hold of the low corner lifted it bodily up; the horse was told to move on, when, as no one was hurt our trouble was over.

The other four mates were greatly relieved at our success at Court. Scarf and party never troubled us after, and the work went on with a will. The Irishman, Phil, who by trade was a cooper, and I had the dressing of the slabs for stabbing the shaft. It was necessary down from the top logs as the ground was very rotten, and treacherous. We worked by day only till we came to water, and a very troublesome white spewy drift, and small gravel which caused us to start night and day shifts. Our progress after that was slow. The slabs we used were only four inches wide. Skilful and lucky was the man who could get in a set in his turn below. Gribble and the major failed utterly to get in their set of slabs. They would send up plenty of dirt, and water but could not manage to get in their set which made it worse for the next man down.

So it was agreed not to let them down at all. I took Gribble's turn down as well as my own, and the Major always got someone to volunteer for him. It was a desperate game sinking through the drift and water as it would keep running in from every open space, and kept the floor always level. The only plan was to put in the side slabs first, one a time, and bank them up with dirt from the middle; even then the side would often get bulged in too far to get the ends in. I had had a little experience of drift at Linton's and advised a trial of a box, but was overruled on the plea that a box, unless made of iron, would soon be battered to pulp by knocking it down, and likely have to be taken out in which case we might loose the shaft. So we struggled on in the old way.

Chinaman's Flat was the liveliest diggings I had been on since I had been in Ballarat, yet more orderly than the latter. Digger hunts were a thing of the past, and robberies were fewer. There were plenty of fights over claims, and numerous helly prize fights; the most notable was between Joe Kitchen and Bill Melody for so much a side - I cannot remember how much. They had it out somewhere near the Alma; thousands went to witness the fight, but none of our party went. Ice Kitchen came off the victor, after several rounds, and punishing Bill severely, who was a much heavier man than himself. Joe became a popular man after that, and opened a shanty which he called "The Old House at Home" and did a roaring business. Many months after, I heard he fought a black man called Black Sellers in Geelong and got licked.

We passed the Christmas of 1856 on Chinaman's Flat. There was no lack of sports, races, Highland sports, Cornish, Cumberland and Irish wrestling, Quoit-throwing, Punch and Judy concerts in plenty, boxing contests; pleasures in fact to suit all tastes.

A few weeks after Christmas three men in three different claims were smothered by falling earth, the goldfields Commissioner committed suicide, an Italian very near our tent in Frying Pan Street one morning was found dead, stabbed to the heart with a stiletto, supposed to have been murdered by one of his country men of whom there was about there, a numerous crowd. The police came to investigate the affair, and made a great fuss and inquiry to discover the murderer, but getting no clue in a couple of days made no further effort and the investigation came to an end. No more notice was taken of it till three weeks later when a notice in large printed letters was tacked on a gum tree near where the body had been found, in burlesque and ridicule of the carelessness, and laissez faire (slow business) of the Government officials as follows -

£1,000 REWARD IS OFFERED TO ANY PERSON OR PERSONS WHO WILL GIVE INFORMATION THAT WILL LEAD TO THE APPREHENSION AND CONVICTION OF THE MURDERER OR MURDERERS OF JACOBI MARONI ON THE NIGHT OF THE OF JANUARY, 1857.

We were getting on well through the troublesome drift and expected to have a change of 'country' soon, as the cousin Jacks call it. The second claim to the right had bottomed shallow, at eighty feet dry and had had no drift. That looked well for us as we were then over ninety feet and still in drift; it showed at least that we were in deep ground, and the gold there lay in deep ground. One night when I was on night shift and on top at the windlass Jimmy McLachlan who was below sang out: "On top." "Yes." "What is it Jim?" "I've struck solid ground," he cried out. "Good on you," we returned. "We are through the drift boys," I said to my other two mates. At twelve o'clock every night a party near us took upon themselves as time-keepers; one of them would crow like a cock, indicating crib time, and the crow would travel from claim to claim each way till it died out in the distance. When I said: "We are through the drift," the Major who was one of the three at the windlass and bearing a spiteful feeling against that drift because he could not contend with it as others did, let out such a ferocious crow from under his moustache that would have startled the Sphinx. "Shut up you fool," I sang out, "you'll be putting everybody out tonight; do you know it's only a little after eleven." Nevertheless the signal was taken up as usual, and went its round.

Before morning we got into a solid stiff red clay and was on firm ground. When the day shift came on, Enoch, who was in that shift suggested the advisability of examining the back of the slabs where the drift had been which must have become cavernous from the continuous washing in of the mud and small stones while sinking. The slabs put in through the drift were all suspended by cleat of hoop iron, and nails but were unsupported from behind. We all considered Enoch to be the best miner in the party, and willing to listen to his advice. We all being together asked him to examine the state of the shaft where we had gone through the drift. He was lowered down till he sang out "hold on." In about half an hour he called out "haul up." He told us with the aid of a tomahawk he had shifted an end slab at either end of the shaft big enough to put his arm through with a lighted candle and could see in for nearly four feet from the spot where the drift first commenced, adding from the rotten class of Chinaman's Flat ground: "I would not

The bones of countless old diggers lie unnoticed and certainly in peace at the Amhurst Cemetery.
It is indicative of the state 150 years later of once exciting towns which are disappearing very rapidly.

be surprised if the overhanging clay collapsed any moment, the slabs you know are hanging on hoop iron; a heavy fall of dirt might put the shaft out of shape or perhaps close it altogether, then where would the man be, working below and water rising, and not being able to bail it." "So what is to be done?" I suggested battening the corners of the shaft; that is running long battens nailed to every slab. "Well," Enoch said, "that is commonly done on many diggings; but my advice boys is to fill up the back of the slabs with dry dirt, throwing it in from the top till it is chock-a-block. It will be safe then." All hands thought Enoch's plan the best, and concluded to adopt it.

So it was arranged that Enoch and his mates should commence the filling up, and we went home to sleep.

A quick walk around Dunolly reveals evidence of its past.

Our tent was only a few yards from the claim. As I went in my wife inquired: "What were you all having such a long confab about this morning?" "Oh," I said, "some considered the part of the shaft where the drift was, was unsafe and we were consulting about the best means of fixing it up." "For goodness sake," she said, "don't you be going down that deep hole if it is not safe." "Don't worry my girl," I replied, "neither I nor any one else is going to sink again till everything is made perfectly safe."

My wife was near her confinement and unusually nervous. After reassuring her there was no danger at all I turned in. The day was Saturday on which day it was not the custom to work in the afternoon nor on Sundays, except in cases where water was troublesome, when the party took turn about at bailing to keep the water under, as often as required. Enoch and his mates had no thought of half-holiday but determined to complete the filling in before they left off. Some cart loads of dirt were sent down and stowed away. The man doing the filling stood on a swing stage suspended by ropes fastened to the top logs.

I got up about two o'clock, and after having had something to eat went out to see how things were progressing. Gribble was on the stage at the time. After a while he sang out for some one to help him and to bring something down to push the dirt back. I manufactured an implement out of a short bit of slab, and sticking a short handle to it went down to his assistance. "Just the thing Henry," he said, "if you hand in the dirt I'll push it back." In a little over an hour we had the cavern filled up, till no more would go in. I said to Gribble: "Now you go up, and send me down the hammer, a few nails and some pegs and I will replace the slabs." In half an hour it was all completed.

Monday morning I was on the day shift. Being at the windlass in the afternoon we saw a crowd gathering around a claim between us and the claim in which our hopes were centred; no doubt it had bottomed. After a time a man came out with a dish filled with dirt in his hand, no doubt of it, to try a prospect. The crowd followed close behind. "By golly," one of my mates said, "they've bottomed and going to pan off a dishful; one of us ought to go and see the result." "You go," I said, "and bring us back good news." In a short time the crowd dispersed, our mate went to the claim to look at the last dirt sent up, and make further inquiries. When he returned we were anxious to learn the result and inquired what's the news. "Well," he said, "they have bottomed, and are on the pipe clay right enough, but the prospect was only a few fine specks; they have no wash, no big round boulders like which are found in the good claims. I tell you boys it looks blue for us. It seems to me the other is the real lead, and that rich claim which encouraged us on and others to sink is only a sweep round at the angle of the turning of the lead." Not any one spoke for some minutes; when the Major spoke cheerfully and said, "That might be only a blank spot, and the lead will make again before it gets to us. Anyway we shall soon know as we cannot be far from bottom, and the holes round and above us are so near down that they are sure to see it out."

That night, towards morning, my wife took ill. I got up immediately and went for her mother who lived not many yards away. A while after I asked her if I had better go for the doctor at once. "Oh no," she said, "I don't think there is any particular hurry, but I wish you would go for Mrs Enoch." The morning was very dark; I had to provide myself with a lantern as it was unsafe going among the holes without a light, so knocking the bottom out of an Old Tom bottle and sticking a piece of candle in, I started. I was soon back with Mrs Enoch (her husband's name was Enoch Holdsworth but we always called her 'Mrs Enoch').

The women advised me to wait till daylight before going for the doctor, who was an acquaintance of mine. I had first met him the first time I was on Brown's diggings. He was a young American doctor who had, like many others of his profession, come to Victoria to make his pile. I had seen him several times since, and always with the same two mates. Doctor Butler or Doc as we used to call him, was fond of appearing in digger's clothes plentifully smeared with pipeclay, always industriously searching for gold but I never knew him to drop on any, except what he got professionally. He was very popular among the ladies as an accoucheur.

A well educated man was Doc and a real gentleman when in his professional togs. As soon as it was light I walked half a mile to the doctor's tent, and putting my head through the front opening called out: "Get up Doc. you're wanted." He knew what was the matter as I had engaged him a fortnight before. He sprang up saying: "All right my boy, I'll be with you in a jiffy." After he had clothed himself and came out he enquired: "Is it urgent, who is with her?" I told him. "What did the women say?" "Oh," I said, "they did not seem in any excited hurry but to tell you to come as soon as possible." "That's all right," he said, "I'll get a bit to eat and a pannikin of tea and tog up for it would not do to go in these togs you know. Better stay and have a bite with me for there is little chance I guess of getting a square meal on these exciting occasions." "No thank you doctor," I said, "but hurry up."

Having had breakfast when the shift came, we started to work. I was one of the three at the windlass. Shortly after the doctor put in his appearance. He nodded to me as he passed into the tent. Jimmy Carr remarking: "Doc. has gone into your tent Mundy in his professional style, is anything the matter?" "Yes I said, "my wife is taken ill." "Oh," was the simple remark. Nothing more was said on the subject for a couple of hours when an unusual voice was heard by us all, in the tent. "By golly," my mates remarked "what lungs the kiddy has got; it's singing out for its daddy." The major joined in: "Got good lungs at any rate." Another remark was: "I hope the little un brings us good luck with it." We all signified "Amen" to that. Later on Doc. made his appearance smiling blandly saying: "Mundy allow me to congratulate you on your son and heir, a fine healthy strapping boy as fine a specimen as I have ever seen for his age."

"How old is he Doc?" the Major asked. "About two hours Major." "Are all things right with the mother Doctor?" I asked. "Tip top my boy, couldn't be better," was his reply. I think the Major joined in: "We ought to wet this important occurrence boys, what do you think?" "All right," I said, "we'll go over to Jimmy Quaids and have a drink, call up MacLachlan," so Jimmy was ordered to come up forthwith. When his head appeared above the logs he enquired: "What's up." After an explanation duly given, he uttered but one word "Jerusalem."

We all, doctor included, adjourned to the shanty of James Quaid, an old acquaintance of mine as the reader will know, if he has read this story through. I shouted drinks round, and after finishing mine I went back to the tent to see if I could be admitted. As I went inside Mrs Enoch ran to the bed, picked up a bundle of clothes containing a small specimen of humanity. All I could see was a little pair of tiny hands and face. "Come dad and kiss your son, take him, and feel his weight, is he not a splendid lad? I'll bet he weighs twenty pounds if an ounce." After doing as requested, I went to my wife's bedside with the prodigy in my arms. She was smiling contentedly as I kissed her, as I asked her how she was. "I feel fine Henry," she said, "I'm so thankful it is all over, I was dreading I should be as I was the last time, but thank God it was nothing this time like that."

After holding the baby for sometime I said to Mrs Gribble: "Here Granny, take your chiel and put it in bed again it's making my back ache." She took it tenderly and after kissing it twenty times, and calling it all the dear little loving names she could think of, put it beside its mother again. I told her I had been shouting for my mates to go and fetch Gribble too. She went but soon returned saying: "He's asleep, I'm not going to wake him, we can have a bottle bye and bye and drink the chiel's health when Enoch and his shift come to work."

In half an hour I went back to the shanty wondering why they had not come back. They had had two shouts round, besides mine, and were talking of having another, nothing for it but I must join them. "All right," I said, "but the next shout will be mine, where's Doc?" "Oh," the Major said, "he left after the second drink, you'll never see Doc. take more than two drinks, and often as not, more than one, at a time." Taking a square bottle of Hollands with me to treat Gribble, Enoch and our other two mates on the night shift, I went home.

I had not been in long before Gribble came inquiring for any news that might be of Ann. Mrs Gribble took the treasure from the bed and handing it to him calling him "grandfather." He took it gingerly with a wondering broad smile all over his kindlooking face, and kissed it several times which the object of his caresses resented with a loud howl; not liking his bristly beard. "Take it," he said to his wife, "he does not know me yet; you'll know me better bye-and-bye won't you sonny." I produced the bottle then, and we all, excepting the mother, pledged baby's health all round, and also the mother's. "I wonder," I said to Gribble, "If my mates are going to stay at Jimmy Quaid's shanty the rest of the shift?" He sprang up saying, "I'll go over and see what they are up to."

Mrs Gribble strongly objected saying: "No don't'e go William, you'll only be getting too much drink; let them stay there the remainder of the shift. I do not suppose by this time they are in a fit condition to go to work; what do you say Henry?" I said: "No doubt it was best, but we would have to keep the water down." Near the end of the shift they left the shanty, "three seas over" the three of them, in a great flurry to go to work again. I said: "Look here boys, I'm not going to do any more work to day, and you'll do best to leave it alone as the three of you are nearly tight; but we'll have to bale out as there must be six or seven feet of water in now; the night shift won't like that when they come to work." "Right you are," the Major hiccupped, "we'll see to that now, bye-the-bye Mundy, how are the wife and bairn progressing?" "Splendidly thank you," I answered.

When they started to bale, I went to do my share at the windlass but neither of them would allow it; so I had to retire. When the water was reduced to half buckets they went home. Enoch came soon after to see how affairs were going, seeing his wife had not come home, when the three of us had a gin round. The other two of the night shift came at the usual time. I told them of the new arrival and the state of affairs and invited them in to our front room which was partitioned off the bedroom by a chintz curtain; producing the Hollands and asking them to drink

JAMES QUAID
Born in Limerick, Ireland. Died in 1877 aged 85.

The gold country has returned to its farming roots, but drought remains a constant problem.

mother's and baby's health, which they did with a hearty good will wishing the pair all kinds of happiness and success. Of course Gribble, Enoch and I had to join them for good manner's sake.

We chatted on after that for a couple of hours, having a drink occasionally till the bottle became exhausted. I took good care that my own were very small. Mrs Gribble claimed the privilege of pouring out her husband's nobbler, which caused a bit of altercation between the two. When the bottle was done Gribble wanted to fetch another, but I objected saying too much talk would disturb Ann. That settled it, as far as another bottle went. Nevertheless the three of them went to the shanty for one more drink. I was requested to go with them, but declined. During the night I heard the water dashing down the water shoot, and was well content to know they had not gone on to work.

The morning following we started work at the usual time, but with depressed hopes; two more duffers had bottomed the position of which boded us bad luck. It was my turn below first. There was no indication of a wash of gravel or boulders, but coarse sand and clay. I put in my set of slabs easily enough by ten o'clock, when I was called to come up when the Major went down. As I was going into the tent the doctor came out who had just visited his patient. "How do you find your charge getting on Doc? Alright?" I inquired. "First class, first class, Mundy," he replied, "couldn't be doing better, good sakes; what a fine healthy boy that is. You must be near the bottom soon I should think with your shaft." He continued, "I hope my boy you'll get a pound weight off the bottom." "Thank you doctor," I said, "but I fear things are looking blue." "Wa-a-al," he said, with a Yankee drawl, "it does not look very encouraging, but there's no telling you know. Good morning." Jimmy Carr relieved me below. There was no alteration in the dirt coming up, no gravel or indication of a gold wash.

The afternoon sinking was the same. We were over 100 feet deeper than any claim that had bottomed round us. The night shift continued sinking and struck the pipe clay, the bottom, about twelve o'clock, overlayed with coarse hungry sand. A bucketful of dirt was skimmed off the pipeclay and sent up; after that the man was hauled up. By the aid of a candle a large dishful was puddled, and panned off with the result of only a few fine specks. It was no good doing anything further till all hands held a consultation, so all went home.

Gribble could not help calling to me to tell me what had happened. I was sleeping, but the wife answered him: "What is it William?" she asked. "We've bottomed at last," he said. I heard that, and got up to let him in, when he told me all about it. "A rank duffer it is, I believe it is," he said, "and so does Enoch. The others are gone home. We'll meet in the morning to talk things over. I'll go now, I thought I'd stop and tell you," and left. A rank duffer. I'd been duffered out many times in shallow holes, but this was the heaviest blow, by far, I had received, and what made it worse, after paying the doctor, our money would be nigh exhausted. And I had wasted over five months for nothing. I went back to bed when my wife said: "I heard what Gribble said, they had bottomed, and a rank duffer." "Oh," I replied, "we can't tell yet, we might get gold by driving our shaft as deep, or deeper than those claims which are yielding the best returns," and told her what I could to cheer her up for in her present state I was afraid the dear soul would be despondent. In my heart of hearts I believed Gribble to be right for deep ground was, as often, as bad an omen as too shallow.

We met altogether in the morning. It was my turn down. I gouged out a bucketful from off top of the pipeclay, and sent it up; then went up in the next bucket myself. The whole bucketful was carefully puddled, and panned off with a very discouraging result. The Major said: "It's all up boys, there is no gravel wash, no boulders, and seeing all the blanks round us, it is evident enough we're off it." Enoch desired to go down and sink a bit in the pipeclay to make sure the bottom was reached. After half an hour he was hauled up and said: "Yes lads it's bottom alright." An hour later each of the party left except Gribble, Enoch and me who talked over future ventures. We concluded to pay Dunolly a visit which had been rushed some little time before Chinaman's Flat broke out. Gribble offered to take us in the dray. We would take a couple of blankets with us each, and stay a day or two if necessary to satisfy ourselves, but I said I should like to wait a few days before we went as I would like to see my wife strong again before I left her. So it was decided to go in a week's time.

My wife and her mother took our disappointed hopes very calmly. Ann said: "What's the good, funking over a duffer, have we not had lots of disappointments before; we'll be lucky yet if we only persevere." "Yes," I said, "my dear girl, I believe in what you say, but this is a poser, five months lost and our money - after Doc. is paid, will be nearly all gone. Five months working, waiting and planning," I growled, "and nothing to show for it." She sprang to a sitting posture, picked up the baby: "Nothing for it?" she cried, holding out the kiddy. "Nothing, what do you call that, nothing, the dear

262

little darling angel." The little angel then had to suffer kisses galore which he did without a murmur. I was glad to see her take our bad luck so lightly for I knew she had entertained higher hopes than usually over our last venture. If I had been a single man I should not have cared a rap, but now I had a wife and child; which seemed a heavy responsibility. But I soon shook off the burden of disappointed hopes and was myself again, I had the pluck and heart of a lion in those days, and a perseverance and persistency that nothing could bluff.

Mrs Gribble had been busy preparing supper for us, and said: "Supper is ready Henry. You see to Ann and I'll go and look after William." After we had finished our supper, and a little talk I took up a book to read, but the contents had little interest for me. The lamp was on a box standing at the head of the bed, baby was lying facing it with wide open eyes, as if wondering what the light could be. Ann had covered her head with the bedclothes as if seeking sleep. Things remained thus for half an hour. I knew my wife could not be asleep from her continual movements. When I lifted the clothes off her head, as she looked at me I saw her eyes were red. "What is it my girl," I said, "you've been crying." "Get out you silly," she said, "what should I be crying for? No I was not crying I was only thinking," she added cheerfully. "Well tell me what you were thinking about then." "You remember when you were carting to Ballarat, when we were courting, mother and Gribble had gone there, Aunt Fanny and I lived by ourselves, we made flannel shirts, and over-shirts for the shops, we earned five shillings a day easily. I understand the work pretty well, if we are hard-pushed, why should not mother and I get work off the draper's shops. There is plenty of that work to be got I know, as a woman told me the other day who was doing that kind of work, that she could get twice as much as she could do." "Ann, my dear," I said, "when I married you I knew it my duty to keep you, what nonsense are you talking of taking in sewing to keep the house. By God, I'll get a living for us if in no other way I'll go fossicking till something better turns up." "Well, well," she said, "don't get in a sputter over it, we've not been long married yet; we do not know what is before us." I told her Gribble, I and Enoch were going to look at Dunolly, as soon as she got strong. "Oh", she said, "go as soon as you like. Mother will be with me, I shall be alright, I hope you will see something good, good enough to shift for I want to be out of this place, I'm weary of it."

Two days after the three of us, with a pair of blankets each, set out for Dunolly. We arrived there about midday; having had a bit of dinner and a pannikin of tea we set out on foot for inspection. The diggings seemed half abandoned, as many of the holes had been worked out, and left; an odd windlass was still standing here and there; some had not quite finished, others were doing a bit of fossicking in claims supposed to be worked out, taking out pillars, working round the edges or taking down more of the wash overhead. A few of the shanties were still hanging out and some stores of which was the most conspicuous was the Red Shirt Store, the sign, not a flag as usual, but a red shirt elevated on a long pole with arms extended like a scare crow. This store was duplicated by another on Chinaman's Flat supposed to be the same owner. In place, a few claims had traced an offshoot from the lead which seemed, after a few successful holes, to have run itself out. We traversed nearly over all Dunolly, and then visited another small diggings farther on, called Inkerman's with the same result. We saw nothing inviting enough to induce us to shift there.

It was getting dusk when we returned to the dray. After discussing some supper and tea, and a long yarn

A careful look at the front of this old crumbling building in Dunolly shows that it was once the booking office for the Cobb & Co coach operation.
These sights are enchanting for those who like to look around at the past, and the tourism industry has not come near these sorts of towns.

263

over the unsatisfactory state of things with our clothes and boots on, we rolled ourselves in our blankets on the bottom of the dray to court sleep. From the turning and tossing about, I do not think there was much sweet repose.

At the break of day each one of us was ready to get

This other Burnt Bridge, over Burnt Creek, lies in the northern goldfields.

out of bed. Enoch was in a bad temper, not usually the case with him, and remarked with a bit of Yorky: "if ah'd a knowed ah'd a ligged on t' ground, it wad ha bin safter; baith ma huggin banes are sair." After having finished breakfast we concluded to return home; but before starting thought it advisable to go to the Red Shirt Store and have a wet. The store was not far; so we walked. As we neared the store we met a man leading a horse just leaving a dray. "Why," Enoch said, "that's Jack the carter's horse, who lives near us." "So it is," I said: "I wonder how that man got him." We passed by the man leading the horse without saying any more. We passed the dray; three men were sitting round a fire smoking, apparently after breakfast. When we had had our drinks, returning passed by the three men again but asked no questions; and thought little farther about it. As we were near home Jack the carter on foot made up to us, seemingly quite crippled as he limped along. He knew us and said: "I've lost my horse these two days, you haven't seen anything of him have you?" "Yes," Enoch said, "we saw him in Dunolly this morning."

"In Dunolly," Jack said surprised, "what direction was he making for?" "He was not making for anywhere of his own accord," we told him, "a man was leading him." "By thecky then," Jack cried out, "he's been stolen." We told him all about what we had seen; the men and the dray and where to find them near the Red Shirt Store, and if he went by night he would probably find his horse feeding at the dray. "I'll go there tonight," he said, "but Lord, my feet are so blistered I can scarcely hobble. I know what I'll do, I'll hire a saddle horse, and ride to Dunolly tonight." We asked him to get up into the dray, Gribble said: "I'll drive you home Jack."

Next day Jack came to see me and asked me where to find Enoch as we two had noticed the most particulars. On taking him to Enoch's tent, this is the story he told. "As I told you I would, I hired a saddle horse and made straight for Dunolly. I reached there a little after sundown, there was still good daylight. Going by your directions I found the dray easily enough, and there was my horse tied up feeding from a bag stretched between the shafts. I passed, pretending to take no notice; four men were sitting round a fire close by having supper. I went straight to the police camp and told them my horse had been stolen from Chinaman's Flat two days ago; and I had just found him tied up to a dray; feeding and four men close by apparently the owner of the dray. "Did you come across your horse accidentally or from information you received?" "By information from two neighbours from Chinaman's Flat," I replied, "who saw a man leading my horse by a rope into the ranges this morning." "When you passed the horse did you say anything to the men?" "No, I passed by as if I took no notice," I said. "You are perfectly satisfied that it is your horse?" "Perfectly." "Have you the receipt of the purchase, for payment with you, brands and description of the horse, in your possession?" "Yes," I said, and handed it to him. Looking the receipt over he said: "I'll send two policemen with you if you will wait a bit. You did quite right in coming to us first before you claimed the horse off them."

In the company of two police we made for the dray, which when I pointed out to them. One of them said to me: "You stay here, we want to ask the men a few questions before you show yourself; when we want you I'll sound my whistle." The conversation that passed they told me after. Examining the horse over, one of the police said to the men: "This horse very much resembles a strayed horse for which so much inquiry has been made; does it belong to you?" "Well, yes for the time being," one of the men answered, "but it is not our own; one of our mates borrowed him off a friend just only to take our dunnage to Mount Moliagul, as we are shifting." "Who and where is your mate's friend? Fetch him that we may have a talk with him." Another man spoke then, saying: "It happens he is not at home; he went to Ballarat this morning, and will not be back for a few days, that's the reason he lent us his horse."

At this point the whistle blew; when Jack marched up, and one of the police introducing him said: "Is this the friend you speak of?" Jack said he never saw men so suddenly shrivel up as they did. They had not another word to say, as they knew he was the owner of the horse. Getting no answer to the last question the policeman said: "This man owns this horse, is he the friend you speak of who lent the horse to you?" One of the four men said: "There must be a great mistake somewhere, this man is not the owner of this horse; to that I take my solemn oath." But the policeman said: "He is willing to swear it is his horse and what is more he has handed to me a written receipt with the description and his brands which tally exactly. This man accuses one or all four of you of stealing his horse; therefore it is our duty to take you, all four in charge, and lock you up, till this matter is investigated." Then putting the men two and two together, handcuffed them together and drawing their revolvers from their belts ordered them to march to the lockup. When they had been locked up safe in the logs, I said: "I suppose I can take my horse now?" "Certainly not," was the reply. "Tomorrow bring the two men who saw the man leading the horse with a rope, we shall be able to decide then what to do; till then he remains in our possession. A policeman has gone for him now."

"So you see lads," Jack said, "how I'm fixed, I will have to trouble you both to go to Dunolly tomorrow if you will be kind enough. If the man that took you in before will take us, we can go together, and I will pay him for it."

In the evening I told Gribble Jack's story, and that he wanted him to take us to Dunolly tomorrow. "Yes," Gribble said, "I'll take you in; as for paying me for it, I should not think of such a thing. Poor devil, I pitied him yesterday when I saw how crippled he was. If any thief stole my horse I should be only too thankful to anyone who would help me."

In the morning we were off to Dunolly the four of us. We reached the police camp before midday. The police brought the four men out and ranged them in a row with their backs against the logs, their faces towards us, and asked us to point out the man we saw leading that horse (the horse was standing there). Neither Enoch nor I had the least hesitation in recognising the man. He was stout-built with florid complexion, and long black hair about thirty-six. The other three were older and bore unmistakable the Van Demonian stamp all over. "That is the man," we both said pointing to the youngest, "that we saw day before yesterday leading the horse into the ranges with a rope round his neck." The police asked us further questions if we had not seen either of the three others handling or feeding the horse. They seemed anxious to implicate the others in the trouble. "No, we had seen nothing more than what we had already told them." This seeming to be the end of the business, Jack inquired if he could not take the horse home. Turning to Enoch and me, one of them asked: "Have you seen this horse in this man's possession, for any length of time?" "Yes," we replied, "we have seen him daily for at least three months." "Yes," he told Jack, "you can take the horse with you; but I shall bind you all three to appear at the next Carisbrook Criminal Sessions to give evidence at this man's trial."

Gribble was not far off feeding his horse; he also had a billy of tea ready. After discussing a snack we started for home. On passing the Red Shirt Store, Jack said: "Hold on a bit," jumping off the dray, went in and presently reappeared with a square bottle of gin. We were all alcoholic-thirsty and straightway uncorked the 'crater' and with a pannikin had stiff drinks round, repeating the dose at intervals till we reached Chinaman's Flat, where we threw the empty bottle overboard. I met my wife at the door of the tent, and granny who was taking baby out for an airing. "Well how did you get on? Did the carter get his horse?" were the first queries. "Yes," I said, "Jack brought his horse back, but I wish now we had not gone to Dunolly at all." "Why?" "Why? Well the diggings offered us no encouragement in the first place and happening to be there we blundered on those horse thieves. There were four of them in the party, one a young man, the other three I know were old lags. The old ones were cunning and cautious enough to let

Moliagul, near Dunolly, is another once exciting gold town which has seen the other side of life, and was captured by John Darbyshire on canvas.

AFTER THE GOLD RUSH
By 1871, 1,539,127 people lived in Australia and by 1881 that had risen to 2,250,194.

The old Dunolly Town Hall remains grand.

the young man do all the handling and taking care of the horse; that is why we saw him leading it. This man is in gaol and has to stand his trial at the next Carisbrook Criminal Sessions; when the other villains are let go, one man is a scapegoat for the other three. Besides Enoch and I are bound to go and give our witness at the trial." "Don't go," my wife said. "Oh but," I replied, "we had to give our names and addresses or Jack would not have been allowed to get his horse, one thing I am glad, he has got him."

"Henry," my wife said suddenly, brightening up, "don't let us bother ourselves so much about other people's troubles; we have enough care of our own just at the present, don't you think?" "Oh I say," she continued, "the doctor came today and told me I looked quite bonnie, "This is the last time I intend visiting you as a patient, you are looking as fresh as a daisy and the boy is as fine a specimen of infantile humanity as any one could wish to see; keep on bathing him well in tepid water every morning." "Thank you doctor," I said, "for your compliments and advice, I might as well pay you now." "Well Mrs Mundy," he answered, "if it is convenient and not putting you about; you can please yourself." I went and took five pounds from under the pillow and said with it in my hand, "Your fee is five pounds isn't it doctor?" "If you please Mrs Mundy," he said. I believed I blushed when I said: "But Doctor you know we have been unlucky lately, and the worst of it is our money is getting low; could you not knock a pound off?" "Yes, Mrs Mundy," he replied, considering your circumstances and our long acquaintance, as far as digger's acquaintances go, I will take four pounds."

When I gave him the four pounds, he remarked: "I hope your son, when he comes to be a man, will find something more reliable to depend on than digging for his success in life." "Oh but doctor," I said, "my husband believes, and so do I, that if we persevere with patience we are sure to be lucky in the long run." "I hope so," he replied, "but my mates and myself have received very little encouragement so far; but as you say, we must hope on, and persevere. No one knows what may turn up."

Later on, Ann said to me: "We will have to get the baby registered; the doctor told me so. So we will have to choose some names for him." "Names," I said, "how many?" "You and I," she said, "were baptised with only one Christian name, but that is old fashioned; every child now has two names or more." "The young brat," I replied, "deserves to be baptised after the old fashioned way. If he had brought us luck when he came I would not have begrudged him half a dozen names, anyhow, I would like his first name to be George after my father; you can give him one or two more if you like. I do not care what they are as long as they are not ridiculous." So that was agreed on. Ann consulted her mother, Gribble and all of her intimate friends and the ultimatum arrived at, the baby was to be named George Francis. I was satisfied; only remarking he is the first of my family that ever I heard of who has been honoured with two names; he ought to feel proud.

The names being settled on, the next thing I had to do was to walk into Maryborough to register George Francis which I did a couple of days after. When in Maryborough I was advised to take a new and far better road to where I lived; which I took on returning. About a quarter of a mile from Chinaman's Flat diggings I saw on the roadside an isolated little township of tents snugly ensconced among the trees, and wondering what it meant, I enquired of the first I came to. "Oh," replied the individual, "That's Hobart Town Poll's establishment, where the aristocratic ladies hang out." "Oh," I said, "is it?" Scenes of revelry were going on by day; the laughing and screeching of men and women was uproarious. If I had been a single man I should probably have passed through the excited crowd to see what the fun was about, but being a married man and father of a family I thought of the proprieties and passed by like a serious benedict. When near home I came across for the hundredth time "Bob the Original Bellman" as he called himself.

Very few old diggers have not seen or heard of Bob the Original. He was said to have been the first mate of a ship and bolted from his vessel in Hobson's Bay for the diggings; a short thick set man about fifty. Bob was always drunk; at least I never saw him sober, his services were very much in demand as a crier (Commissionaire). At the present time when I met him Bob was holding forth profusely over a concert to be held at the Gold-diggers Hall this evening when the celebrated and popular comic singer Thatcher will sing his best songs composed by himself, all particularly adapted, Australian taste etc. Roll up, roll up and enjoy a pleasant evening. Doors open at seven o'clock sharp. "God bless her most illustrious Majesty the Queen, and all the little queens." At the finish he made a peculiar burr with his lips which no pen could imitate.

"Well, did you register the baby?" was the first salute from Ann, as I entered our tent. "Yes," I said, "if I die worth twenty thousand pounds he'll be my heir, and can claim the lot unless I leave a will for his mother to have some of it." She laughed, and replied: "Get the twenty thousand first Henry, it will be time enough then to think about making a will. I can trust him, I know he will never be unkind to his mother; nor to your father either will you my darling?"

"There is another performance yet my girl," I said: "He has to be vaccinated within a month of his birth, or we will be subjected to a heavy penalty." "Well," she answered, "I suppose it is for the child's good and it will have to be done. The Government vaccinator lives in Maryborough, you will have to go there yourself with him." "As for that," she answered, "Gribble will take us in if I ask him, and mother can go with us."

About this time Gribble met with an accident in freaking his wheel with a load of washdirt on. The tyre came off when he was within a few yards of his destination. When he ventured to chance the remaining distance with the tyre, the consequence was he smashed one of the felloes (part of wooden rim) and broke two spokes. "Here's a mess Henry," he said in the evening. "I'll have to cart that wheel to Maryborough, the nearest place to find a wheelwright." "Nonsense." I said, "get me a piece of curly box long and wide enough and two bullock spokes as dry as you can and I'll fix it up for you." "Can you?" he said, seeming rather incredulous. He looked on me as a bit of a genius but this was almost too much for him to swallow. At any rate he went into the bush and after a pretty long time arrived with a lump of wood nearly taxing his whole strength to carry it: "There," he said, dumping it down, "that's curly enough I should think." "Could you not get a smaller piece or chop it smaller?" I told him, "there's enough wood there to make felloes for a whole wheel."

"It is a good piece of wood for the purpose. We must try and split it down the middle. Will you get the maul and wedges." With the aid of wedges and chopping on both sides, we managed to separate the block nearly into two halves; when I started with the adze to make a face on one side. When Gribble told me he had found a splendid piece of she-oak he knew it would split like a match, and off he went. He soon returned with two splendid pieces split nearly to the size for the occasion. While he was extracting the old spokes and dowels I thinned the felloe with the aid of the axe to its required thickness. We worked till dark and early next morning we had the spokes and the felloe nicely fitted ready for the tyre to go on. The blacksmith was not far away so we rolled the two wheels down to have both tyres fitted. The blacksmith being a skilful hand at that kind of work turned out a splendid job, remarking, although the new work was not over elegant, it was the strongest and most durable part of the wheel. Gribble was in ecstasies. He never doubted my cleverness after that.

Gribble, I and the blacksmith forthwith went to Jimmy Quaids to wet the job.

Samuel Thomas Gill's depiction of Thatcher performing.

WHAT HAPPENED TO THE REST OF THEIR LIVES?
HENRY WROTE ABOUT THE FIRST TWENTY-SIX YEARS OF HIS LIFE
– BUT WHAT HAPPENED AFTER THAT?

Writing the words: "Gribble, I and the blacksmith forthwith went to Jimmy Quaid's to wet the job" was the last thing Henry Mundy did - he died very soon after at his daughter Rose's house at Binney Street, Euroa in Northern Victoria. His Death Certificate states that the doctor, who was called for assistance but confirmed his passing, had not treated him before that day. If he had, that would be stated on the certificate, so his passing was a sudden event, even if Henry was frail at that stage.

The date was January 28, 1912 making him eighty years and six months of age, but after becoming so acquainted with the man and his tale, there had to be more. He couldn't leave us to wonder what happened to him in the next fifty-three years. What too of his family and the many people who also now knew him so well?

It was clearly impossible to know all of his intimate details in the same fashion as he had retold them up until he was twenty-six, but it has been possible to piece together the happy, but often very sad, continuing story which Henry didn't get the chance to relive in words - as he predicted.

We now know Henry and Ann's first living child, George Francis, was born in the goldfields near Dunolly in 1857, and firmly believe that the Mundys and Gribbles did succeed in their efforts to strike it rich in the Maryborough and Dunolly regions because they stayed there for many more years. In fact, Henry and Ann had four more children, all born in the goldfields before fate took a cruel hand.

The scene of the old diggings close to Clunes.

The grandeur of the old Bull and Mouth Hotel in Maryborough, a town built on the importance of gold, and where the birth of George was registered.

The Dunolly Town Hall has changed dramatically, the tower having been demolished.

Most country towns in Australia now are generally in steep decline, and many of the smaller townships which once bustled with industry and with a massive population, have slipped to become a ghostly shadow of their former selves, or even totally disappeared without trace. In the 1850s the opposite was true, and in 1871 Ballarat boasted 477 pubs to service the thirsts of its 48,000 residents!

In Melbourne's then outer suburb of Newmarket, the largest sheep and cattle yard in Australia operated from 1871, but as an example of how things have turned, in the late 1990s the huge site, opposite the world famous Flemington horse racing course (home of the Melbourne Cup), was demolished and turned over to townhouse development.

Henry lived through many eras, and while once the majority of the population of Australia lived and worked in country regions, today people who are born there are now generally forced into the cities for employment.

However, between 1857 and 1864 the Mundys continued to live and work around Amhurst and Talbot (or 'Back Creek' as it was originally known and described by Henry). However, far from being isolated from their families in Geelong, the train had now pushed itself throughout rural Victoria, making a journey to Geelong from Dunolly, Talbot, Clunes or elsewhere an exciting thing which only took a few hours. Gone already were the days of mandatory tiresome foot slogging or even horse and carriage travel.

The first train line in Australia was opened between Melbourne and Sandridge (St Kilda) in 1854 and only covered two and a half miles. In 1857 the forty-five mile long track between Geelong and Melbourne became a reality, and in 1859 a line was opened to what must have been the very remote town of Sunbury to the north west of Melbourne.

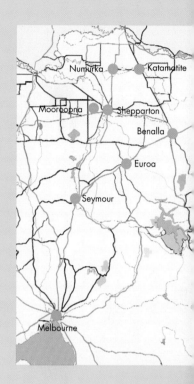

The growth of the rail was enormously quick, and in 1862 the line between Geelong and Ballarat alleviated the need for major horse and cart transport between these two large rural cities. In that same year the one hundred mile stretch between Melbourne and the very rich gold city of Bendigo was made easy because of the railway. The squatters and those businesses and individuals in the goldfields were beneficiaries of the ease of travel.

Gold rushes continued to break out in all of those years, and at Moliagul near where George was born, the huge 'Welcome Stranger' nugget was found only a few inches below the surface as late as 1869. It weighed 2520 ounces.

However, alluvial gold was becoming more difficult to come across easily, and the average weekly wage for miners in that chancy occupation was down from five pounds per week in 1852 to one pound sixteen shillings in 1858. Between 1859 and 1864 the number of miners on the goldfields declined from 125,000 to 83,000, one third of whom were Chinese.

Large companies were now formed to mine for deep deposits, and they transformed mining into a huge and expensive industry. One mine alone had 5000 horses used to work its puddling machines in 1857! Naturally, many of those former gold rush miners became company employees, and a once floating population began to congregate in towns like Clunes where the work was plentiful. From that time many of the smaller townships went into decline.

Ann and Henry did well though, and their four other children had their births registered in Talbot, Amhurst and Clunes - towns which were all very close in proximity.

Emma Elizabeth's entry into the world was recorded at Amhurst in 1860, Mary Matilda in the same town in 1862, while Caroline Mary Anne's birth was registered in Talbot in 1865. More precisely, she was born at Mt Greenock, while in 1868 Rose Helena came into the world at Clunes.

Just as they did in Geelong only a few years earlier, the Mundys tried their hand at running a grocery business, and in early 1860 they operated a shop in Clunes. On March 9, 1860 it was reported in the Creswick Advertiser that Joseph T. Braithwaite had been charged with stealing a pair of shoes and a packet of nails from the Mundy store. Henry was holding the man when the police arrived, and while the man was charged, that venture would be short lived - but not be their last as shopkeepers.

This sign states 'Dunach' but it is the only evidence of a community. However, the old school building which Henry was instrumental in having built and recognised by the government, lies in good condition in the yard of a Talbot private home.

Sadly, there is nothing left of Dunach today, and this it Mt Greenock - once a busy company mining community.

Henry and Anne, with their George, Emma and Mary went back to mining, mixed increasingly with carpentry. Around 1863 they stablised their lifestyle and settled permanently in the newly established mining town known as Mt Greenock. It was later renamed Dunach, and was located several miles south of Talbot and about five miles north of Clunes.

Mt Greenock was one of dozens of towns which sprung up because of gold, and within a three mile radius seven schools operated to cater for the education of the children of miners.

Each of those new communities would elect its own school committee, build a room, supply the basic needs and even appoint a teacher. After establishing the school they would seek a

recommendation from the District Inspector to apply to the Board of Education for aid from the government in the form of two pounds for the teacher in return for one pound raised by the parents.

By 1861 a small chapel and school room was built on the side of Mt Greenock and the Reverend Symons applied for aid. The school was finally recognised in 1865 as '772 Mt Greenock', and Margaret Whitehead was the head teacher with twenty-seven boys and nineteen girls were under her care.

Eight year old George Mundy, and probably five year old Emma were students there when aid was finally granted in January 1865. Henry Mundy headed the school board, which is not surprising in light of the importance he placed on formal education.

In 1866 he gave away mining to become a full time carpenter and builder, as he has told us in his own words. Mt Greenock was expanding rapidly, and his skills were in demand.

Henry's brother John Mundy too had taken up carpentry, a trade with stayed with the Mundy family for many generations. However, John remained in Geelong where he married Catherine Ward in 1858.

John supported his mother and sister Jane who was twelve when he married, but he and Catherine had their own share of sadness.

As was so often the case in those times, child mortality was a constant fear and occurrence in people's lives, and their first child, Henry John, who was born in Newtown, Geelong, died that same year at seven months. They had two more children however, Annette who was born in Ashby in 1861, and Henry George at Ballarat in 1863.

With both of her sons married and living away from home, their mother Mary and seventeen year old sister Jane were left on their own in Geelong, and Mary, wanting the best for her daughter, seems to have encouraged her to find a husband who could guarantee a good future rather than true love.

Sadly, as we will see later, Jane's fortunes went down hill very quickly after her marriage, prompting Henry to remark briefly about 'Mother's foolish teaching' and lamenting the fact that it might almost have been better if Jane had not been born. More of that later.

In 1868 Henry and Ann moved from Mt Greenock with their almost completed family, and purchased a fine timber home at 21 Service Street, Clunes.

That town was probably the most exciting gold centre in the region, and was going through a massive population and building boom. Evidence of its prosperity is still very clear today, despite only a tiny population remaining there.

The Port Phillip Mining Company, whose senior engineer was one John Munday (no relation), was the major employer and operated a very large scale mining, refining and smelting business on the hill behind the town

This is the old Mundy home in Service Street, Clunes.

on the site where gold had been first discovered in Victoria on June 28, 1851.

1860 saw Clunes with a population of 40,000, and in 1873 it had forty licensed hotels, and by 1870 Henry had a shop on the corner of Fraser and Service Streets from where he operated his building business. It is not known whether that included an undertaking service which then went hand in hand with building. The Mundy families of Henry and John would be associated with both aspects of that business for decades to come and earned a good living from it.

The Short Street home where Ann died.

The house Henry and Ann owned was built in 1858 by Joseph Stubbs, a draper in the town. Today it is a Heritage Listed building known as 'The Poplars' and is a bed and breakfast business.

Soon after the Mundys moved in, Henry, no doubt with the assistance of young George who would also become a fine and successful builder, added to

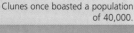

Clunes once boasted a population of 40,000.

The Port Phillip Mine originally and 140 years on.

the house which increased in official value from fifteen pounds to thirty during the two years the Mundys lived there.

Their final living child, Rose Helena, was born in that home in 1868, but in 1870 they sold it to Joseph Tarrant, and moved to a new home which Henry had built at 2 Short Street, Clunes.

Short Street is at the top of what is effectively Service Street, the main road from Ballarat leading into Clunes. Like its name, it is a very tiny dead-end road opposite the Clunes railway station. Their neighbours were Charles Webb, Richard Jose, Archibald Bruce and John Boyle - all miners. Strangely, and probably for monetary reasons, the Mundy house was owned in the name of their son George even though the boy was only thirteen and working for his father.

When Henry went to Clunes in 1868, his brother John and his wife Catherine, with their daughter Annette, moved from Ballarat and purchased Henry's house. John took over his work. Following his father's passing in 1856, John had principally taken over George's milking cows and continued to supply milk to residents in Newtown and Ashby.

After the move to Mt Greenock it is probable that the two brothers worked with and for each other for the next five or six years, but two heart-rending tragedies were to beset Henry and Ann.

In 1871 Ann became pregnant at thirty-two for the seventh time, but endured a repetition of the birthing troubles she suffered in her first pregnancy during the mid-1850s. For the last month of this impending birth she required medical supervision from Dr Joshua Rowbottom. He treated her at the Short Street house on July 3, and two days later the birth occurred at their home, but the unnamed baby died - and Henry's beloved Ann died too.

The baby was premature, but Ann died of complications in labour and 'exhaustion'.

As can well be imagined, Henry and the rest of the family were shattered, and on the next day (July 6) Ann and the baby were both buried in the Church of England section of the Clunes cemetery. Such was the profundity of Henry's loss that for the only time in his life he erected a headstone, and its message is very sad and clear. It remains today in splendid condition, and even if nobody else understands the tragedy behind the words, its size clearly shows that Henry, who did not even have a headstone for himself or his mother despite being a builder and undertaker, found it necessary to have this imposing monument erected in that isolated graveyard.

He remained in Clunes at Short Street, with his children who were aged fourteen, eleven, nine, seven and three. More devastating tragedy was in store though in only three years time. On June 22, 1874 Henry's daughter Mary Matilda, who preferred to be called Polly, drowned in Clunes.

It has not been possible to find out how this accident occurred, but she was only twelve years of age, and it happened at a time of year when floods might have struck at the bottom of the hill in the centre of the town. Polly was buried in the same grave as her mother and unnamed sibling, and her name was added to the headstone along with the very sad line - 'Short Was Their Time'.

On a visit back to Geelong following their deaths Henry met, or perhaps re-met, Caroline Wilkinson who lived in Ashby near his mother and Jane. She had been born Caroline Moore in Surrey, and married John William Wilkinson there in about 1854.

They had two sons in Surrey before emigrating to Australian in 1860 when they settled in Newtown (Ashby), Geelong. They later had two more boys, Charles Arthur in 1861, and Matthew Norman in 1863.

Perhaps it was mutual tragedy which drew Henry and Caroline together, for surely they both needed each other then. Unfortunately, Henry didn't get the

The old Clunes Cemetery with most of its graves now unmarked and in need of restoration. A look around the various denominations gives a very clear idea of the international nature of the inhabitants in the goldrush times - and the massive rate of childhood mortality.

The saddest sight of all for the Mundy family is this headstone erected by Henry for his wife and unnamed stillborn child - then three years later his daughter Mary Matilda or 'Polly'. The grave has been unattended for over 120 years.

The two storey building in Main Street, Mooroopna is the home and business which Henry constructed in 1876. This contained his building and undertaking enterprises. It was taken over by his son, became Hill's newsagency and was demolished in the mid-1980s.

chance to introduce us to Caroline to whom he would be married for the next thirty years, and who must have played a major roll in bringing up the Mundy girls in particular. She would also look after Henry's mother until her passing. She and Henry married in Geelong in 1876.

The losses people incurred until modern medicines were developed were unbelievable, and could not be better illustrated more than by Henry's new wife. In 1861 her sons John Charles aged five, and Wilson William seven, both died in Geelong. Caroline had another son that same year named Charles Arthur, but he died aged five in Geelong too.

Worse was to follow for Caroline though, and also in 1866 her husband John passed away at only thirty-four! She now had only one relative left in Australia, her fourth son Matthew Norman who was born at Ashby in 1863. He remained in Geelong when Henry and Caroline moved away when the boy was thirteen. In 1886 he married Anne Parkinson in Geelong.

Then in 1876 the entire Mundy family took the decision to make a new start, and left Clunes, gold mining and even Geelong forever.

With Henry newly married, his family, that of John's and also their mother Mary, left Jane and her husband of ten years, William Pierce behind. In some ways perhaps, their leaving sealed Jane's fate in the long term?

The Mundys moved north east to the newly developing town of Mooroopna in central Victoria. It was opening up to the fruit industry, and tinned fruit in particular.

Mooroopna is situated about fifty miles east of Bendigo, and has a wonderfully mild climate which is perfect for fruit growing. That part of Victoria had previously been very dry, but was made vastly more productive by two Americans, the Chaffey brothers, who set up a fantastic irrigation system of open channels which brought water there from the Murray River in the north.

Mooroopna is situated on the opposite bank of the Goulburn River to Shepparton, and the border between the twin towns is a flood prone area several miles wide. Today it is linked by a long bridge, but then there was a punt and a rough road through the swampy river flats.

In 1876 the now principal city of Shepparton did not exist, and only came to the prominence it now enjoys because of politicking.

The area was first opened up in 1841 by Edward Curr for sheep grazing, and the life between the aborigines and white settlers was very harmonious. By 1870 many new settlers occupied farms in the area and so the need for a town arose. That place was named Mooroopna, and was situated on the old main route to the gold rushes in Bendigo, Clunes and Ballarat. It is doubtful if Henry or John visited the area until now though as gold was not found

Examples of George and John Mundy's advertising in the Toolamba and Mooroopna newspaper. John was clearly keen to distance himself from his nephew's identical business.

Plans and Specifications prepared on the shortest notice. Estimates of Cost given.

H. MUNDY AND SON,

CARPENTERS, GENERAL BUILDERS, and

UNDERTAKERS,

MOOROOPNA.

THE GOULBURN VALLEY BREWERY COMPANY.

TOOLAMBA TELEGRAPH

Business Addresses.

JOHN MUNDY,
(Not H. Mundy and Son),
CARPENTER, BUILDER, & UNDERTAKER,
Mooroopna.

FUNERALS CONDUCTED
At moderate charges.

Apply at Mr. Lambert's office, Athenæum, or on the premises, near Chinamen's gardens

MOOROOPNA COACH FACTORY.

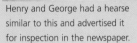

Henry and George had a hearse similar to this and advertised it for inspection in the newspaper.

Original buildings in the Mooroopna Hospital built by H. Mundy and Son - and still existing over a century later.

there.

The beginnings of the town can be traced to W.S. Archer in 1851 when he opened the first hotel in the area. It remained the only building in the future town, apart from the Archers home, until nearly 1870. In 1871 a second hotel was built, and in the next seven or eight years the township developed rapidly, and was far more important than Shepparton. However, in 1879 the rail reached Mooroopna and pushed up the prices of land in the main street to such an extent that future settlers purchased cheaper properties on former government land in Shepparton.

When Henry and John moved to Mooroopna they arrived as professional builders and undertakers. Henry built a very prominent two story weatherboard shop and residence in Main Street Mooroopna, while John and Catherine with their two boys opted to live on the opposite side of the Goulburn River in what was termed the 'Village Settlement'.

Chinaman's Gardens 120 years after John ran his business here.

Henry's shop became a famous landmark in Mooroopna until being demolished in the 1980s. It was later a newsagency, but was replaced with a characterless brick shop which in 2003 was a pizza parlour. John operated his business from a building near what was a market garden known as Chinaman's Garden on the banks of the Goulburn River at the start of the town. The spot received its name after being developed by the very popular Ah Wong who was also a prominent civic leader in Mooroopna. John specialised in buildings, and funerals for the poor who died at the Mooroopna Hospital. He was also the official Building Inspector for the hospital in 1885, a position which would bring him into conflict with his nephew, George.

This, sadly, is now the site of Henry and George's old shop in Mooroopna.

In 1878 Henry turned to farming, and selected 320 acres of land on two properties at Naringaningalook, near Katamatite about thirty miles north east of Mooroopna. He turned his healthy Mooroopna business over to twenty-one year old George.

With children still needing an education, in September 1878 Henry and nine others began moves to establish a school in Naringaningalook - also known for a time as Dunblane.

A two acre site was purchased from Mr E. Bentley, and on May 28, 1880 the school was gazetted with a portable classroom erected. State School 2366 had an enrollment of fifty children by 1894, but as the years progressed the building fell into disrepair and attendance dropped to only twenty.

Repairs were finally made in 1908 and the ground graded and drained in 1914, but with enrollment as low as eight in 1922 the school became unstaffed in July 1924, and closed on April 22, 1925.

Henry happily farmed there for many years, and his mother Mary is buried in Katamatite Cemetery. She died at their home in 1888, aged eighty. Mary was buried in an unmarked grave as was the Mundy way, but in 1913 John Mundy erected a small marble headstone to his mother from 'Jack'.

Where the ANZ bank building stands is the location John Mundy moved his business to in Main Street.

Henry remained on the property for many years, but today no signs can be found of the Mundy home, or his two properties.

In 1893 he purchased Lot 7 at the new Kialla Settlement, a new town just outside Shepparton, while John purchased Lot 8 next door. John built there, but it is unclear whether Henry ever lived at that address - it is nice to think that the brothers remained good friends despite John's rivalry with George.

Soon after Henry turned his business over to George, who clearly was a very astute businessman, they turned into bitter rivals. John later opened his shop and funeral parlour close to George's in Main Street. The rivalry lasted until the late 1890s when George moved to Shepparton and continued in business there. 'H. Mundy and Son' was then taken over by one of John's sons. A great grandson would later direct the funeral of his grandfather, Henry.

George Mundy was recognised in writing as a significant pioneer of Mooroopna, and was more prominent there than his father who moved away after only four years. George worked tirelessly for the community as well as his own benefit, and was a senior member of the Methodist Church - one of whose ministers was ironically, a Reverend Gribble!

The Mooroopna Hospital was established in 1876, the same year the Mundys arrived, and both Henry and George's businesses were instrumental in the construction of many new sections of the hospital for more than twenty-five years - and its funeral business. George served with distinction, and some controversy, on the Board of the hospital while winning major building and funeral tenders. In 1885 John Mundy was Clerk of Works for the same hospital, and also was the favoured undertaker for many of its burials.

This perceived conflict of interest led to a huge amount of public quarrelling in the newspaper between George and his uncle. In 1882 and 1884 George won £362/10/0 worth of building contracts for the expansion of the hospital, and in 1885 'Henry Mundy and Son' won another job worth £476/7/0. George was on the hospital Board from 1880 when the earliest minute book recorded its business, and was a member of the 1880 Mooroopna Australian Rules Football team - the first recorded, was a member of the Rifle Club and many other organisations.

He was a Board member of the Mooroopna Water Trust, Patron of the Mooroopna Football Club, Director of the Mooroopna Butter Factory and in 1888 made Life Governor of the Mooroopna Hospital at only thirty-one.

Under the business name of 'H. Mundy and Son', George built many prominent buildings in Mooroopna and Shepparton, and in 1892 had the centre of very wide Main Street Mooroopna planted out with trees and grass landscaping. They remain a strong character point of the town.

The public brawling between uncle and nephew often spilled into the Mooroopna and Toolamba Telegraph newspaper. George was strong-minded enough to take a customer to court after he had been accused in a sign placed in a shop window, of not replacing a leaking tap! He won the case and was awarded one shilling in damages, after which the judge stated to both parties that this paltry case should never have wasted his and the court's time.

John often felt cheated in hospital business in favour of George, and claimed that his nephew was awarded tenders for funerals and building business even when John's prices were better. Such was his outrage that he would regularly advertise on the front that page of the newspaper that it should be noted his business was not 'H. Mundy and Son'!

George married Esther Johnson in 1876, his bride being one year older (1856), and having been born in Dunolly - the same area as George. They had three girls and two boys, all born and bred in Mooroopna. Their first child was Mary Matilda, born in 1879, five years after the death of George's sister Mary Matilda. Sadly, she died at only twenty-one in 1899.

Their second child was Esther Elizabeth who came into the world at nearby Rushworth in 1880. Percival George Mundy was born in 1884, and Reginald Clarence Rupert in 1888. The latter son would be killed in Scotland in 1915 in training to be a pilot in WW1 - another irony in light of Henry's stated dislike of aeroplanes only a few years before. Their final child was Sylvia Vivian who came into the world in 1892.

Esther married Arthur Long, Sylvia wed Hal Northcott, and Percival lived until March 1961 when he was cremated in Melbourne after living in the leafy suburb of Montmorency. Emily died in July 1952, having lived at Lower Plenty. She was taken to Ararat in the early 1920s, probably to the large asylum there, having not fully recovered from the birth of her daughter Esther. There must have been a deep issue as her father directed family members never to mention her name! One of her sisters visited her regularly though.

Henry and Ann's other surviving children all had successful lives and seemingly happy ones. Emma married Charles Tully in 1878 when she was only eighteen, and they lived in Geelong for

Henry died in this street at Euroa in 1912, and two days later was buried in an unmarked pauper's grave at Mooroopna Cemetery on the left. We like to think he would have been very pleased to see his last major work now published, and his time in Bow Brickhill brought back to life.

much of their married life, having seven children there.

After George left Mooroopna for Shepparton he and his family operated a steam joinery works, and in 1907 built the stage for His Majesty's Movie Theatre Company. He died in the Melbourne suburb of Preston in 1923 where his daughter Sylvia also lived. He passed away only two years after his uncle John. He was only sixty-five, a modest age by Mundy standards.

When Henry died on January 28, 1912 in Euroa at the home of his daughter of his daughter Caroline Donovan, he left behind nineteen grandchildren.

George was then fifty-four, Emma fifty-one, Caroline forty-six and Rose forty-three.

For the final six years of his life after Caroline died, Henry must have remained fairly fit and he moved regularly between his children at Euroa, St Kilda (Rose Carnie) and Emma Tully who then lived in Numurkah close to her old home town of Katamatite.

Henry not only moved around covering large distances, but wrote the final one-third of his manuscript in the final six months of his life. Interestingly, when he died an obituary was included in the newspaper, and a highlight of the piece was that Henry had written much of his life history!

He requested he be buried at the Mooroopna Cemetery, so his body had to be brought around thirty miles to Shepparton, and then to Mooroopna for burial two days later. Not surprisingly, Henry was buried in an unmarked pauper's grave - the same as countless of his ancestors had been buried in Bow Brickhill for generations.

THE OTHERS

We cannot conclude such a personal story without knowing what became of the other people in Henry's life who we now know so well.

JOHN MUNDY

To conclude with Henry's brother John, he retired to Kialla, a then new settlement on the outskirts of Shepparton where he died on March 31, 1921 aged eighty-seven. As was the case with Henry, John too was buried in an unmarked pauper's grave at the Mooroopna Cemetery. His service was conducted by the Seventh Day Adventist Church, although like Henry he was not a religious type in the years we knew him, and it is doubtful if he changed.

ANN GRIBBLE

Ann Gribble was born Ann Gillingham, and for very many generations the Gillinghams lived at East Coker in Somerset where the women were mostly all weavers. A constant number of their children were given the names George, Matilda and Nathan, and those would continue to

275

This headstone for Mary Mundy is believed to have been placed on her grave at the Katamatite Cemetery by her son John in 1913 after Henry's passing the year before. Perhaps this illustrates that Henry was always the 'big brother' despite their ages, but it does show that Mary's grave was not anonymous as those of most of the Mundy and Munday families. We have seen John referred to as 'Jack' only when Henry met Tom Poole - but it must have been his preference, while the family continued to call him 'John'.

favoured in Australia.

Ann Gribble, Henry's mother-in-law, was baptised in East Coker, Someset near Yeovil, on September 9, 1814, and married William Masters, the son of a weaver, at Lopen on April 16, 1836. They had no children, but unofficially adopted Ann before arriving in Melbourne on the 'Tasman' on October 18, 1848. Ann's birth parents were John Gillingham and Elizabeth Young, and they were married in Lopen on May 13, 1837.

Ann and William were contracted to work for six months for Henry Anderson at his property 'Borriyallock' at Skipton, a station covering 50,000 acres and carrying 18,000 head of sheep. Their wages were thirty-five pounds a year with rations provided.

William Masters died on June 29, 1850, and Ann remarried on December 12, 1850 to William Gribble. We know a good deal about her tough life with Gribble through Henry, and she died in 1878 aged sixty-four. It seems from Henry's small hint that she did not approve of his marrying Caroline Wilkinson five years after Ann's passing. Ann must have known Caroline because they lived very close to each other.

WILLIAM GRIBBLE

William Gribble was born in Cornwall, and despite his years of hard drinking, he must have moderated sufficiently to outlive his tormented wife by seven years. He died in the Melbourne suburb of Northcote in 1885 aged seventy-four.

JOHN CROSSLEY

The lovable old rogue John Crossley probably never formally divorced the wife he left behind in England, but as we have seen, he finally married his younger sweetheart Fanny Wills in Geelong in 1856. He died in 1862.

FANNY CROSSLEY NEE WILLS NEE-GILLINGHAM

Fanny was a favourite of her niece Ann, and also much liked by Henry despite the occasional run-in. She was born Fanny Wills in Somerset and married Nathan Gillingham at Lopen on May 27, 1834. They came to Australia with their children Edwin and Nathan on the ship the 'Sir Edward Perry', arriving in Geelong on October 23, 1852. Nathan died in Geelong on December 15, 1852 soon after arriving from England and returning from prospecting on the Ovens River in rugged north western Victoria. Fanny finally renegged and married John Crossley in 1856. There are no records of Fanny's passing before 1888 and it is believed she lived to a fine old age with her sons.

EDWIN GILLINGHAM

As mentioned by Henry, his best friend was Edwin Gillingham, son of Fanny and Nathan. Edwin was born in Somersetshire in 1834, and lived until seventy years of age when he died in 1904 at the Bendigo Hospital. Edwin's wife Mary Ann, who was born in 1839, died in Bendigo in 1906.

NATHAN GILLINGHAM

Nathan Gillingham, Edwin's younger brother by ten years (1844), married Frances Charlotte Hands in 1870, and lived his life with her at mostly Camperdown in the Western District. They had nine children who principally stayed in and around their home town and Geelong. He died in Camperdown in 1915 aged eighty-one years, while his wife died in Geelong on February 22, 1929 aged seventy-seven.

JAMES GILLINGHAM

James Gillingham, Ann Mundy's uncle, was baptised in East Coker on July 21, 1822. He married Susan Stukeley Templeman on August 29, 1846 at Lopen. They had Henry who was born in 1847 and died the following year, Lavinia (1849-1933), Emily Susan, Mary Elizabeth, George William, Henry Thomas Templeman, Charles Edward, Emma Jane, Annie Marie, Isaac John and Charlotte. James and Susan came to Geelong on the 'William Stewart' and arrived in Geelong on May 15, 1848. Their children all married in quick succession - Lavinia in 1866 to William Panther, Louisa in 1867 to MP Brackwell, Suzanne in 1868 who teamed with Charles Baker while her sister Mary Elizabeth married Charles baker's brother Edward in the following year - 1869.

JANE PIERCE (MUNDY)

The saddest story has been left until last.

While a novel might end up happy with smiles all round, the truth about Henry's young sister Jane could not be further removed.

As we have mentioned, it seems her mother Mary encouraged Ann to marry for security rather than true love, and in her marrying William Pierce when she was nineteen her life slipped from one low point to an even more despairing one.

Her father-in-law was a Swedish sea captain named Hans Pehrsson who came to Australia in 1838 and married Tipperary-born Irish woman Catherine Cleary in 1842. She was a former convict who had been transported for stealing a cow! Pehrsson got in and out of serious trouble and changed his name at least five times before settling on Pierce. Nothing definitive is known about him however, other than he died in Creswick in 1886 aged sixty - and as will be realised, he had little or no contact with his son or daughter-in-law.

The Goulburn Railway Station where the Pierce's would have arrived from Geelong, and from where Jane's husband finally departed for New Zealand.

His son William Pierce was a lame bootmaker who walked with the aid of a silver-topped cane. It is difficult to know who was most to blame with their ailing marriage, but it seems that Jane was extravagant, drank very heavily, and had what she described as 'an excitable temper'.

Pierce too was a very heavy drinker and a violent man, and that combination, added to the fact that four of their seven children died when they were all very young, provided the ingredients for an unhappy and eventually fatal relationship.

William was a good provider for the first ten years of their lives together, and owned houses in Geelong plus land in at Ifield. He later owned a restaurant in Newcastle north of Sydney, a pub in New Zealand and perhaps another pub back in Australia.

Ann demanded a stylish life in Geelong, but began to drink heavily there, and the Pierces became notorious for their fighting. William had a bootmaking business in Geelong known as Pierce and Strong.

Old residences in Goulburn restored and looking fine.

After they left Geelong in about 1880 and went to Goulburn, the Pierces lived in boarding houses and other rented accommodation with their children Albert (born 1871), Alfred (1873) and Florence (1876). Still though, the family was in constant serious turmoil.

William established another bootmaking business, but Goulburn is and was a very remote major town. It is nestled in a mountainous region which also yielded a lot of gold and can be bitterly cold in the winter.

She and William had no contact with Henry, John or her mother, and they were unaware of her plight or even where she was. For over one hundred and

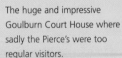

The huge and impressive Goulburn Court House where sadly the Pierce's were too regular visitors.

ten years future generations of the Pierce family were unaware of any Mundys or their links back in Geelong.

There are a very telling series of reports in the Goulburn Herald between 1881 and 1885, in which their tragic lives are laid bare.

It was reported on July 30, 1881 that Jane had charged her husband with threatening language. She was in the process of having a separation drawn up, but in the following few days she accused him of claiming he would shoot her and 'stick me with a knife' after coming home from heavy drinking sessions. Jane had taken her children and moved into a boarding house owned by Mrs Osborne, where she claimed he had arrived drunk and 'said I had his studs'. As she rushed out he had grabbed her and broke her silver fob watch.

The police station where Jane sought protection from her husband.

She told the magistrate that he was earning a good living from his trade, and from rents derived from their properties in Geelong. She also claimed they had not left Geelong because of her extravagances and heavy drinking, but because he was constantly beating her up.

Jane had a servant in Goulburn named Margaret Spillane, who told the magistrate she had never seen Mrs Pierce drunk, and corroborated the threats made by William Pierce, adding that she had gone to the lockup with Mrs Pierce for protection. She later admitted that she had gone to McInnes's Hotel 'for porter and beer for my mistress'.

Senior Constable Emerton told the magistrate that Jane Pierce had arrived at his station that Sunday night excited and crying. According to her husband: "I had a business in Geelong which I had to give up through my wife's extravagance; my wife has a very excitable temper; she has lately not been satisfied with our mode of living; since I have not been able to keep her in the position she used to occupy, she has been nasty; we have not lived happily for the last three months."

In their talks over separation William claimed he offered her 30/- a week if she wanted to keep her daughter and he would take the two boys. He added that her solicitor Mr Gannon told her not to take less than 50/- a week, and if he accepted that she would leave. He said he had not been drunk for five months, and had not threatened her. The case was dismissed.

Then on January 19, 1882 Mrs Thomas Lehane, who owned the boarding house in Goldsmith Street, next to the Pierces, was charged with having assaulted their thirteen year old son Albert. It was claimed she had kicked him without warning or provocation while he sat on the front path near the gate. She said he had insulted her boarders, but Helena Lehane, a daughter, told the court that her mother had been in dispute with Jane Pierce over water.

William Pierce rented three rooms from Mrs Ann Lehane, but said he had disagreements with her for the previous four weeks and had been given notice to quit the place.

The judge believed the assault had taken place, and fined the Lehane's 1/- with 5/10 costs.

Sadly, trouble was never far from the Pierce's lives, and appearances in court became a regular thing. Only nine days later William Pierce appeared before Mr Voss, Captain Rossi and Mr Chisholm, having this time had an argument with Thomas Lehane. Piece told the court that Lehane told him: "You — Wesleyan cripple, what did you break my gate for?"

Piece claimed he had broken a padlock owned by him, with an axe, and Lehane had insulted him for the previous five weeks over being a cripple.

He had stopped living at the Lehane boarding house a few days before, and it seems had returned for some reason only to find the place locked. One charge was dismissed and the other withdrawn.

Syd Hill, with his wife Lena, is the great grandson of Jane and William Pierce. Until he began to investigate his family's background he had never heard of the Mundys.

Two weeks later William Pierce was charged by Thomas Lehane with breaking a glass door by throwing a brick through it. The Pierces had moved next door after being ordered out two weeks before.

Pierce was ordered to pay 10/- with 5/10 costs or seven days in prison.

The next court appearance came on November 3, 1882 when John O'Brien, owner of the Imperial Hotel, was charged with insulting language towards William Pierce, and hitting him over the head with a bottle on October 14. Pierce had been on medical treatment

The tiny gaol behind the old Goulburn police station where Jane spent time.

since, and appeared in court on November 3 with his head bandaged. The case was dismissed, but William Pierce claimed he was taking the assault charge to the Supreme Court for damages.

Following all of those problems, and clearly more which went unrecorded, William Pierce left his family without warning or support, and went to New Zealand after selling all of his properties and business in Geelong. That included two houses for £900 and a third for £250, plus the land which was sold for an undisclosed sum. He purchased a hotel in New Zealand with the proceeds, but still his wife and children remained unsupported in Goulburn.

Twelve months later he sold the hotel for £375, and moved back to Australia where he purchased a restaurant in Newcastle. It is not known if his family derived any income from the business he had owned in Goulburn, but did not according to his wife's testimony. She found he was in Newcastle, and charged him with desertion and leaving her and his children with no means of support. He was remanded to appear in Goulburn Court in early January 1885, and ordered to pay £10 per quarter for one year for the maintenance of his daughter Florence. Presumably the boys were now working and could support themselves. The money had to be paid directly to the police superintendent who would then pass it to the Wesleyan clergyman. Pierce had claimed that money he gave to his wife previously to pay bills or for the children was spent on alcohol. The case for desertion was held two days later and postponed for a week in an endeavour that the pair would settle out of court.

Another case was heard against him in early March when Mary McCarroll was trying to recover £9 for the board of his wife and three children. She had not been paid for ten weeks, and while a hearing had taken place several weeks before, and a judgment made against Pierce, he had not appeared because he was back in Newcastle. William Pierce was ordered to pay on the previous judgment and a new trial was ordered.

Jane Pierce's tormented time was almost through however.

On July 11, 1885 she was imprisoned for one month after being arrested for vagrancy. She was so intoxicated that she could not walk, and was suffering badly from delirium tremens (DT's). When she was taken to jail she was immediately put into medical care, but her condition deteriorated, and three weeks later, at 5.45 pm, she died of heart failure and 'serious apoplexy'.

For many years the Mundy family was oblivious to her dilemmas and ultimate fate. When her mother died three years later it was declared on her death certificate that Jane was still living, and it is not known how and when Henry came to know about his sister's tragic end.

It is also not clear what had become of the children during all of these family upsets, but both Albert and Florence did live up in Brisbane. Florence was a cook at a hotel in Beaudesert, south west of Brisbane, dying in Sydney's Woollahra aged sixty-three, and it is known that she would not touch alcohol.

Albert was married at Singleton north west of Newcastle indicating that his father may have taken his children to Newcastle. After moving to Brisbane where he spent the rest of his life, Albert became deeply involved with the Salvation Army, and while he too would not touch alcohol, he did not spurn others for doing so, and kept a bottle of brandy in the house at all times. He would happily go into a pub with friends, but drink only lemonade.

His grandson Syd Hill recalls that following a sudden death in the family Albert brought out the brandy and gave some to those were suffering from the shock and loss - but he would not take any.

Their other child Alfred disappeared from sight after his mother died, and it is possible his father returned New Zealand to start afresh and took Alfred with him. There are no known records relating to William Pierce following his wife's terrible ending.

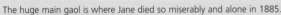

The huge main gaol is where Jane died so miserably and alone in 1885.

Finale

tire to go on. The blacksmith was not far away as we rolled the two wheels down to have both tires fitted The blacksmith being a skillful hand at that kind of work turned out a splendid job remarking, although the new work was not over elegant, it was the strongest, and most durable part of the wheel Gribble was in extacies. He never doubted my cleverness after that

Gribble, I and the blacksmith forthwith to Jimmy Quaid's to wet the job

Henry Mundy's final page.
Written on January 28, 1912. He died the same day.